ZATCH BELL!™

ZATCH BELL!
Vol. 2

STORY AND ART BY
MAKOTO RAIKU

English Adaptation/Fred Burke
Translation/David Ury
Touch-up Art & Lettering/Melanie Lewis
Design/Izumi Hirayama
Special Thanks/Jessica Villat, Miki Macaluso, and Mitsuko Kitajima
Editor/Frances E. Wall

Managing Editor/Annette Roman
Director of Production/Noboru Watanabe
Vice President of Publishing/Alvin Lu
Sr. Director of Acquisitions/Rika Inouye
Vice President of Sales & Marketing/Liza Coppola
Publisher/Hyoe Narita

Published by VIZ Media, LLC
P.O. Box 77010
San Francisco, CA 94107

10 9 8 7 6 5 4 3 2 1
First printing, July 2005

ZATCH'S PAST OPPONENTS

GOFURE **BRAGO** **REYCOM**

THE STORY THUS FAR

Kiyo is a junior high student who's so intelligent that he's bored by life and doesn't even go to school. As a birthday present, Kiyo's father sends him an amazing child named Zatch who has vowed to bring the pompous Kiyo back down to earth and help him make friends. With Zatch by his side, Kiyo thwarts a bully and foils a bank robbery...each time saving Suzy in the process!

As these events unfold, Kiyo's view of the world begins to change—and Zatch's secret becomes more evident. Although Zatch is completely unaware that he's not a normal kid, when Kiyo holds the red book (which only Kiyo can read) and utters a spell, Zatch displays awesome powers. Soon the duo learns that Zatch is one of many mamodo children chosen to fight in a battle which will determine who is king of the mamodo world for the next 1000 years. Now Kiyo and Zatch's rivals are appearing, one after the other, challenging them to fight!

ZATCH BELL! 2

CONTENTS

LEVEL.9 **MY TURN** 7

LEVEL.10 **THE BATTLE WITH DESTINY** 25

LEVEL.11 **KIYO IN THE HOSPITAL** 43

LEVEL.12 **WHERE IS THE BOOK?!** 61

LEVEL.13 **A MOVING TARGET** 79

LEVEL.14 **A HEROIC HEART** 97

LEVEL.15 **THE LIMIT OF STRENGTH** 115

LEVEL.16 **A REAL FAMILY** 133

LEVEL.17 **A MAMODO'S TEARS** 151

LEVEL.18 **A GENTLE KING** 171

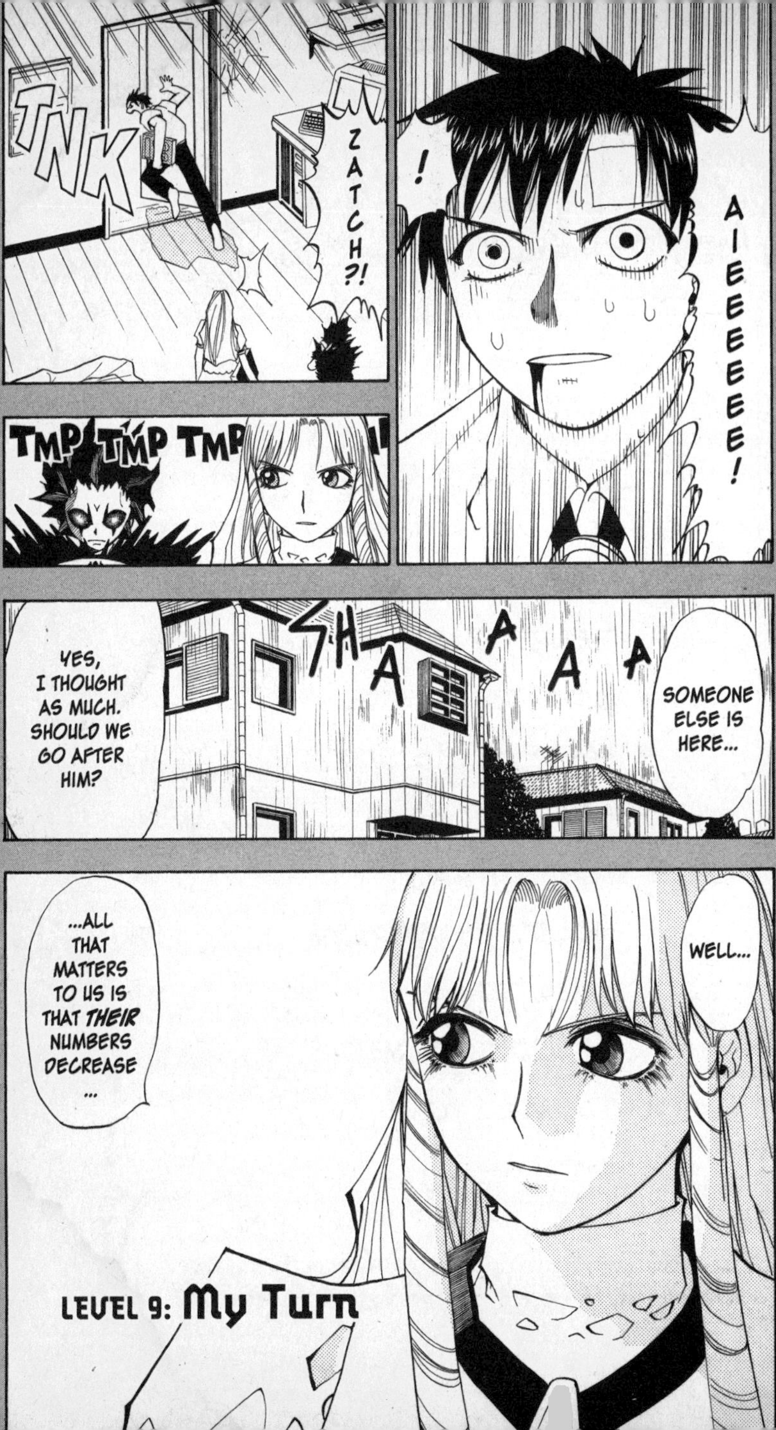
!
AIEEEEEEE!
TNK
ZATCH?!
TMP TMP TMP
SOMEONE ELSE IS HERE...
SHAAAA
YES, I THOUGHT AS MUCH. SHOULD WE GO AFTER HIM?
WELL...
...ALL THAT MATTERS TO US IS THAT *THEIR* NUMBERS DECREASE...

LEVEL 9: My Turn

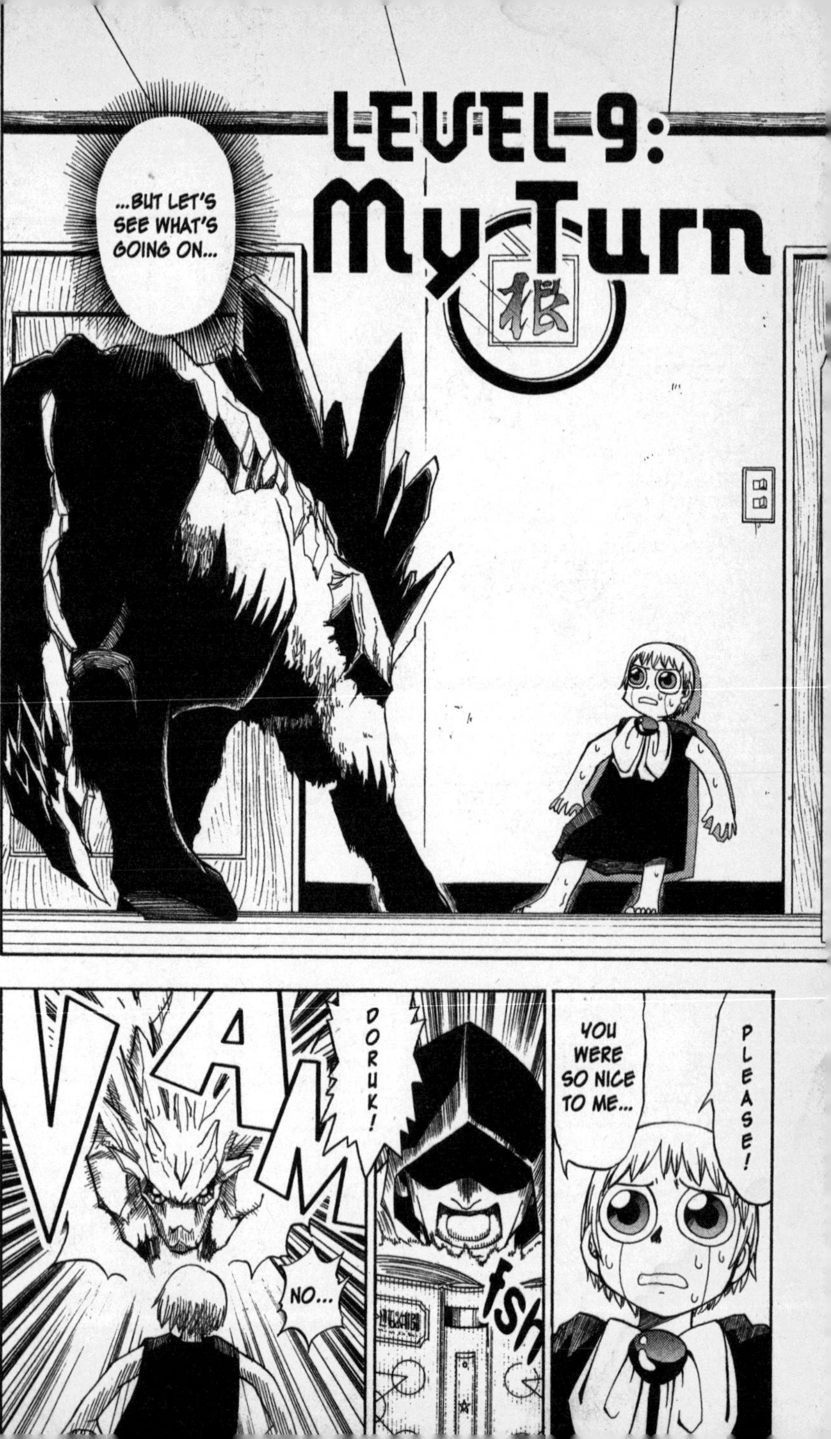
LEVEL 9: My Turn
...BUT LET'S SEE WHAT'S GOING ON...
PLEASE!
YOU WERE SO NICE TO ME...
DORUK!
fsh
VAM
NO...

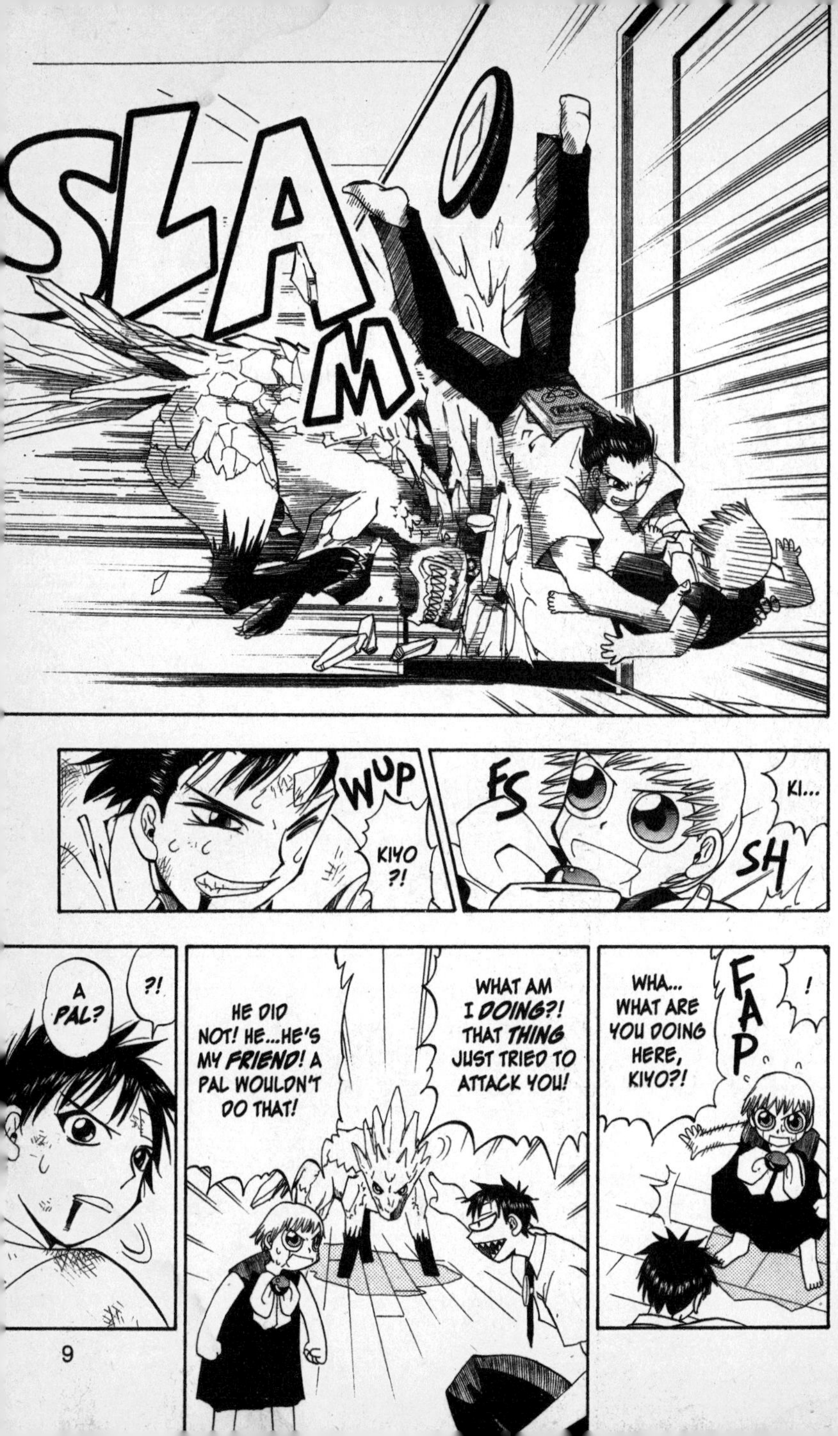
SLAM
FS
KI...
SH
WUP
KIYO ?!
FAP
!
WHA... WHAT ARE YOU DOING HERE, KIYO?!
WHAT AM I DOING?! THAT THING JUST TRIED TO ATTACK YOU!
HE DID NOT! HE...HE'S MY FRIEND! A PAL WOULDN'T DO THAT!
?!
A PAL?

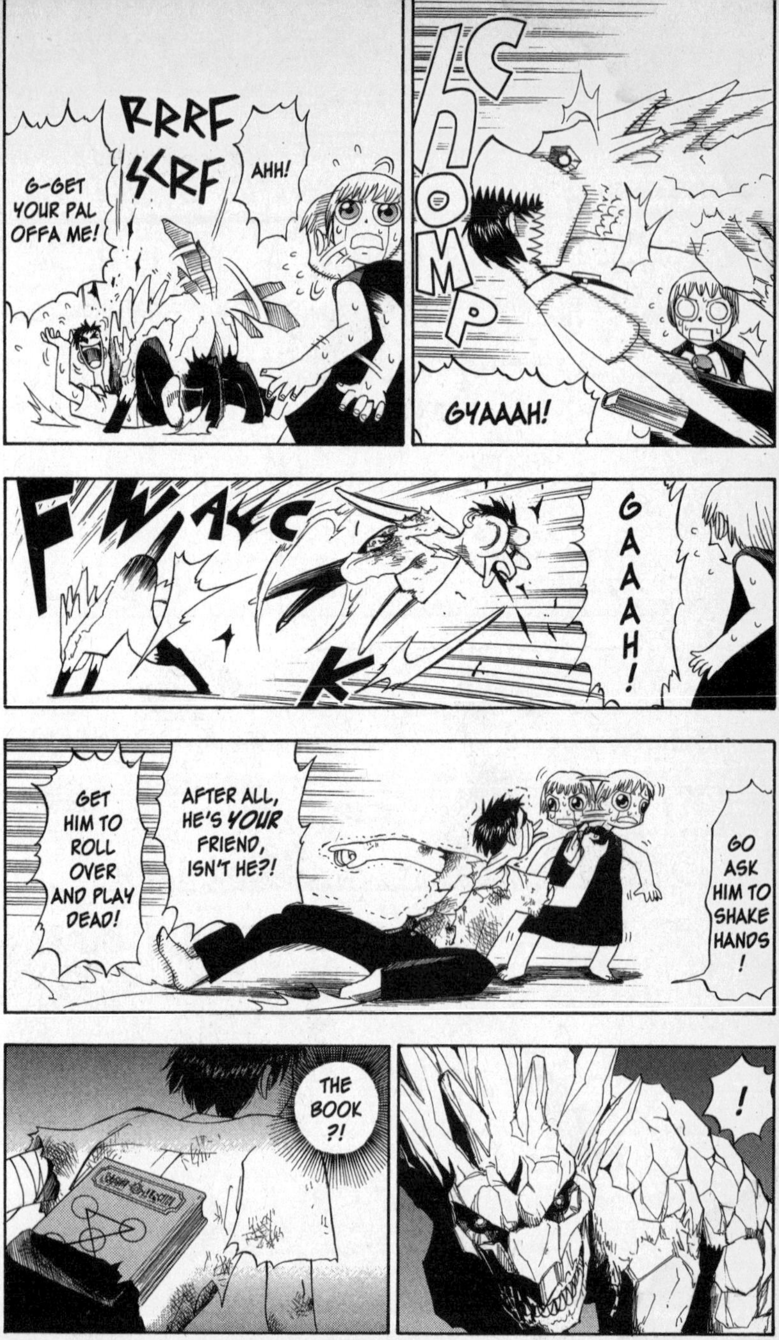
CHOMP
GYAAAH!
AHH!
RRRF SCRF
G-GET YOUR PAL OFFA ME!
GAAAAH!
FWACK
GO ASK HIM TO SHAKE HANDS!
AFTER ALL, HE'S *YOUR* FRIEND, ISN'T HE?!
GET HIM TO ROLL OVER AND PLAY DEAD!
!
THE BOOK?!

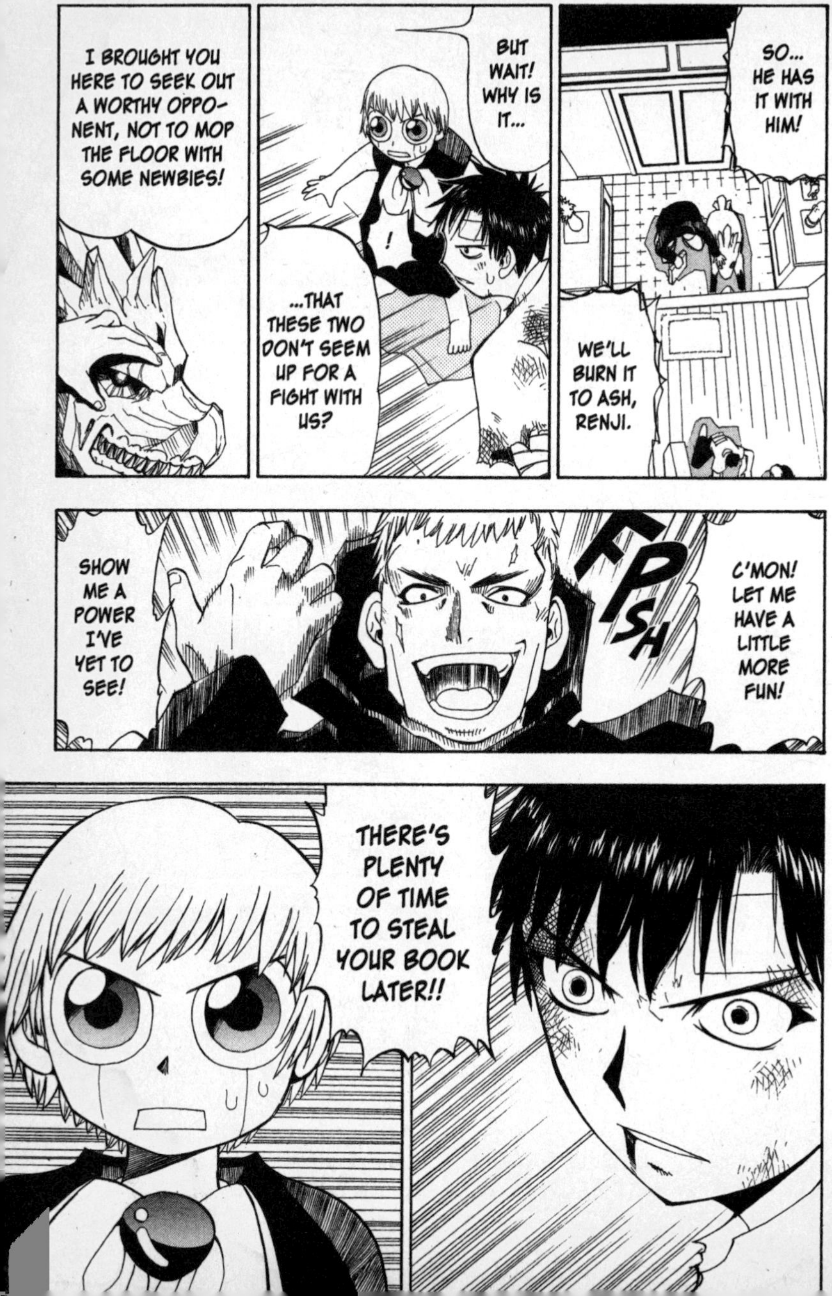
SO... HE HAS IT WITH HIM!
WE'LL BURN IT TO ASH, RENJI.
BUT WAIT! WHY IS IT...
!
...THAT THESE TWO DON'T SEEM UP FOR A FIGHT WITH US?
I BROUGHT YOU HERE TO SEEK OUT A WORTHY OPPO-NENT, NOT TO MOP THE FLOOR WITH SOME NEWBIES!
C'MON! LET ME HAVE A LITTLE MORE FUN!
FPSH
SHOW ME A POWER I'VE YET TO SEE!
THERE'S PLENTY OF TIME TO STEAL YOUR BOOK LATER!!

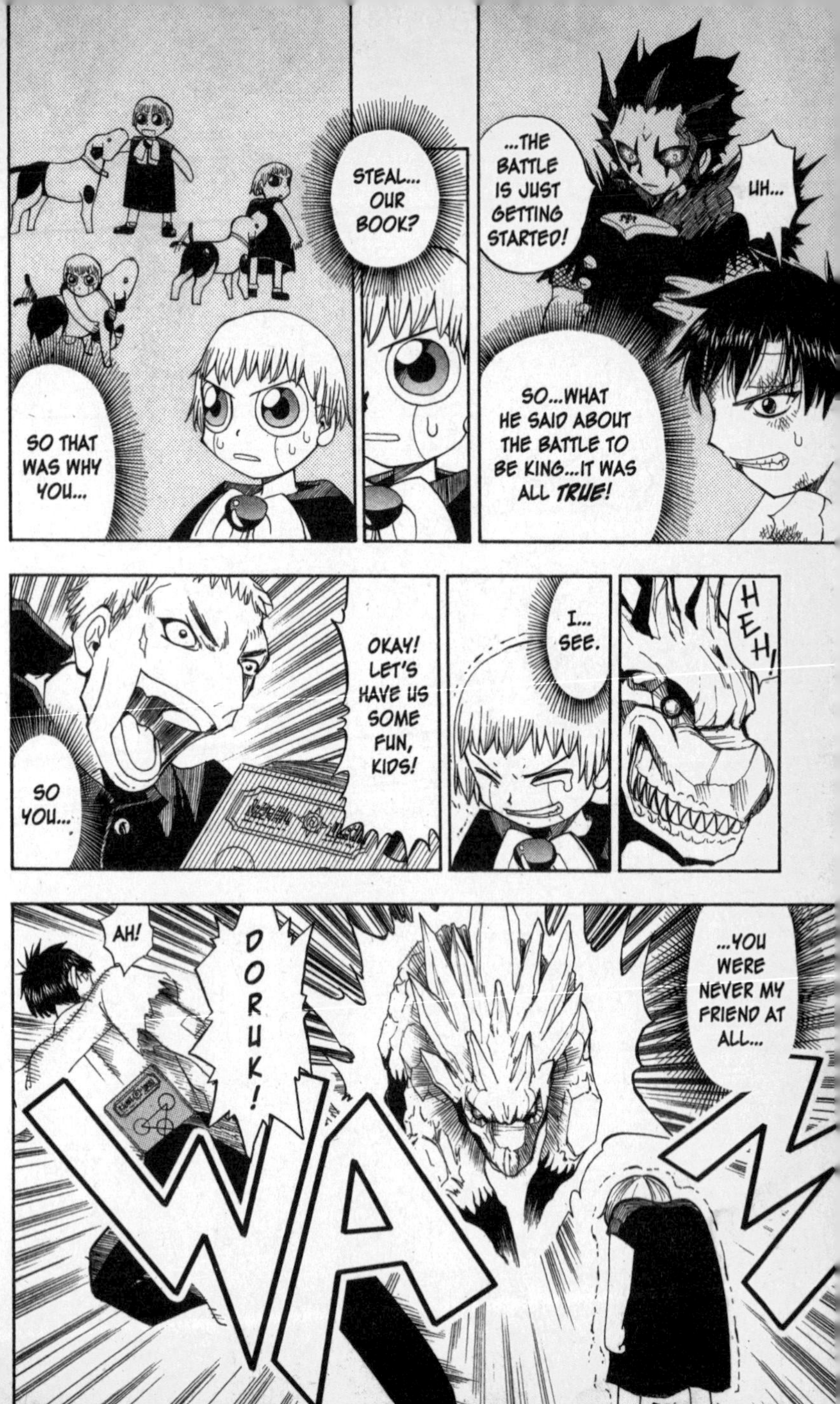
UH...
...THE BATTLE IS JUST GETTING STARTED!
SO...WHAT HE SAID ABOUT THE BATTLE TO BE KING...IT WAS ALL TRUE!
STEAL... OUR BOOK?
SO THAT WAS WHY YOU...
HEH!
I... SEE.
OKAY! LET'S HAVE US SOME FUN, KIDS!
SO YOU...
...YOU WERE NEVER MY FRIEND AT ALL...
DORUK!
AH!
WAM

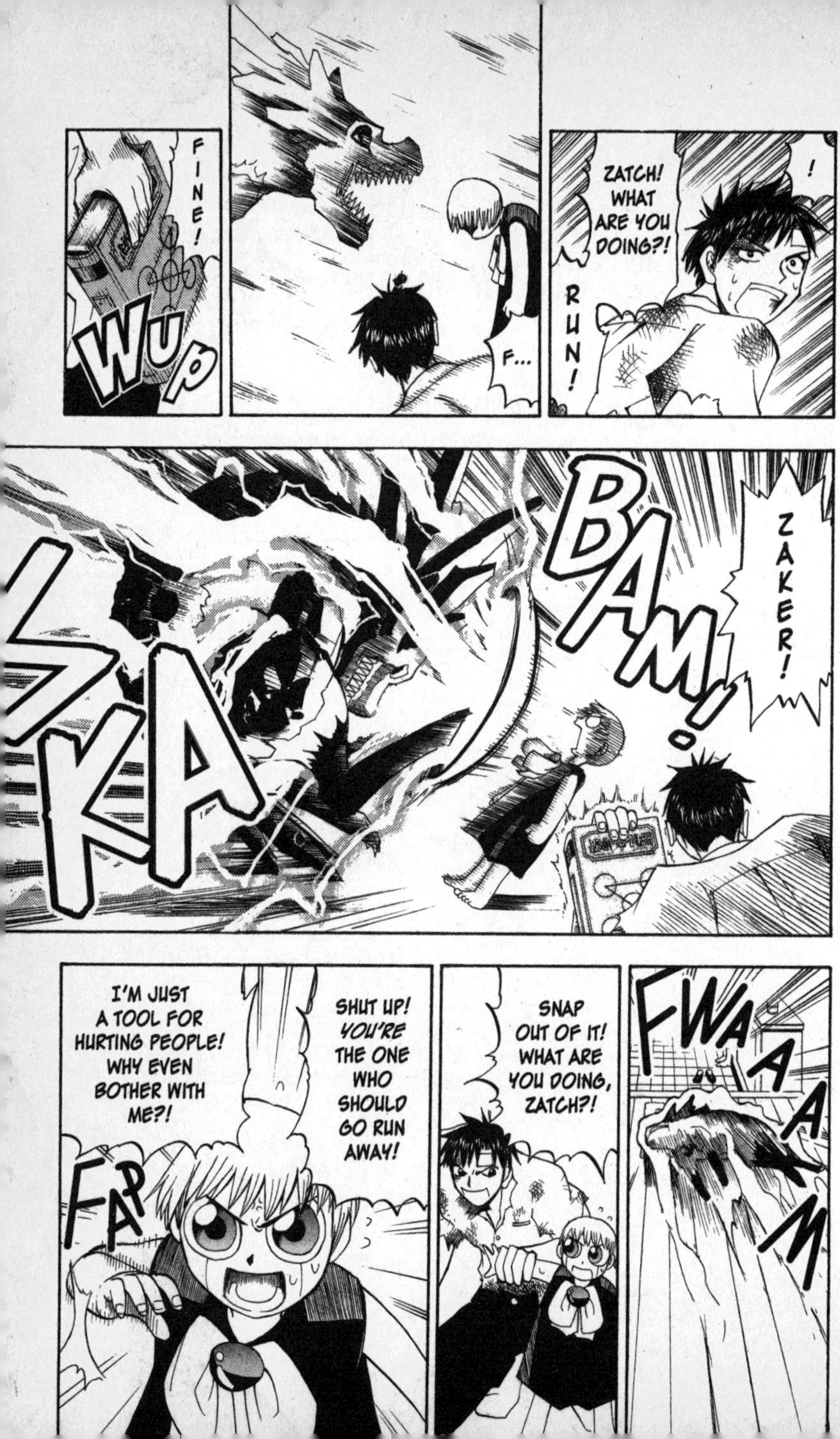
!
ZATCH! WHAT ARE YOU DOING?!
RUN!
F...
FINE!
WUP
ZAKER!
BAM!
KA
FWAAAAM
SNAP OUT OF IT! WHAT ARE YOU DOING, ZATCH?!
SHUT UP! YOU'RE THE ONE WHO SHOULD GO RUN AWAY!
I'M JUST A TOOL FOR HURTING PEOPLE! WHY EVEN BOTHER WITH ME?!
FAP

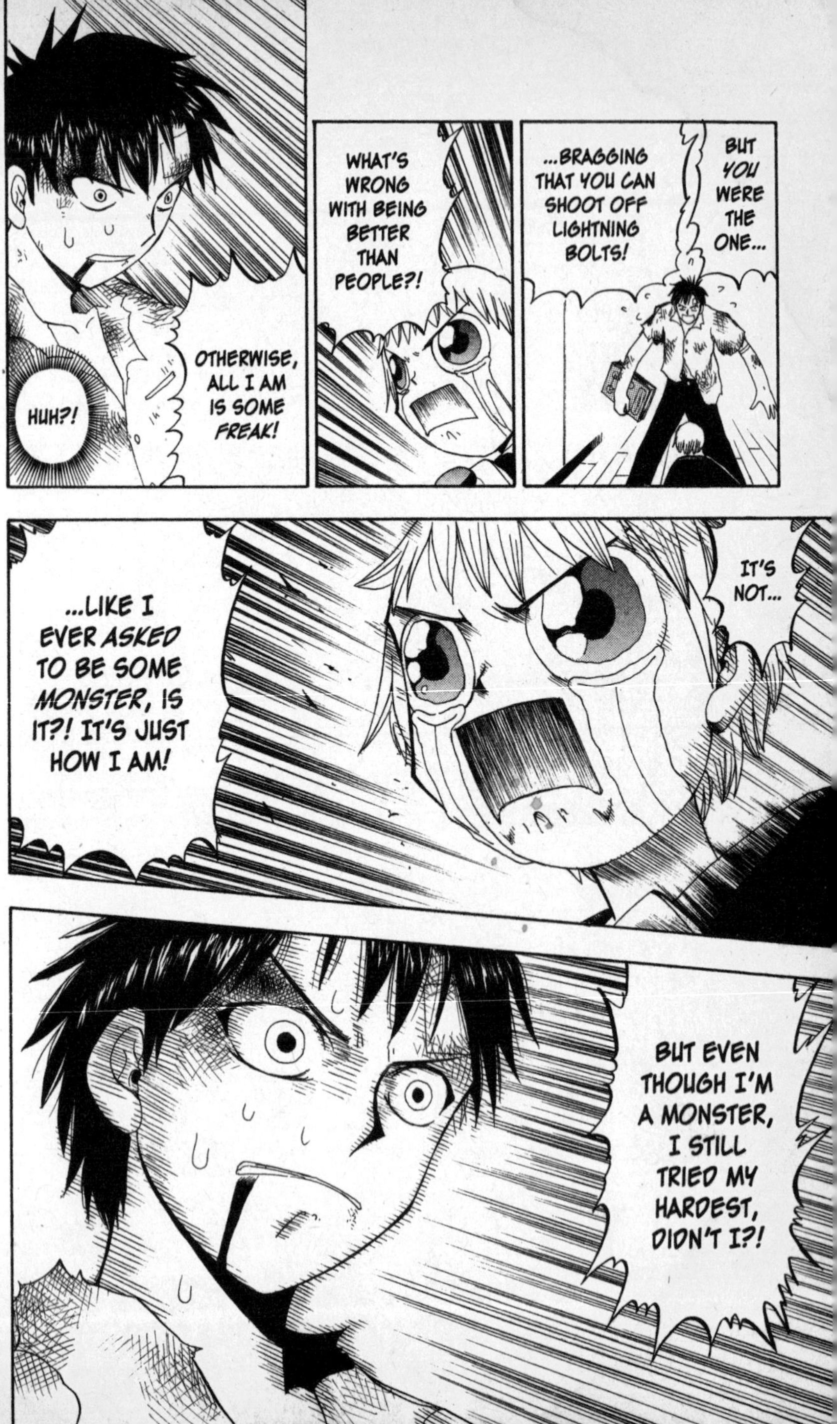
BUT *YOU* WERE THE ONE...
...BRAGGING THAT YOU CAN SHOOT OFF LIGHTNING BOLTS!
WHAT'S WRONG WITH BEING BETTER THAN PEOPLE?!
OTHERWISE, ALL I AM IS SOME *FREAK!*
HUH?!
IT'S NOT...
...LIKE I EVER *ASKED* TO BE SOME *MONSTER*, IS IT?! IT'S JUST HOW I AM!
BUT EVEN THOUGH I'M A MONSTER, I STILL TRIED MY HARDEST, DIDN'T I?!

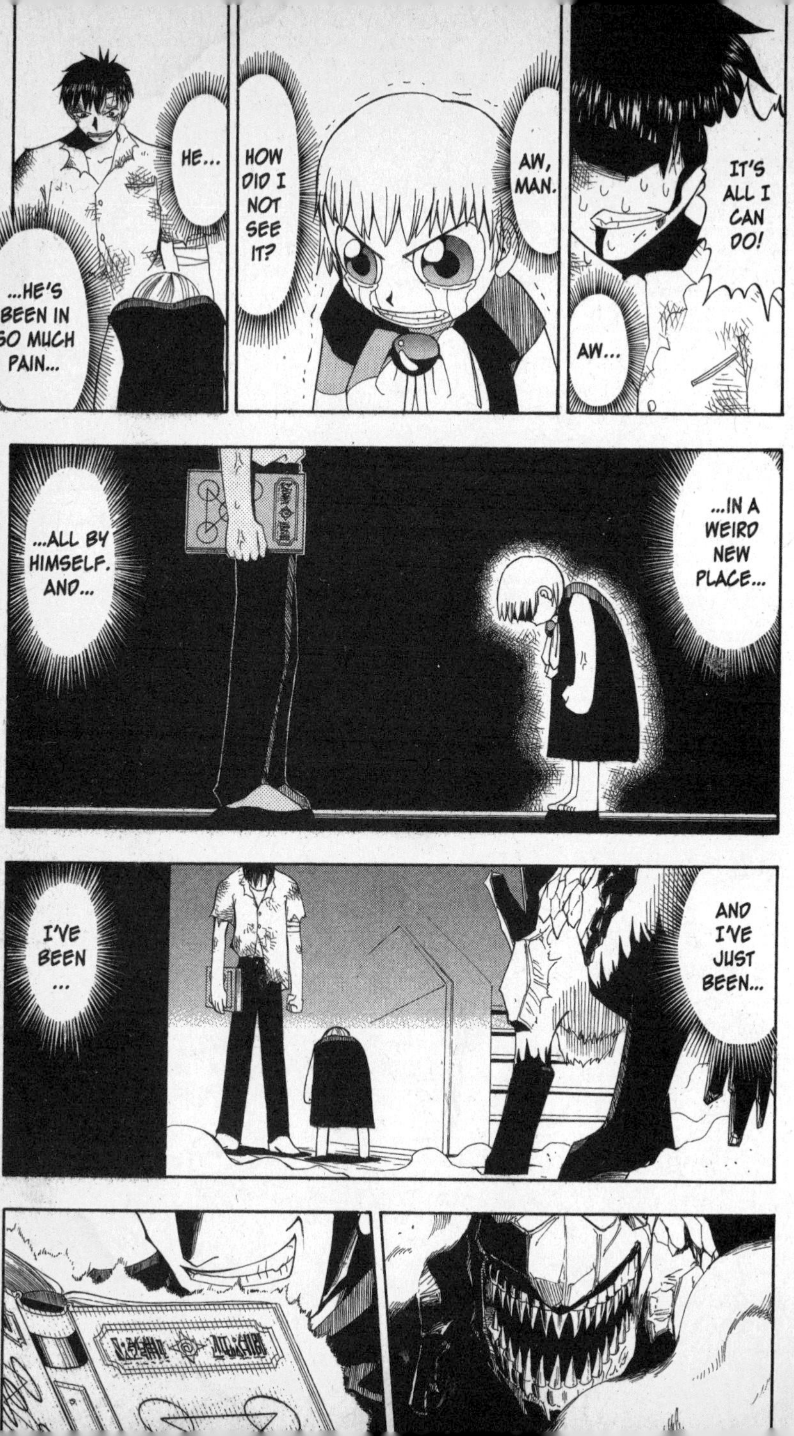
IT'S ALL I CAN DO!
AW...
AW, MAN.
HOW DID I NOT SEE IT?
HE...
...HE'S BEEN IN SO MUCH PAIN...
...IN A WEIRD NEW PLACE...
...ALL BY HIMSELF. AND...
AND I'VE JUST BEEN...
I'VE BEEN ...

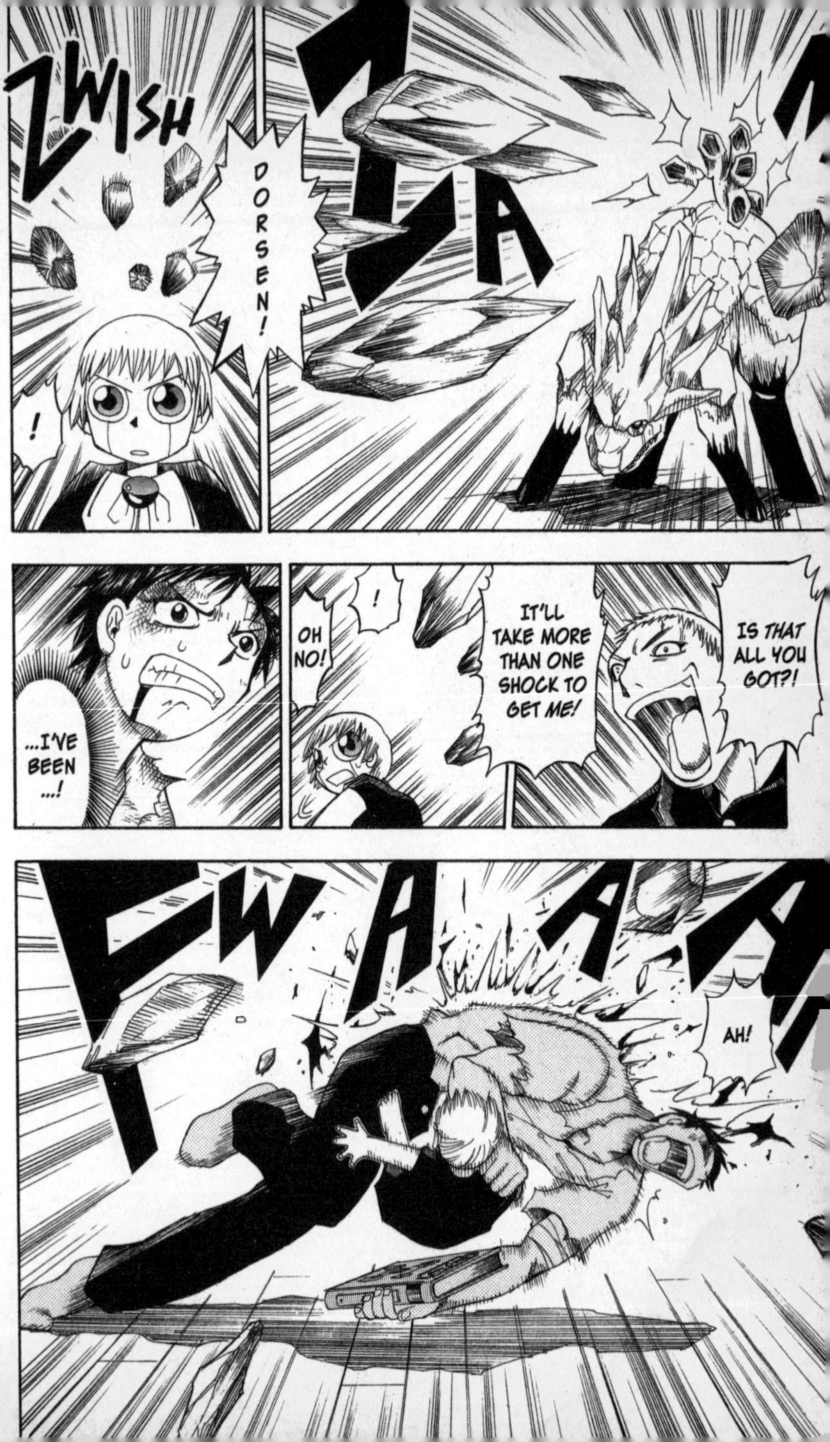
ZWISH
DORSEN!
!
IS THAT ALL YOU GOT?!
IT'LL TAKE MORE THAN ONE SHOCK TO GET ME!
!
OH NO!
...I'VE BEEN ...!
FWAAA
AH!

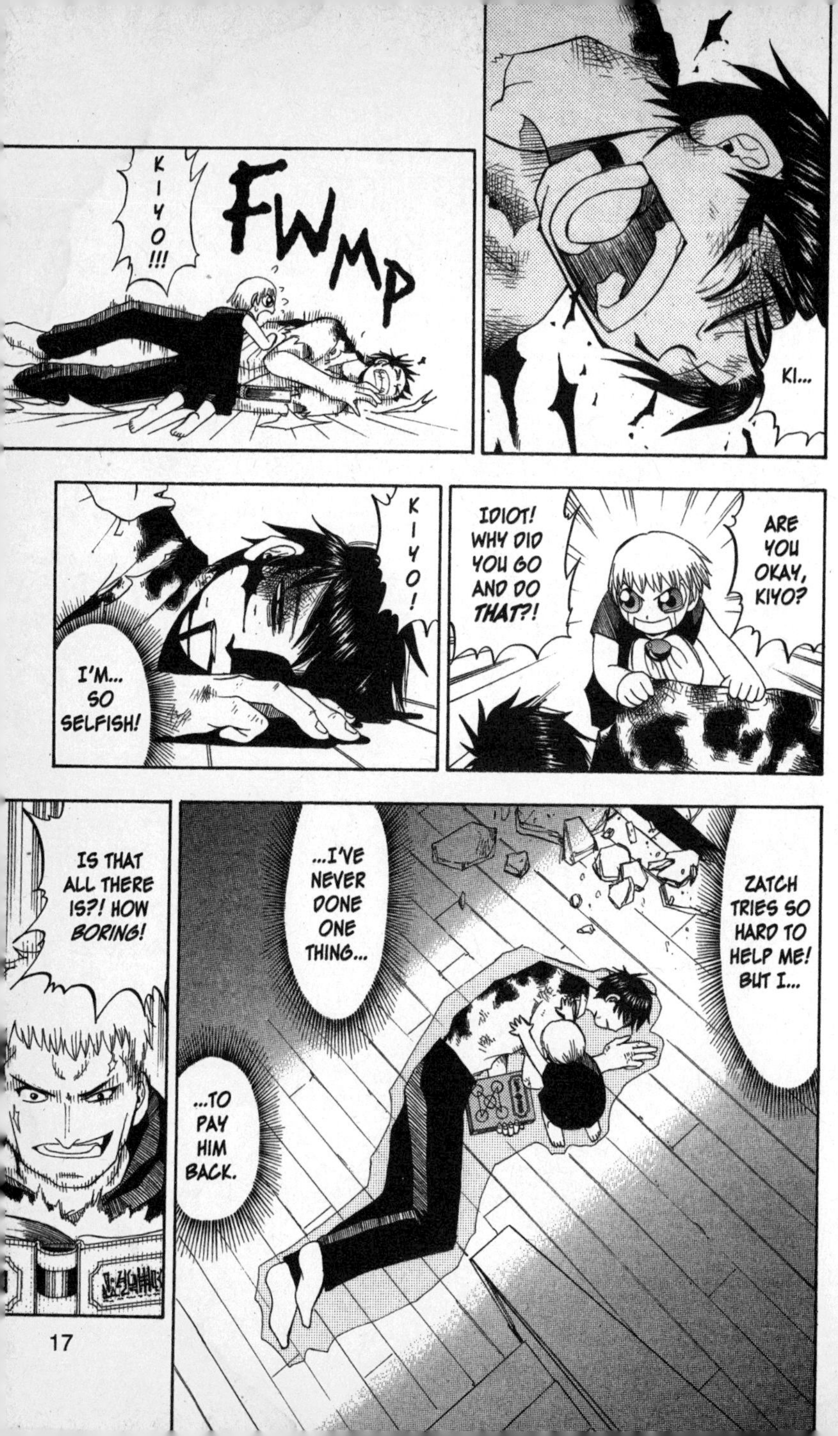
KI...
KIYO!!!
FWMP
ARE YOU OKAY, KIYO?
IDIOT! WHY DID YOU GO AND DO *THAT*?!
KIYO!
I'M... SO SELFISH!
ZATCH TRIES SO HARD TO HELP ME! BUT I...
...I'VE NEVER DONE ONE THING...
...TO PAY HIM BACK.
IS THAT ALL THERE IS?! HOW *BORING*!

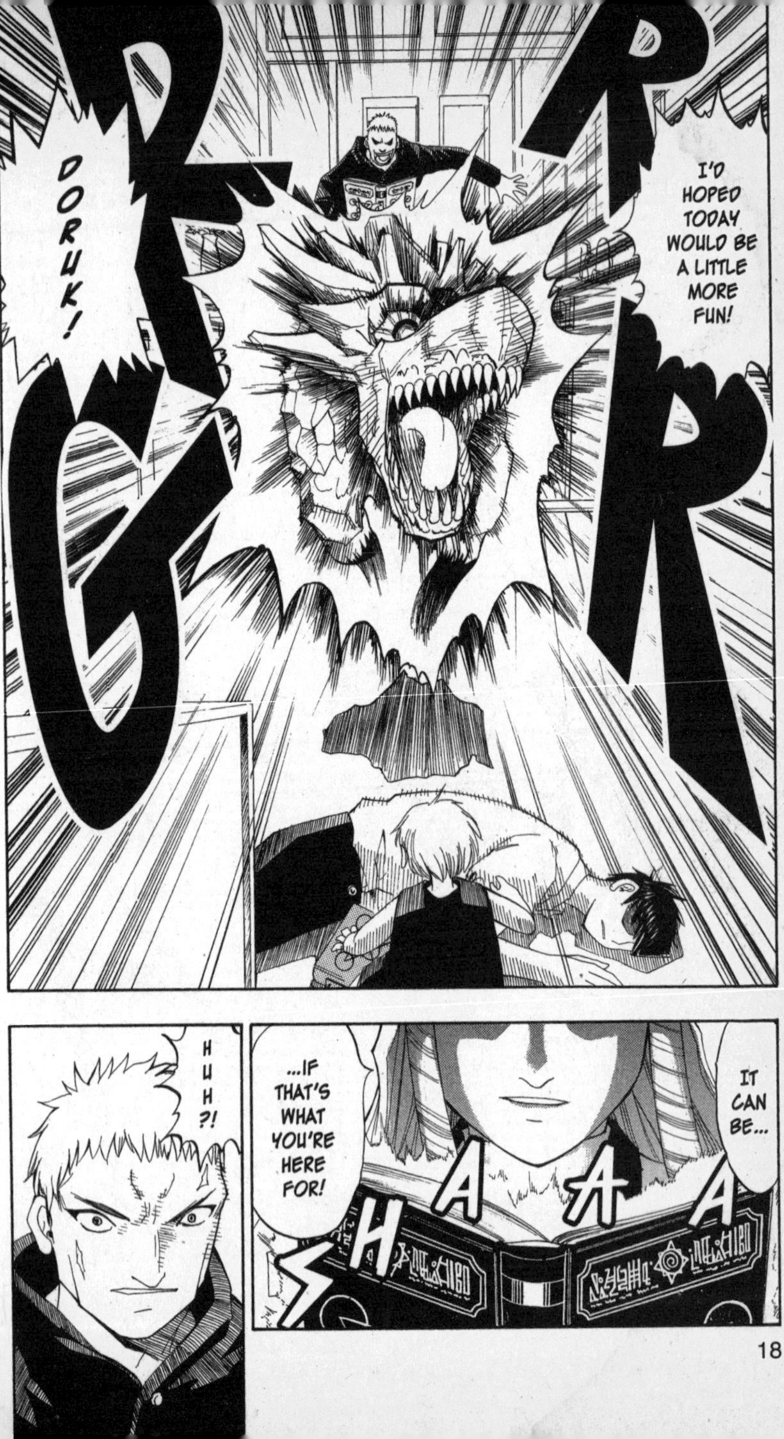
I'D HOPED TODAY WOULD BE A LITTLE MORE FUN!
DORUK!
IT CAN BE...
...IF THAT'S WHAT YOU'RE HERE FOR!
HAAA
HUH?!

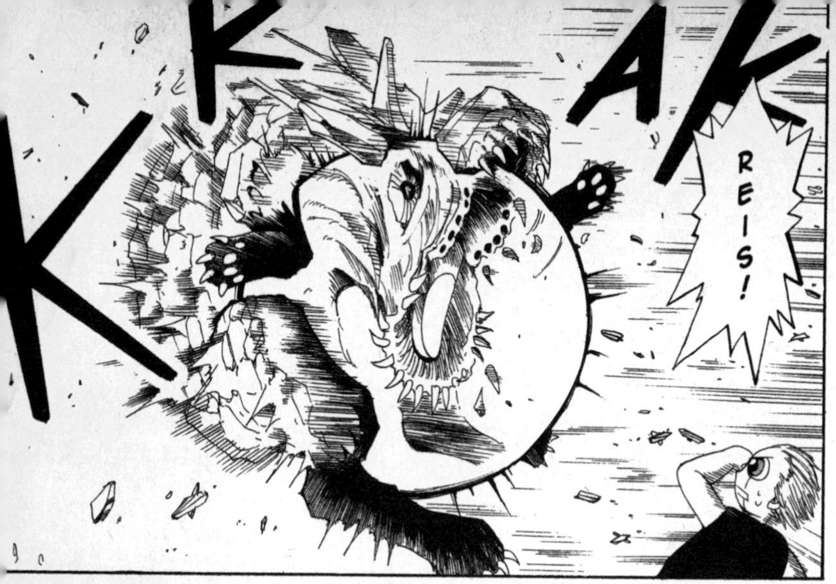
REIS!
K
K
AK

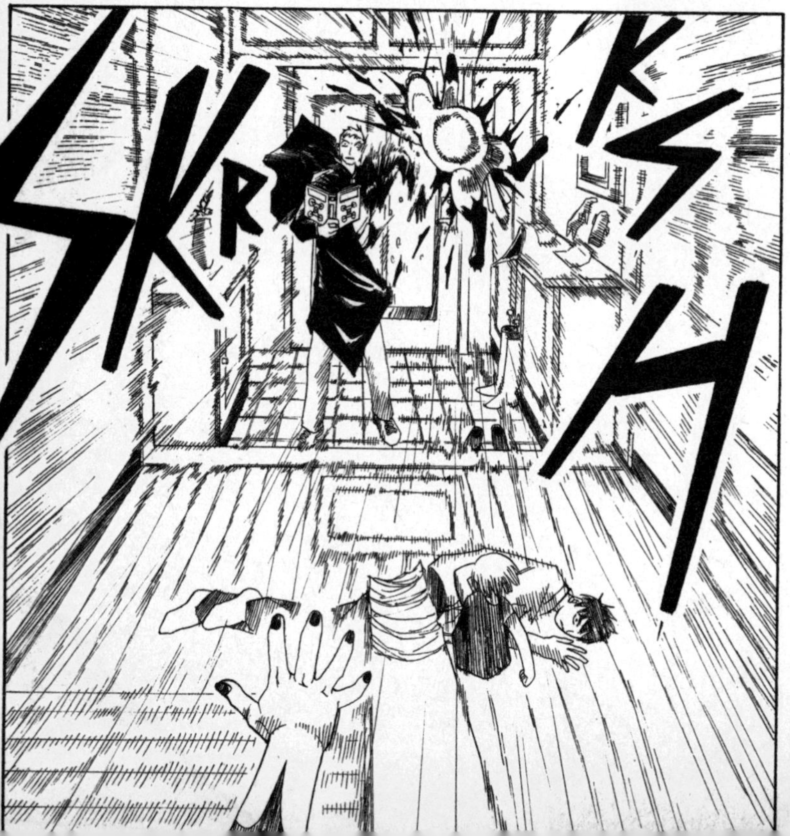
SKR
KSH

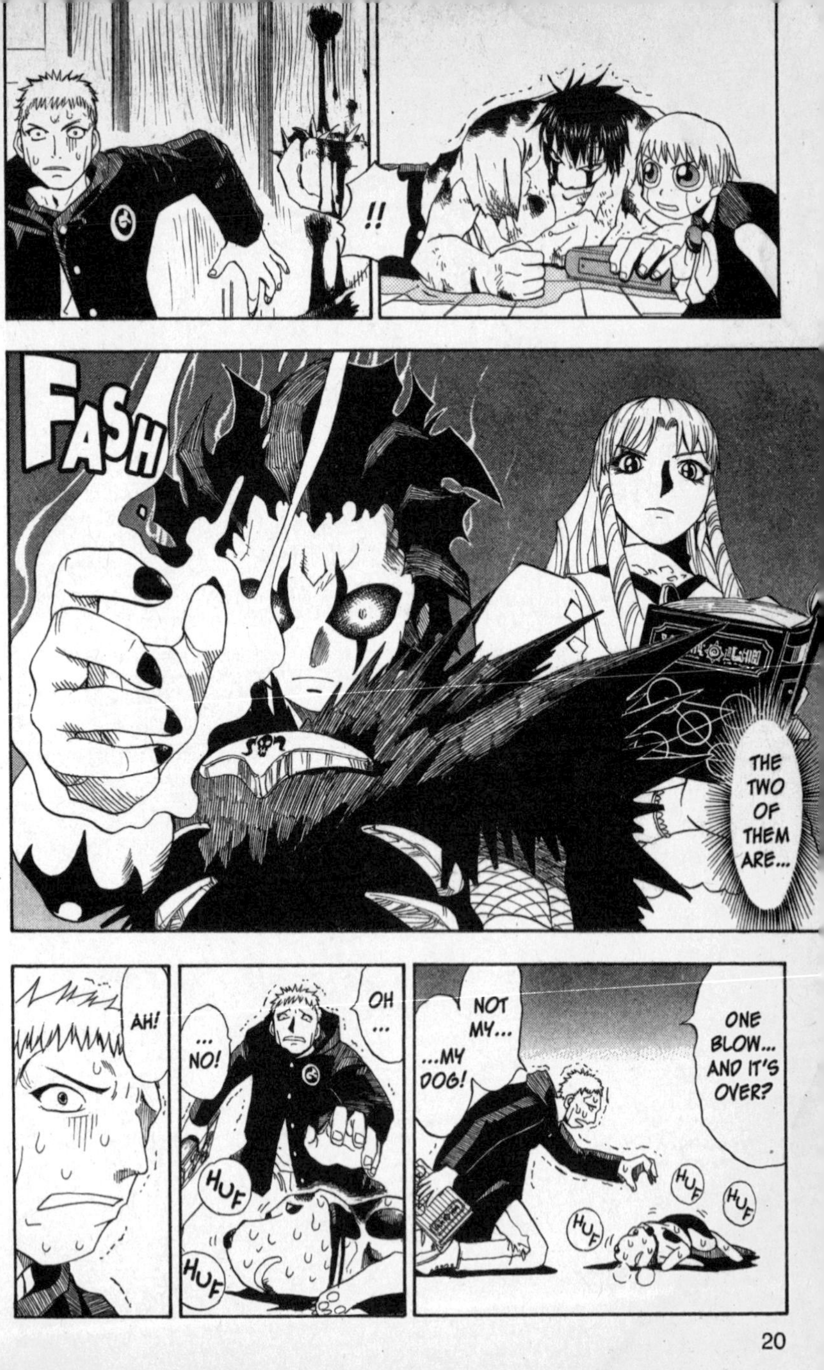
!!
FASH
THE TWO OF THEM ARE...
ONE BLOW... AND IT'S OVER?
NOT MY...
...MY DOG!
HUF
HUF
HUF
OH ...
... NO!
HUF
HUF
AH!

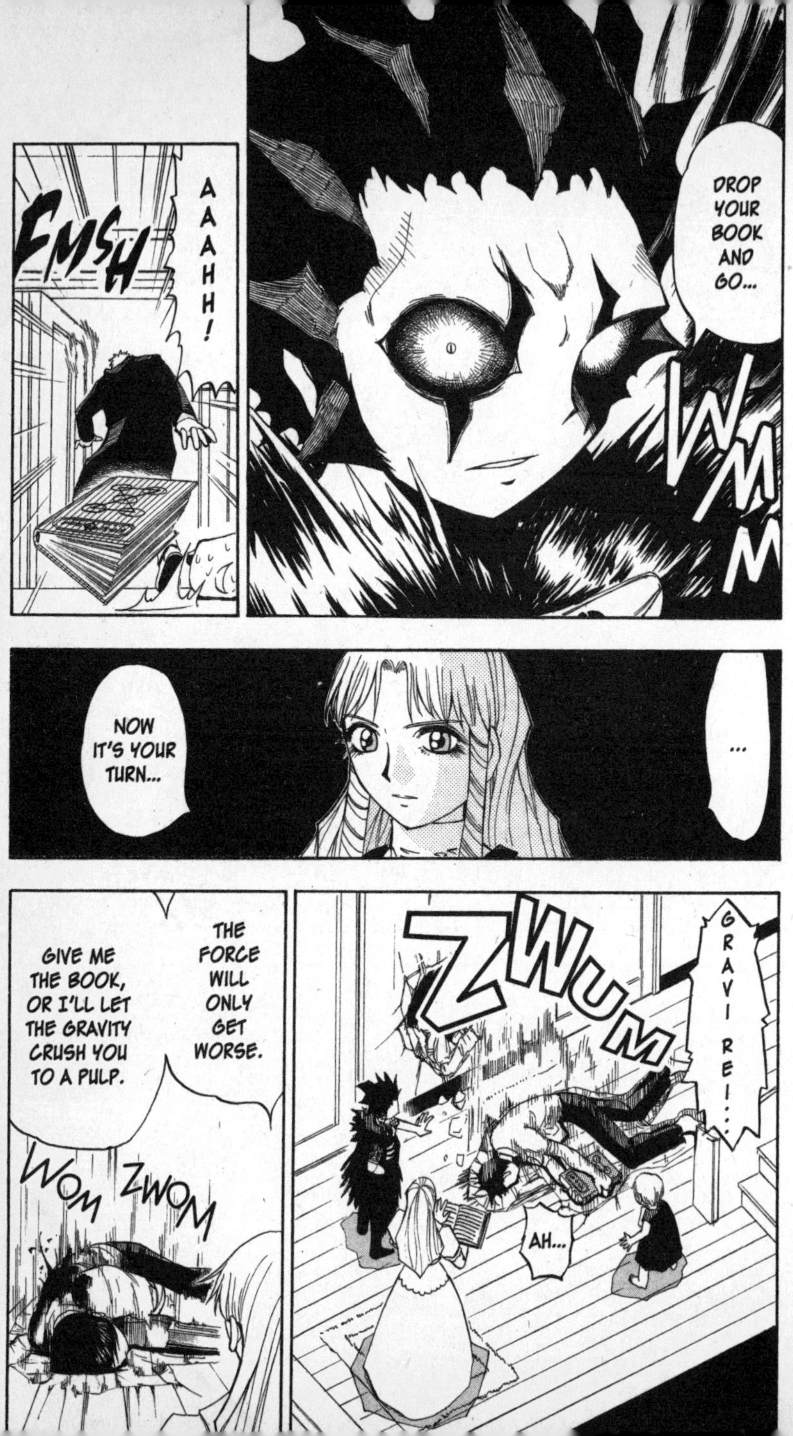
DROP YOUR BOOK AND GO...
WMM
AAAHH!
FMSH
...
NOW IT'S YOUR TURN...
GRAVI REI...
ZWUM
AH...
THE FORCE WILL ONLY GET WORSE.
GIVE ME THE BOOK, OR I'LL LET THE GRAVITY CRUSH YOU TO A PULP.
ZWOM
WOM

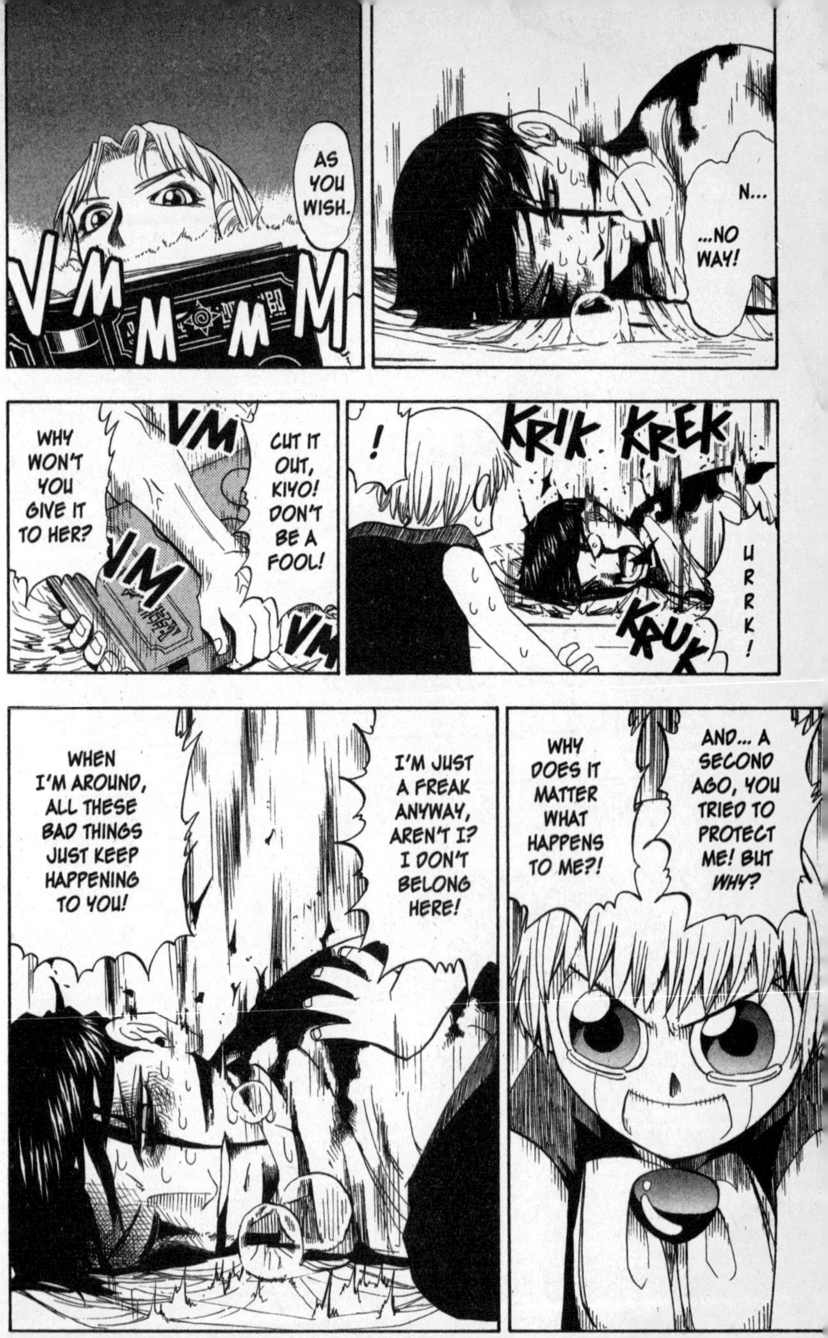
N...
...NO WAY!
VMMMM
AS YOU WISH.
!
KRIK KREK
URRK!
KRUK
VM
CUT IT OUT, KIYO! DON'T BE A FOOL!
WHY WON'T YOU GIVE IT TO HER?
VM
VM
AND... A SECOND AGO, YOU TRIED TO PROTECT ME! BUT *WHY?*
WHY DOES IT MATTER WHAT HAPPENS TO ME?!
I'M JUST A FREAK ANYWAY, AREN'T I? I DON'T BELONG HERE!
WHEN I'M AROUND, ALL THESE BAD THINGS JUST KEEP HAPPENING TO YOU!

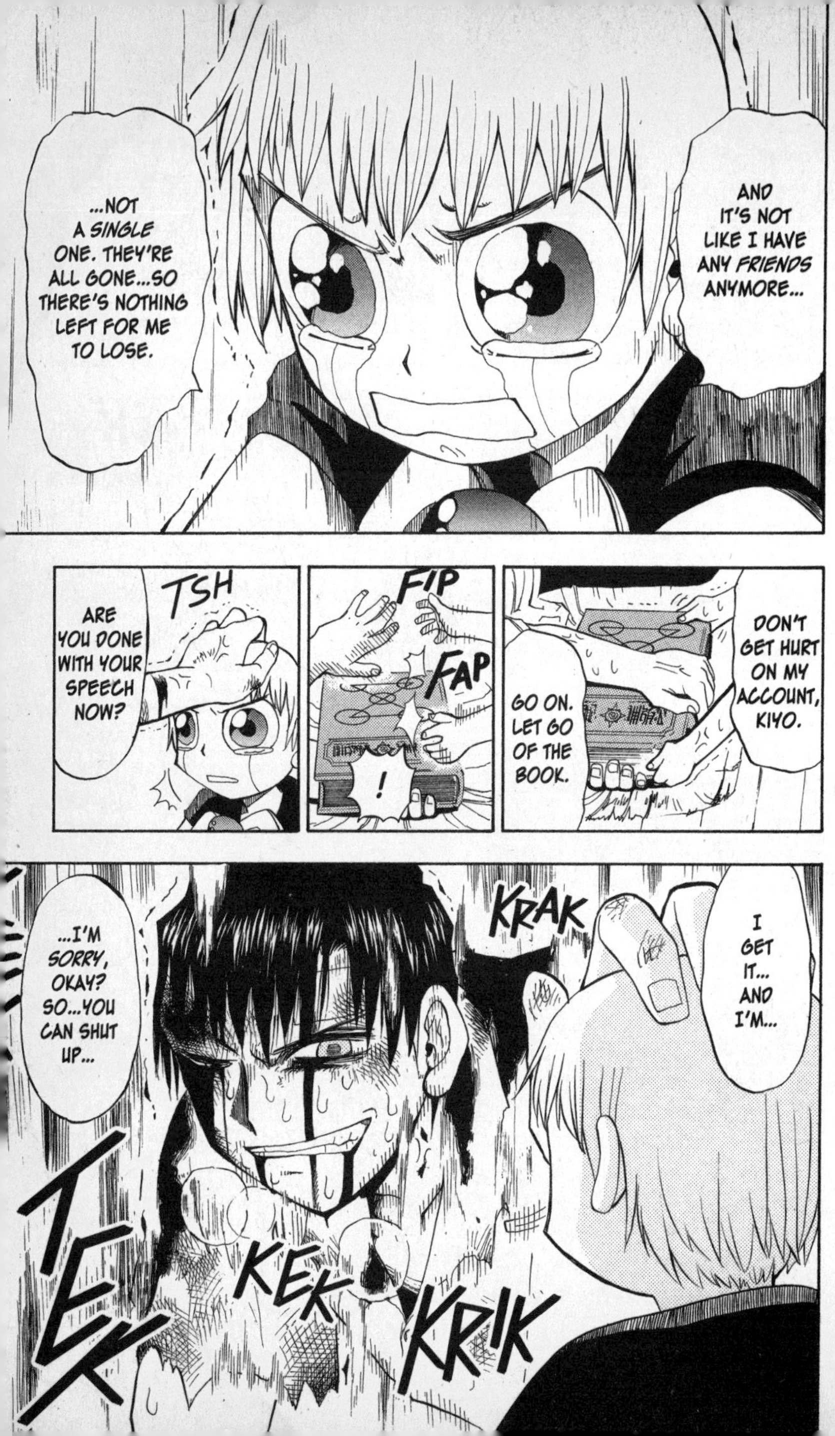
AND IT'S NOT LIKE I HAVE ANY *FRIENDS* ANYMORE...
...NOT A *SINGLE* ONE. THEY'RE ALL GONE...SO THERE'S NOTHING LEFT FOR ME TO LOSE.
DON'T GET HURT ON MY ACCOUNT, KIYO.
GO ON. LET GO OF THE BOOK.
FIP
FAP
!
TSH
ARE YOU DONE WITH YOUR SPEECH NOW?
I GET IT... AND I'M...
KRAK
...I'M *SORRY*, OKAY? SO...YOU CAN SHUT UP...
TEK
KEK
KRIK

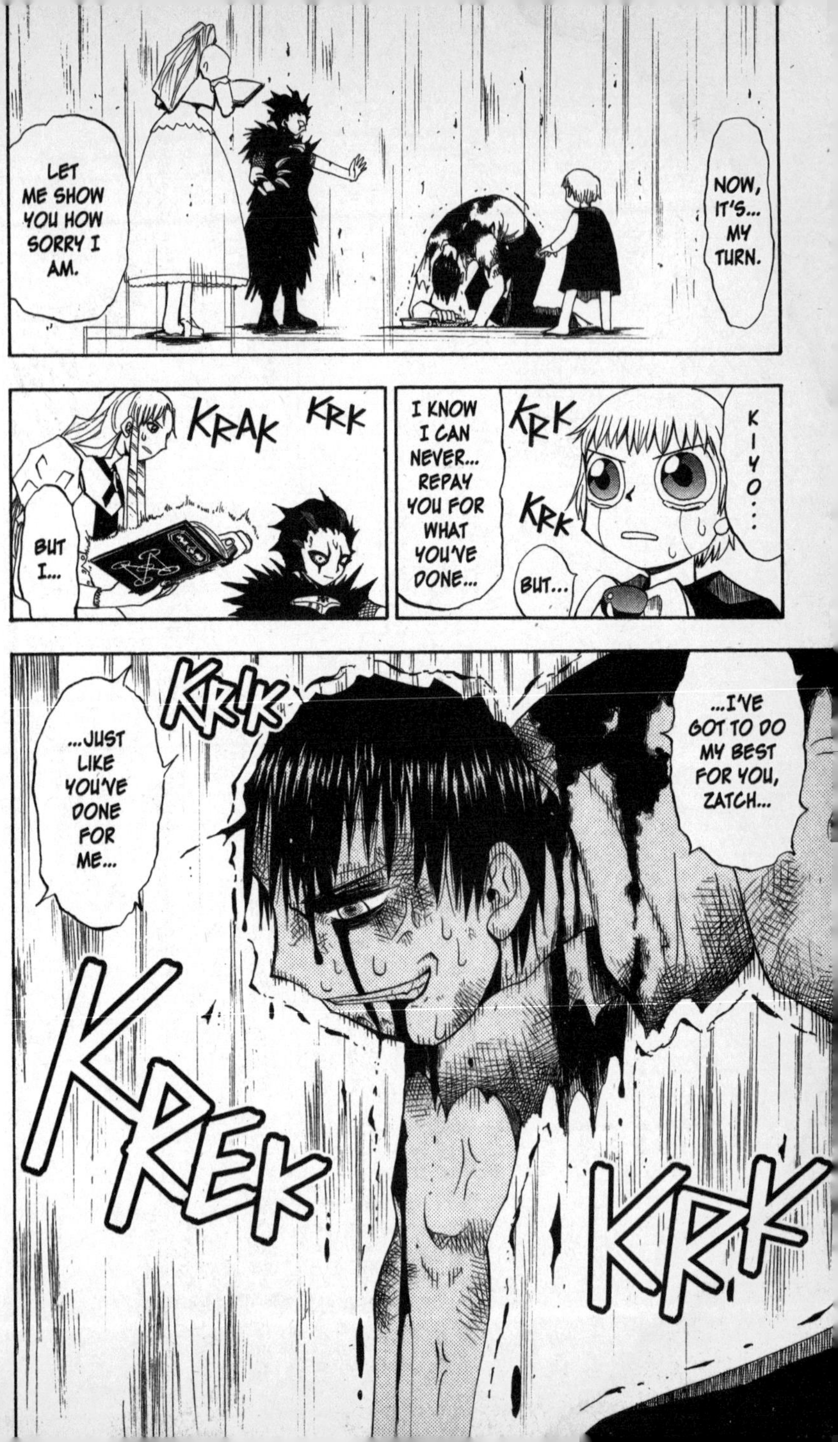
NOW, IT'S... MY TURN.
LET ME SHOW YOU HOW SORRY I AM.
KIYO...
KRK
KRK
I KNOW I CAN NEVER... REPAY YOU FOR WHAT YOU'VE DONE...
BUT...
KRK
KRAK
BUT I...
...I'VE GOT TO DO MY BEST FOR YOU, ZATCH...
KRIK
...JUST LIKE YOU'VE DONE FOR ME...
KRK
KREK

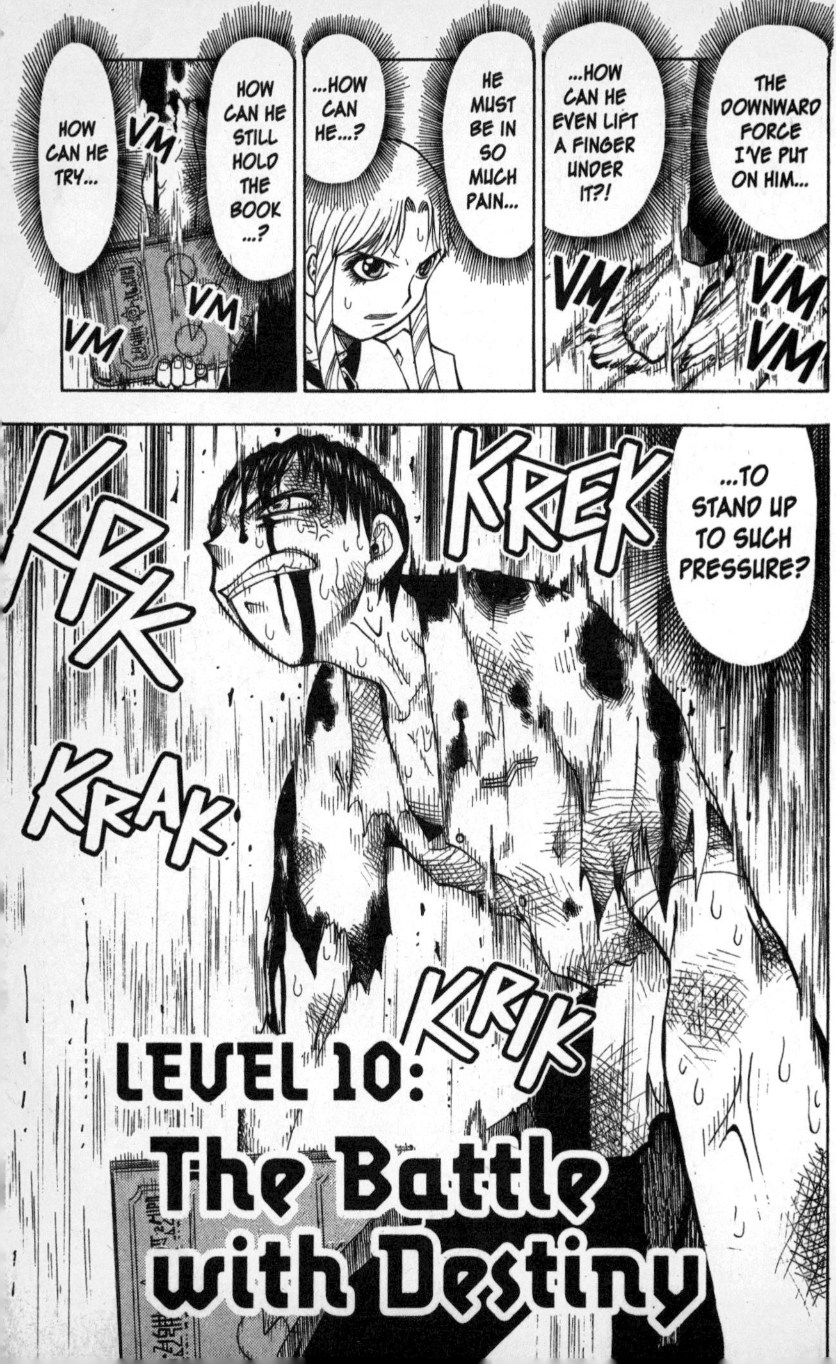
THE DOWNWARD FORCE I'VE PUT ON HIM...
VM
VM
VM
...HOW CAN HE EVEN LIFT A FINGER UNDER IT?!
VM
HE MUST BE IN SO MUCH PAIN...
...HOW CAN HE...?
HOW CAN HE STILL HOLD THE BOOK...?
VM
HOW CAN HE TRY...
VM
VM
...TO STAND UP TO SUCH PRESSURE?
KREK
KRK
KRAK
KRIK
LEVEL 10:
The Battle with Destiny

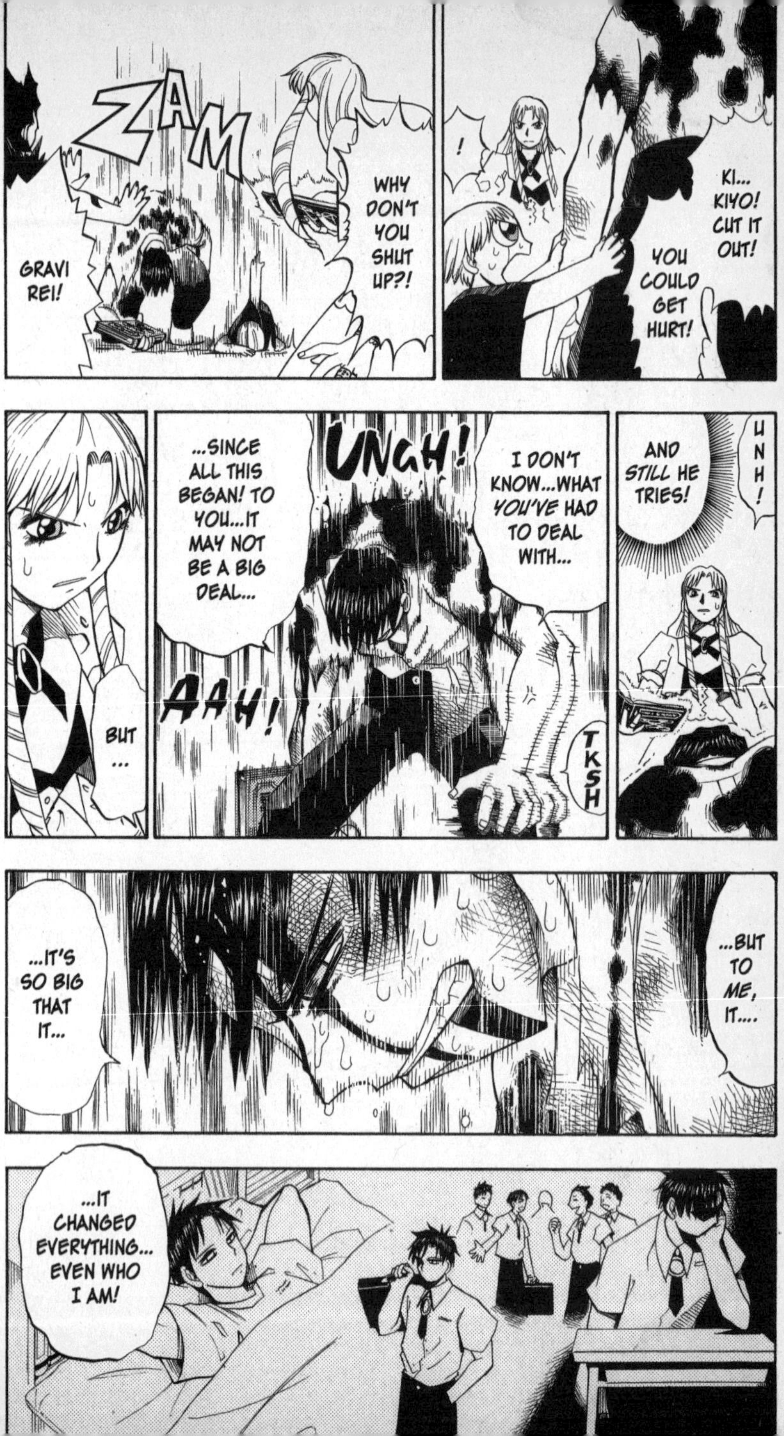
!
KI... KIYO! CUT IT OUT!
YOU COULD GET HURT!
WHY DON'T YOU SHUT UP?!
ZAM
GRAVI REI!
UNH!
AND STILL HE TRIES!
I DON'T KNOW...WHAT YOU'VE HAD TO DEAL WITH...
UNGH!
...SINCE ALL THIS BEGAN! TO YOU...IT MAY NOT BE A BIG DEAL...
TKSH
AAH!
BUT ...
...BUT TO ME, IT....
...IT'S SO BIG THAT IT...
...IT CHANGED EVERYTHING... EVEN WHO I AM!

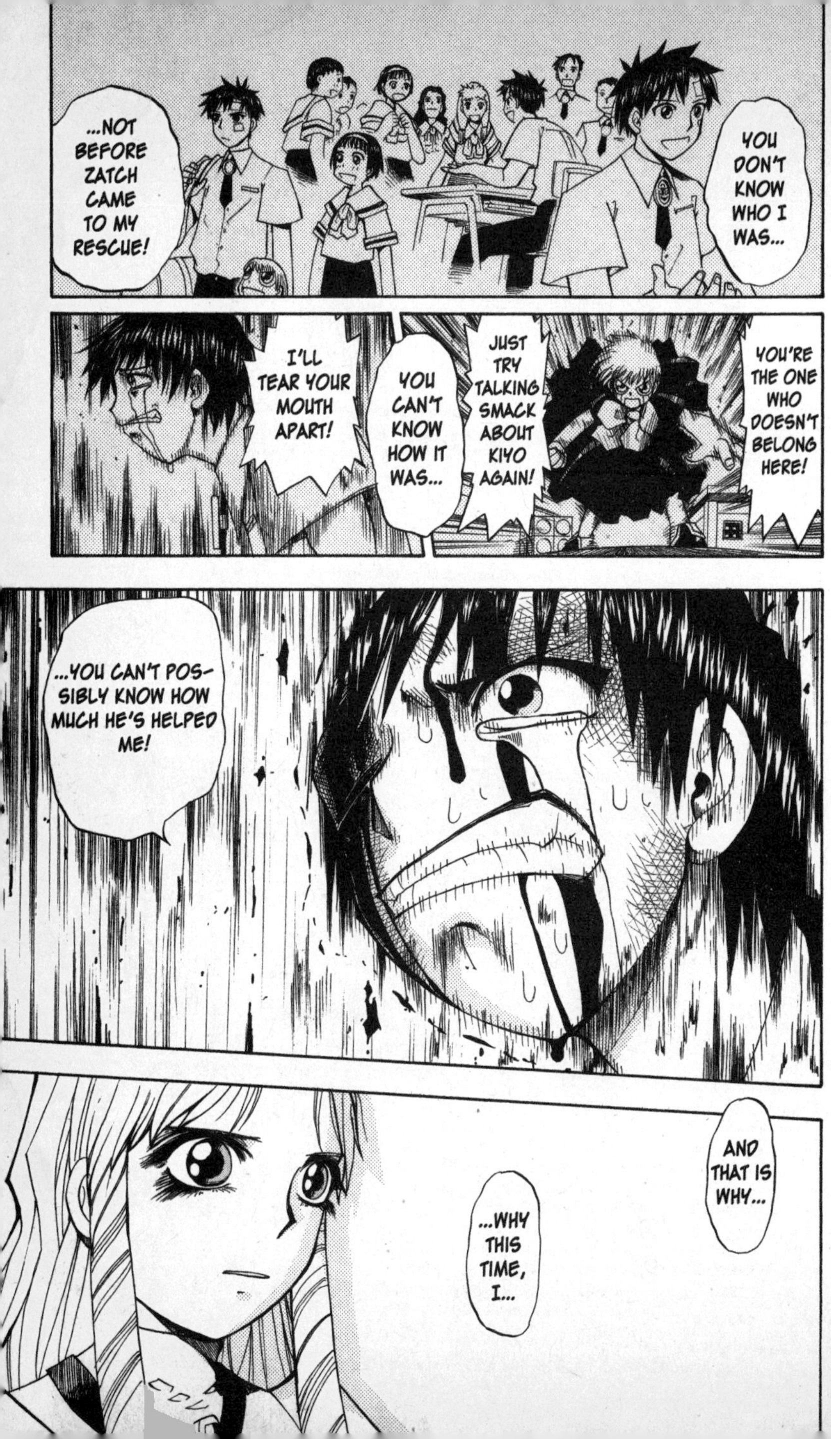
YOU DON'T KNOW WHO I WAS...
...NOT BEFORE ZATCH CAME TO MY RESCUE!
YOU'RE THE ONE WHO DOESN'T BELONG HERE!
JUST TRY TALKING SMACK ABOUT KIYO AGAIN!
YOU CAN'T KNOW HOW IT WAS...
I'LL TEAR YOUR MOUTH APART!
...YOU CAN'T POS-SIBLY KNOW HOW MUCH HE'S HELPED ME!
AND THAT IS WHY...
...WHY THIS TIME, I...

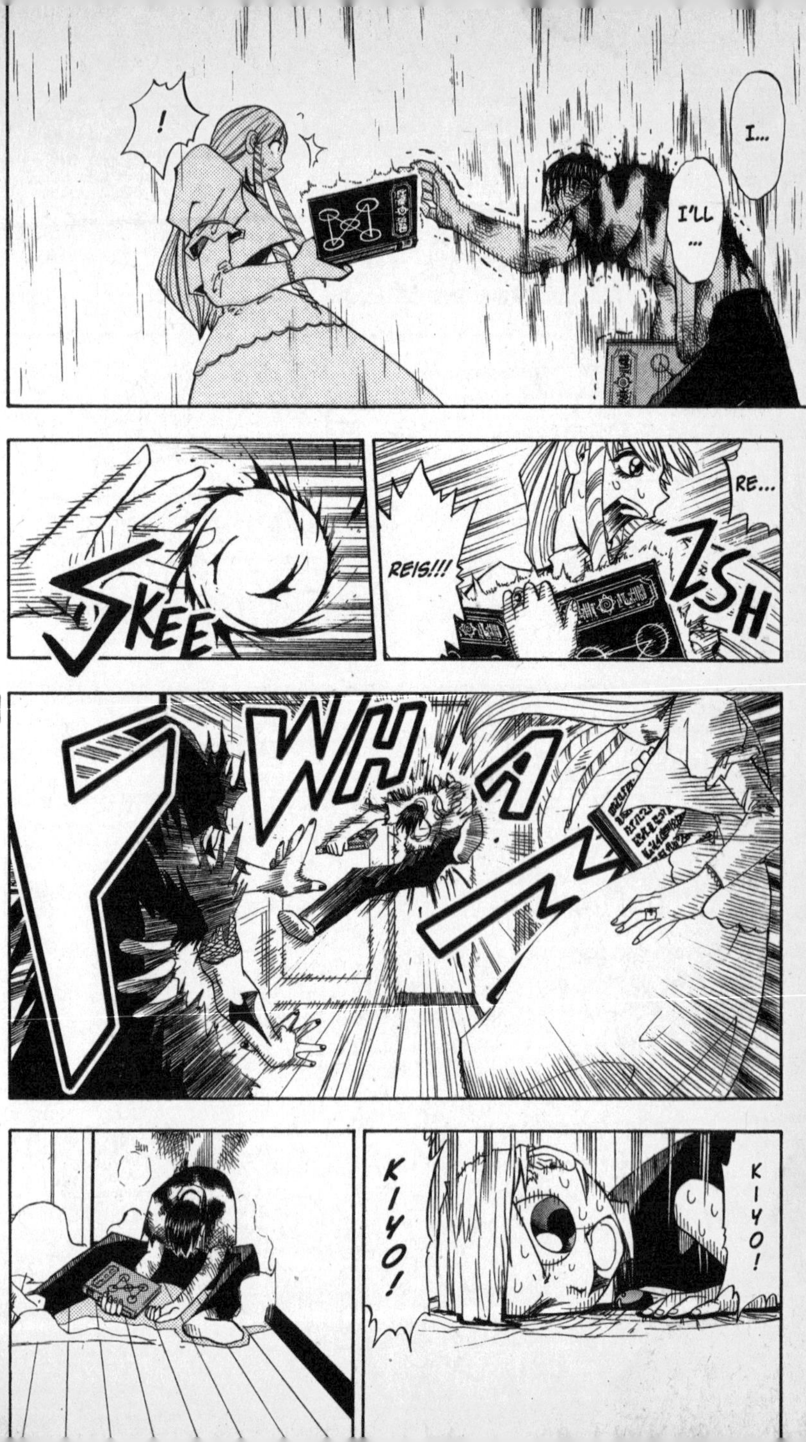
I...
I'LL ...
!
RE...
REIS!!!
ZSH
SKEE
WHAM
KIYO!
KIYO!

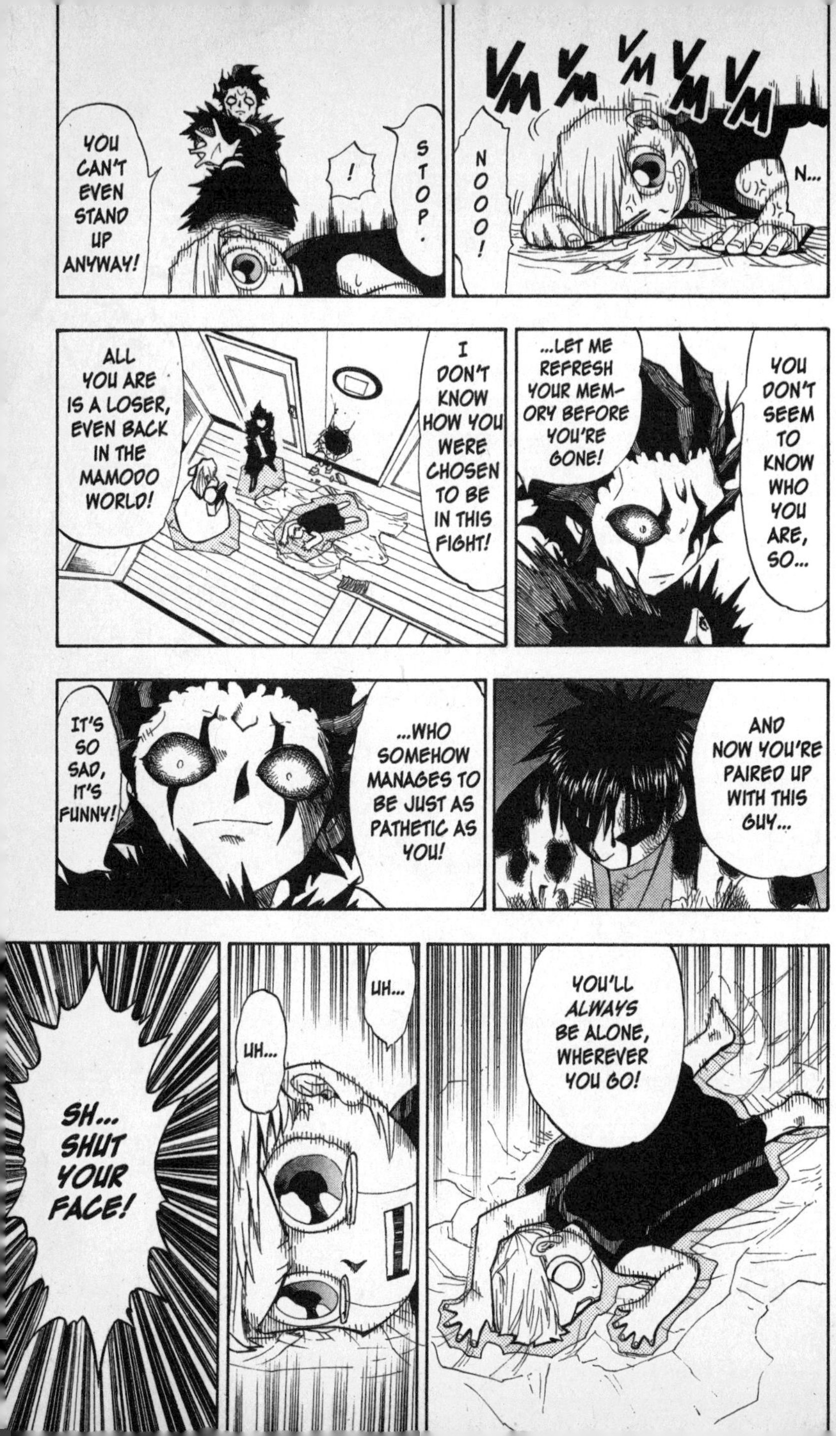
VM VM VM VM VM
N...
NOOOO!
STOP.
!
YOU CAN'T EVEN STAND UP ANYWAY!
YOU DON'T SEEM TO KNOW WHO YOU ARE, SO...
...LET ME REFRESH YOUR MEMORY BEFORE YOU'RE GONE!
I DON'T KNOW HOW YOU WERE CHOSEN TO BE IN THIS FIGHT!
ALL YOU ARE IS A LOSER, EVEN BACK IN THE MAMODO WORLD!
AND NOW YOU'RE PAIRED UP WITH THIS GUY...
...WHO SOMEHOW MANAGES TO BE JUST AS PATHETIC AS YOU!
IT'S SO SAD, IT'S FUNNY!
YOU'LL ALWAYS BE ALONE, WHEREVER YOU GO!
UH...
UH...
SH... SHUT YOUR FACE!

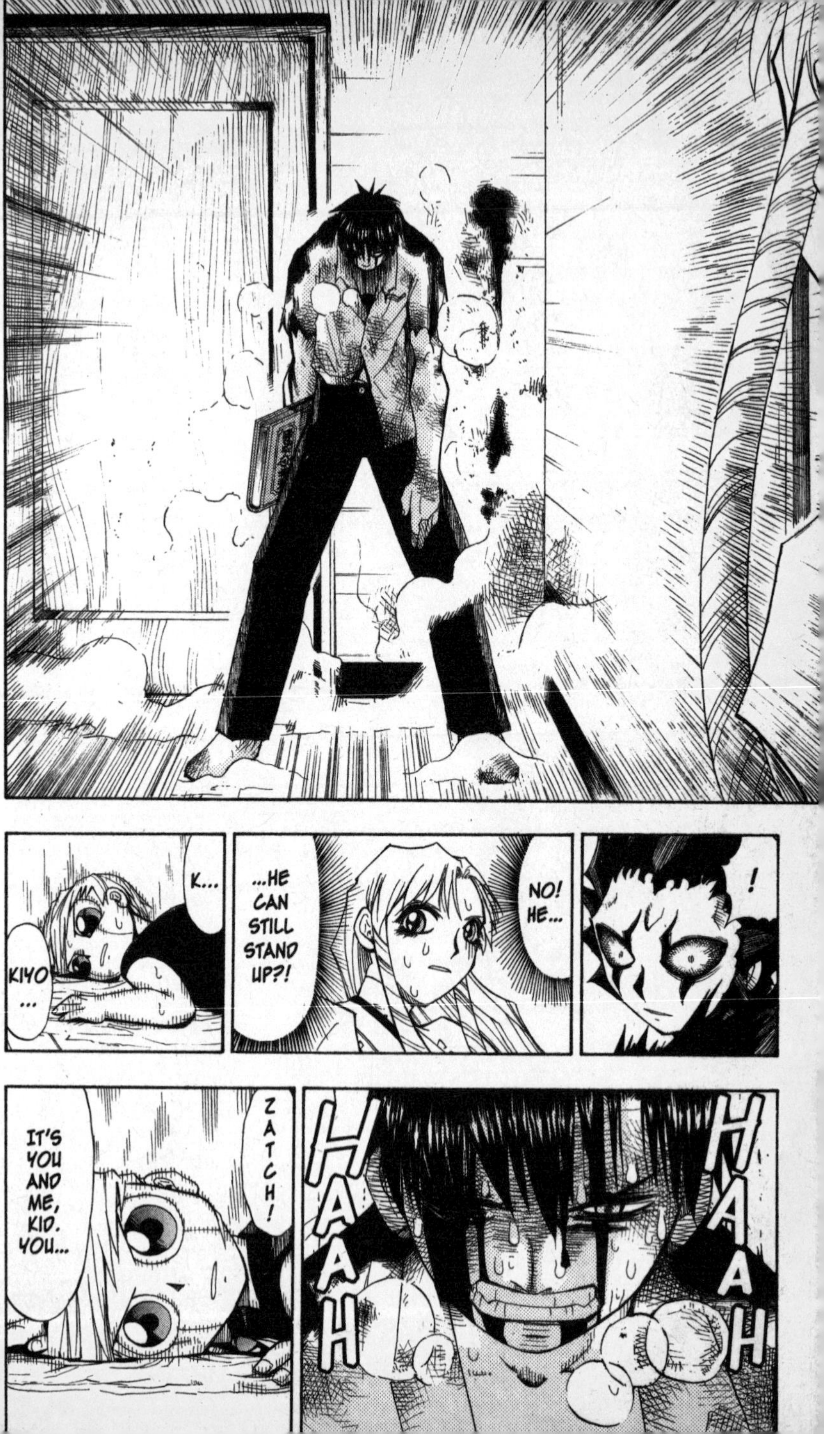
!
NO! HE...
...HE CAN STILL STAND UP?!
K...
KIYO ...
HAAAH
HAAAH
ZATCH!
IT'S YOU AND ME, KID. YOU...

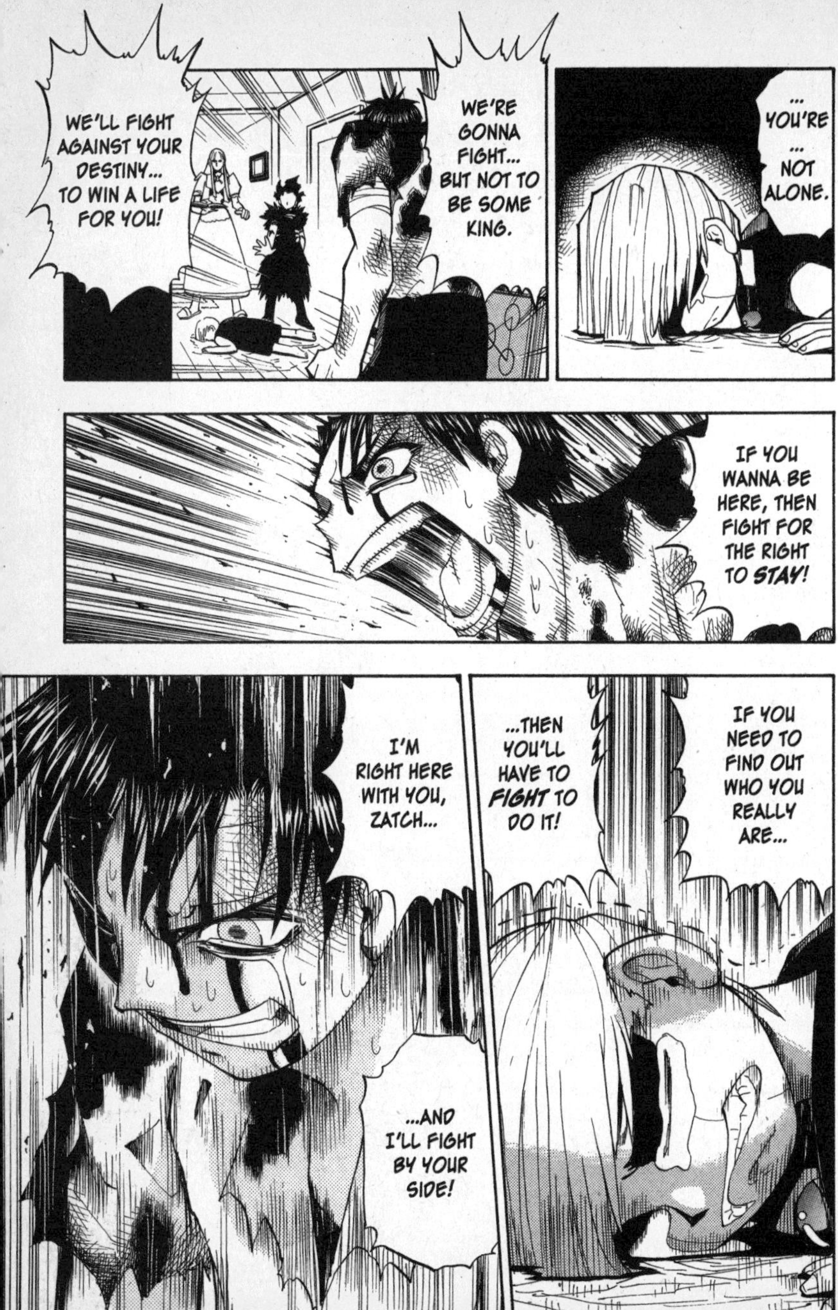
... YOU'RE ... NOT ALONE.
WE'RE GONNA FIGHT... BUT NOT TO BE SOME KING.
WE'LL FIGHT AGAINST YOUR DESTINY... TO WIN A LIFE FOR YOU!
IF YOU WANNA BE HERE, THEN FIGHT FOR THE RIGHT TO STAY!
IF YOU NEED TO FIND OUT WHO YOU REALLY ARE...
...THEN YOU'LL HAVE TO FIGHT TO DO IT!
I'M RIGHT HERE WITH YOU, ZATCH...
...AND I'LL FIGHT BY YOUR SIDE!

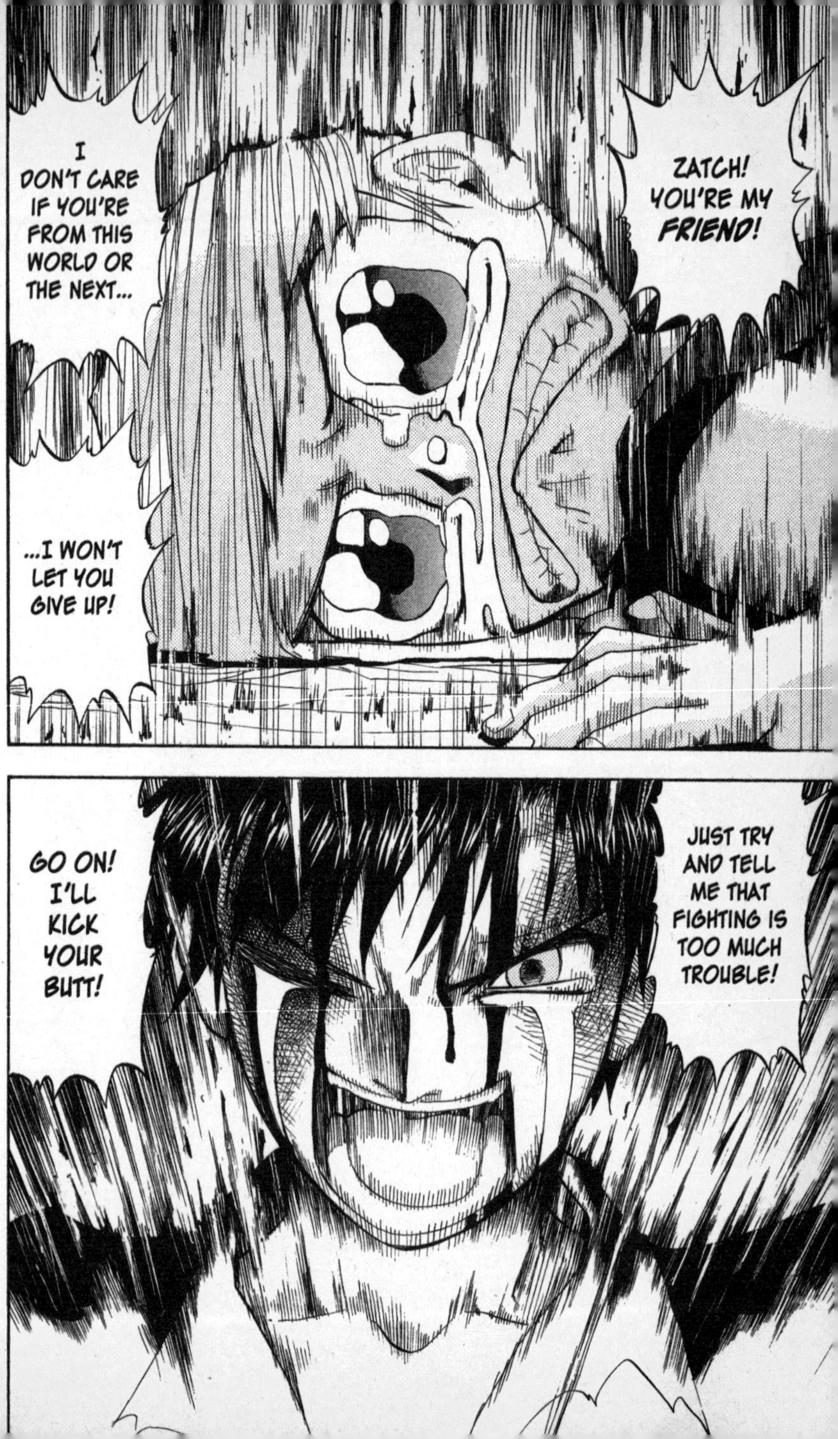
ZATCH! YOU'RE MY FRIEND!
I DON'T CARE IF YOU'RE FROM THIS WORLD OR THE NEXT...
...I WON'T LET YOU GIVE UP!
JUST TRY AND TELL ME THAT FIGHTING IS TOO MUCH TROUBLE!
GO ON! I'LL KICK YOUR BUTT!

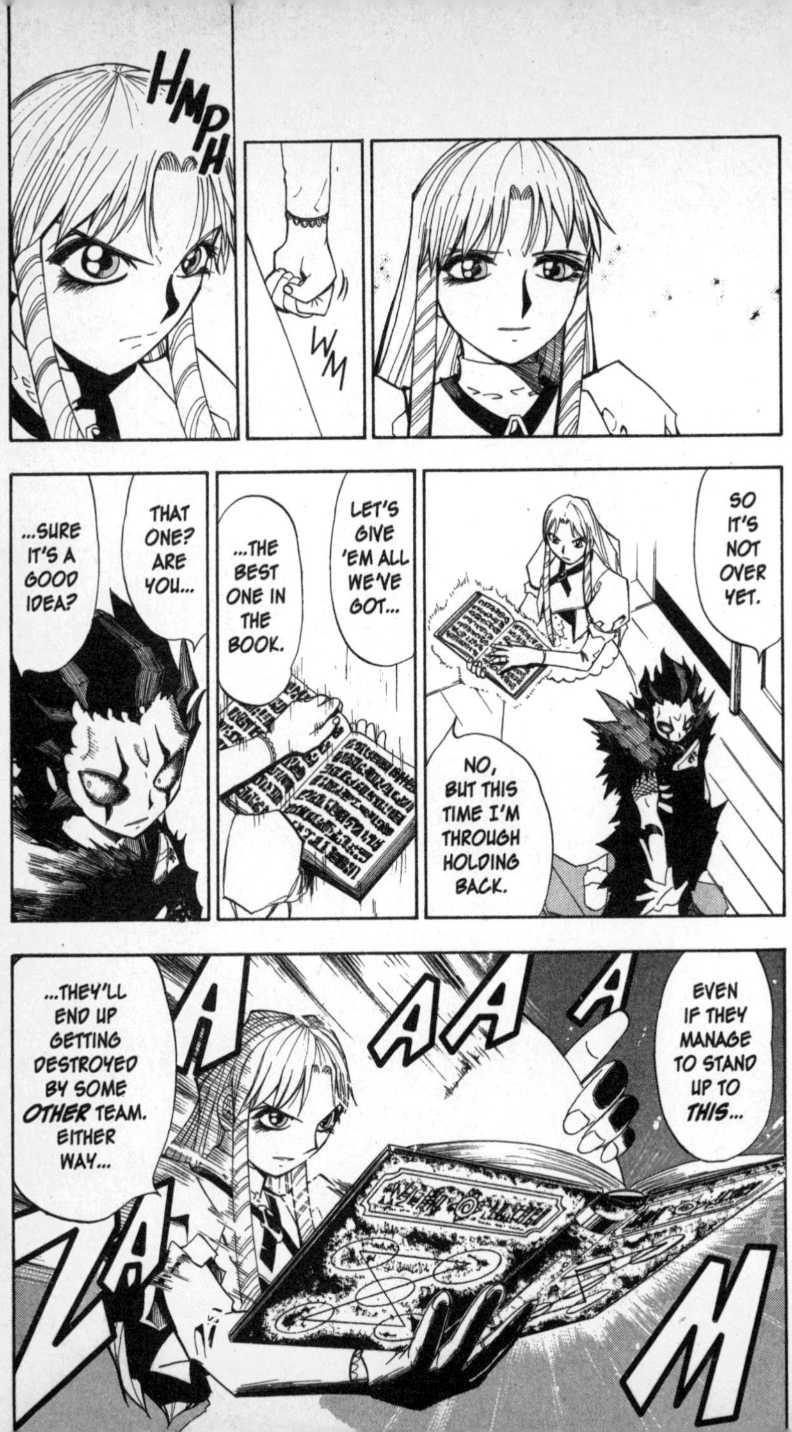
WM
HMPH
SO IT'S NOT OVER YET.
NO, BUT THIS TIME I'M THROUGH HOLDING BACK.
LET'S GIVE 'EM ALL WE'VE GOT...
...THE BEST ONE IN THE BOOK.
THAT ONE? ARE YOU...
...SURE IT'S A GOOD IDEA?
EVEN IF THEY MANAGE TO STAND UP TO *THIS*...
...THEY'LL END UP GETTING DESTROYED BY SOME *OTHER* TEAM. EITHER WAY...
ZAAAAAM

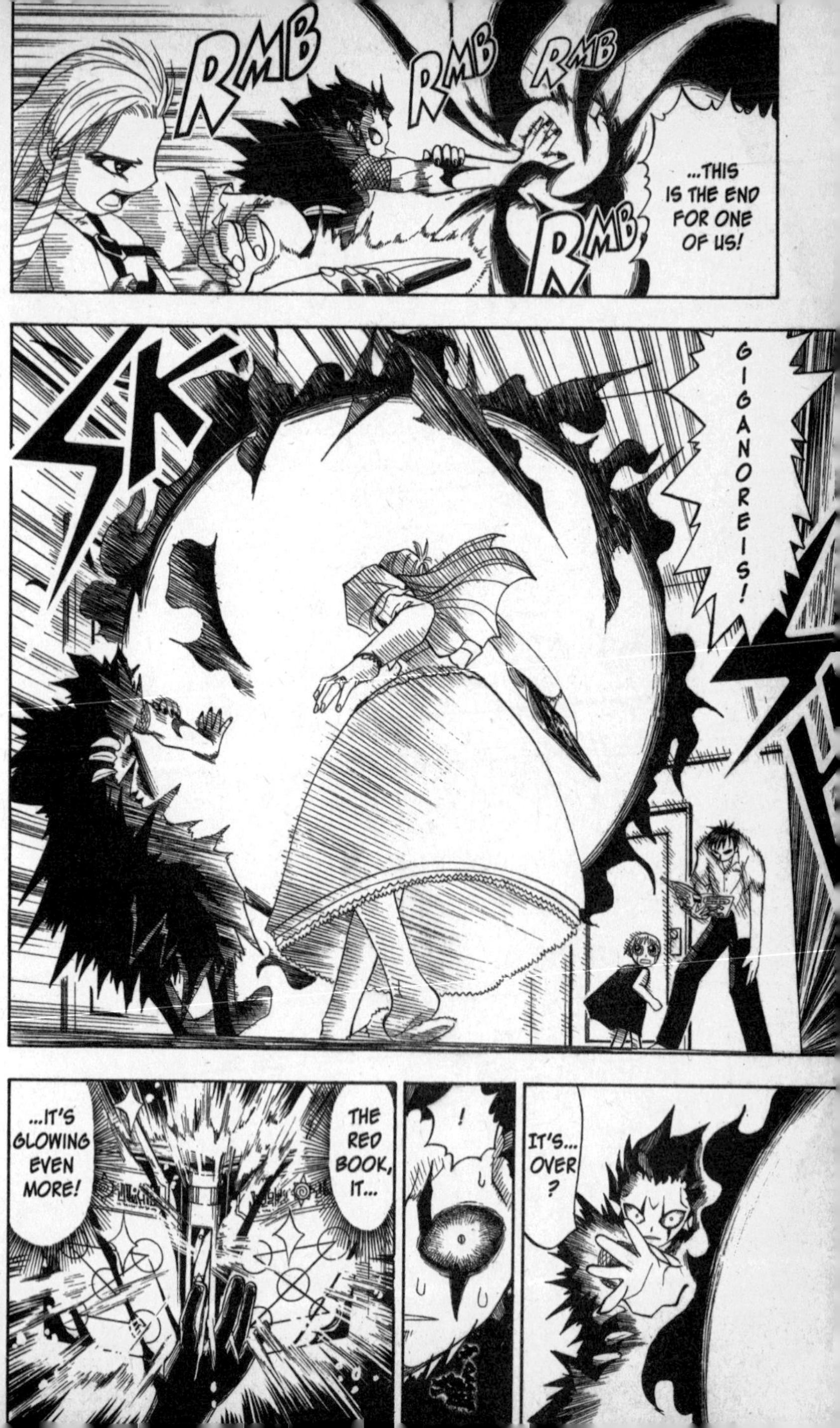
RMB
RMB
RMB
...THIS IS THE END FOR ONE OF US!
RMB
GIGANOREIS!
IT'S... OVER?
!
THE RED BOOK, IT...
...IT'S GLOWING EVEN MORE!

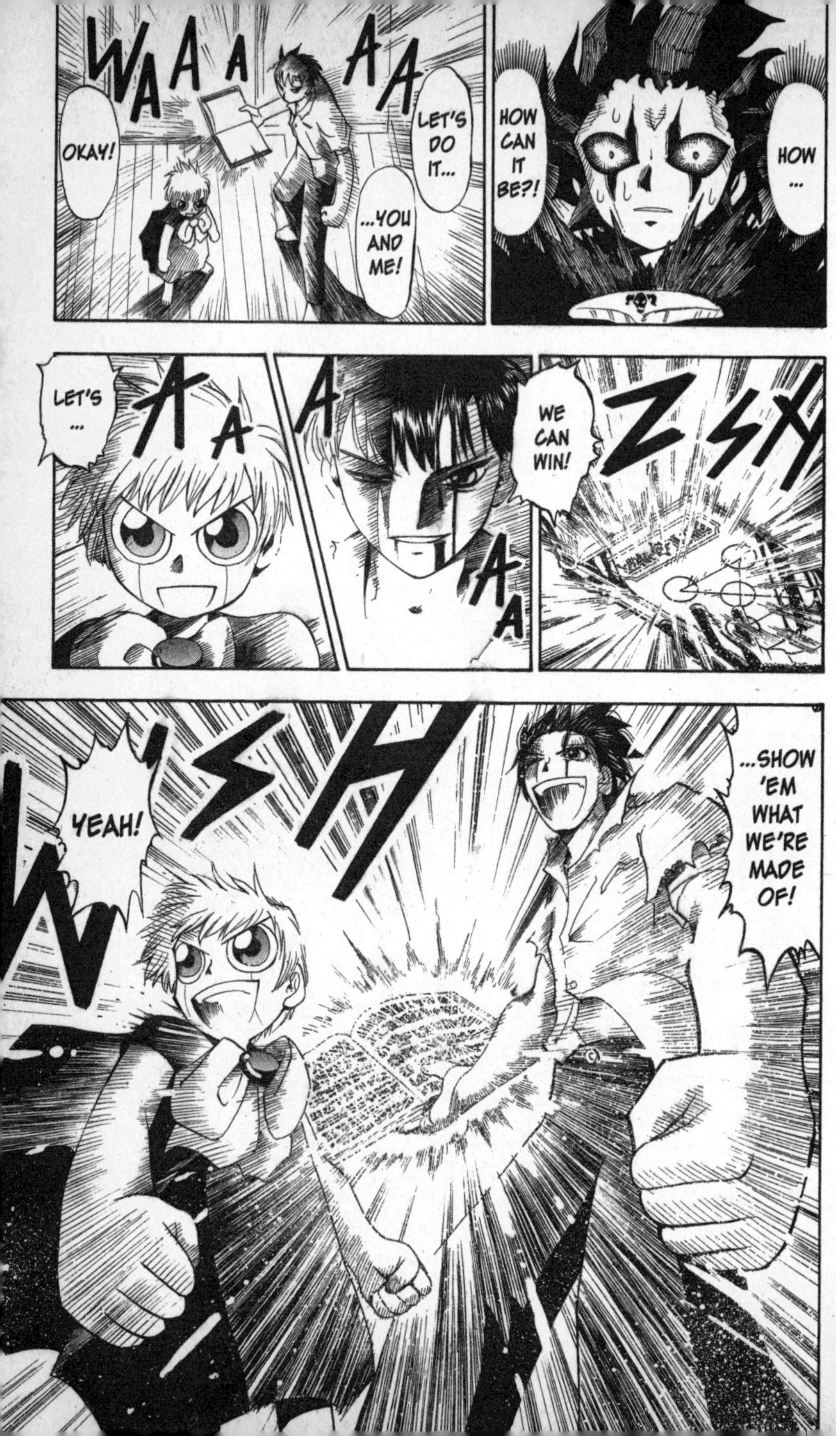
HOW ...
HOW CAN IT BE?!
WAAAAAA
LET'S DO IT...
...YOU AND ME!
OKAY!
WE CAN WIN!
ZSH
AAA
LET'S ...
AA
...SHOW 'EM WHAT WE'RE MADE OF!
YEAH!
SH

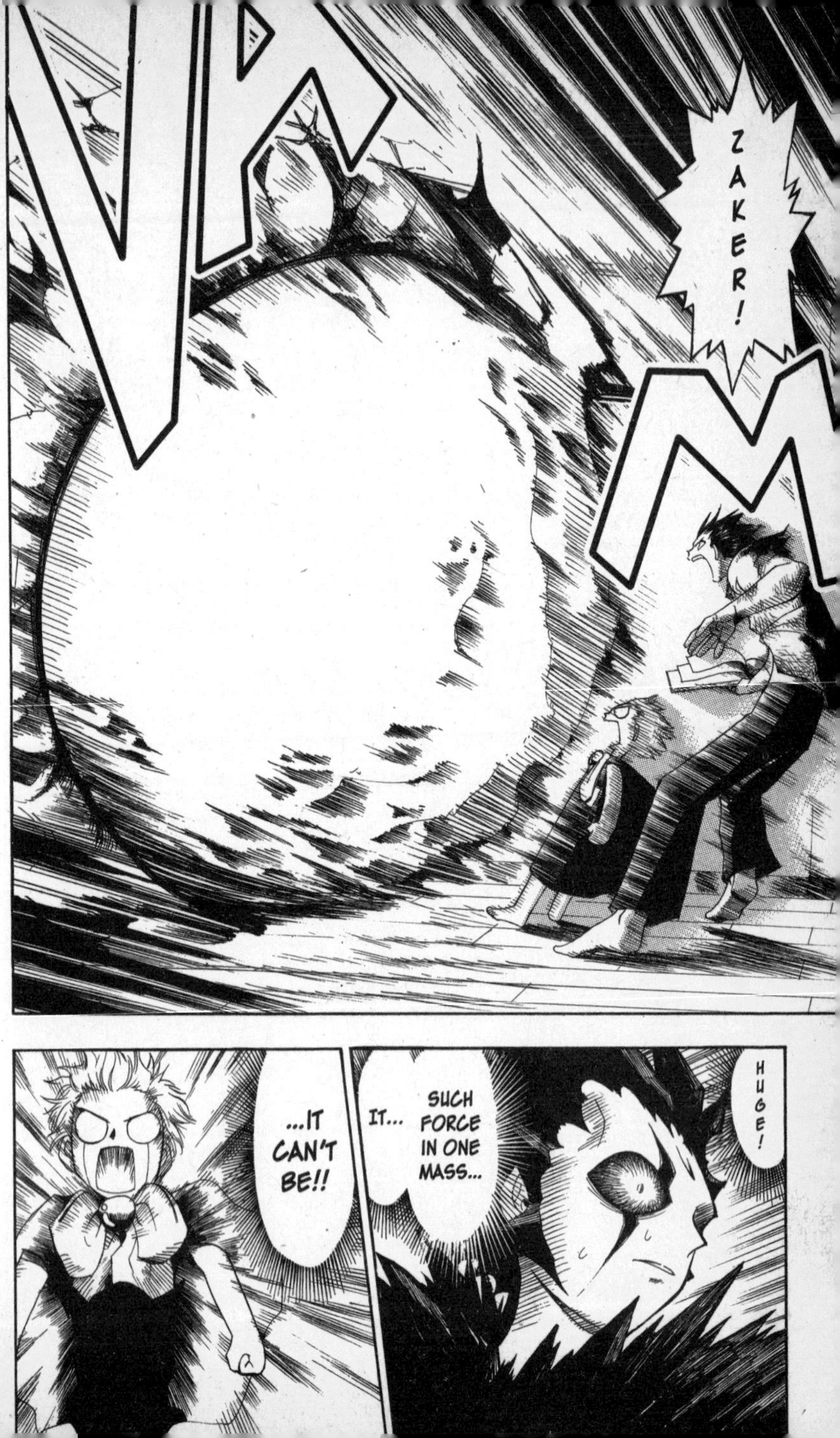
ZAKER!
HUGE!
SUCH FORCE IN ONE MASS...
IT...
...IT CAN'T BE!!

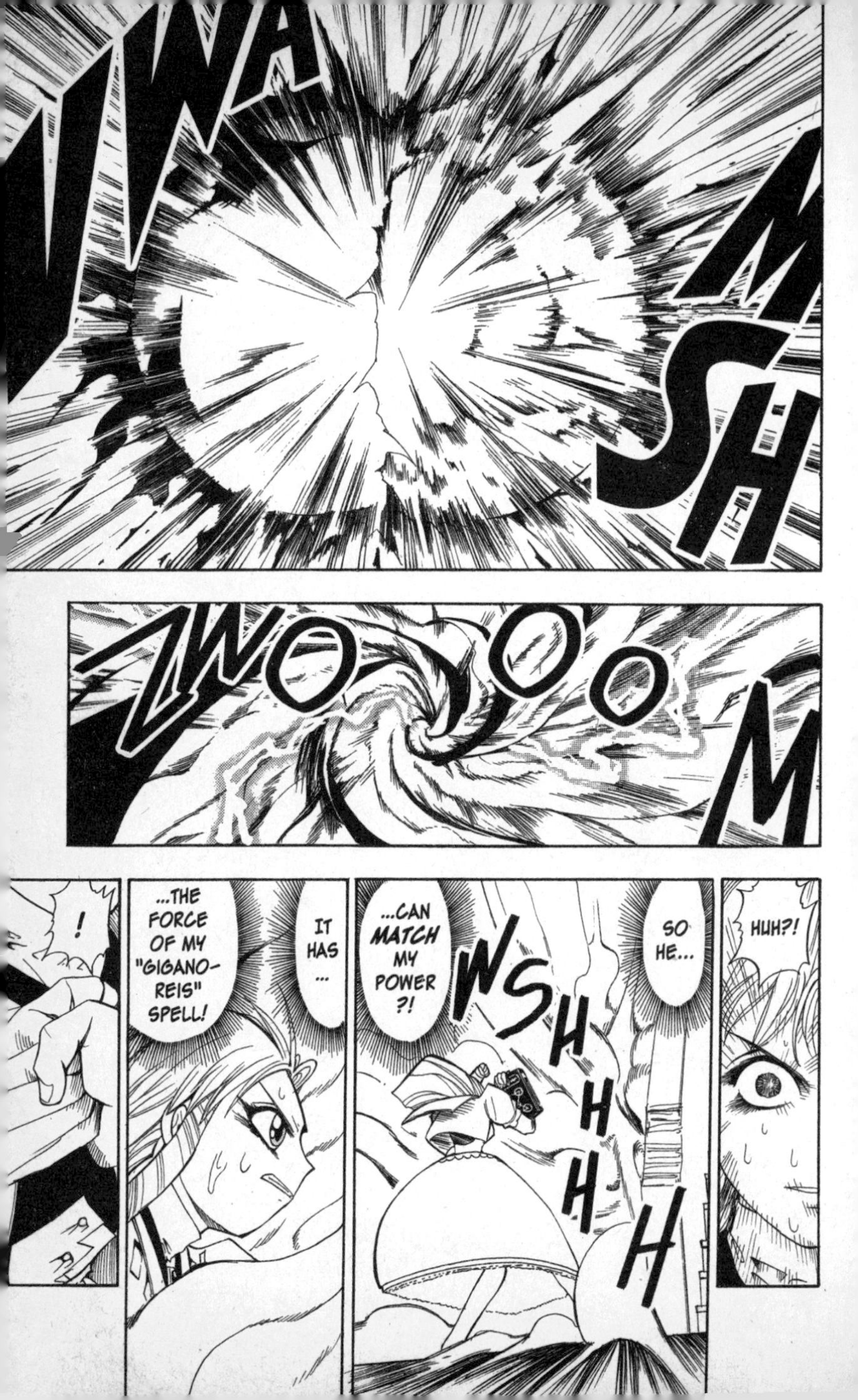
ZWOOOOM
HUH?!
SO HE...
...CAN MATCH MY POWER ?!
WSHHHHH
IT HAS...
...THE FORCE OF MY "GIGANO-REIS" SPELL!
!

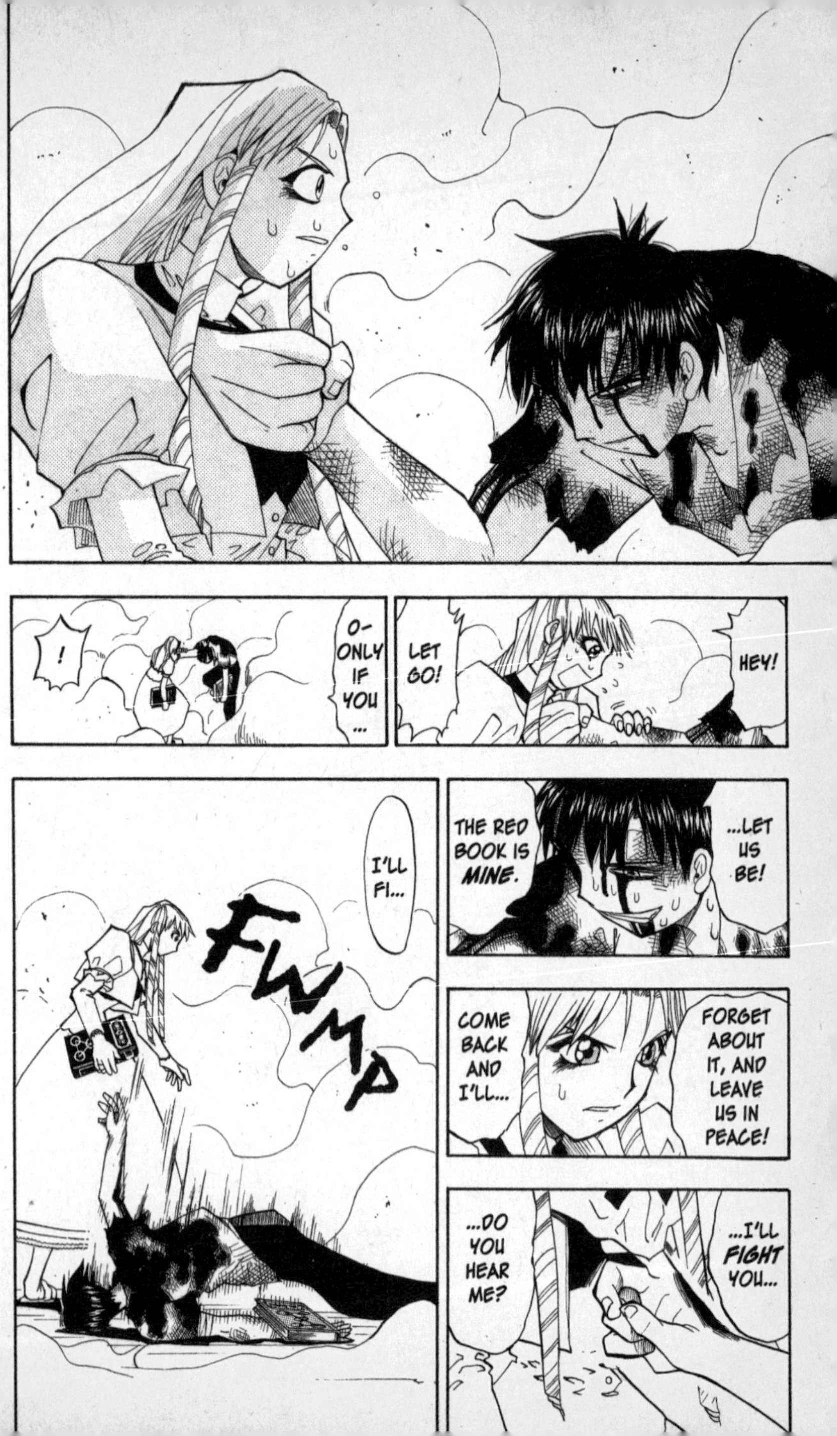
HEY!
LET GO!
O-ONLY IF YOU...
!
...LET US BE!
THE RED BOOK IS MINE.
FORGET ABOUT IT, AND LEAVE US IN PEACE!
COME BACK AND I'LL...
...I'LL FIGHT YOU...
...DO YOU HEAR ME?
I'LL FI...
FWUMP

IF YOU'RE GOING TO FAINT NOW, YOU SHOULD HAVE JUST...

FOOL.

...

...IT CHANGED EVERYTHING... EVEN WHO I AM!

I WON'T LET YOU GIVE UP!

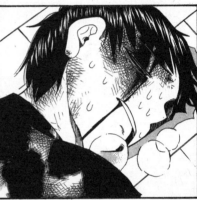

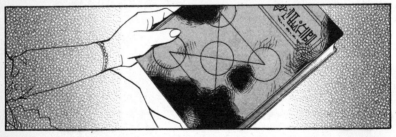

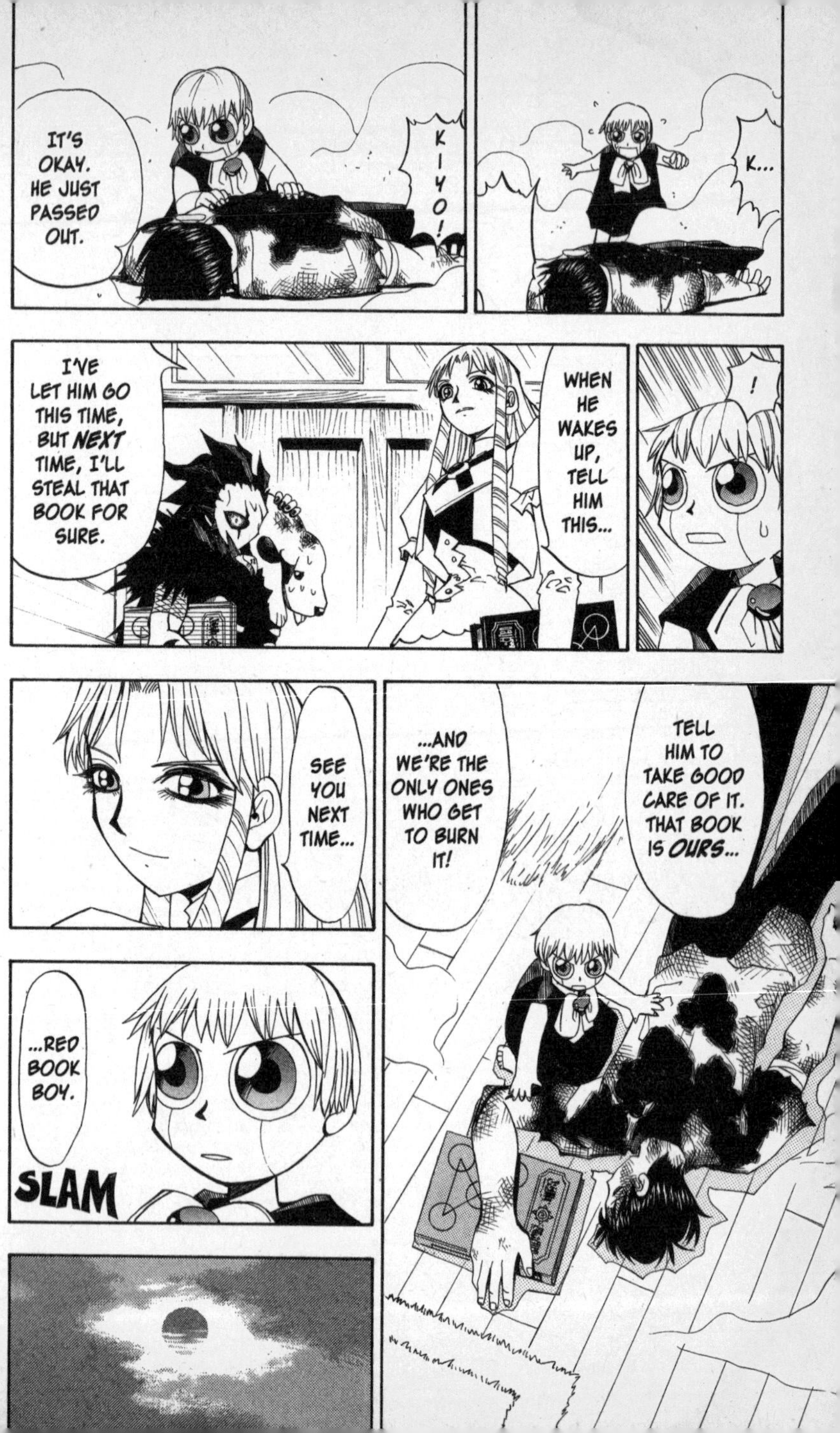
K...
KIYO!
IT'S OKAY. HE JUST PASSED OUT.
!
WHEN HE WAKES UP, TELL HIM THIS...
I'VE LET HIM GO THIS TIME, BUT NEXT TIME, I'LL STEAL THAT BOOK FOR SURE.
TELL HIM TO TAKE GOOD CARE OF IT. THAT BOOK IS OURS...
...AND WE'RE THE ONLY ONES WHO GET TO BURN IT!
SEE YOU NEXT TIME...
...RED BOOK BOY.
SLAM

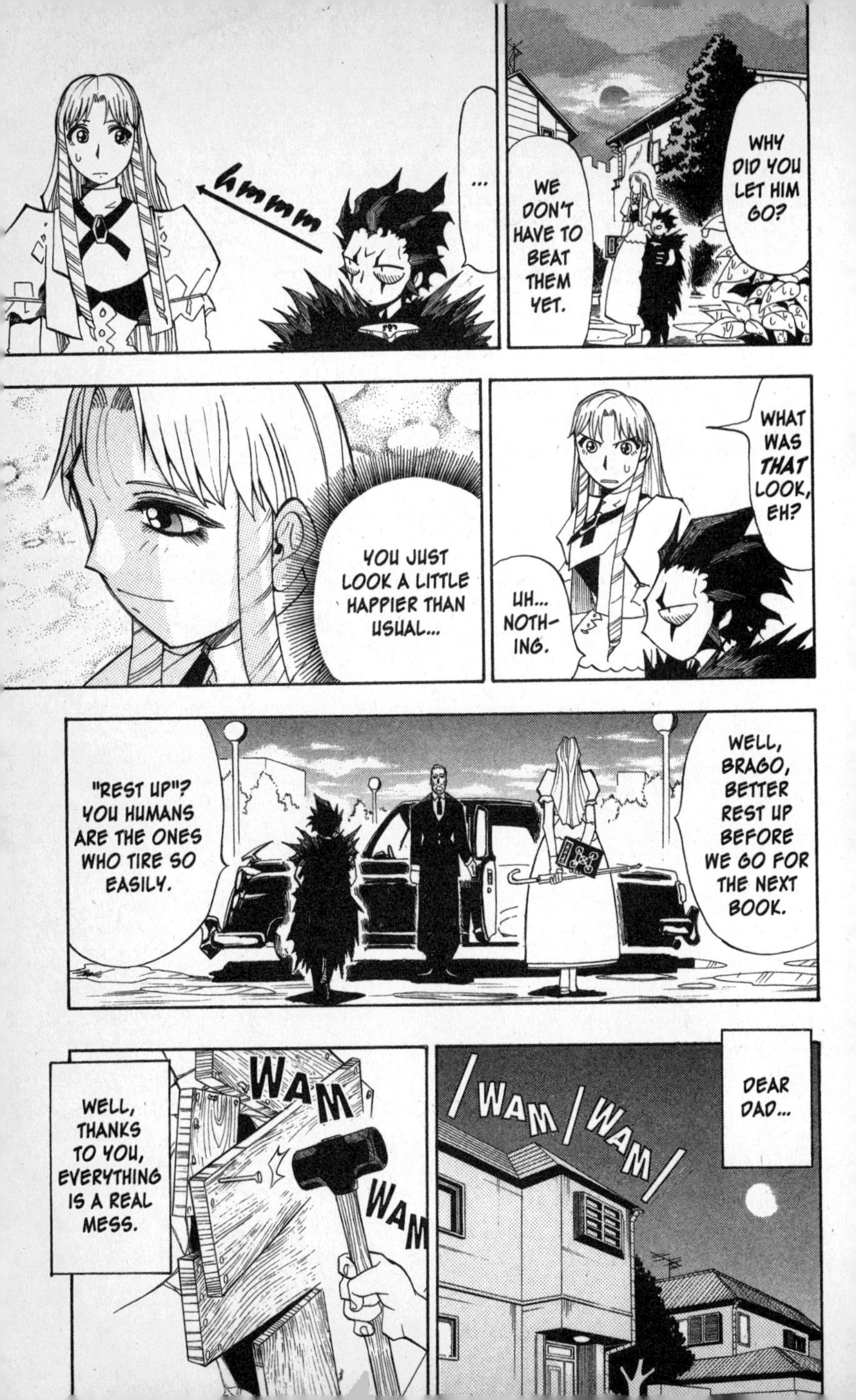
WHY DID YOU LET HIM GO?
WE DON'T HAVE TO BEAT THEM YET.
...
hmmm
WHAT WAS *THAT* LOOK, EH?
UH... NOTH-ING.
YOU JUST LOOK A LITTLE HAPPIER THAN USUAL...
WELL, BRAGO, BETTER REST UP BEFORE WE GO FOR THE NEXT BOOK.
"REST UP"? YOU HUMANS ARE THE ONES WHO TIRE SO EASILY.
DEAR DAD...
WAM WAM
WELL, THANKS TO YOU, EVERYTHING IS A REAL MESS.
WAM
WAM

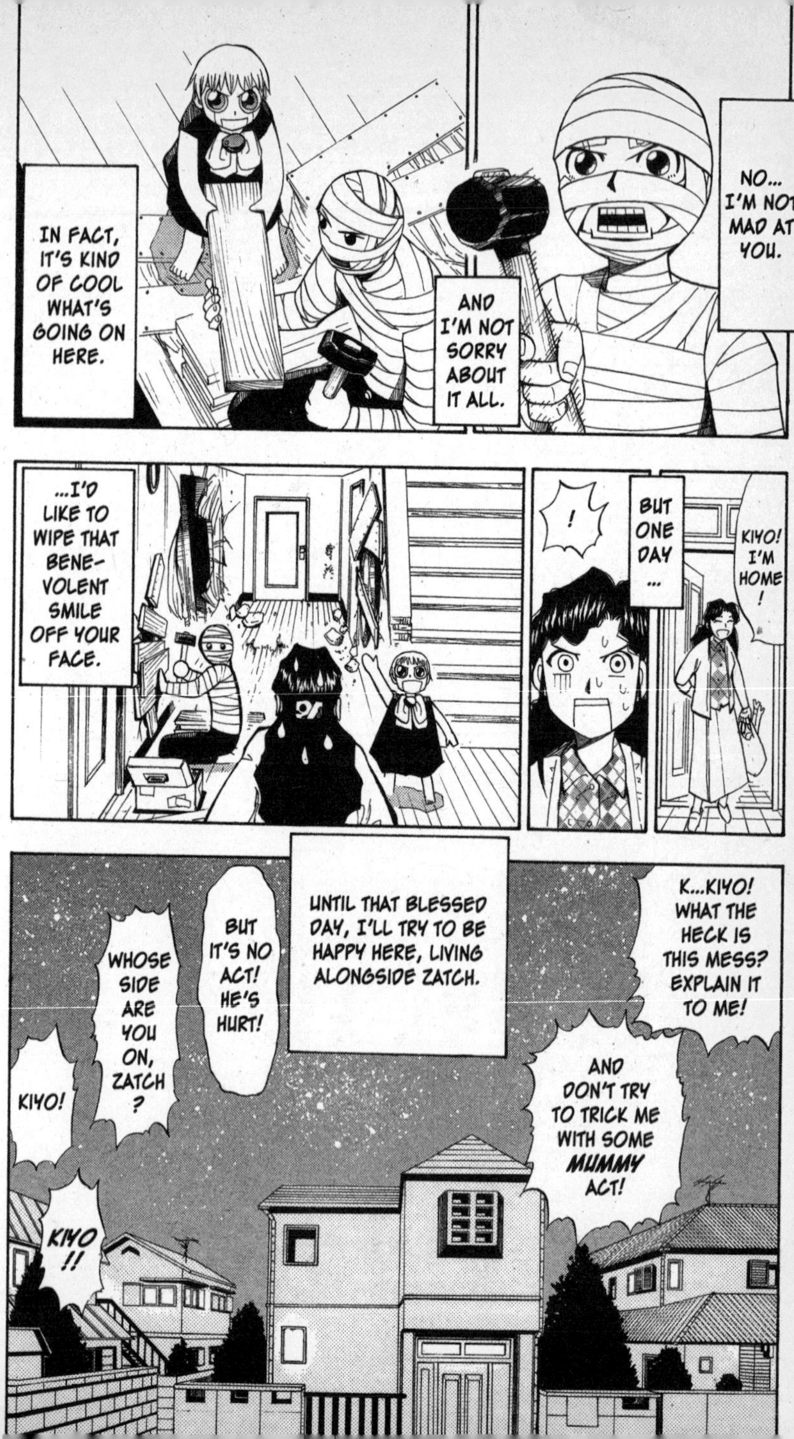
NO... I'M NOT MAD AT YOU.
AND I'M NOT SORRY ABOUT IT ALL.
IN FACT, IT'S KIND OF COOL WHAT'S GOING ON HERE.
KIYO! I'M HOME!
BUT ONE DAY ...
!
...I'D LIKE TO WIPE THAT BENE-VOLENT SMILE OFF YOUR FACE.
K...KIYO! WHAT THE HECK IS THIS MESS? EXPLAIN IT TO ME!
UNTIL THAT BLESSED DAY, I'LL TRY TO BE HAPPY HERE, LIVING ALONGSIDE ZATCH.
AND DON'T TRY TO TRICK ME WITH SOME *MUMMY* ACT!
BUT IT'S NO ACT! HE'S HURT!
WHOSE SIDE ARE YOU ON, ZATCH?
KIYO!
KIYO!!

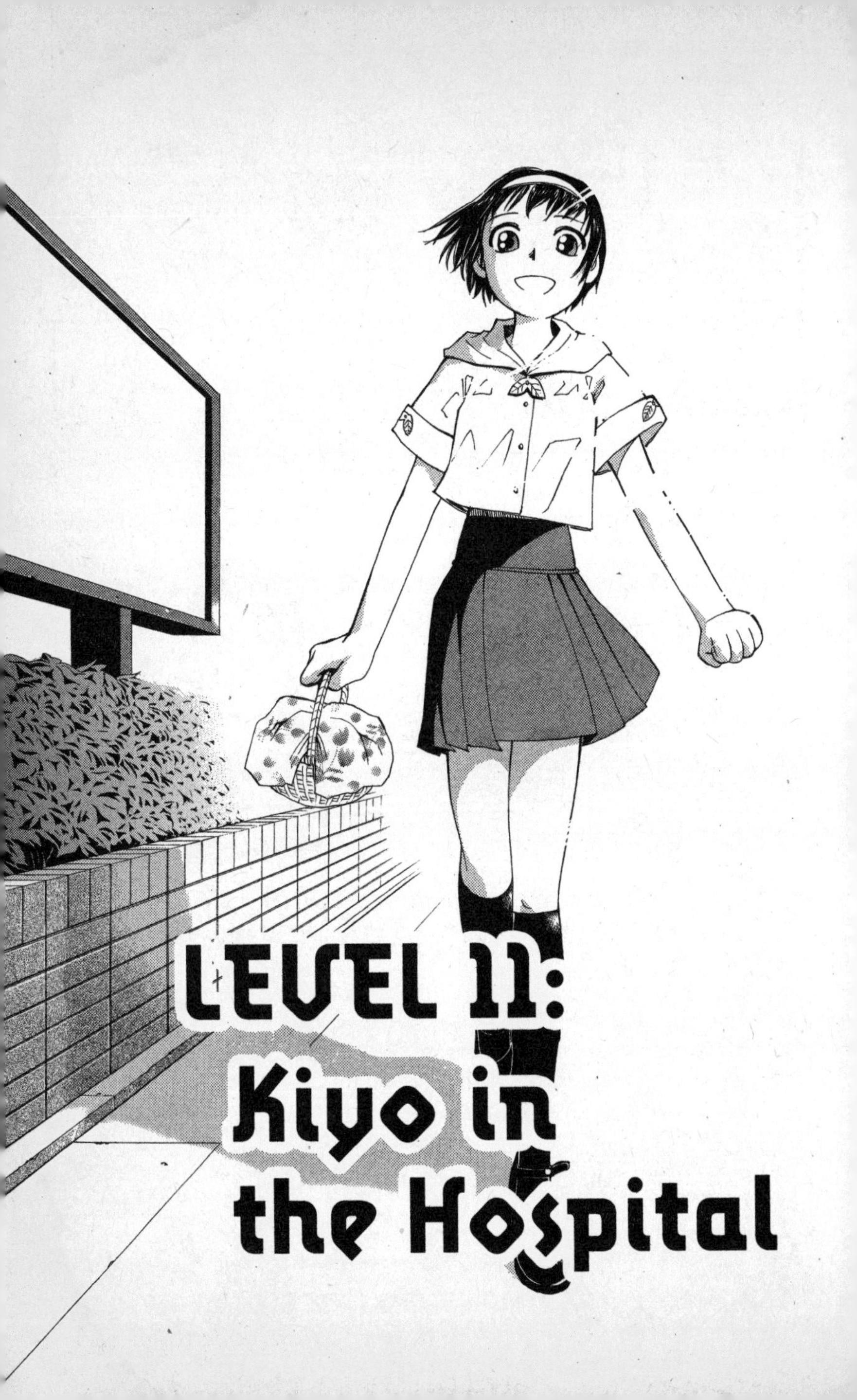
LEVEL 11:
Kiyo in the Hospital

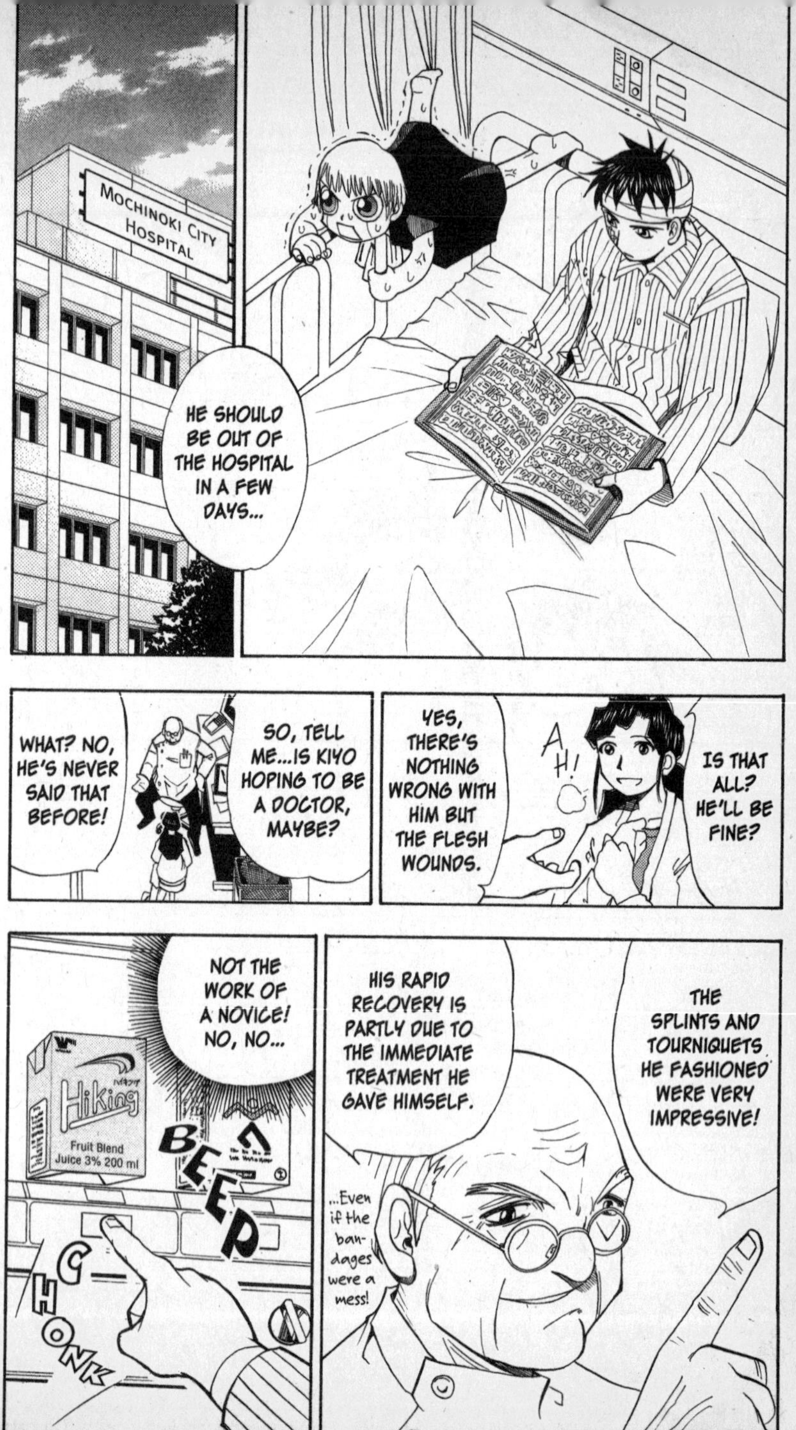
HE SHOULD BE OUT OF THE HOSPITAL IN A FEW DAYS...
MOCHINOKI CITY HOSPITAL
IS THAT ALL? HE'LL BE FINE?
AH!
YES, THERE'S NOTHING WRONG WITH HIM BUT THE FLESH WOUNDS.
SO, TELL ME...IS KIYO HOPING TO BE A DOCTOR, MAYBE?
WHAT? NO, HE'S NEVER SAID THAT BEFORE!
THE SPLINTS AND TOURNIQUETS HE FASHIONED WERE VERY IMPRESSIVE!
HIS RAPID RECOVERY IS PARTLY DUE TO THE IMMEDIATE TREATMENT HE GAVE HIMSELF.
...Even if the bandages were a mess!
NOT THE WORK OF A NOVICE! NO, NO...
Hiking
Fruit Blend
Juice 3% 200 ml
BEEP
CHONK

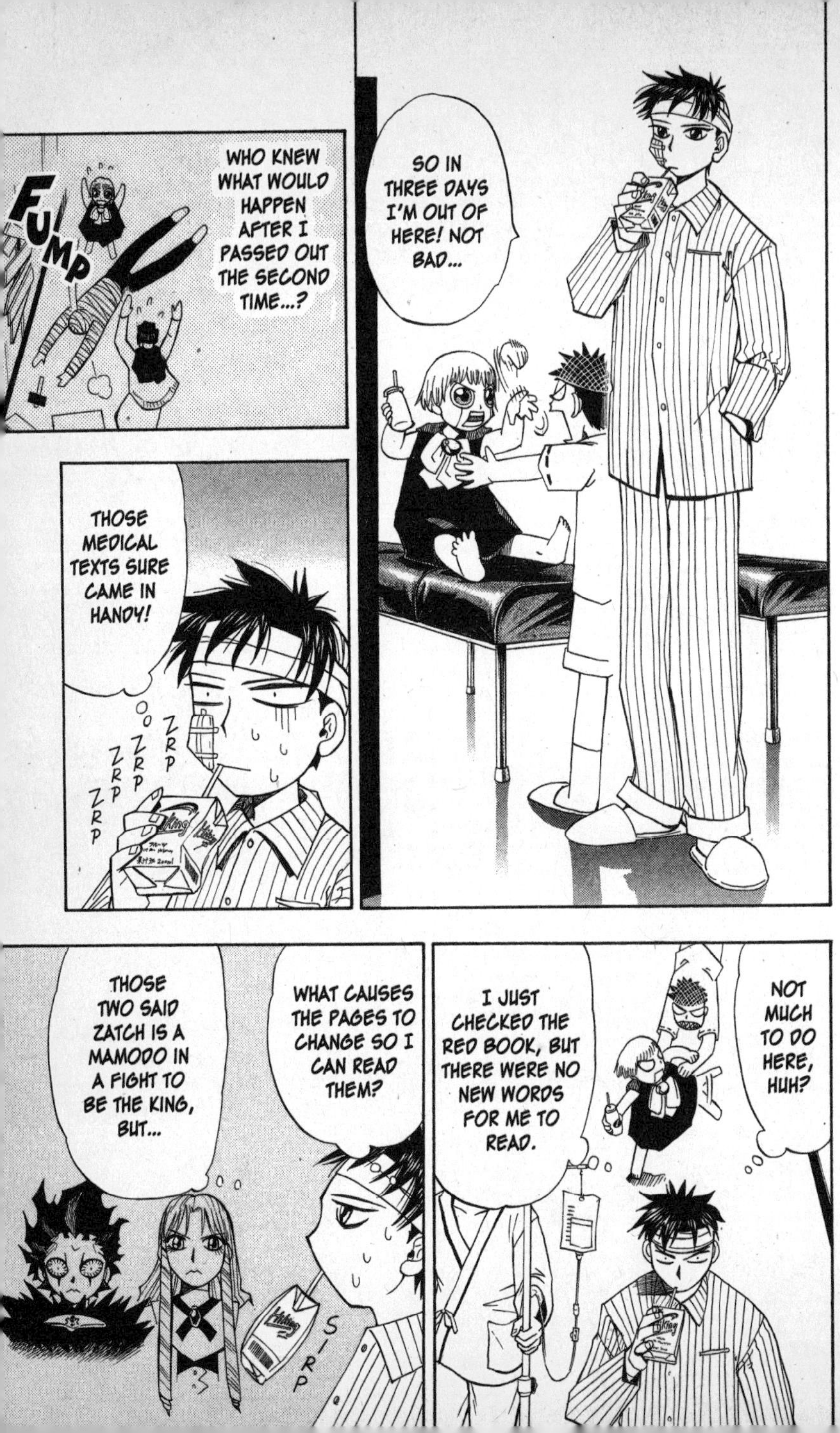
SO IN THREE DAYS I'M OUT OF HERE! NOT BAD...
WHO KNEW WHAT WOULD HAPPEN AFTER I PASSED OUT THE SECOND TIME...?
FUMP
THOSE MEDICAL TEXTS SURE CAME IN HANDY!
ZRP ZRP ZRP ZRP
NOT MUCH TO DO HERE, HUH?
I JUST CHECKED THE RED BOOK, BUT THERE WERE NO NEW WORDS FOR ME TO READ.
WHAT CAUSES THE PAGES TO CHANGE SO I CAN READ THEM?
THOSE TWO SAID ZATCH IS A MAMODO IN A FIGHT TO BE THE KING, BUT...
SIRP

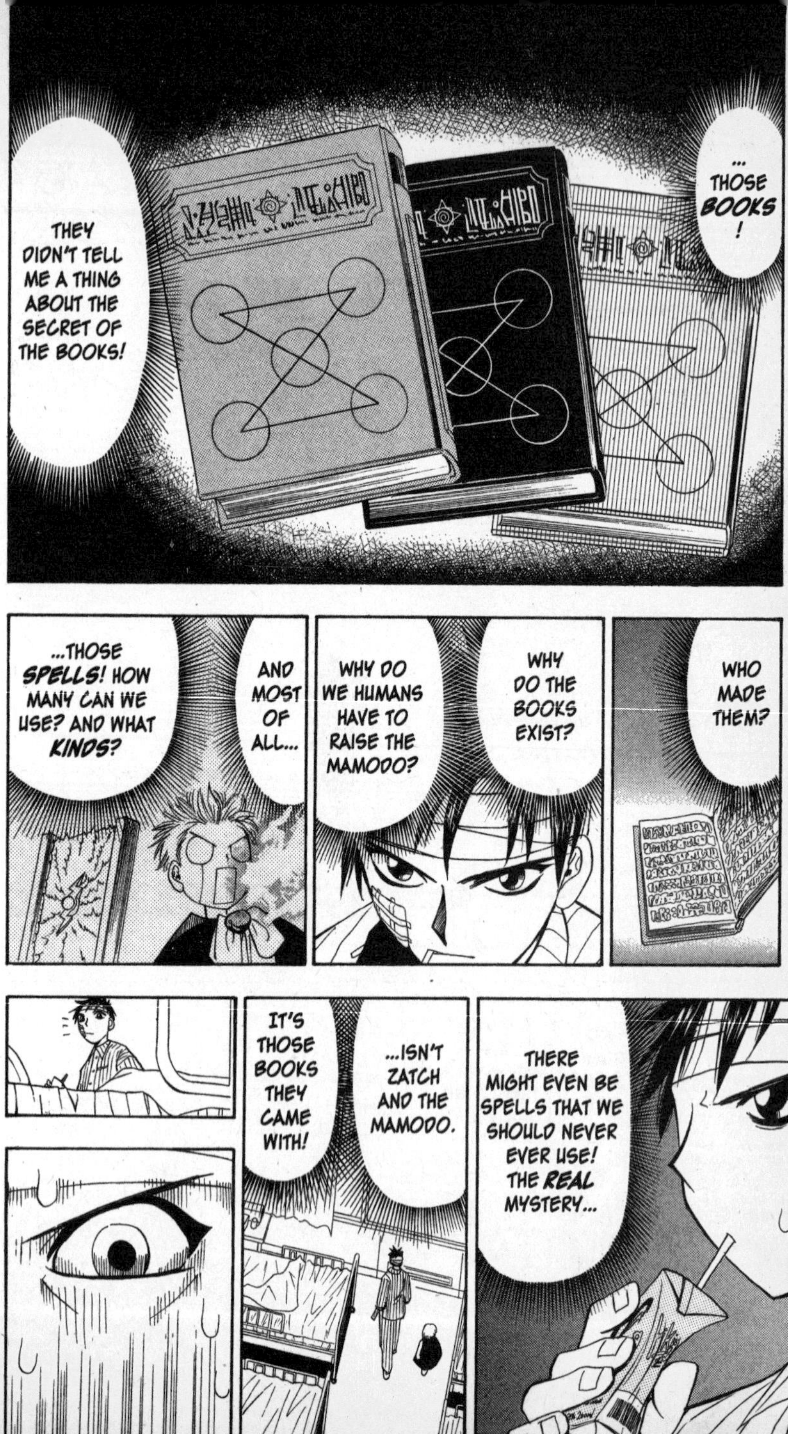
... THOSE BOOKS!
THEY DIDN'T TELL ME A THING ABOUT THE SECRET OF THE BOOKS!
WHO MADE THEM?
WHY DO THE BOOKS EXIST?
WHY DO WE HUMANS HAVE TO RAISE THE MAMODO?
AND MOST OF ALL...
...THOSE SPELLS! HOW MANY CAN WE USE? AND WHAT KINDS?
THERE MIGHT EVEN BE SPELLS THAT WE SHOULD NEVER EVER USE! THE REAL MYSTERY...
...ISN'T ZATCH AND THE MAMODO.
IT'S THOSE BOOKS THEY CAME WITH!

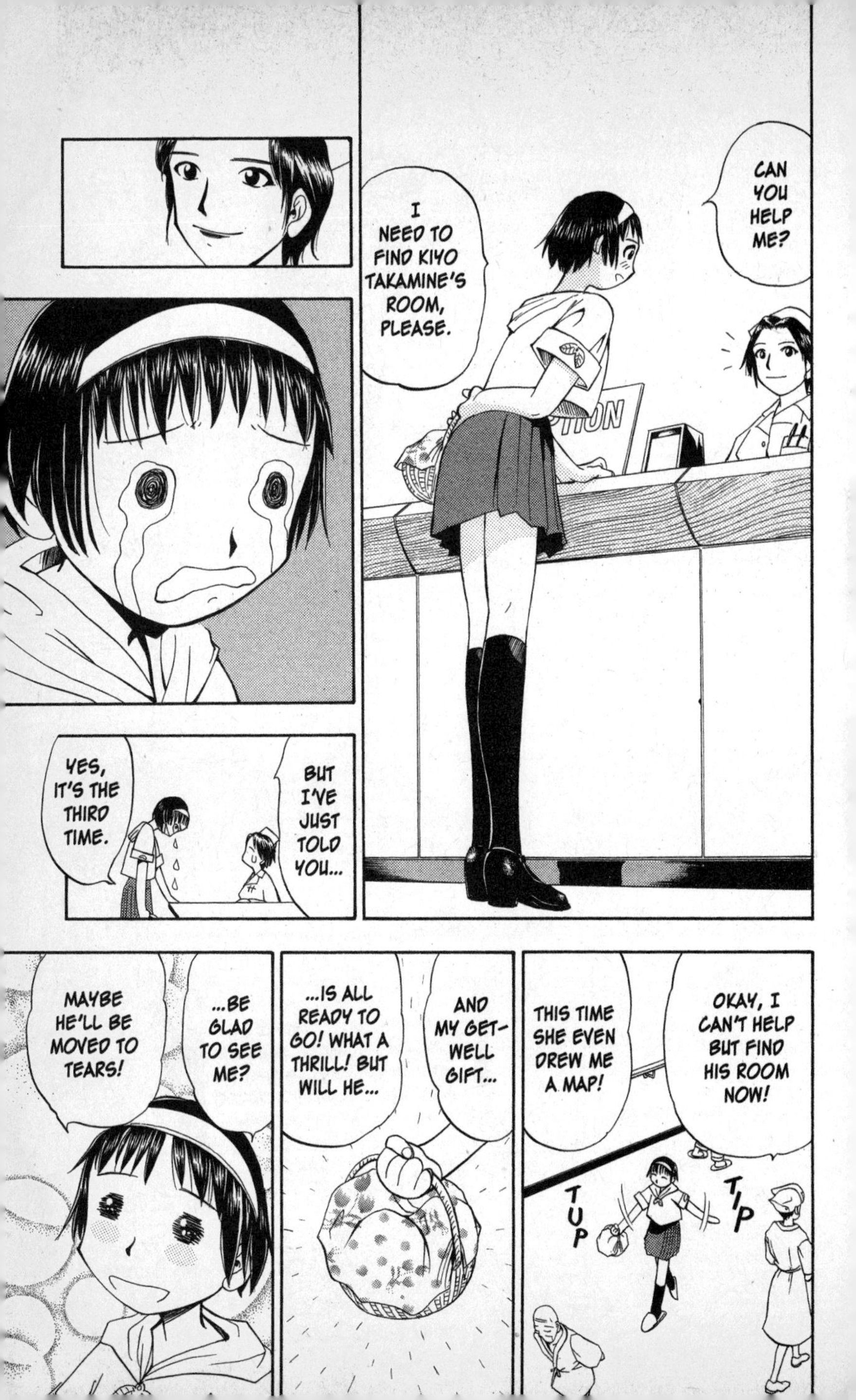
CAN YOU HELP ME?
I NEED TO FIND KIYO TAKAMINE'S ROOM, PLEASE.
BUT I'VE JUST TOLD YOU...
YES, IT'S THE THIRD TIME.
OKAY, I CAN'T HELP BUT FIND HIS ROOM NOW!
THIS TIME SHE EVEN DREW ME A MAP!
TIP
TUP
AND MY GET-WELL GIFT...
...IS ALL READY TO GO! WHAT A THRILL! BUT WILL HE...
...BE GLAD TO SEE ME?
MAYBE HE'LL BE MOVED TO TEARS!

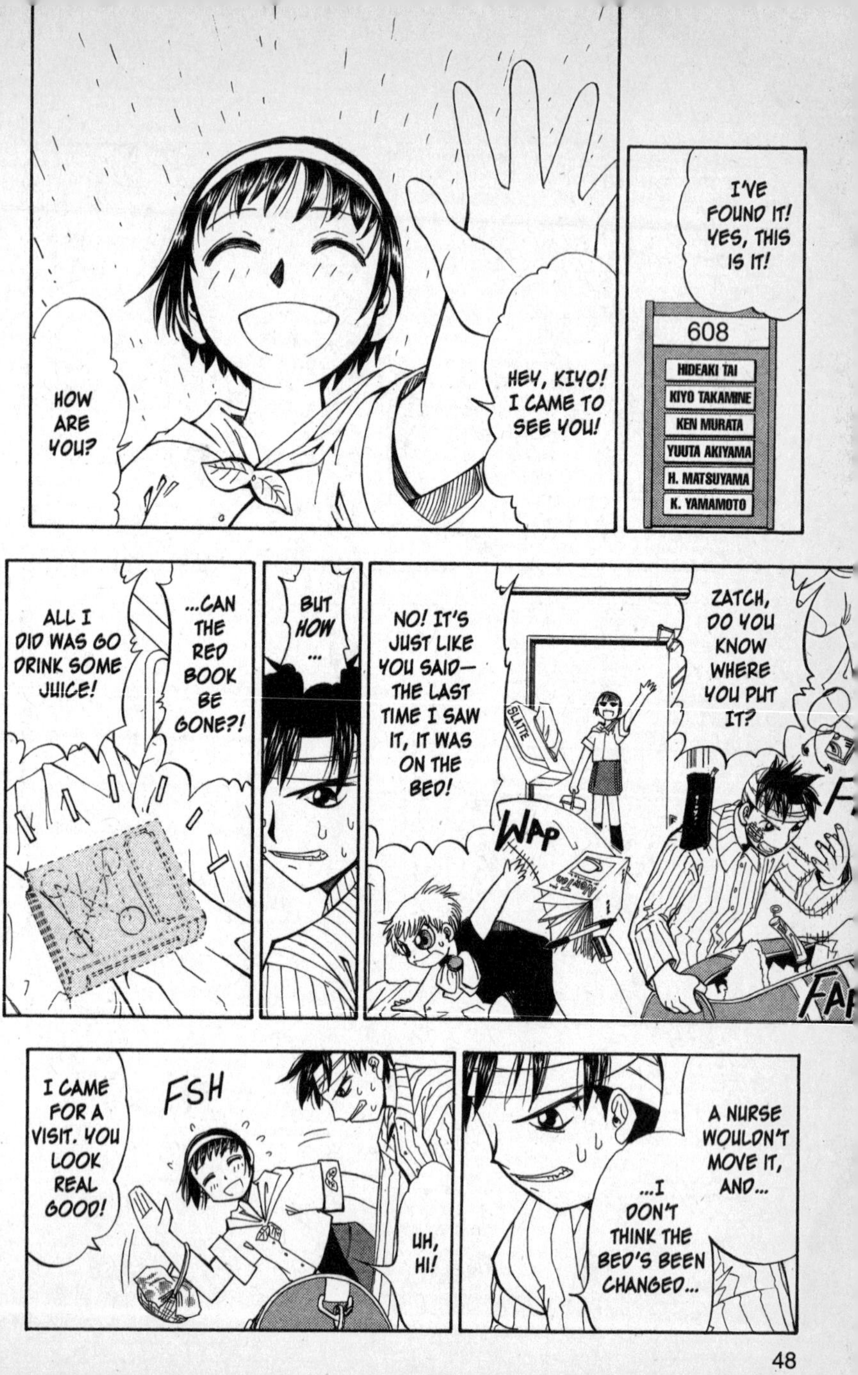
I'VE FOUND IT! YES, THIS IS IT!
608
HIDEAKI TAI
KIYO TAKAMINE
KEN MURATA
YUUTA AKIYAMA
H. MATSUYAMA
K. YAMAMOTO
HEY, KIYO! I CAME TO SEE YOU!
HOW ARE YOU?
ZATCH, DO YOU KNOW WHERE YOU PUT IT?
NO! IT'S JUST LIKE YOU SAID— THE LAST TIME I SAW IT, IT WAS ON THE BED!
WAP
BUT HOW ...
...CAN THE RED BOOK BE GONE?!
ALL I DID WAS GO DRINK SOME JUICE!
A NURSE WOULDN'T MOVE IT, AND...
...I DON'T THINK THE BED'S BEEN CHANGED...
UH, HI!
FSH
I CAME FOR A VISIT. YOU LOOK REAL GOOD!

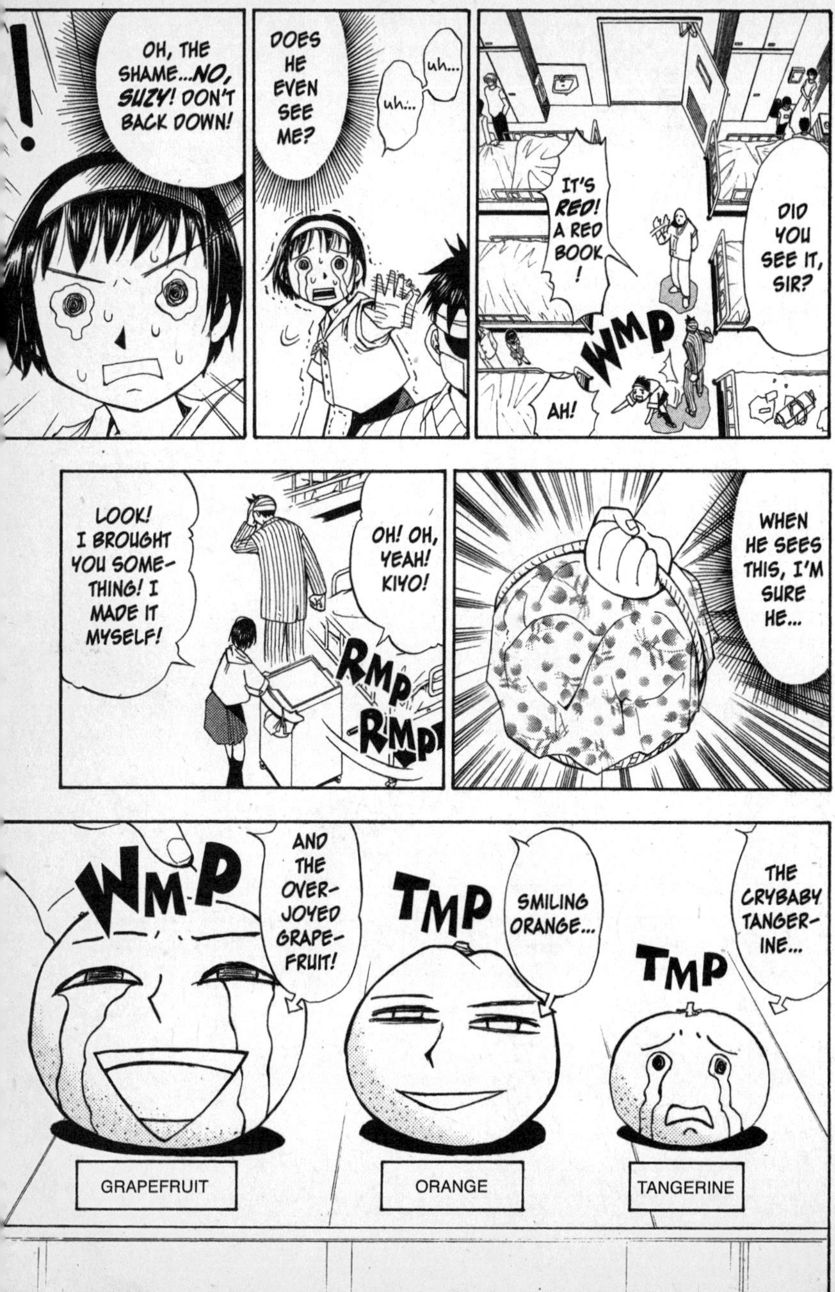
DID YOU SEE IT, SIR?
IT'S RED! A RED BOOK!
WMP
AH!
DOES HE EVEN SEE ME?
uh...
uh...
!
OH, THE SHAME...NO, SUZY! DON'T BACK DOWN!
WHEN HE SEES THIS, I'M SURE HE...
OH! OH, YEAH! KIYO!
LOOK! I BROUGHT YOU SOME-THING! I MADE IT MYSELF!
RMP
RMP
THE CRYBABY TANGER-INE...
TMP
TANGERINE
SMILING ORANGE...
TMP
ORANGE
AND THE OVER-JOYED GRAPE-FRUIT!
WMP
GRAPEFRUIT

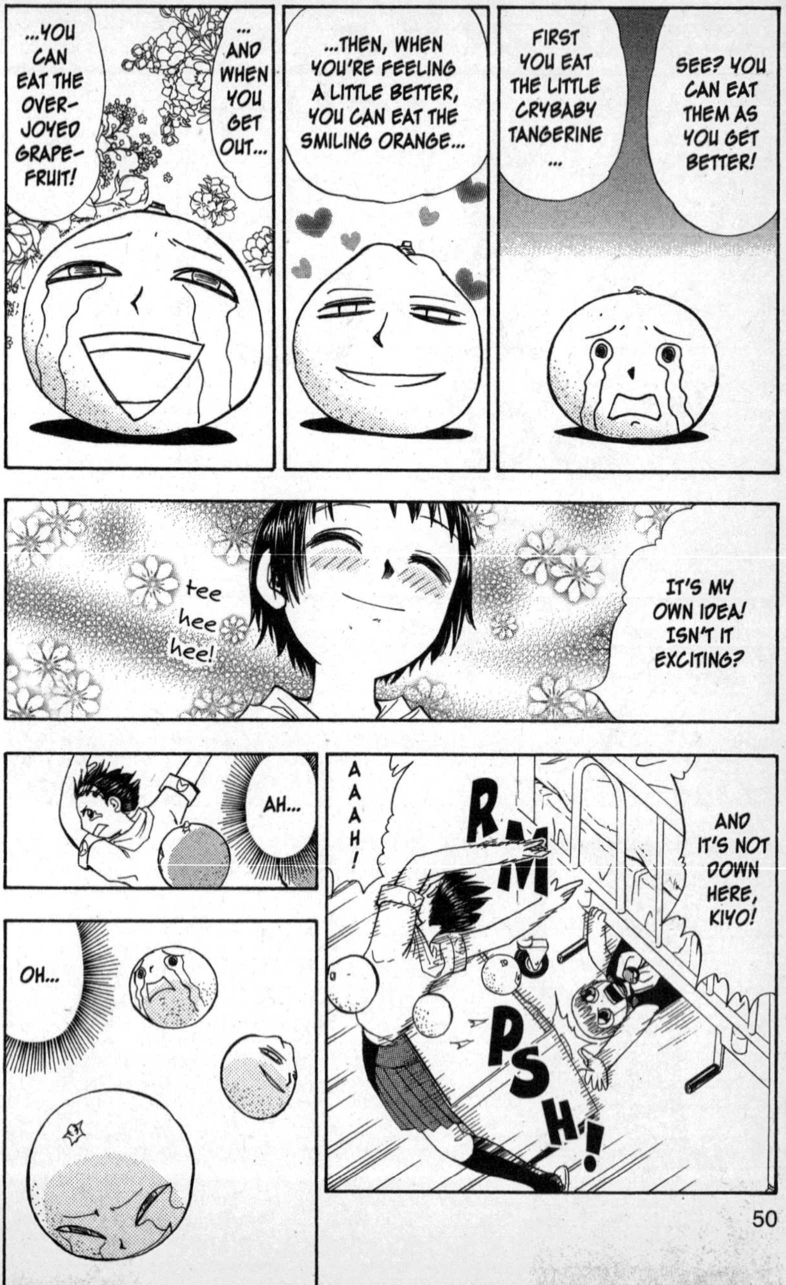
SEE? YOU CAN EAT THEM AS YOU GET BETTER!
FIRST YOU EAT THE LITTLE CRYBABY TANGERINE ...
...THEN, WHEN YOU'RE FEELING A LITTLE BETTER, YOU CAN EAT THE SMILING ORANGE...
... AND WHEN YOU GET OUT...
...YOU CAN EAT THE OVER-JOYED GRAPE-FRUIT!
IT'S MY OWN IDEA! ISN'T IT EXCITING?
tee hee hee!
AND IT'S NOT DOWN HERE, KIYO!
AAAAH!
RMPSH!
AH...
OH...

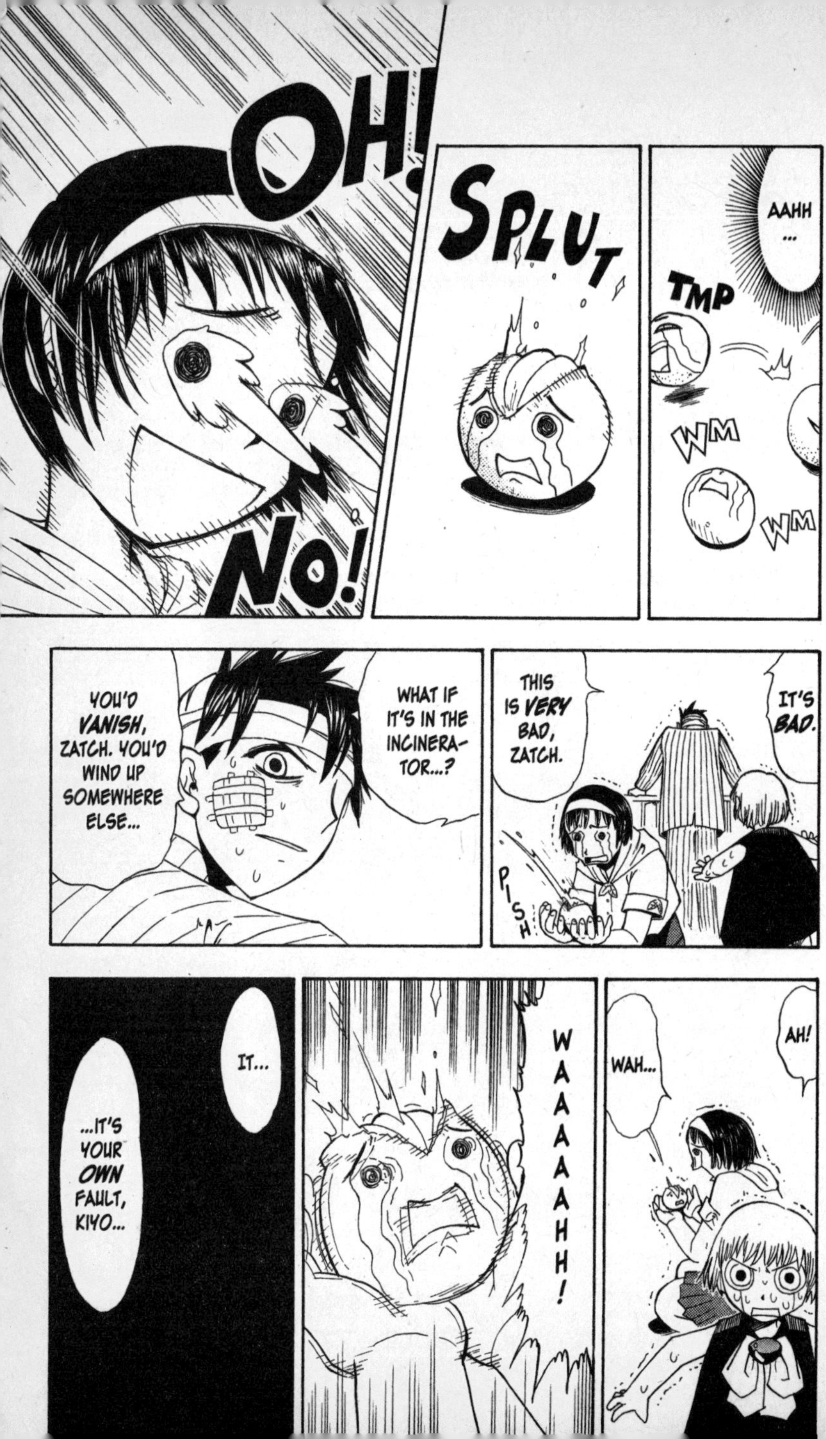
AAHH ...
TMP
WM
WM
SPLUT
OH!
NO!
IT'S BAD.
THIS IS VERY BAD, ZATCH.
PISH
WHAT IF IT'S IN THE INCINERATOR...?
YOU'D VANISH, ZATCH. YOU'D WIND UP SOMEWHERE ELSE...
AH!
WAH...
WAAAAAAAHH!
IT...
...IT'S YOUR OWN FAULT, KIYO...

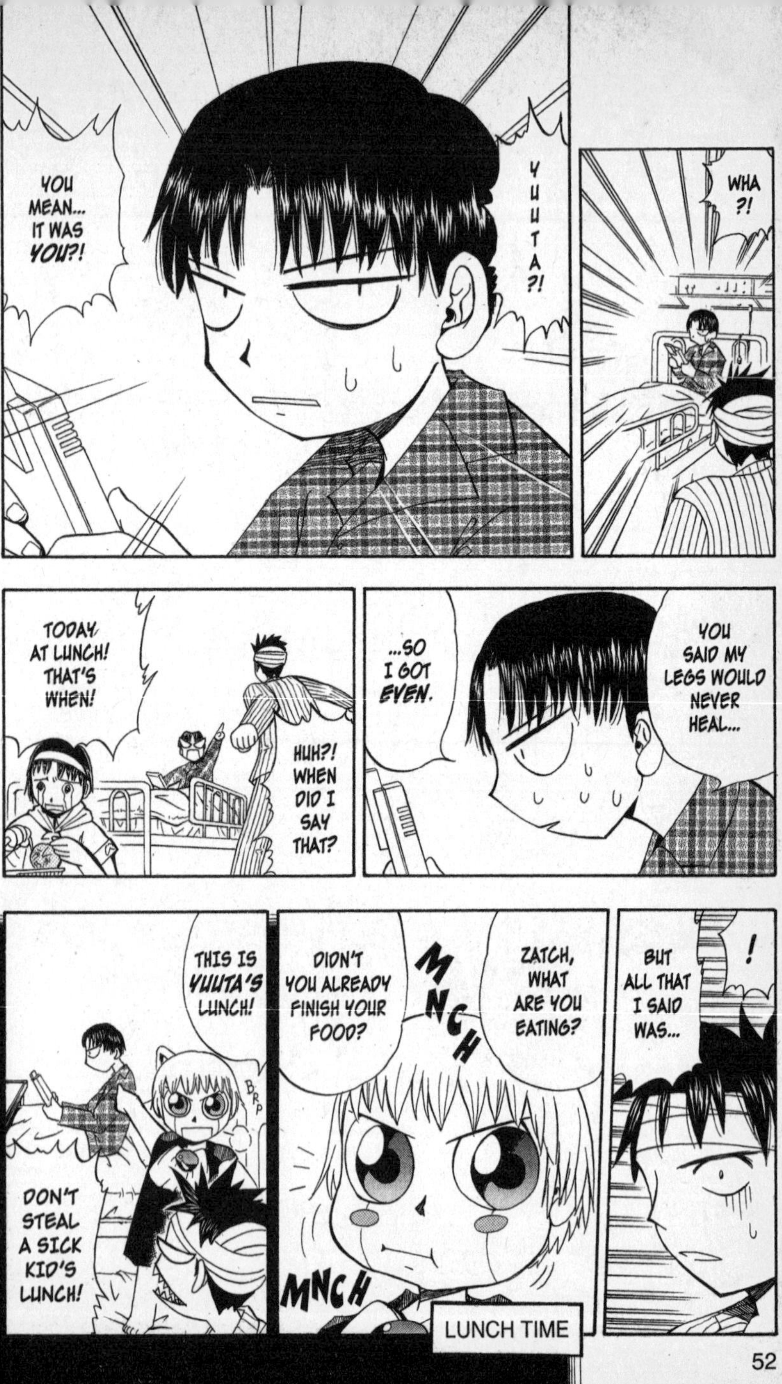
WHA ?!
YUUTA?!
YOU MEAN... IT WAS YOU?!
YOU SAID MY LEGS WOULD NEVER HEAL...
...SO I GOT EVEN.
HUH?! WHEN DID I SAY THAT?
TODAY AT LUNCH! THAT'S WHEN!
!
BUT ALL THAT I SAID WAS...
ZATCH, WHAT ARE YOU EATING?
MNCH
DIDN'T YOU ALREADY FINISH YOUR FOOD?
MNCH
THIS IS YUUTA'S LUNCH!
BRP
DON'T STEAL A SICK KID'S LUNCH!
LUNCH TIME

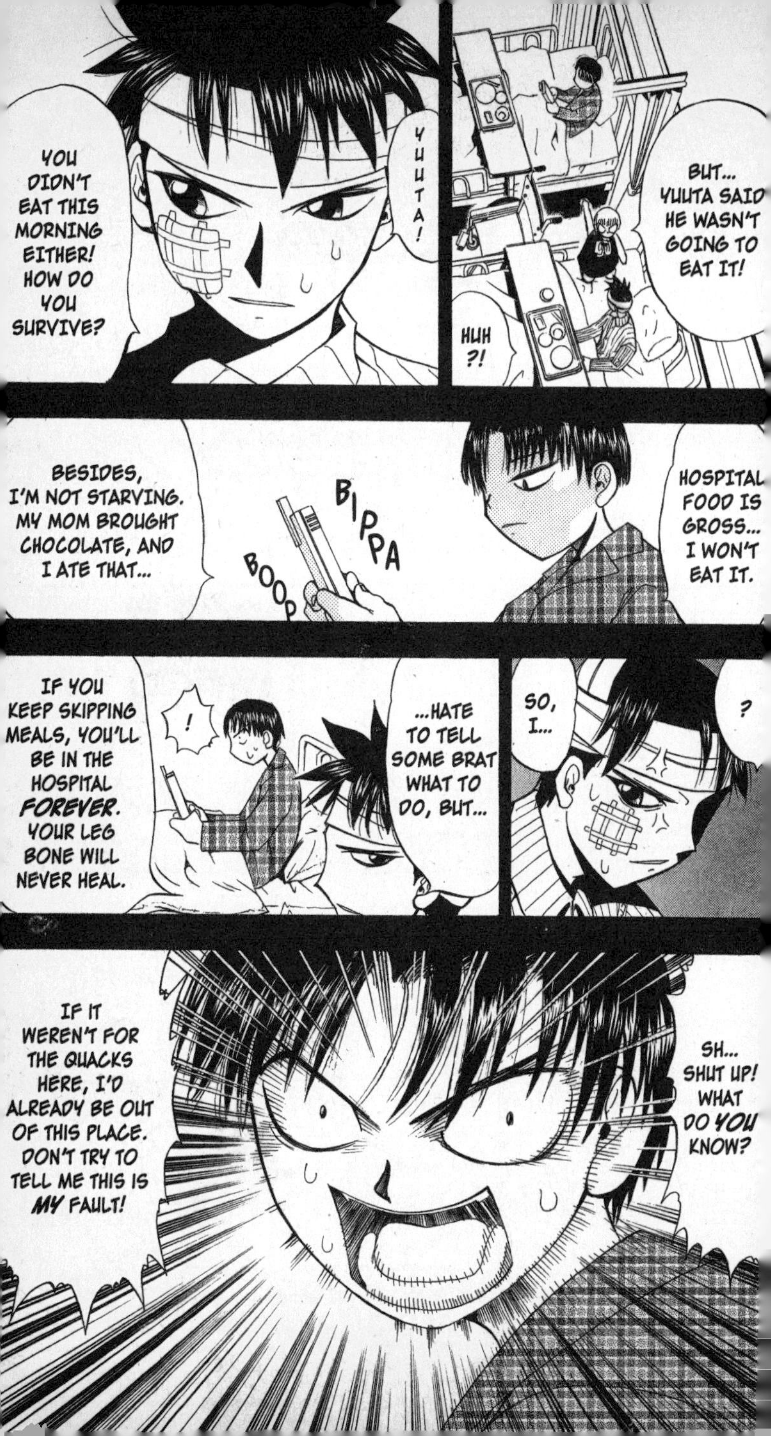
BUT... YUUTA SAID HE WASN'T GOING TO EAT IT!
HUH ?!
YUUTA!
YOU DIDN'T EAT THIS MORNING EITHER! HOW DO YOU SURVIVE?
HOSPITAL FOOD IS GROSS... I WON'T EAT IT.
BIPPA
BOOP
BESIDES, I'M NOT STARVING. MY MOM BROUGHT CHOCOLATE, AND I ATE THAT...
?
SO, I...
...HATE TO TELL SOME BRAT WHAT TO DO, BUT...
!
IF YOU KEEP SKIPPING MEALS, YOU'LL BE IN THE HOSPITAL FOREVER. YOUR LEG BONE WILL NEVER HEAL.
SH... SHUT UP! WHAT DO YOU KNOW?
IF IT WEREN'T FOR THE QUACKS HERE, I'D ALREADY BE OUT OF THIS PLACE. DON'T TRY TO TELL ME THIS IS MY FAULT!

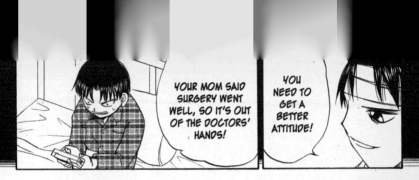

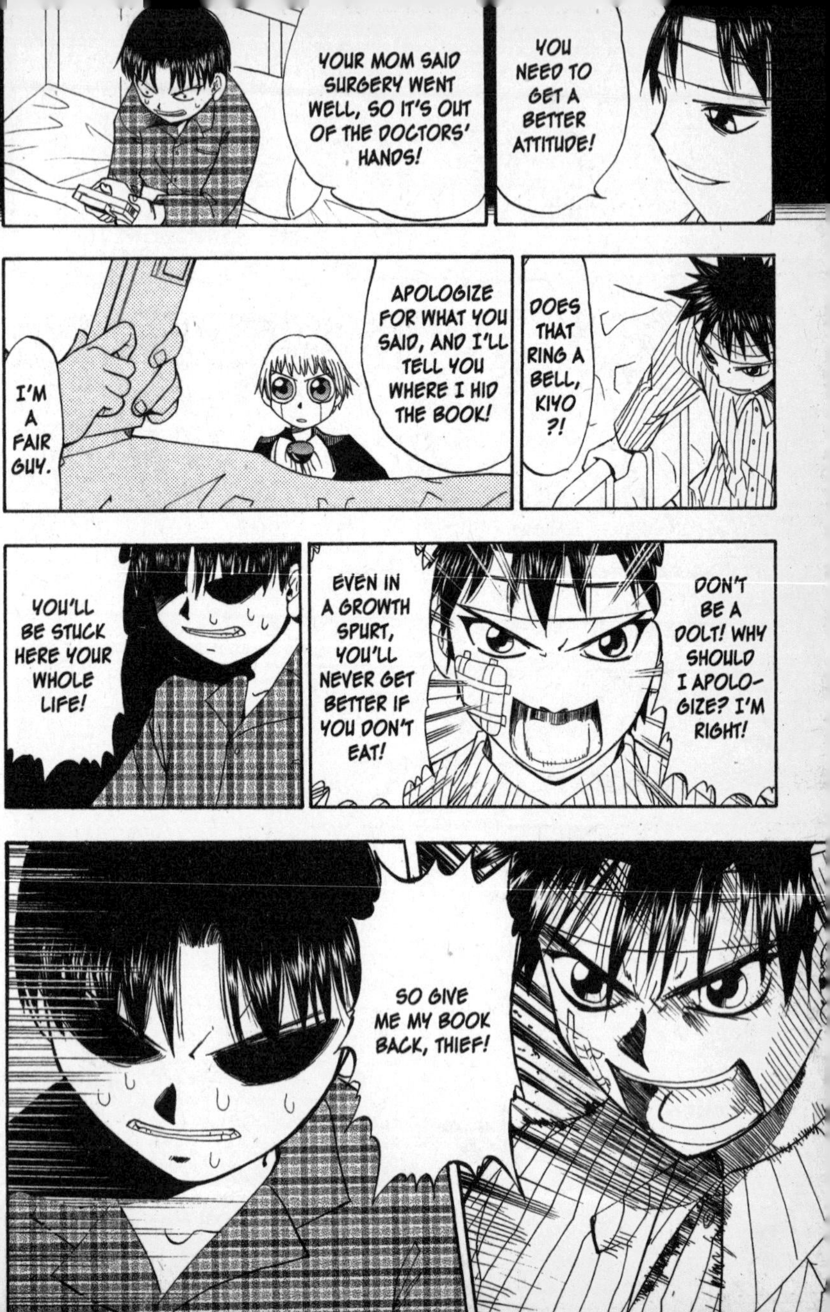
YOU NEED TO GET A BETTER ATTITUDE!
YOUR MOM SAID SURGERY WENT WELL, SO IT'S OUT OF THE DOCTORS' HANDS!
DOES THAT RING A BELL, KIYO ?!
APOLOGIZE FOR WHAT YOU SAID, AND I'LL TELL YOU WHERE I HID THE BOOK!
I'M A FAIR GUY.
DON'T BE A DOLT! WHY SHOULD I APOLOGIZE? I'M RIGHT!
EVEN IN A GROWTH SPURT, YOU'LL NEVER GET BETTER IF YOU DON'T EAT!
YOU'LL BE STUCK HERE YOUR WHOLE LIFE!
SO GIVE ME MY BOOK BACK, THIEF!

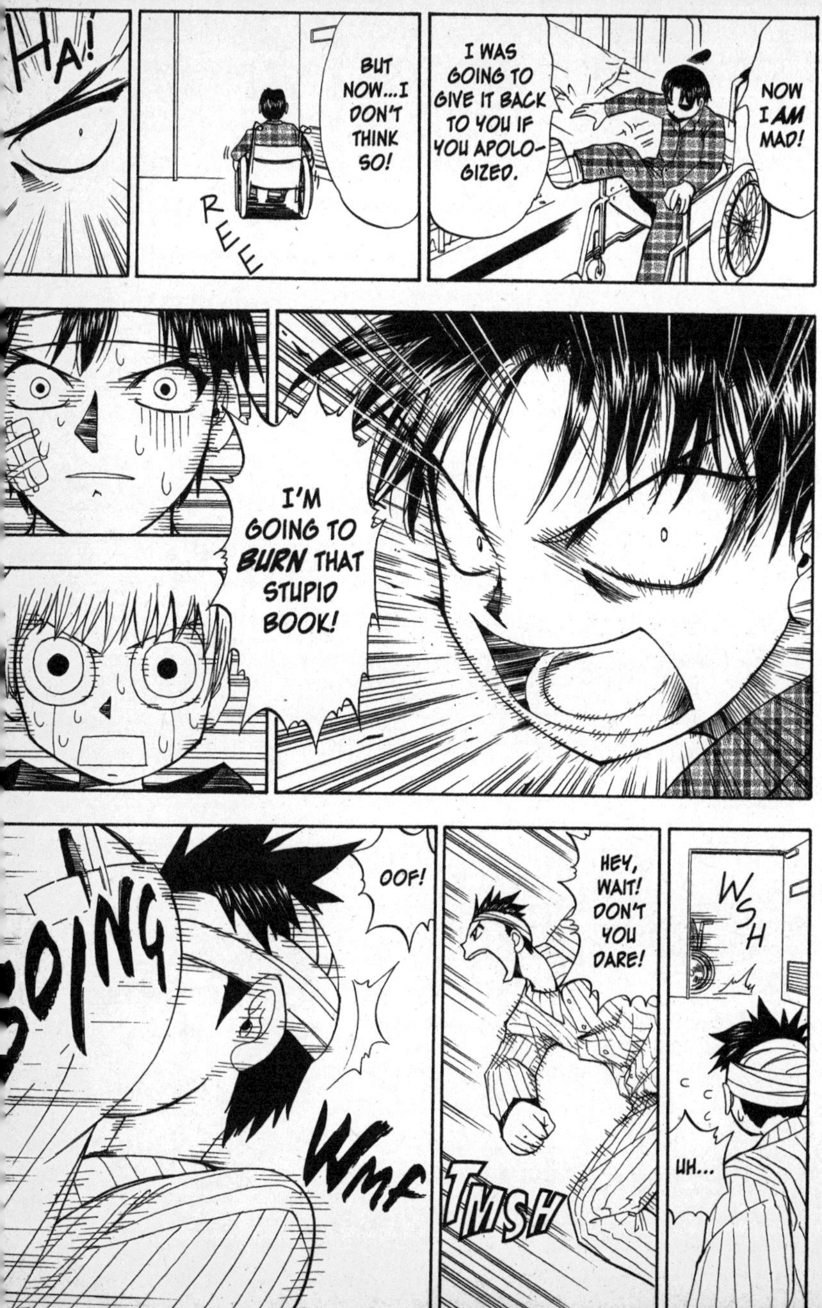
NOW I **AM** MAD!
I WAS GOING TO GIVE IT BACK TO YOU IF YOU APOLOGIZED.
BUT NOW...I DON'T THINK SO!
REEE
HA!
I'M GOING TO **BURN** THAT STUPID BOOK!
WSH
UH...
HEY, WAIT! DON'T YOU DARE!
TMSH
OOF!
BOING
WMF

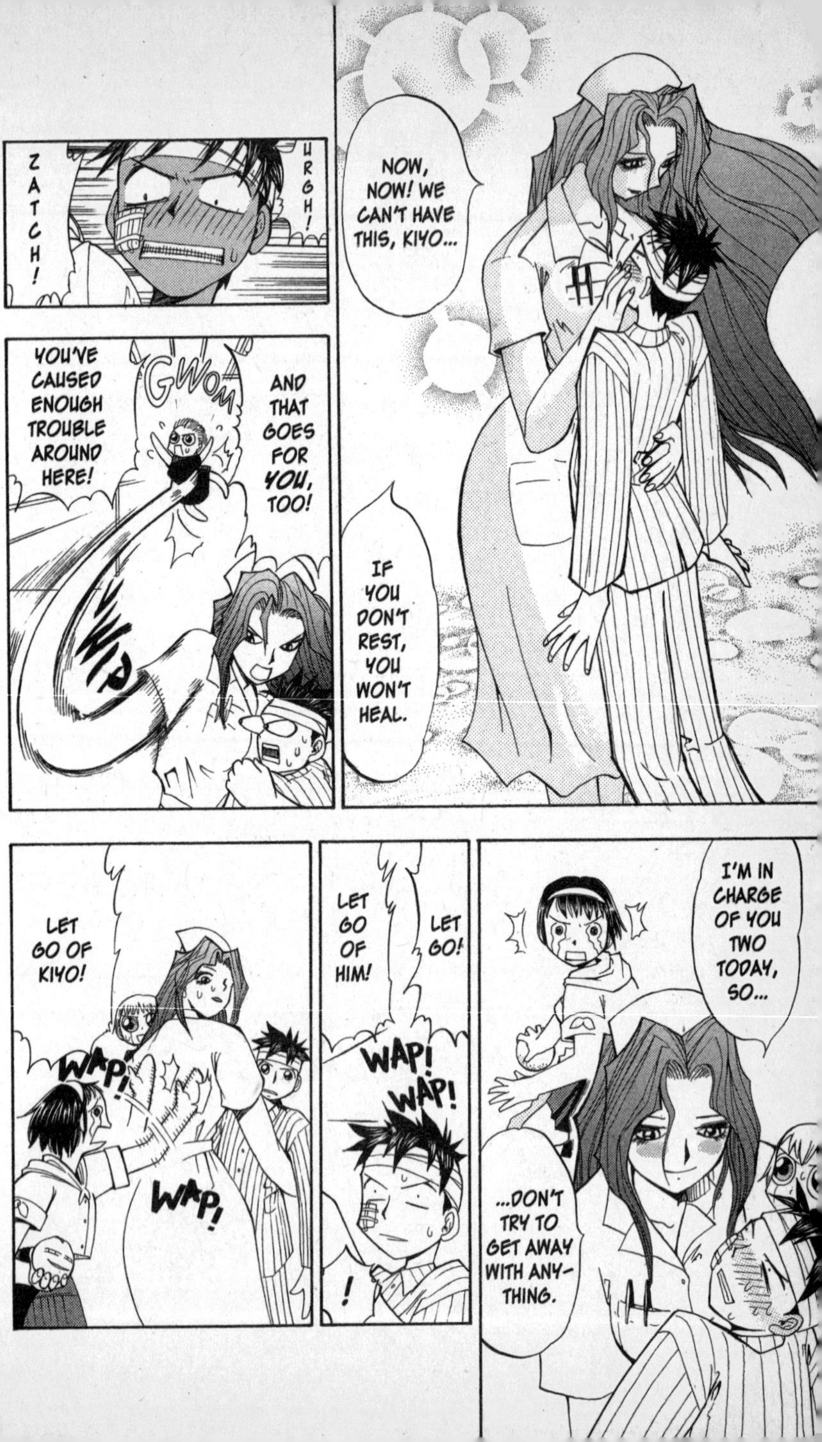
NOW, NOW! WE CAN'T HAVE THIS, KIYO...
IF YOU DON'T REST, YOU WON'T HEAL.
URGH!
ZATCH!
YOU'VE CAUSED ENOUGH TROUBLE AROUND HERE!
GWOM
AND THAT GOES FOR YOU, TOO!
WHIP
I'M IN CHARGE OF YOU TWO TODAY, SO...
...DON'T TRY TO GET AWAY WITH ANYTHING.
LET GO!
LET GO OF HIM!
WAP! WAP!
!
LET GO OF KIYO!
WAP!
WAP!

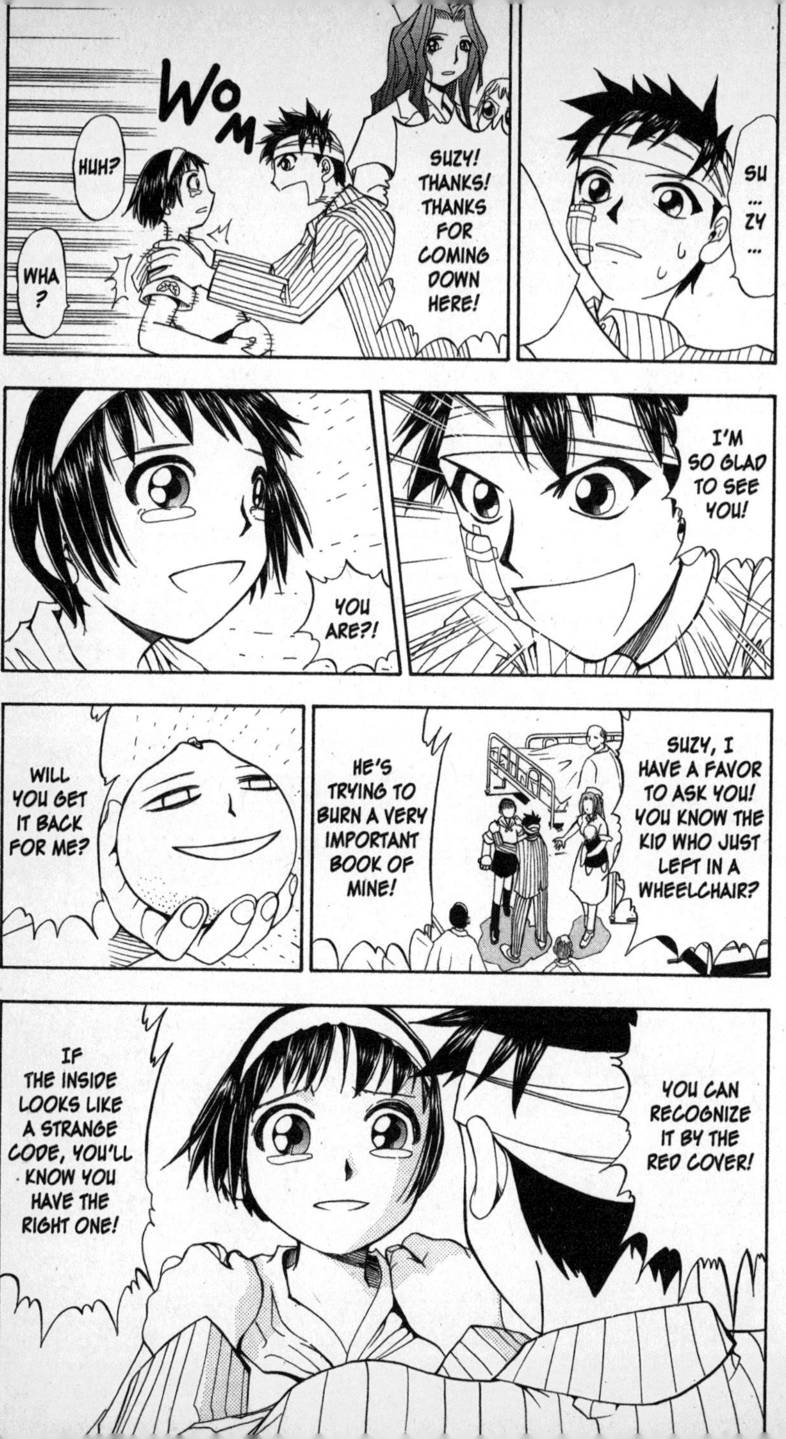
SU ... ZY ...
SUZY! THANKS! THANKS FOR COMING DOWN HERE!
WOM
HUH?
WHA ?
I'M SO GLAD TO SEE YOU!
YOU ARE?!
SUZY, I HAVE A FAVOR TO ASK YOU! YOU KNOW THE KID WHO JUST LEFT IN A WHEELCHAIR?
HE'S TRYING TO BURN A VERY IMPORTANT BOOK OF MINE!
WILL YOU GET IT BACK FOR ME?
YOU CAN RECOGNIZE IT BY THE RED COVER!
IF THE INSIDE LOOKS LIKE A STRANGE CODE, YOU'LL KNOW YOU HAVE THE RIGHT ONE!

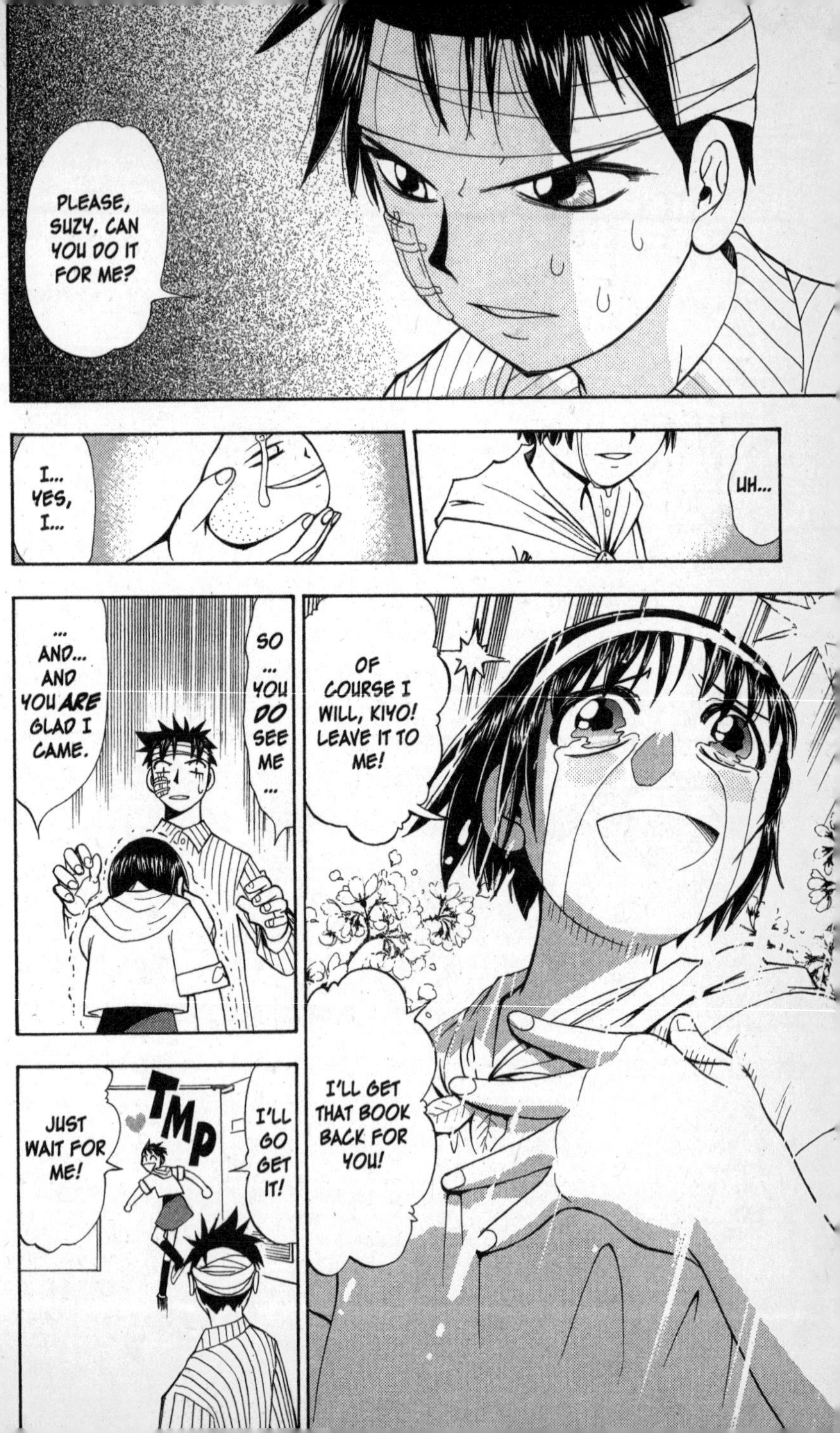
PLEASE, SUZY. CAN YOU DO IT FOR ME?
UH...
I... YES, I...
OF COURSE I WILL, KIYO! LEAVE IT TO ME!
I'LL GET THAT BOOK BACK FOR YOU!
SO ... YOU DO SEE ME ...
... AND... AND YOU ARE GLAD I CAME.
I'LL GO GET IT!
TMP
JUST WAIT FOR ME!

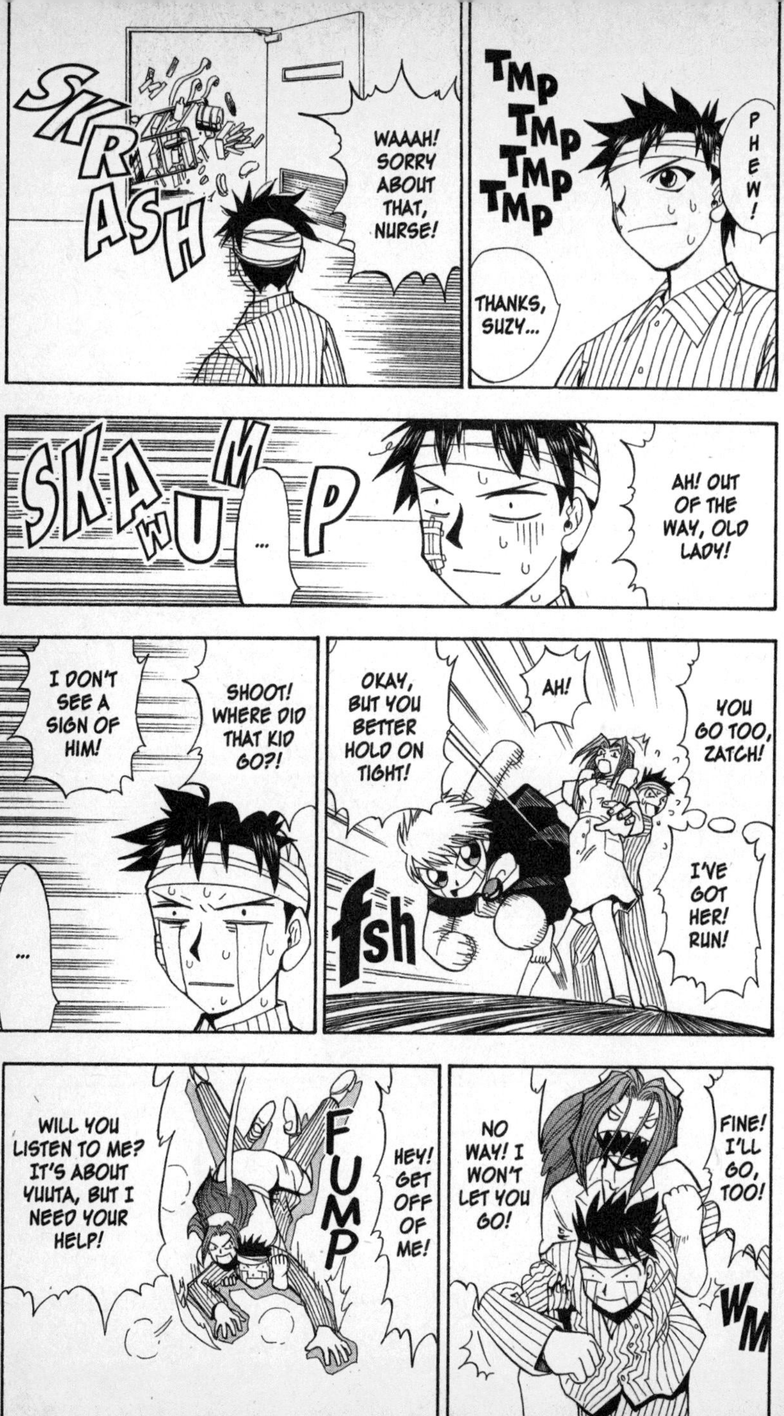
PHEW!
TMP TMP TMP TMP
THANKS, SUZY...
WAAAH! SORRY ABOUT THAT, NURSE!
SKRASH
AH! OUT OF THE WAY, OLD LADY!
...
SKAWUMP
YOU GO TOO, ZATCH!
AH!
OKAY, BUT YOU BETTER HOLD ON TIGHT!
I'VE GOT HER! RUN!
fsh
SHOOT! WHERE DID THAT KID GO?!
I DON'T SEE A SIGN OF HIM!
...
FINE! I'LL GO, TOO!
NO WAY! I WON'T LET YOU GO!
WM
HEY! GET OFF OF ME!
FUMP
WILL YOU LISTEN TO ME? IT'S ABOUT YUUTA, BUT I NEED YOUR HELP!

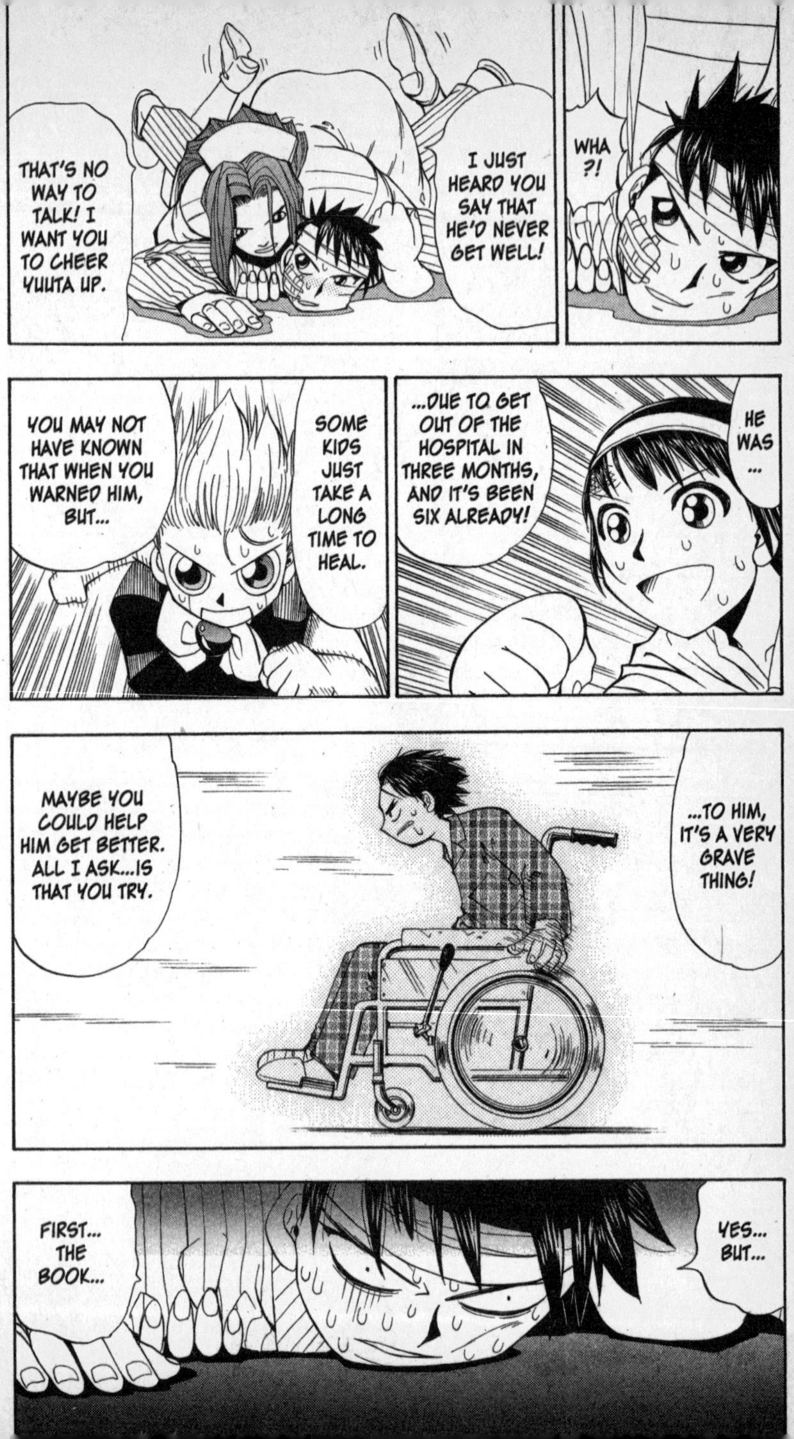
WHA ?!
I JUST HEARD YOU SAY THAT HE'D NEVER GET WELL!
THAT'S NO WAY TO TALK! I WANT YOU TO CHEER YUUTA UP.
HE WAS...
...DUE TO GET OUT OF THE HOSPITAL IN THREE MONTHS, AND IT'S BEEN SIX ALREADY!
SOME KIDS JUST TAKE A LONG TIME TO HEAL.
YOU MAY NOT HAVE KNOWN THAT WHEN YOU WARNED HIM, BUT...
...TO HIM, IT'S A VERY GRAVE THING!
MAYBE YOU COULD HELP HIM GET BETTER. ALL I ASK...IS THAT YOU TRY.
YES... BUT...
FIRST... THE BOOK...

LEVEL 12: Where Is the Book?!

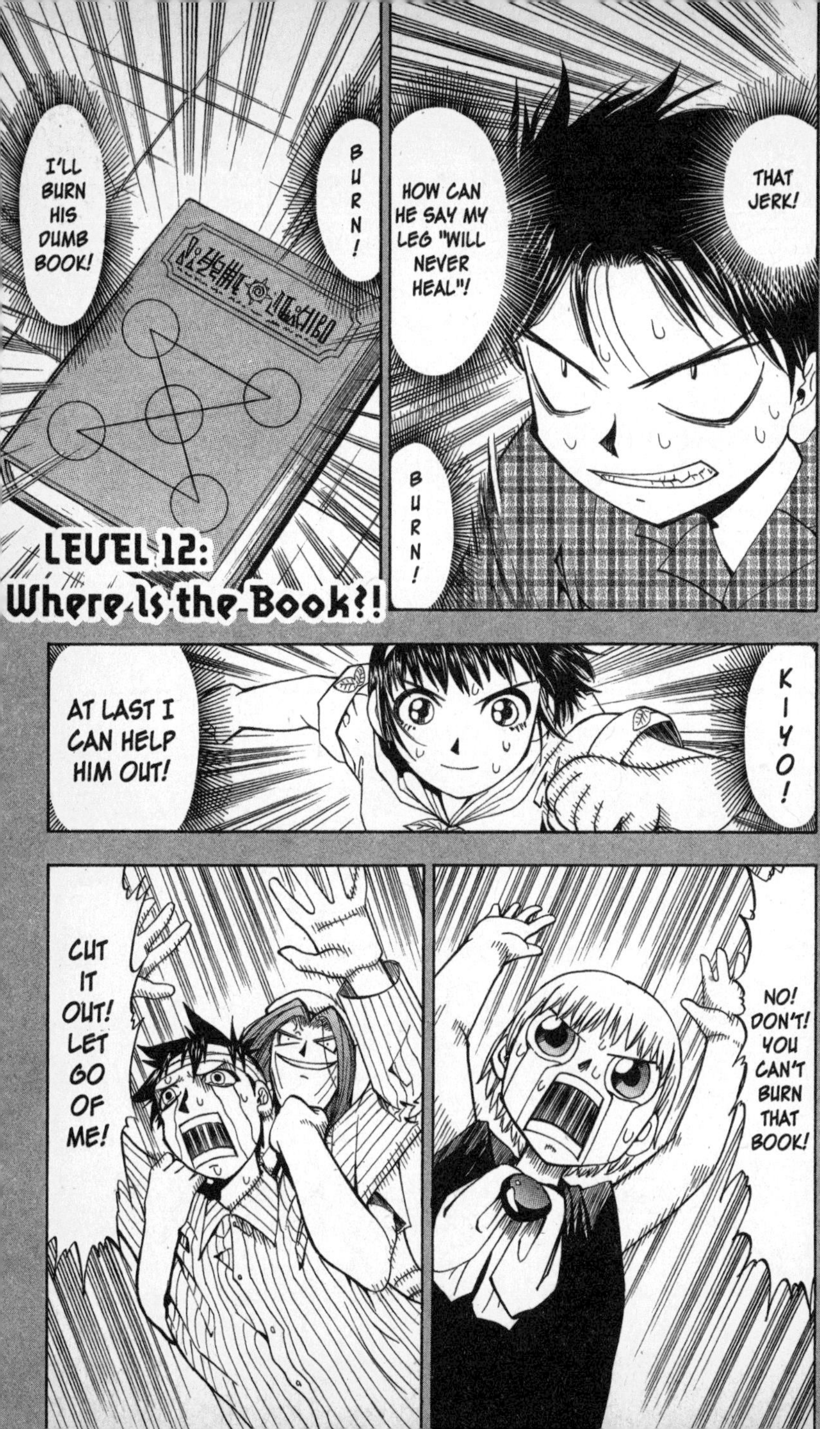

THAT JERK!
HOW CAN HE SAY MY LEG "WILL NEVER HEAL"!
BURN!
BURN!
I'LL BURN HIS DUMB BOOK!
KIYO!
AT LAST I CAN HELP HIM OUT!
NO! DON'T! YOU CAN'T BURN THAT BOOK!
CUT IT OUT! LET GO OF ME!

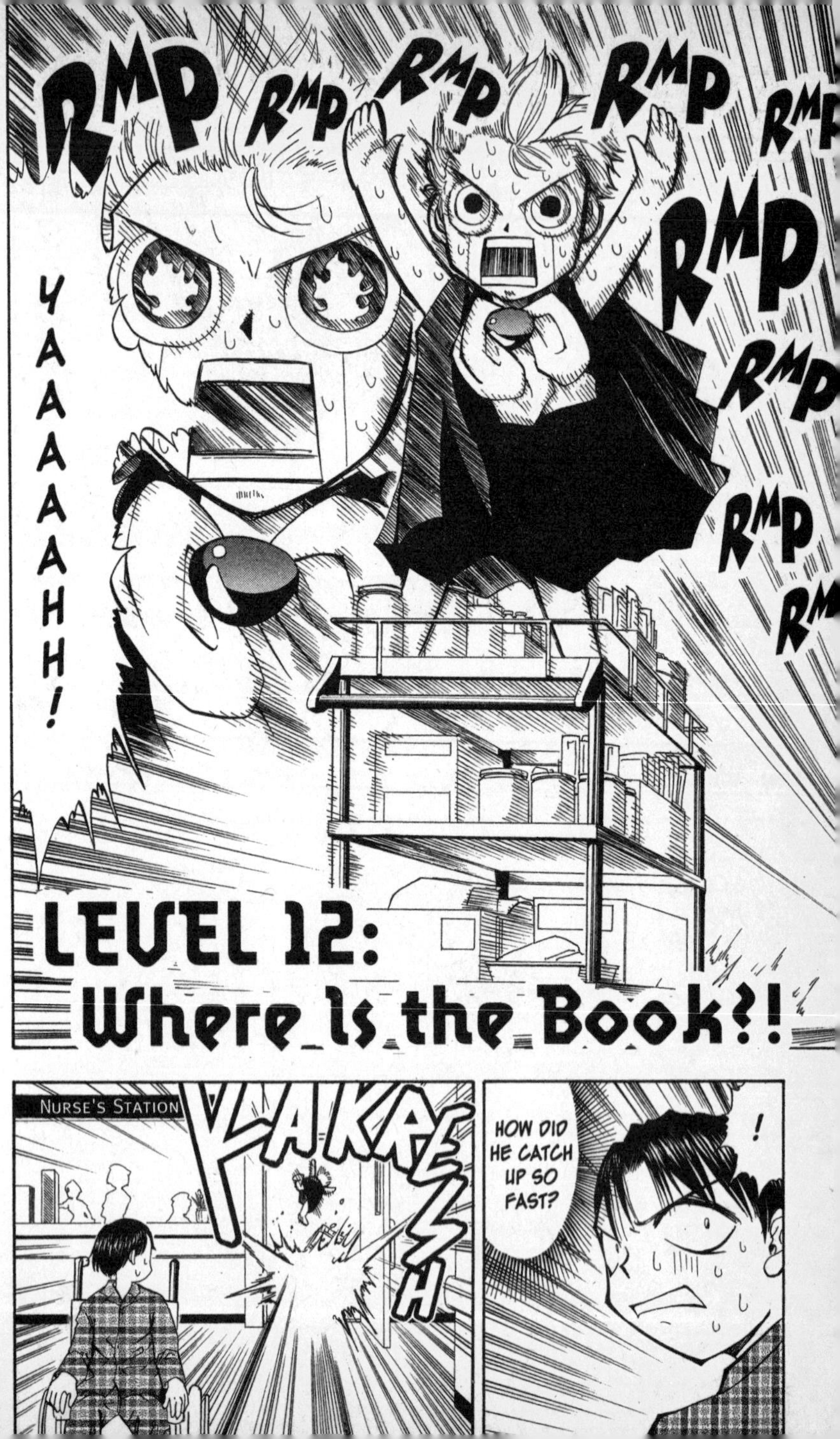
RMP RMP RMP RMP RMP RMP RMP RMP RM
YAAAAAAHH!
LEVEL 12: Where Is the Book?!
!
HOW DID HE CATCH UP SO FAST?
NURSE'S STATION
YAKRESH

TMP TMP TMP TMP TMP TMP TMP

You little brat!

...

NOOOOO!

MAN!

ZSH

...

TM TM TM TM TM

THAT'S WHY I WANT *YOU* TO CHEER HIM UP SOMEHOW.

YES!

608
HIDEAKI TAI
KIYO TAKAMINE
KEN MURATA
YUUTA AKIYAMA
H. MATSUYAMA
K. YAMAMOTO

SO HE'S JUST SLOW TO HEAL?

AAAH!

GISH

Tangerine mace!

I KNOW JUST THE THING TO PUT A SMILE ON HIS FACE!

OKAY!

WOM

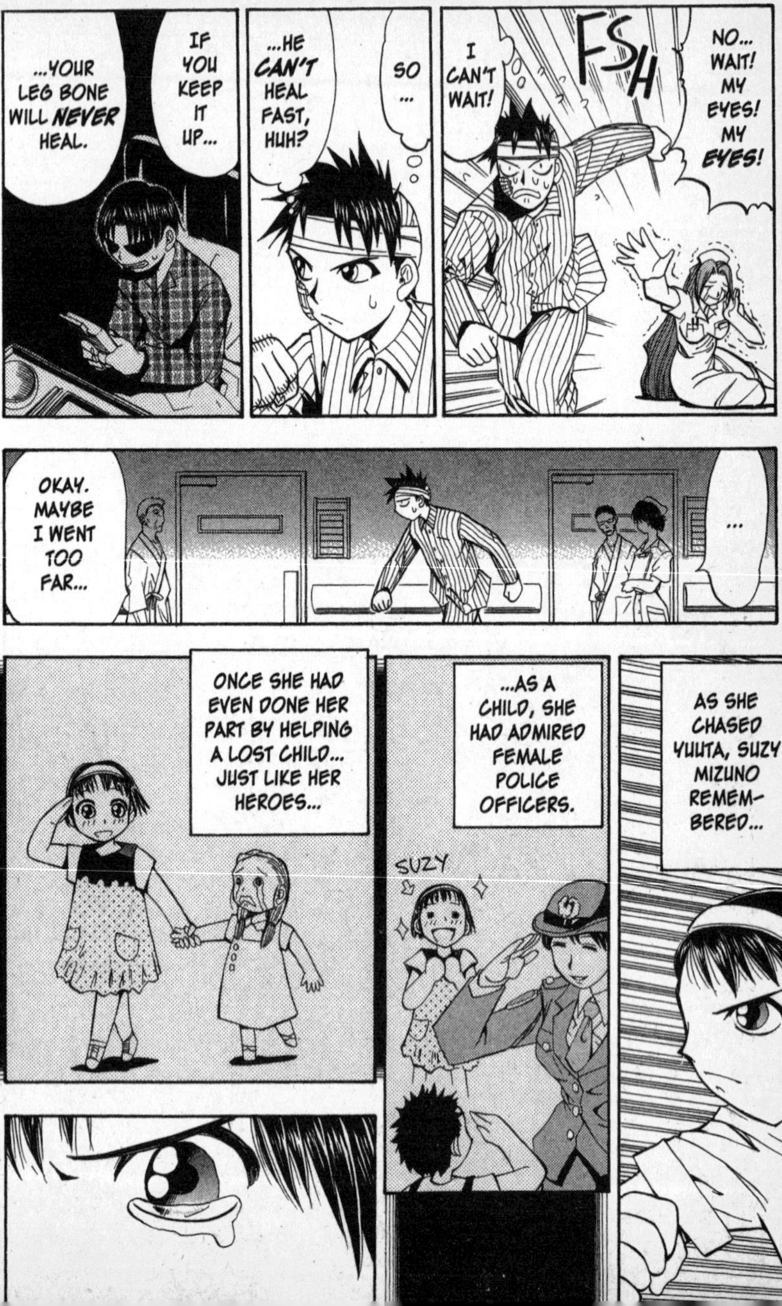
NO... WAIT! MY EYES! MY EYES!
FSH
I CAN'T WAIT!
SO ...
...HE CAN'T HEAL FAST, HUH?
IF YOU KEEP IT UP...
...YOUR LEG BONE WILL NEVER HEAL.
...
OKAY. MAYBE I WENT TOO FAR...
AS SHE CHASED YUUTA, SUZY MIZUNO REMEMBERED...
...AS A CHILD, SHE HAD ADMIRED FEMALE POLICE OFFICERS.
SUZY
ONCE SHE HAD EVEN DONE HER PART BY HELPING A LOST CHILD... JUST LIKE HER HEROES...

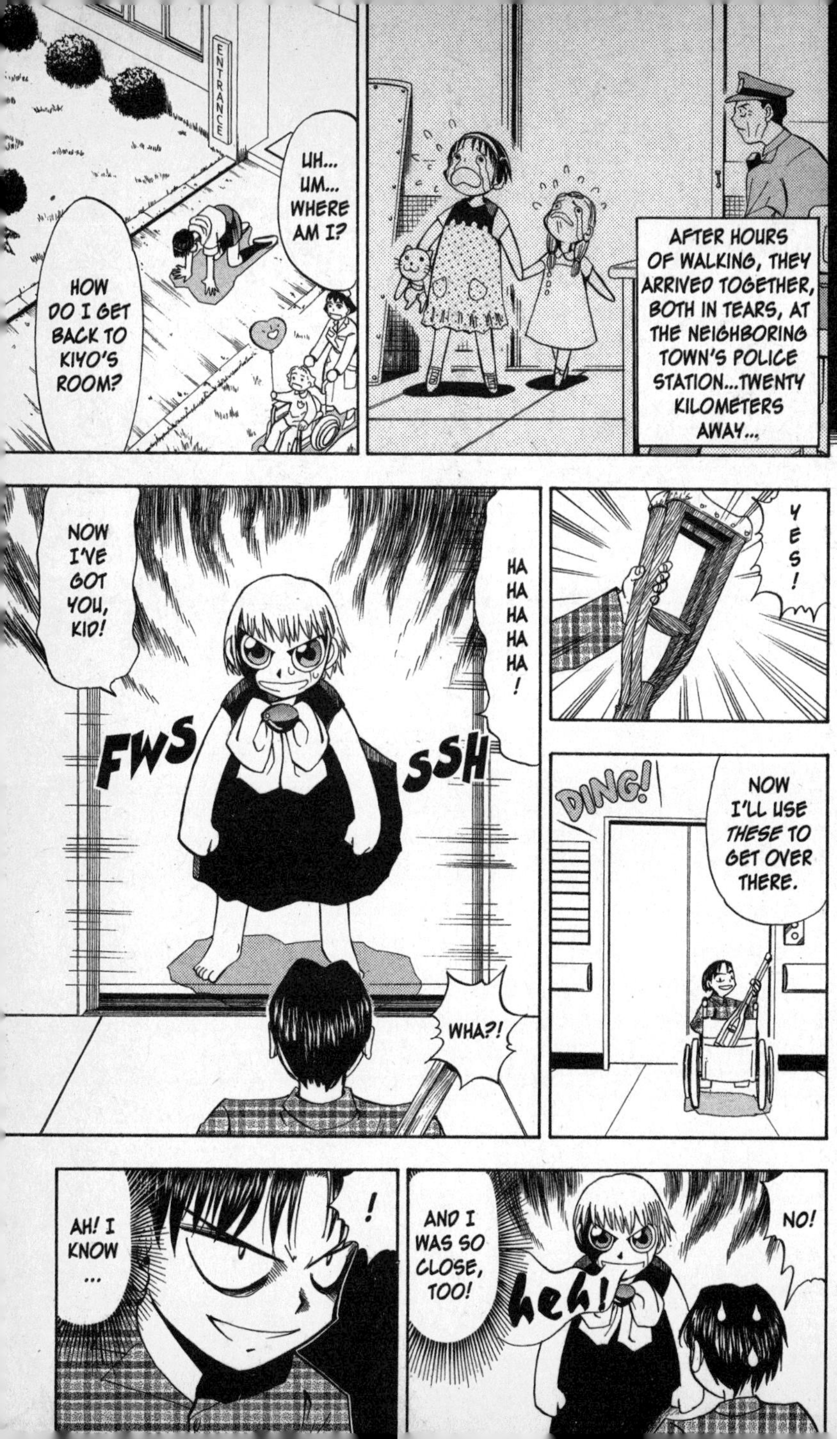

AFTER HOURS OF WALKING, THEY ARRIVED TOGETHER, BOTH IN TEARS, AT THE NEIGHBORING TOWN'S POLICE STATION...TWENTY KILOMETERS AWAY...
ENTRANCE
UH... UM... WHERE AM I?
HOW DO I GET BACK TO KIYO'S ROOM?
YES!
DING!
NOW I'LL USE THESE TO GET OVER THERE.
HA HA HA HA HA!
NOW I'VE GOT YOU, KID!
FWSSSH
WHA?!
NO!
AND I WAS SO CLOSE, TOO!
heh!
!
AH! I KNOW ...

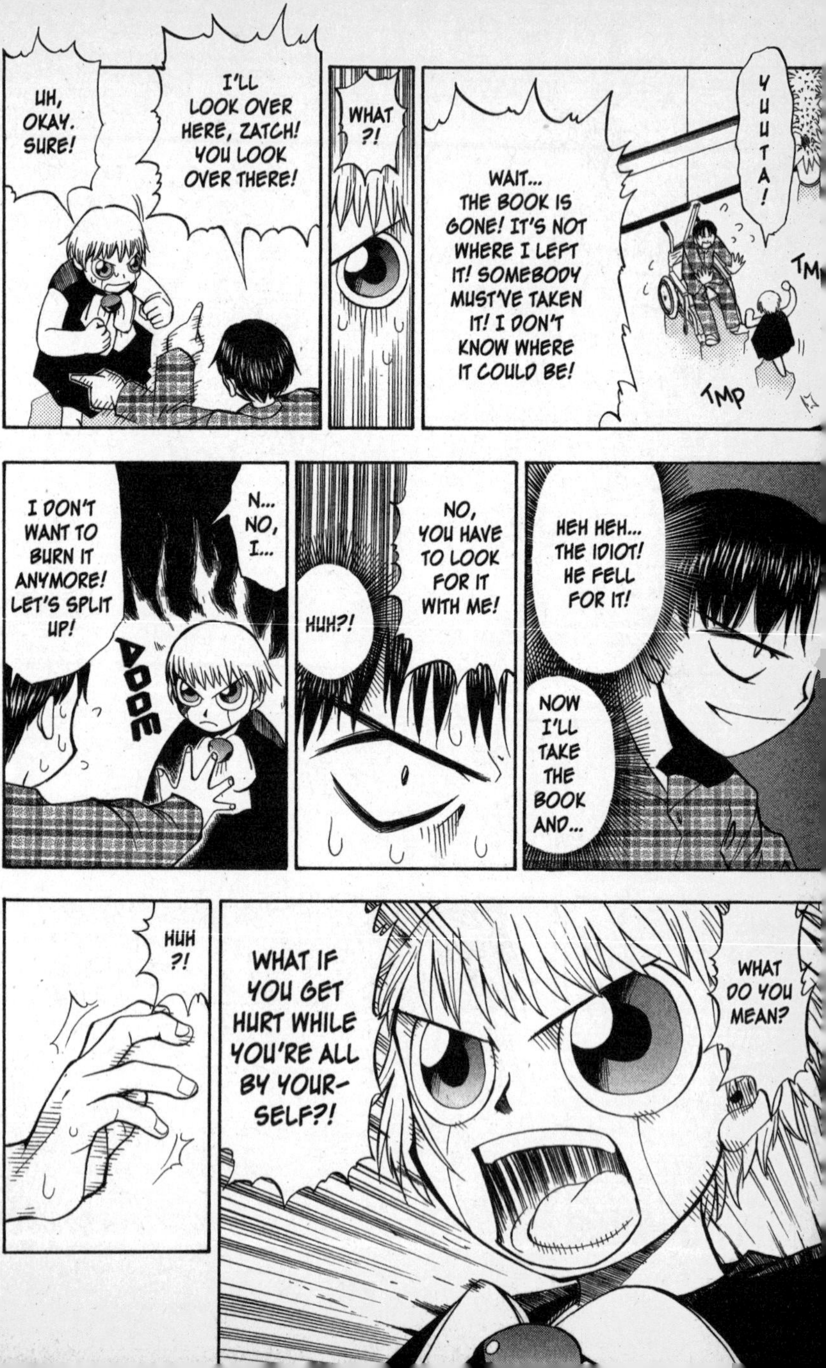
YUUTA!
TMP
WAIT... THE BOOK IS GONE! IT'S NOT WHERE I LEFT IT! SOMEBODY MUST'VE TAKEN IT! I DON'T KNOW WHERE IT COULD BE!
TMP
WHAT?!
I'LL LOOK OVER HERE, ZATCH! YOU LOOK OVER THERE!
UH, OKAY. SURE!
HEH HEH... THE IDIOT! HE FELL FOR IT!
NOW I'LL TAKE THE BOOK AND...
NO, YOU HAVE TO LOOK FOR IT WITH ME!
HUH?!
N... NO, I...
I DON'T WANT TO BURN IT ANYMORE! LET'S SPLIT UP!
DOOM
WHAT DO YOU MEAN?
WHAT IF YOU GET HURT WHILE YOU'RE ALL BY YOURSELF?!
HUH?!

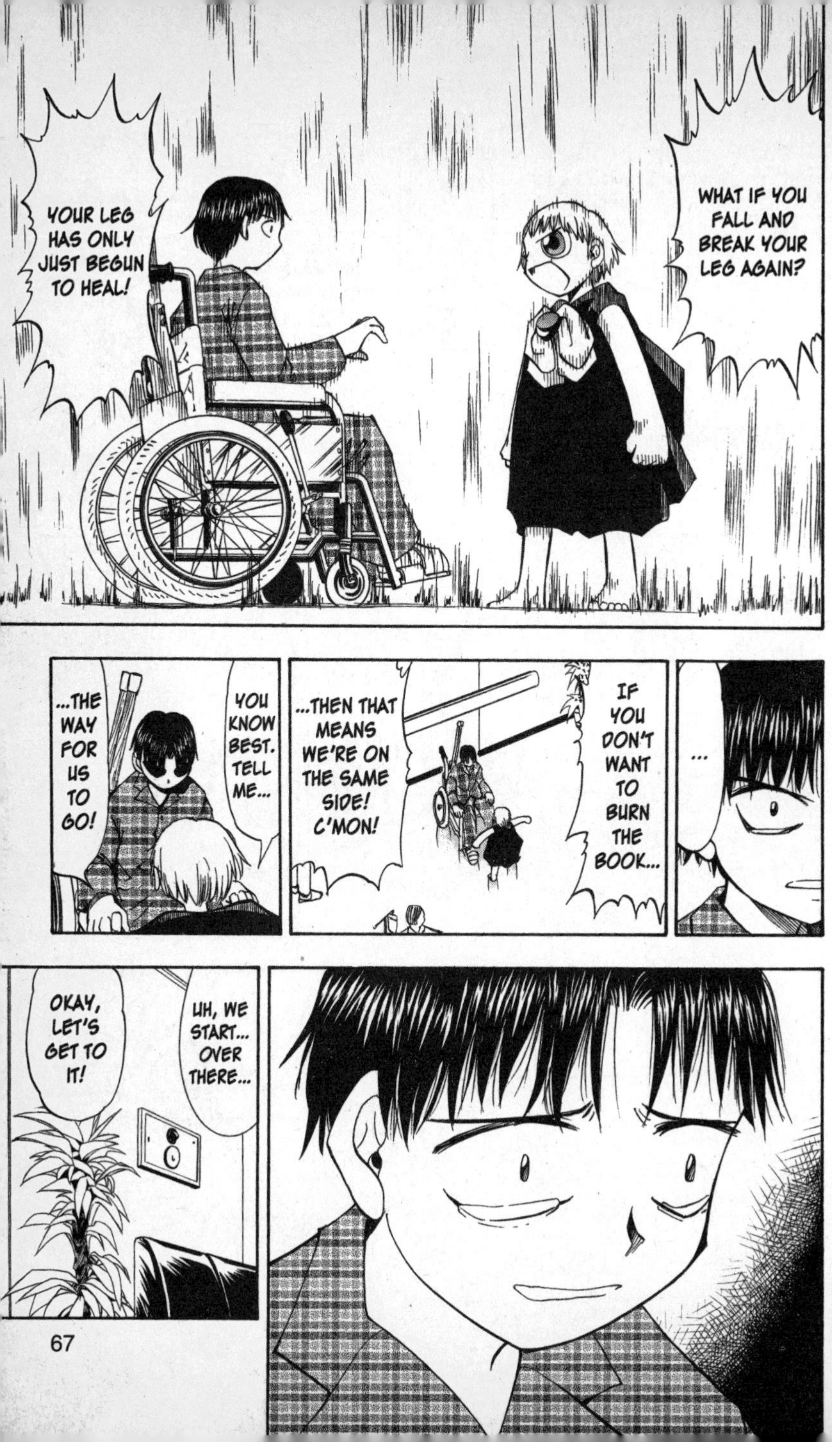
WHAT IF YOU FALL AND BREAK YOUR LEG AGAIN?
YOUR LEG HAS ONLY JUST BEGUN TO HEAL!
...
IF YOU DON'T WANT TO BURN THE BOOK...
...THEN THAT MEANS WE'RE ON THE SAME SIDE! C'MON!
YOU KNOW BEST. TELL ME...
...THE WAY FOR US TO GO!
UH, WE START... OVER THERE...
OKAY, LET'S GET TO IT!

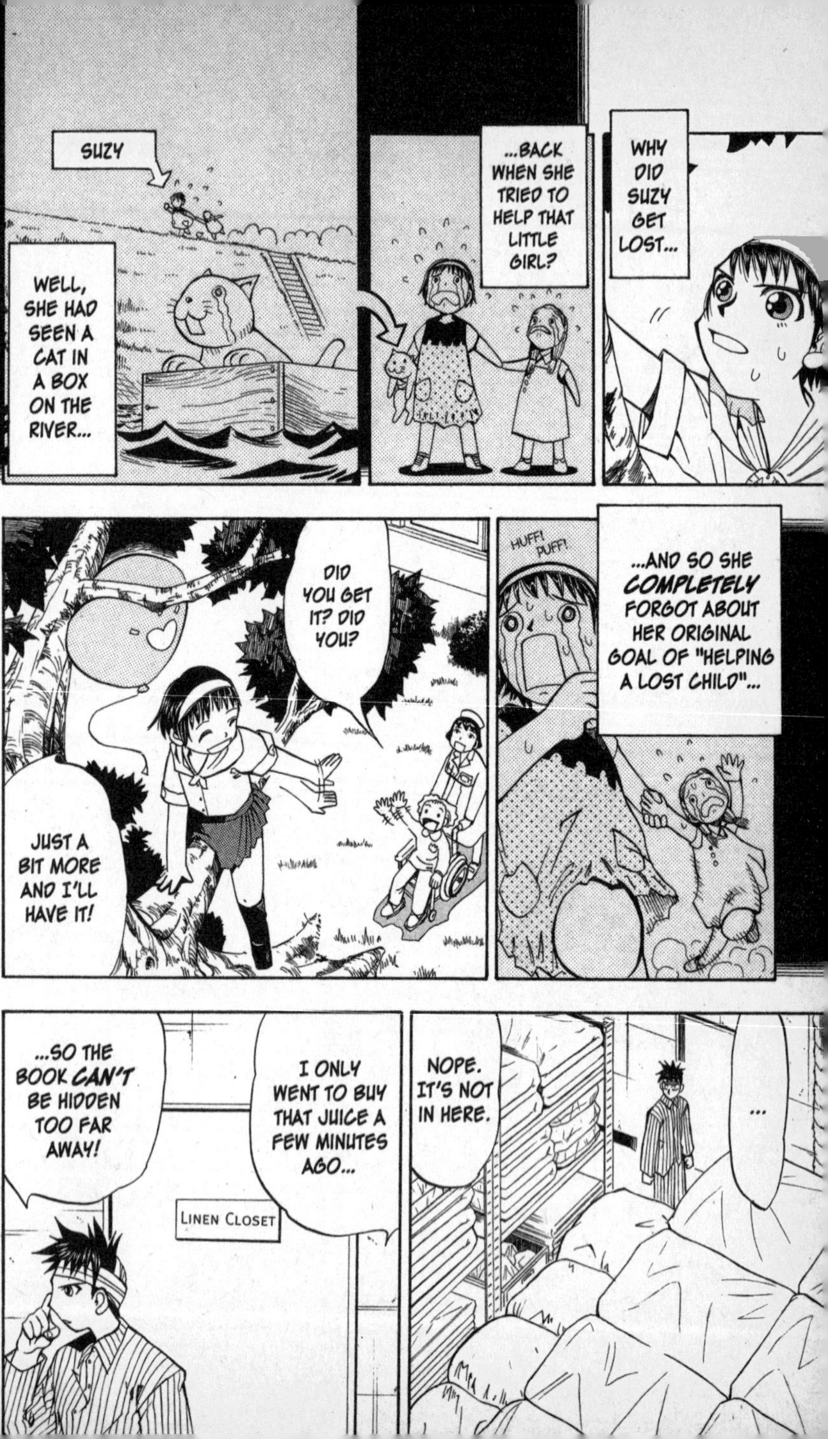
WHY DID SUZY GET LOST...
...BACK WHEN SHE TRIED TO HELP THAT LITTLE GIRL?
SUZY
WELL, SHE HAD SEEN A CAT IN A BOX ON THE RIVER...
HUFF! PUFF!
...AND SO SHE COMPLETELY FORGOT ABOUT HER ORIGINAL GOAL OF "HELPING A LOST CHILD"...
DID YOU GET IT? DID YOU?
JUST A BIT MORE AND I'LL HAVE IT!
...
NOPE. IT'S NOT IN HERE.
I ONLY WENT TO BUY THAT JUICE A FEW MINUTES AGO...
LINEN CLOSET
...SO THE BOOK CAN'T BE HIDDEN TOO FAR AWAY!

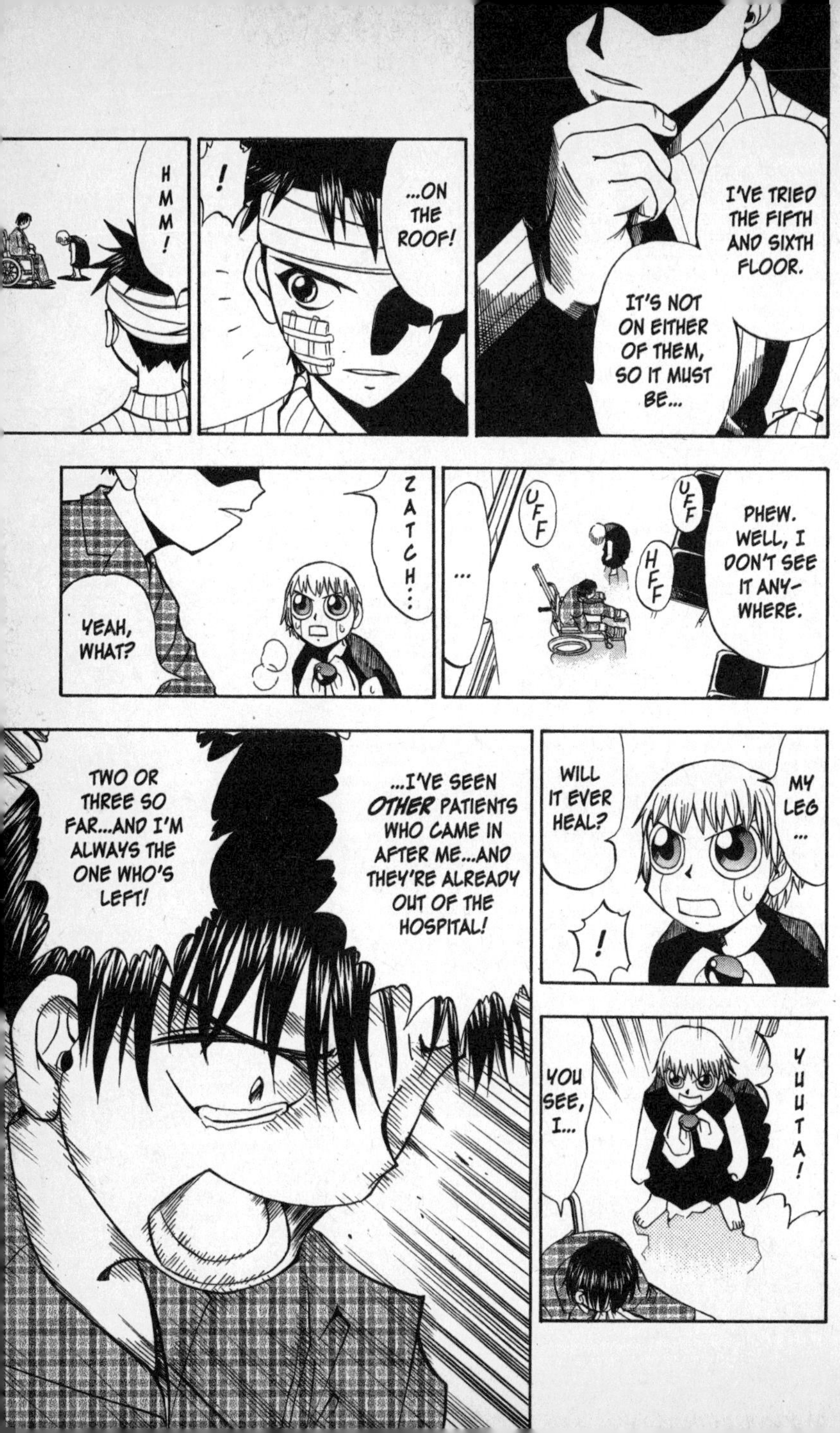
I'VE TRIED THE FIFTH AND SIXTH FLOOR.
IT'S NOT ON EITHER OF THEM, SO IT MUST BE...
...ON THE ROOF!
!
HMM!
PHEW. WELL, I DON'T SEE IT ANY-WHERE.
UFF
HFF
UFF
...
ZATCH...
YEAH, WHAT?
MY LEG...
WILL IT EVER HEAL?
!
YUUTA!
YOU SEE, I...
...I'VE SEEN OTHER PATIENTS WHO CAME IN AFTER ME...AND THEY'RE ALREADY OUT OF THE HOSPITAL!
TWO OR THREE SO FAR...AND I'M ALWAYS THE ONE WHO'S LEFT!

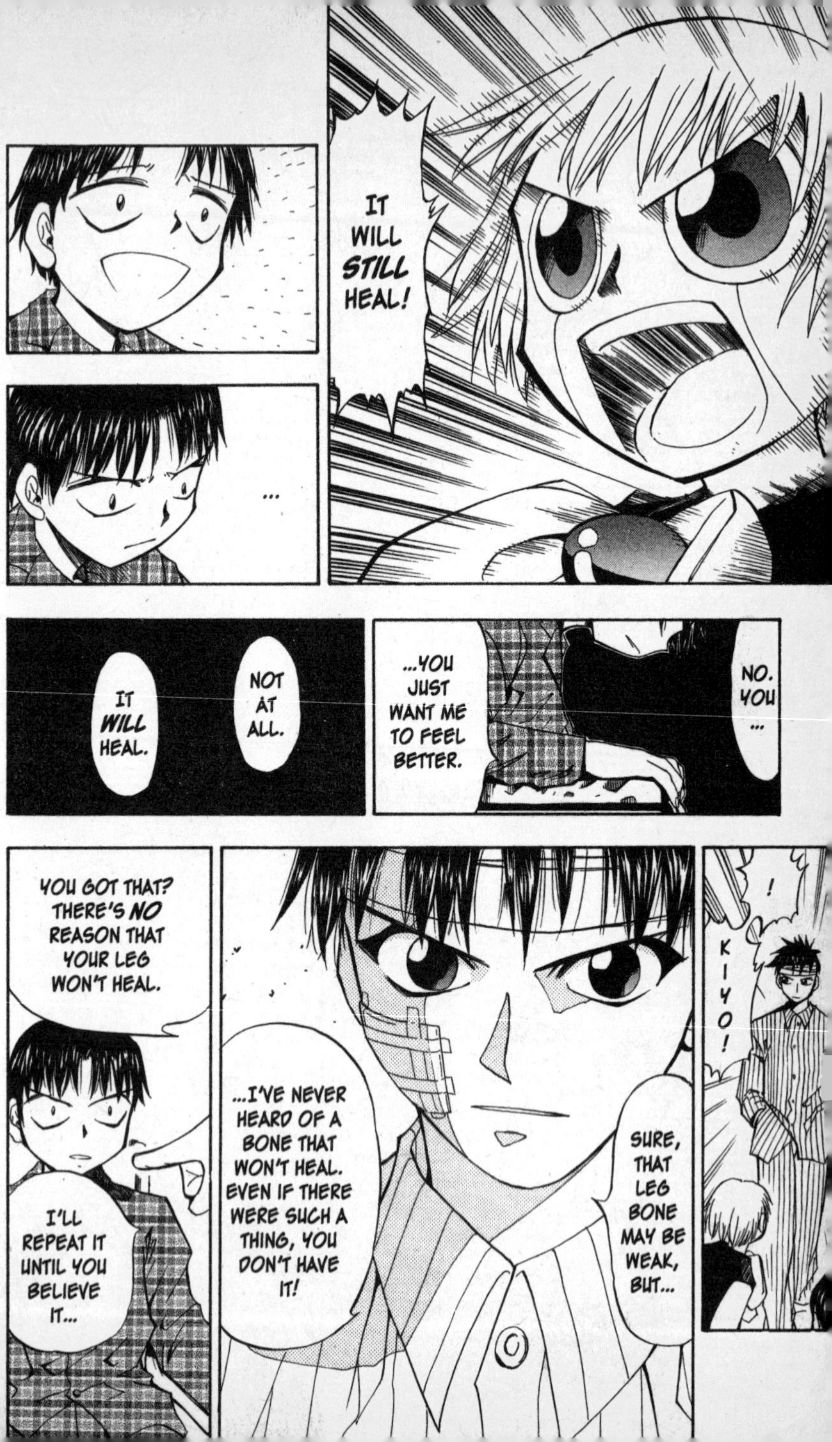
IT WILL STILL HEAL!
...
NO. YOU ...
...YOU JUST WANT ME TO FEEL BETTER.
NOT AT ALL.
IT WILL HEAL.
!
KIYO!
SURE, THAT LEG BONE MAY BE WEAK, BUT...
...I'VE NEVER HEARD OF A BONE THAT WON'T HEAL. EVEN IF THERE WERE SUCH A THING, YOU DON'T HAVE IT!
YOU GOT THAT? THERE'S NO REASON THAT YOUR LEG WON'T HEAL.
I'LL REPEAT IT UNTIL YOU BELIEVE IT...

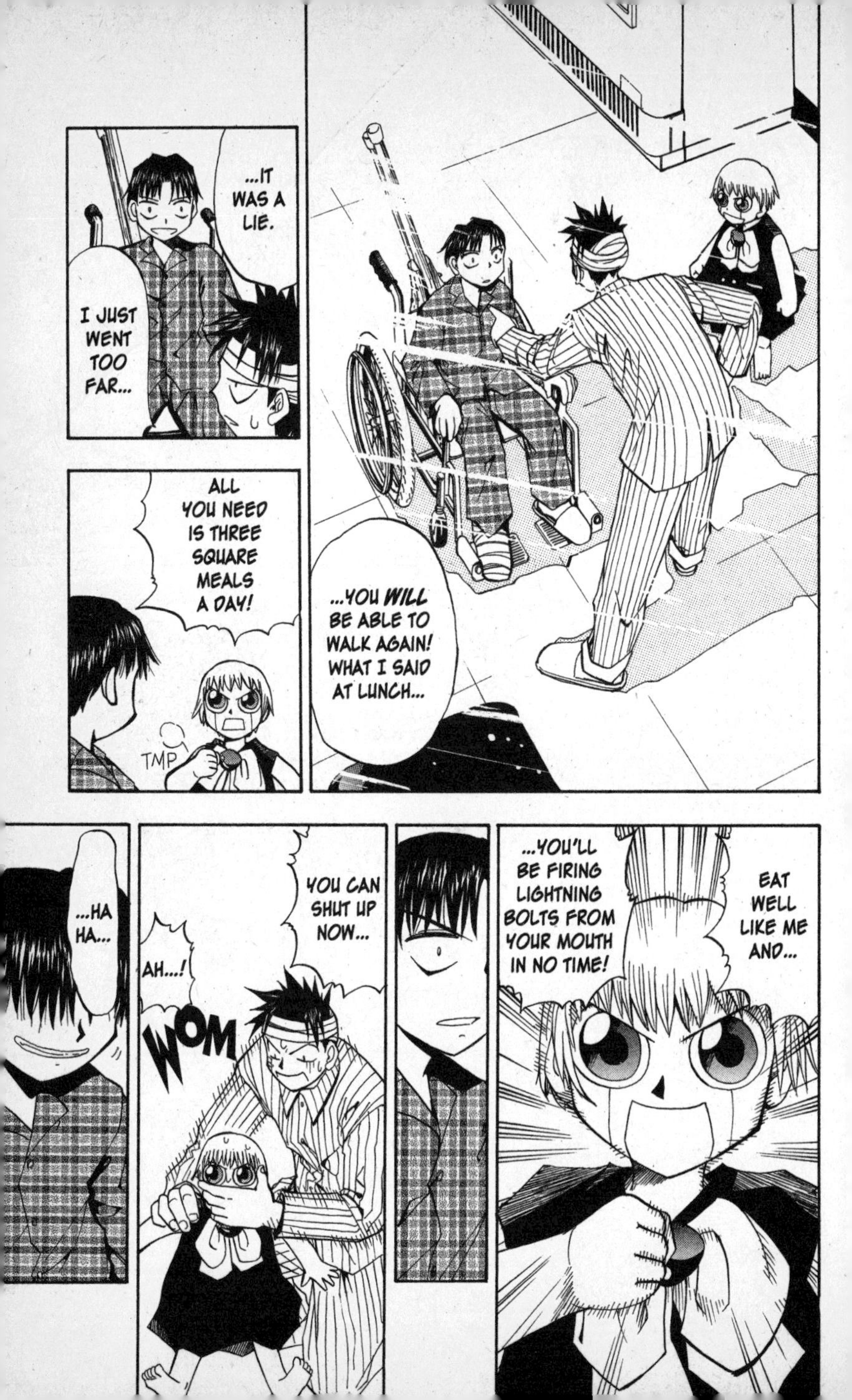
...YOU WILL BE ABLE TO WALK AGAIN! WHAT I SAID AT LUNCH...
...IT WAS A LIE.
I JUST WENT TOO FAR...
ALL YOU NEED IS THREE SQUARE MEALS A DAY!
TMP
EAT WELL LIKE ME AND...
...YOU'LL BE FIRING LIGHTNING BOLTS FROM YOUR MOUTH IN NO TIME!
YOU CAN SHUT UP NOW...
AH...!
WOM
...HA HA...

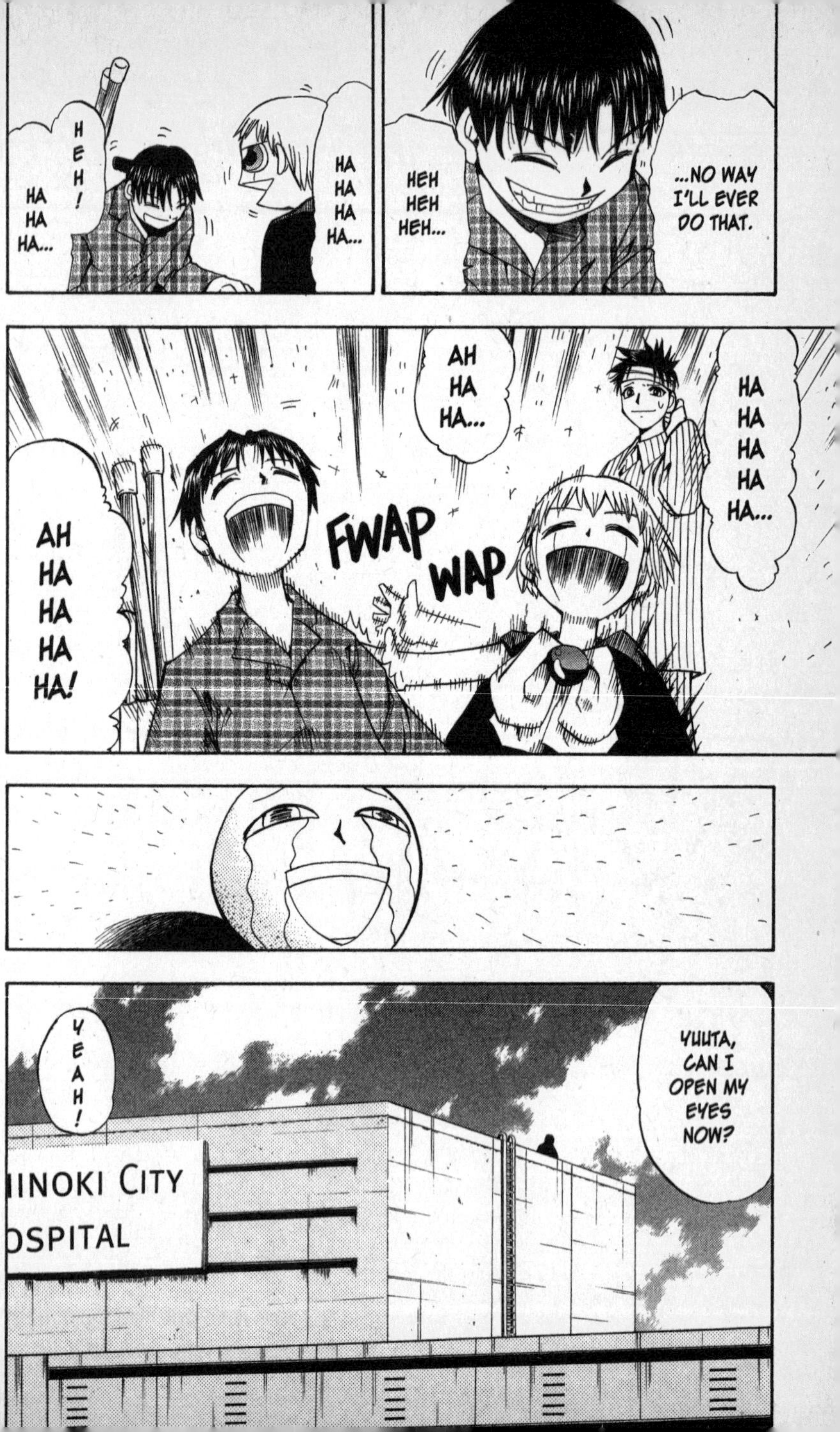
...NO WAY I'LL EVER DO THAT.
HEH HEH HEH...
HA HA HA HA...
HEH!
HA HA HA...
HA HA HA HA HA...
AH HA HA...
FWAP
WAP
AH HA HA HA HA HA!
YUUTA, CAN I OPEN MY EYES NOW?
YEAH!
INOKI CITY
OSPITAL

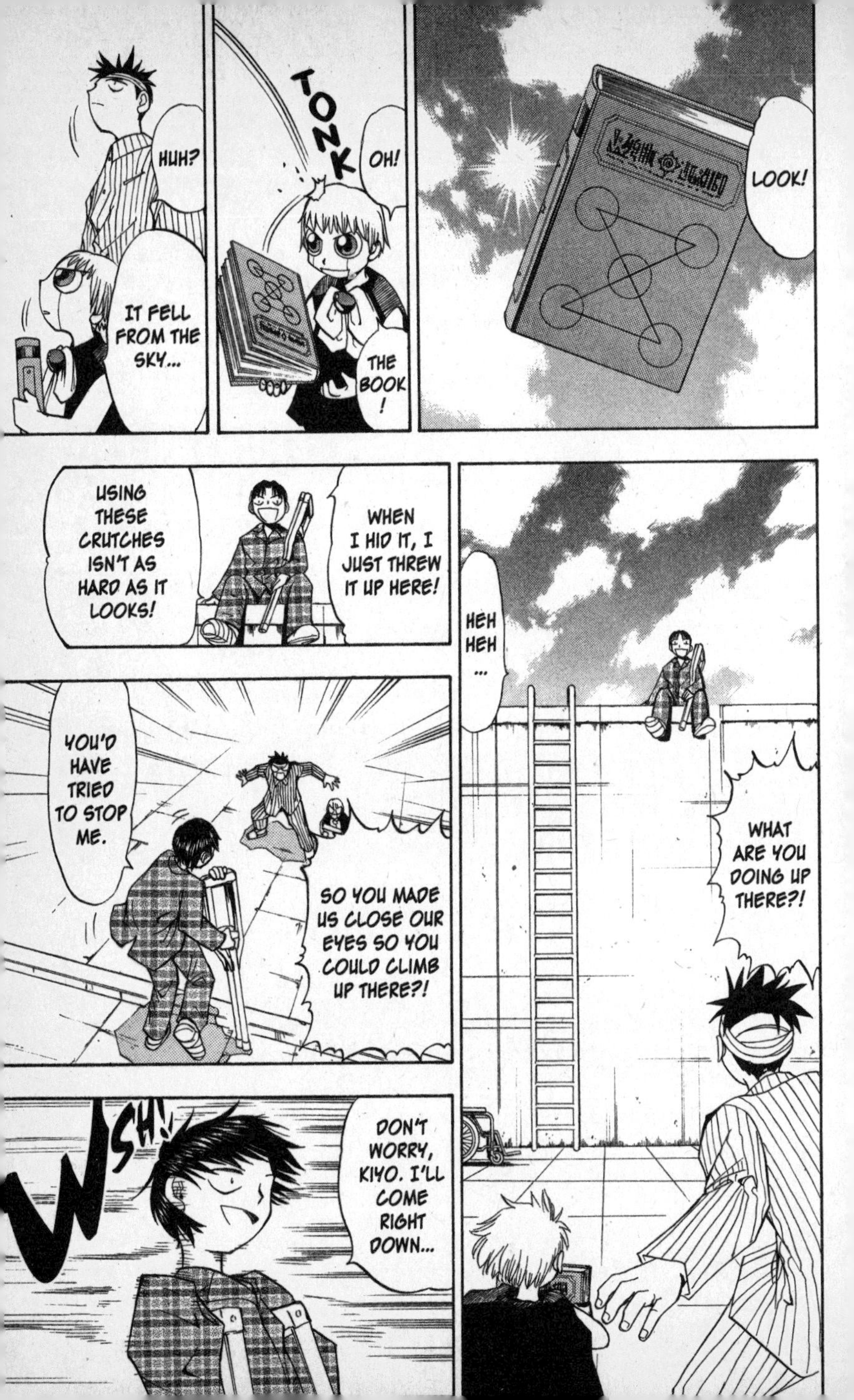
LOOK!
TONK
OH!
THE BOOK!
HUH?
IT FELL FROM THE SKY...
WHAT ARE YOU DOING UP THERE?!
HEH HEH...
WHEN I HID IT, I JUST THREW IT UP HERE!
USING THESE CRUTCHES ISN'T AS HARD AS IT LOOKS!
SO YOU MADE US CLOSE OUR EYES SO YOU COULD CLIMB UP THERE?!
YOU'D HAVE TRIED TO STOP ME.
DON'T WORRY, KIYO. I'LL COME RIGHT DOWN...
WSH!

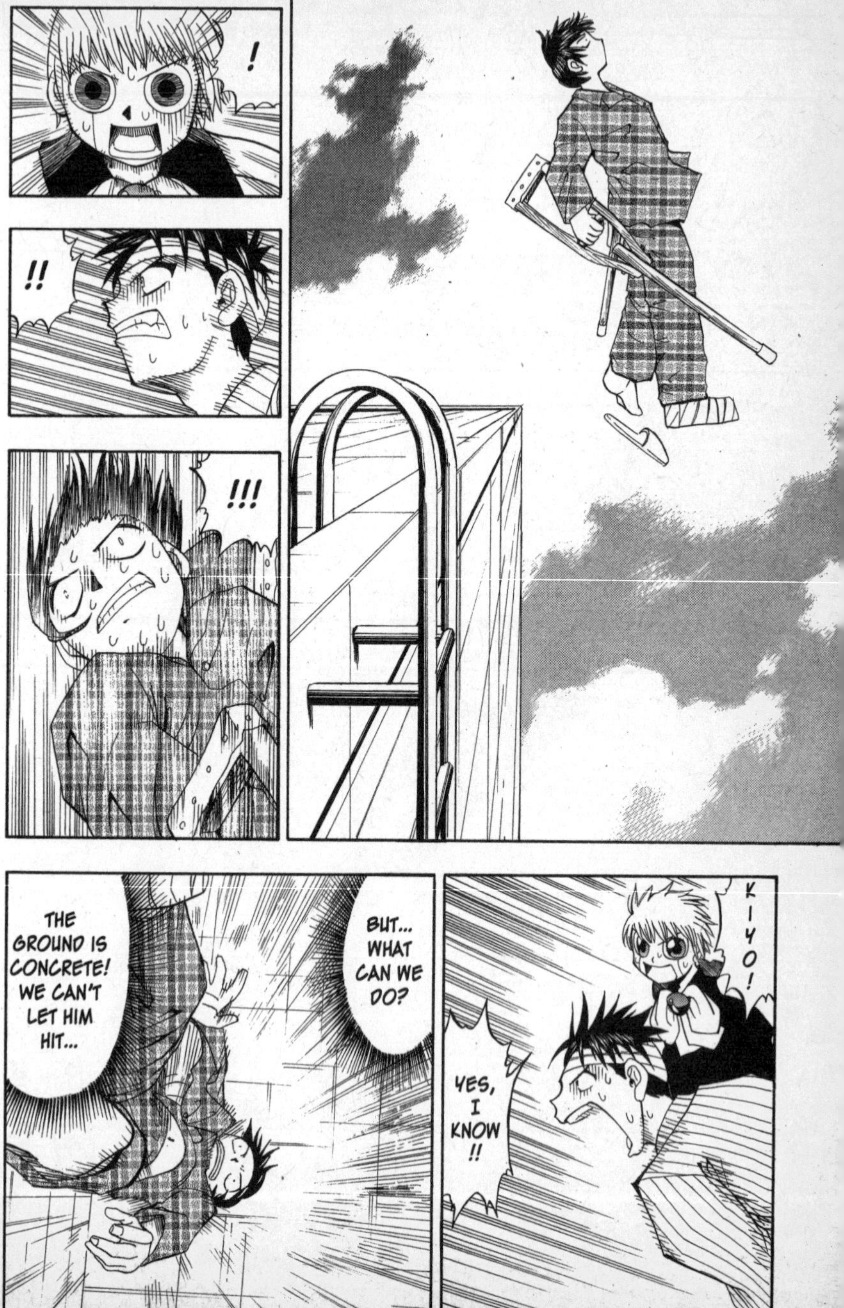
!
!!
!!!
KIYO!
YES, I KNOW!!
BUT... WHAT CAN WE DO?
THE GROUND IS CONCRETE! WE CAN'T LET HIM HIT...

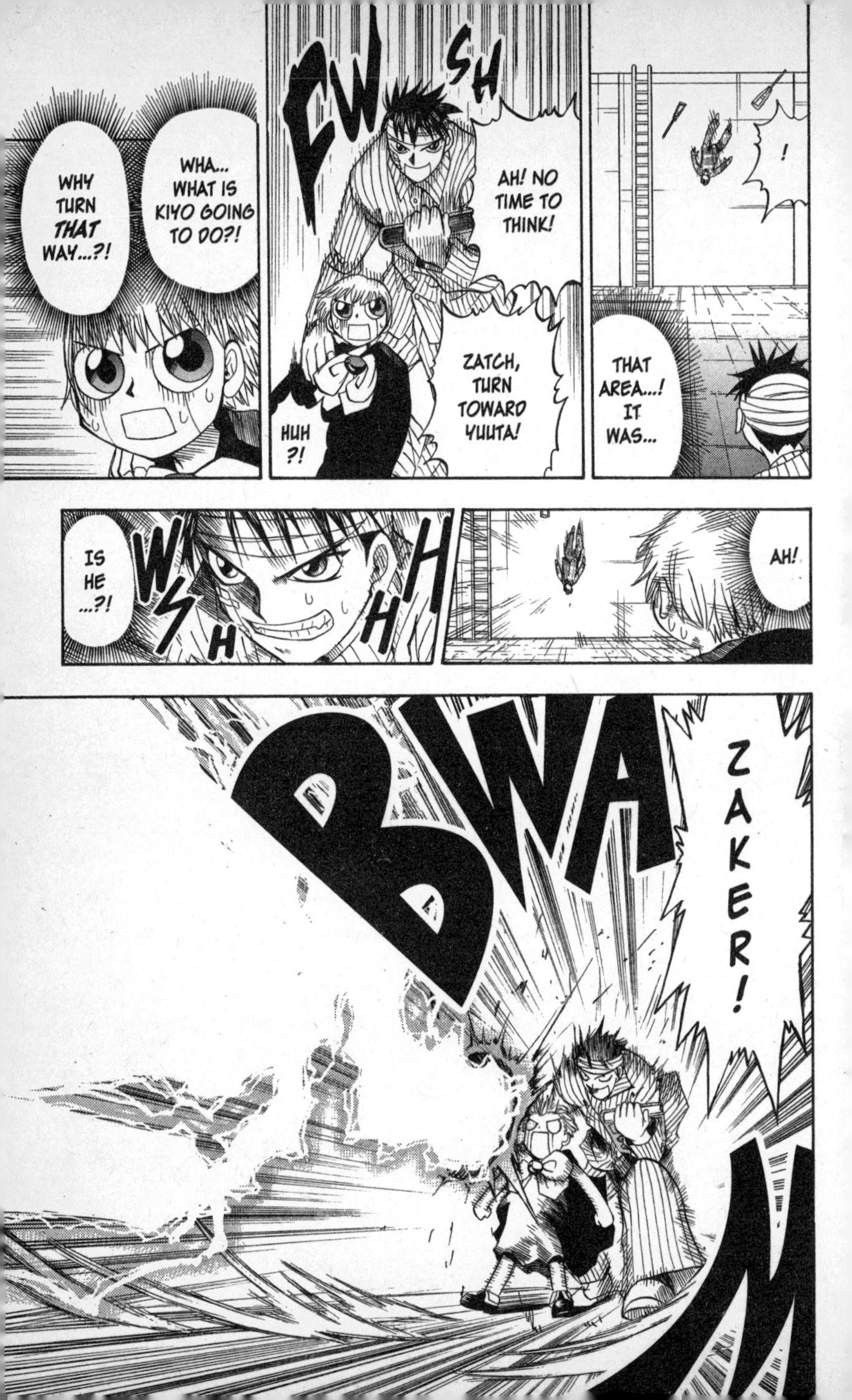
!
THAT AREA...! IT WAS...
AH! NO TIME TO THINK!
FWSH
ZATCH, TURN TOWARD YUUTA!
HUH ?!
WHA... WHAT IS KIYO GOING TO DO?!
WHY TURN THAT WAY...?!
AH!
IS HE ...?!
WSHHH
ZAKER!
BWAM

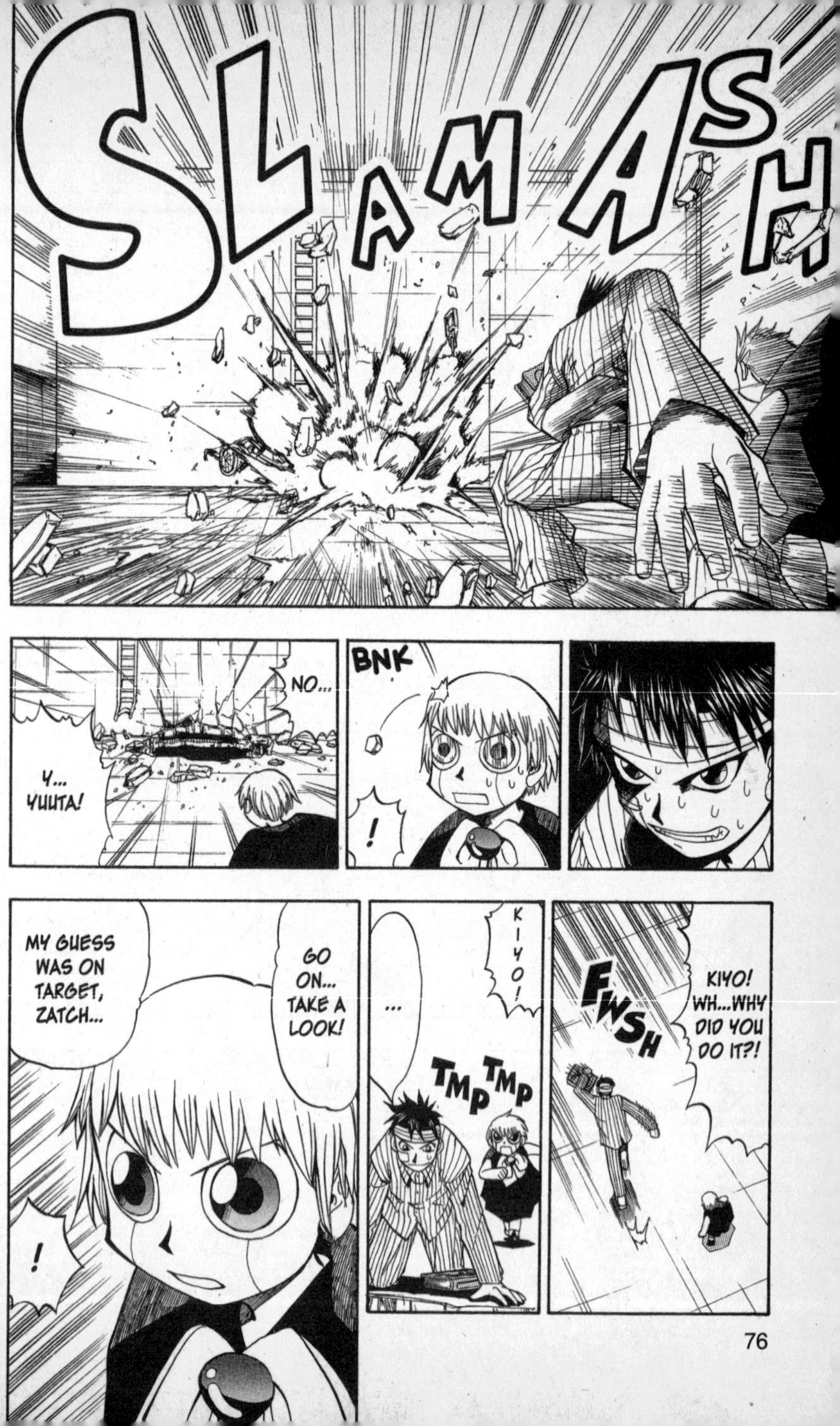
SLAMASH
BNK
!
NO...
Y... YUUTA!
FWSH
KIYO! WH...WHY DID YOU DO IT?!
KIYO!
TMP TMP
...
GO ON... TAKE A LOOK!
MY GUESS WAS ON TARGET, ZATCH...
!

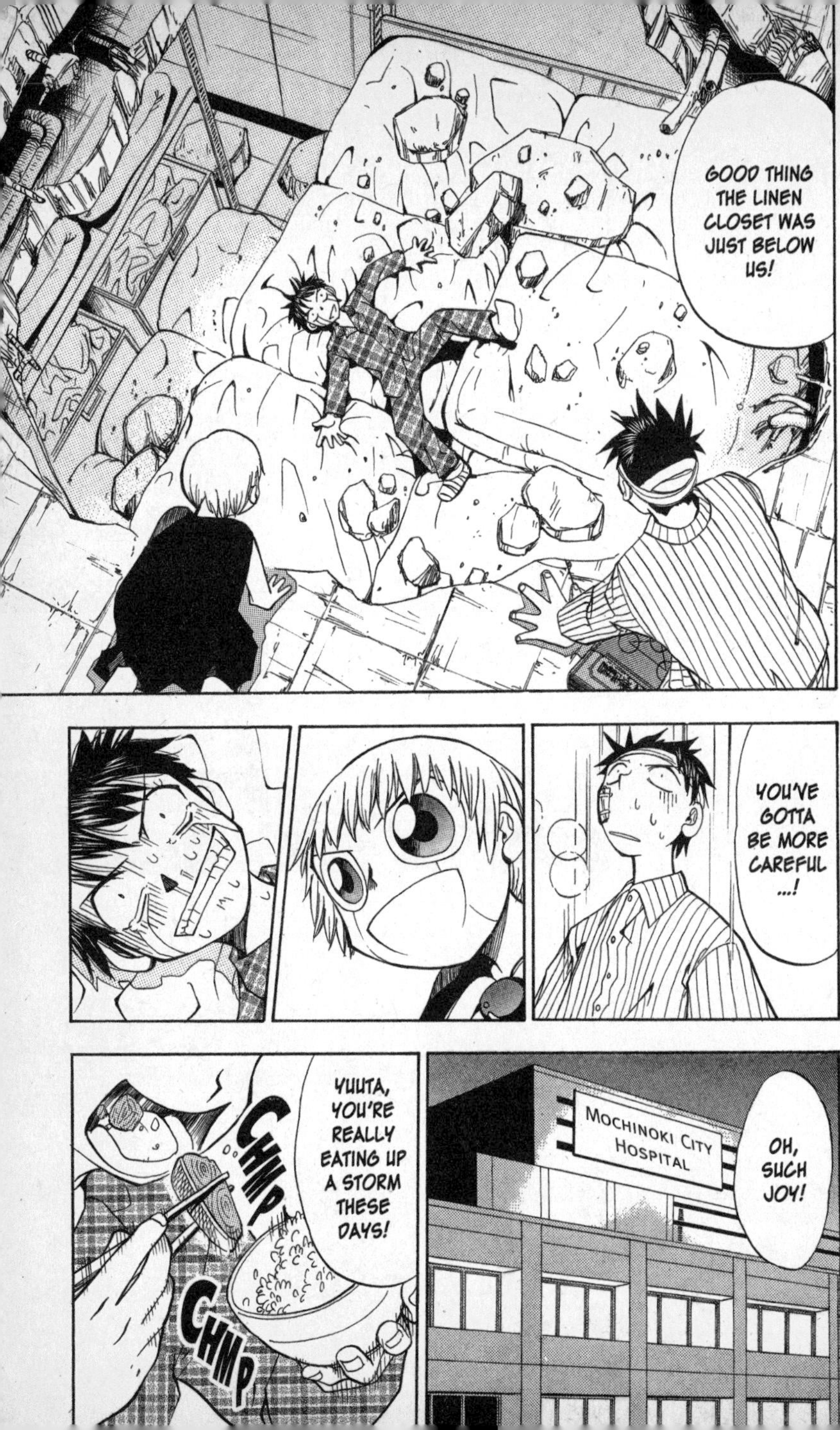
GOOD THING THE LINEN CLOSET WAS JUST BELOW US!
YOU'VE GOTTA BE MORE CAREFUL ...!
OH, SUCH JOY!
MOCHINOKI CITY HOSPITAL
YUUTA, YOU'RE REALLY EATING UP A STORM THESE DAYS!
CHMP
CHMP

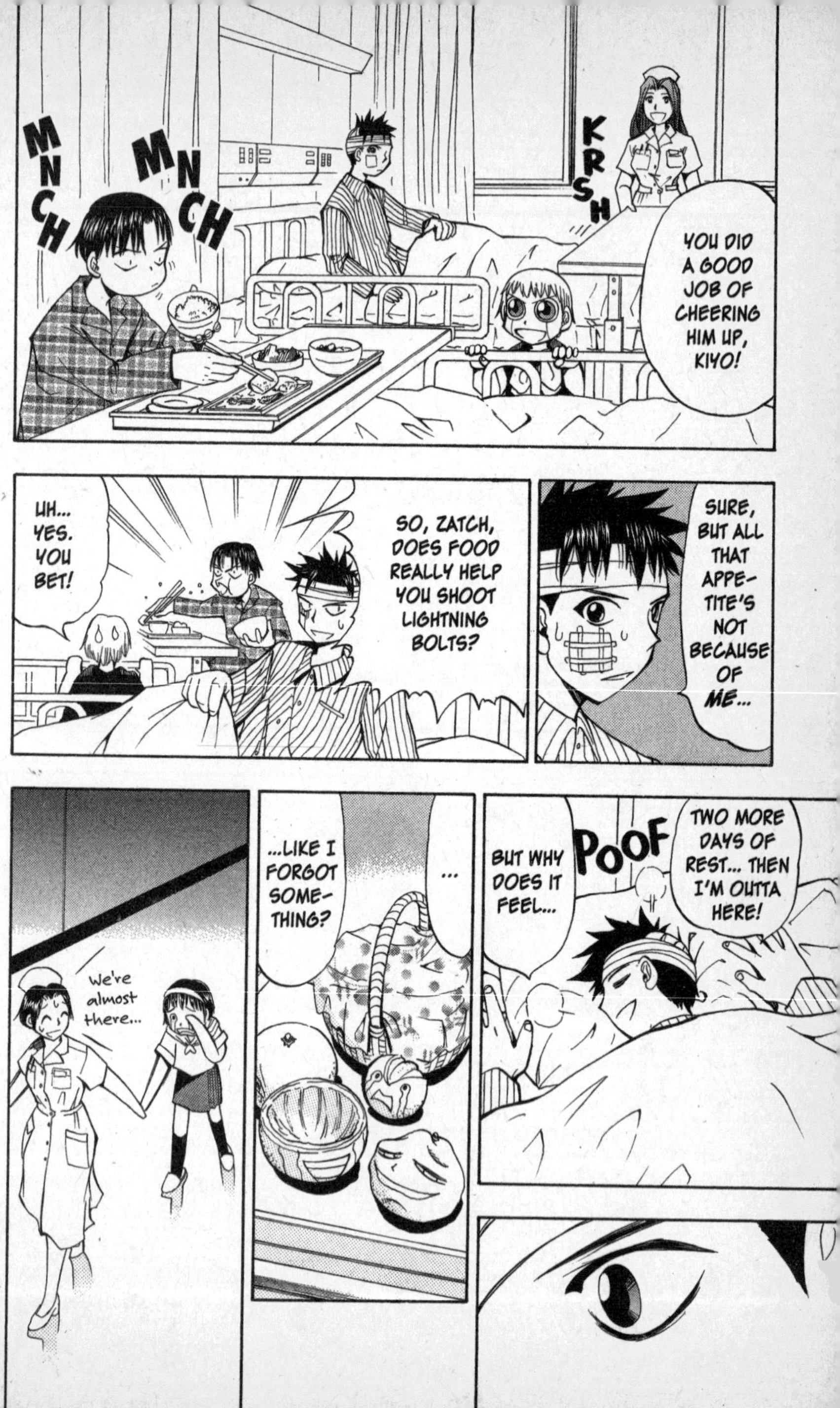
YOU DID A GOOD JOB OF CHEERING HIM UP, KIYO!
KRSH
MNCH MNCH
SURE, BUT ALL THAT APPETITE'S NOT BECAUSE OF ME...
SO, ZATCH, DOES FOOD REALLY HELP YOU SHOOT LIGHTNING BOLTS?
UH... YES. YOU BET!
TWO MORE DAYS OF REST... THEN I'M OUTTA HERE!
POOF
BUT WHY DOES IT FEEL...
...
...LIKE I FORGOT SOME-THING?
We're almost there...

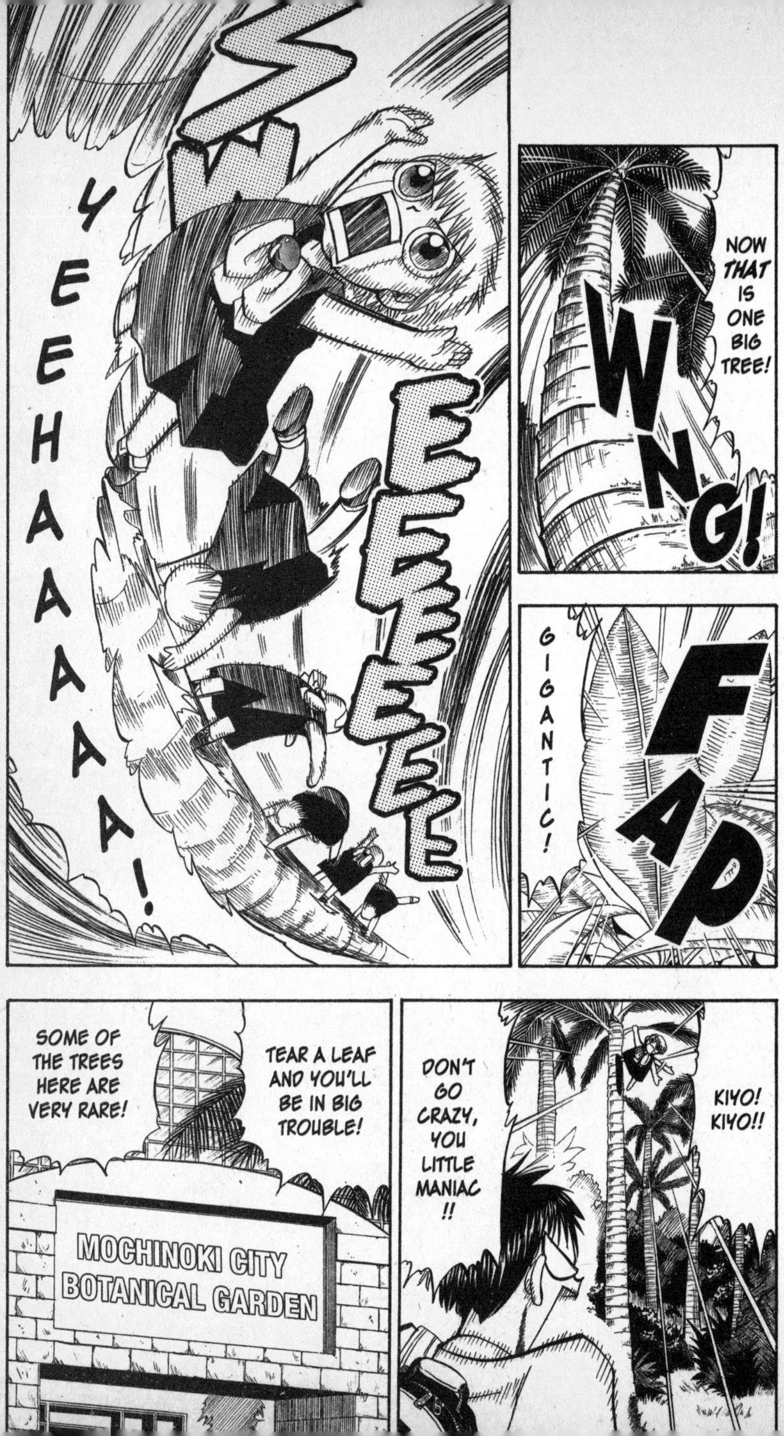
NOW THAT IS ONE BIG TREE!
WING!
FAP
GIGANTIC!
SWEEEEEEE
YEEHAAAAA!
KIYO! KIYO!!
DON'T GO CRAZY, YOU LITTLE MANIAC!!
TEAR A LEAF AND YOU'LL BE IN BIG TROUBLE!
SOME OF THE TREES HERE ARE VERY RARE!
MOCHINOKI CITY BOTANICAL GARDEN

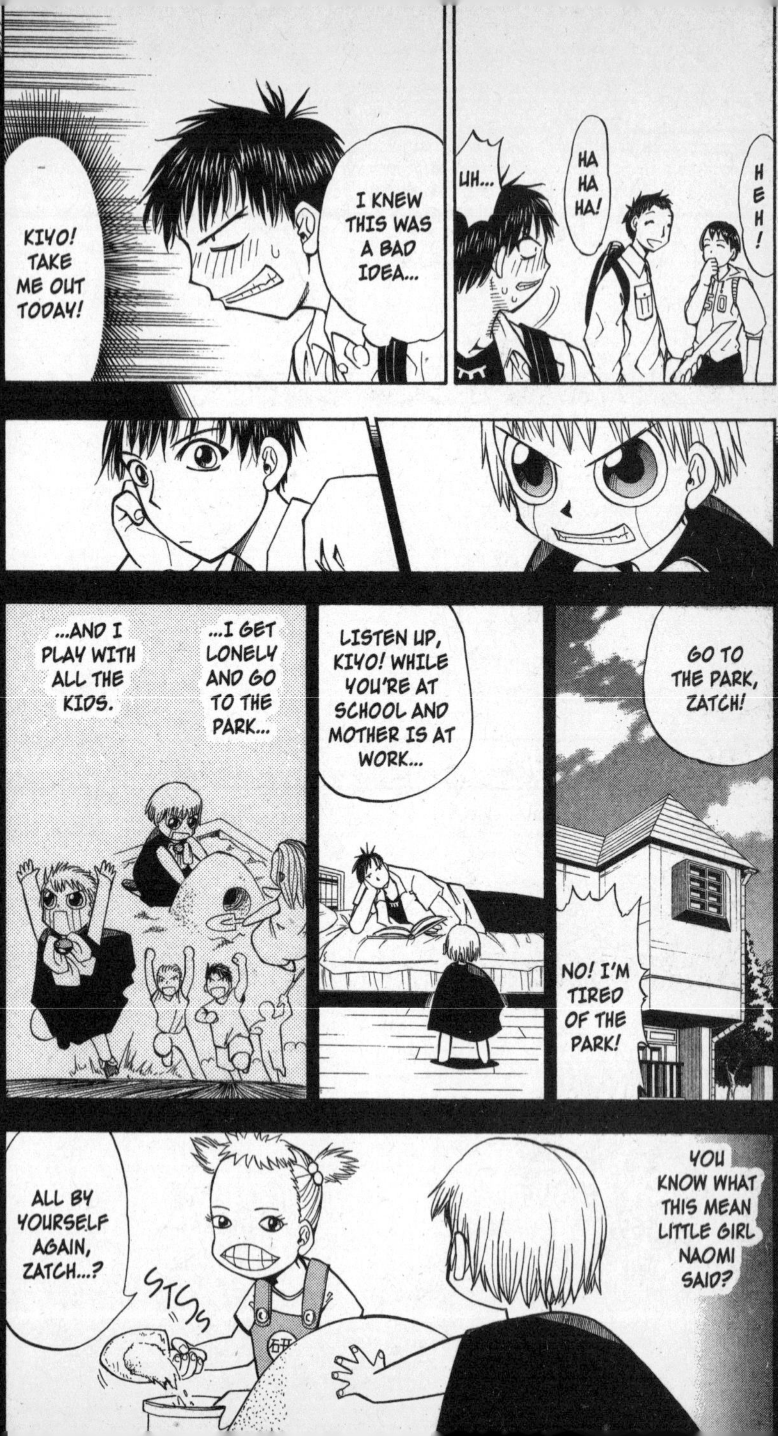
HEH!
HA HA HA!
UH...
I KNEW THIS WAS A BAD IDEA...
KIYO! TAKE ME OUT TODAY!
GO TO THE PARK, ZATCH!
NO! I'M TIRED OF THE PARK!
LISTEN UP, KIYO! WHILE YOU'RE AT SCHOOL AND MOTHER IS AT WORK...
...I GET LONELY AND GO TO THE PARK...
...AND I PLAY WITH ALL THE KIDS.
YOU KNOW WHAT THIS MEAN LITTLE GIRL NAOMI SAID?
STSS
ALL BY YOURSELF AGAIN, ZATCH...?

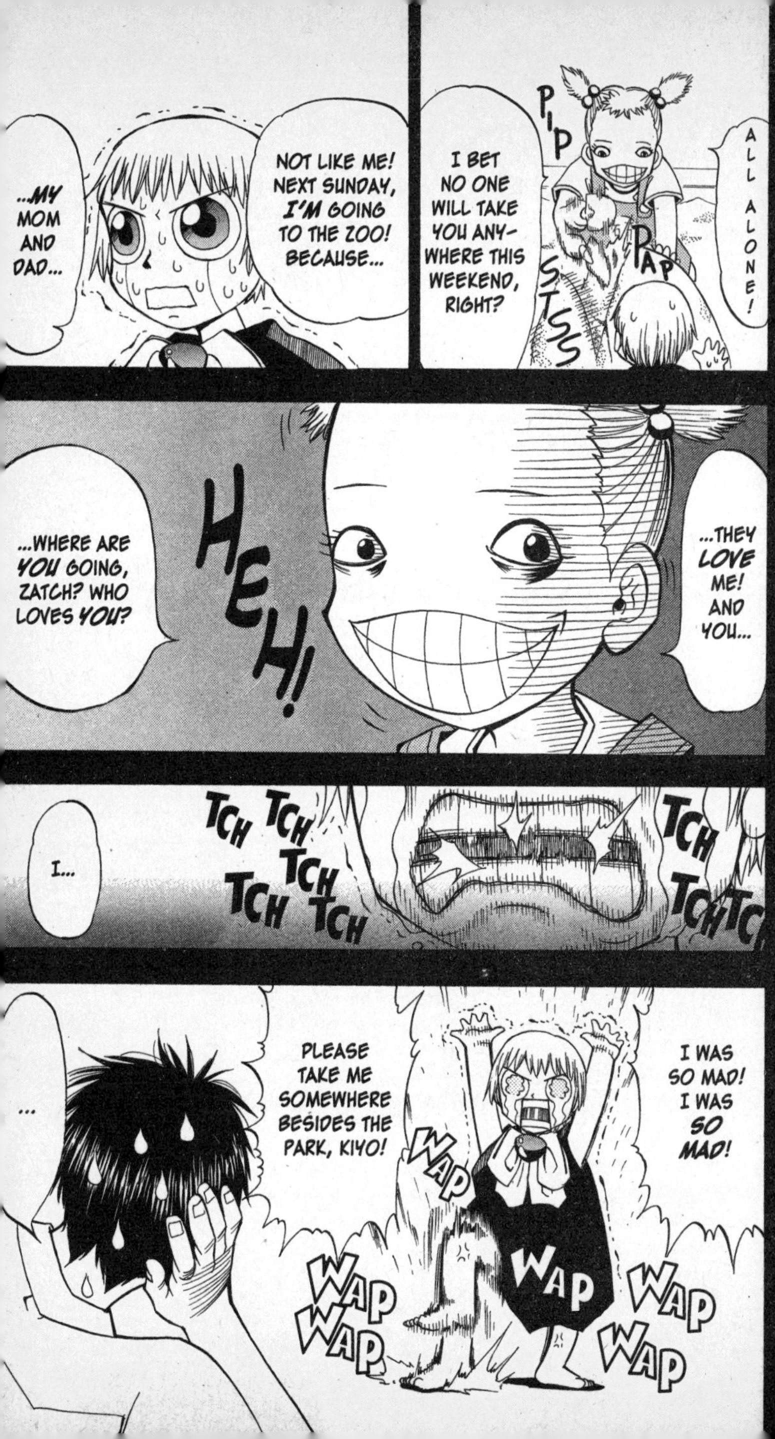
ALL ALONE!
I BET NO ONE WILL TAKE YOU ANYWHERE THIS WEEKEND, RIGHT?
PIP
PAP
STSS
NOT LIKE ME! NEXT SUNDAY, I'M GOING TO THE ZOO! BECAUSE...
...MY MOM AND DAD...
...THEY LOVE ME! AND YOU...
HEH!
...WHERE ARE YOU GOING, ZATCH? WHO LOVES YOU?
TCH TCH TCHTC
TCH TCH TCH TCH TCH
I...
I WAS SO MAD! I WAS SO MAD!
PLEASE TAKE ME SOMEWHERE BESIDES THE PARK, KIYO!
WAP WAP WAP WAP WAP WAP WAP
...

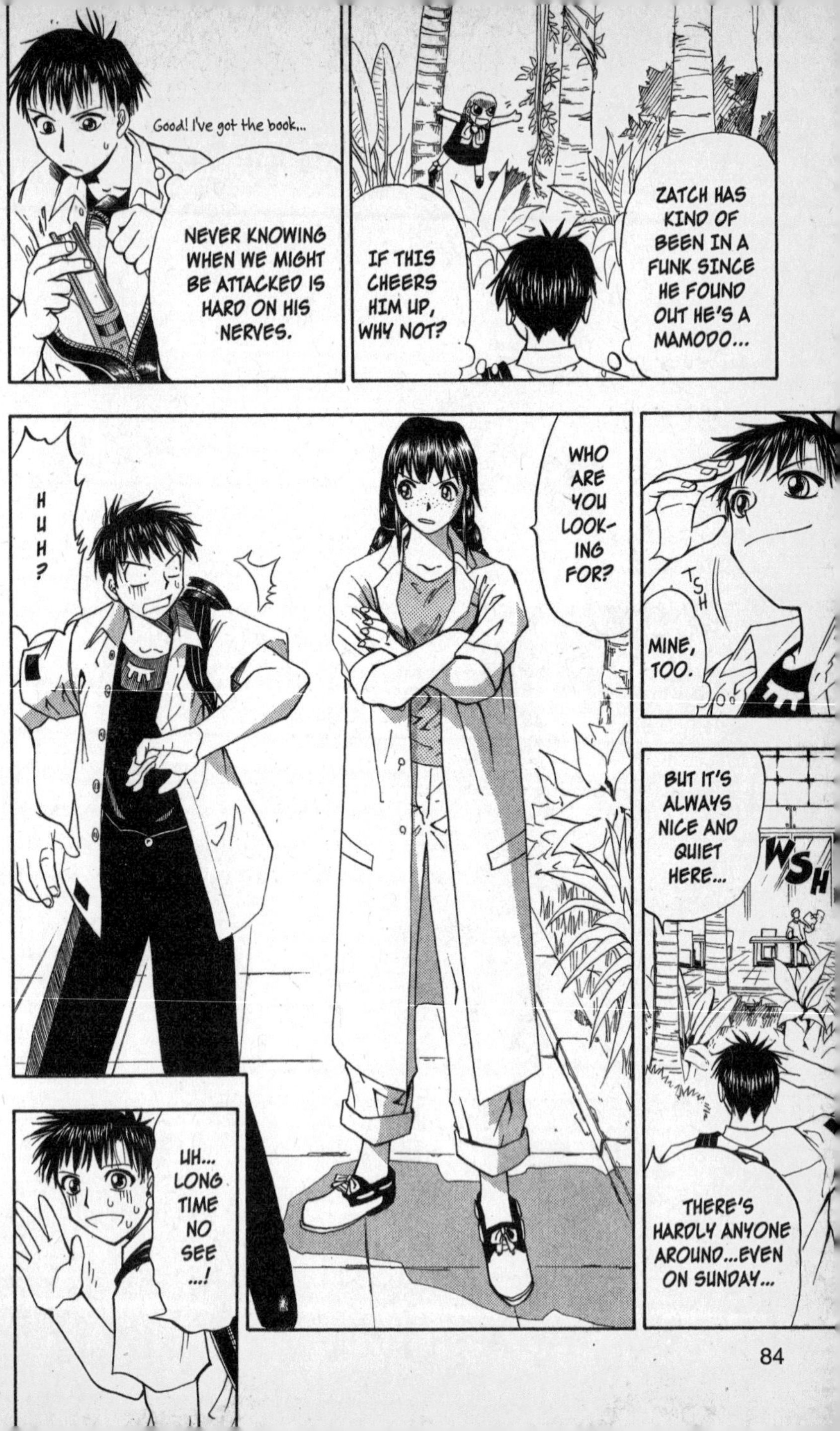
ZATCH HAS KIND OF BEEN IN A FUNK SINCE HE FOUND OUT HE'S A MAMODO...
IF THIS CHEERS HIM UP, WHY NOT?
NEVER KNOWING WHEN WE MIGHT BE ATTACKED IS HARD ON HIS NERVES.
Good! I've got the book...
TSH
MINE, TOO.
BUT IT'S ALWAYS NICE AND QUIET HERE...
WSH
THERE'S HARDLY ANYONE AROUND...EVEN ON SUNDAY...
WHO ARE YOU LOOKING FOR?
HUH?
UH... LONG TIME NO SEE...!

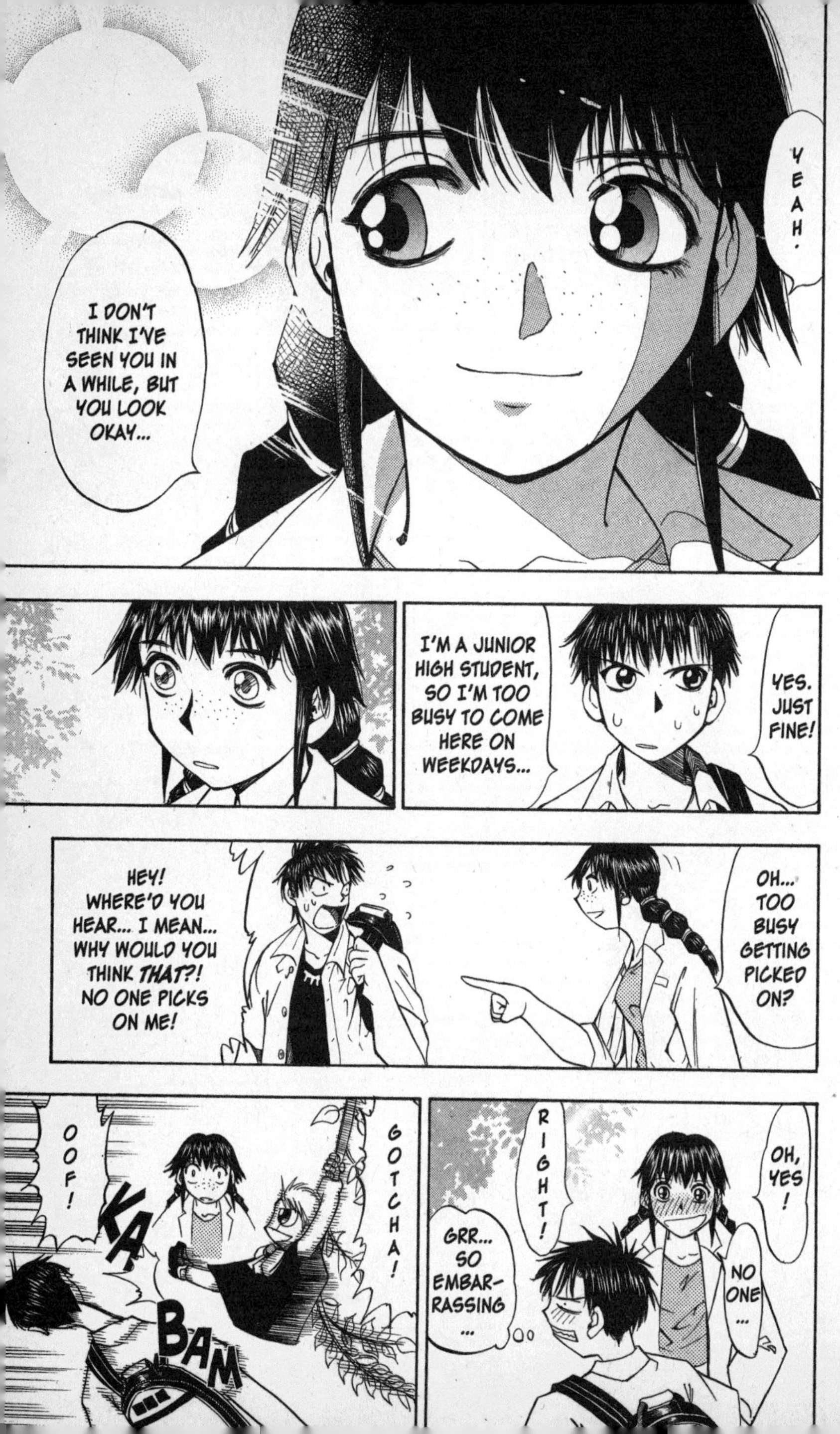
YEAH.
I DON'T THINK I'VE SEEN YOU IN A WHILE, BUT YOU LOOK OKAY...
YES. JUST FINE!
I'M A JUNIOR HIGH STUDENT, SO I'M TOO BUSY TO COME HERE ON WEEKDAYS...
OH... TOO BUSY GETTING PICKED ON?
HEY! WHERE'D YOU HEAR... I MEAN... WHY WOULD YOU THINK *THAT*?! NO ONE PICKS ON ME!
OH, YES!
NO ONE...
RIGHT!
GRR... SO EMBARRASSING...
GOTCHA!
KA
BAM
OOF!

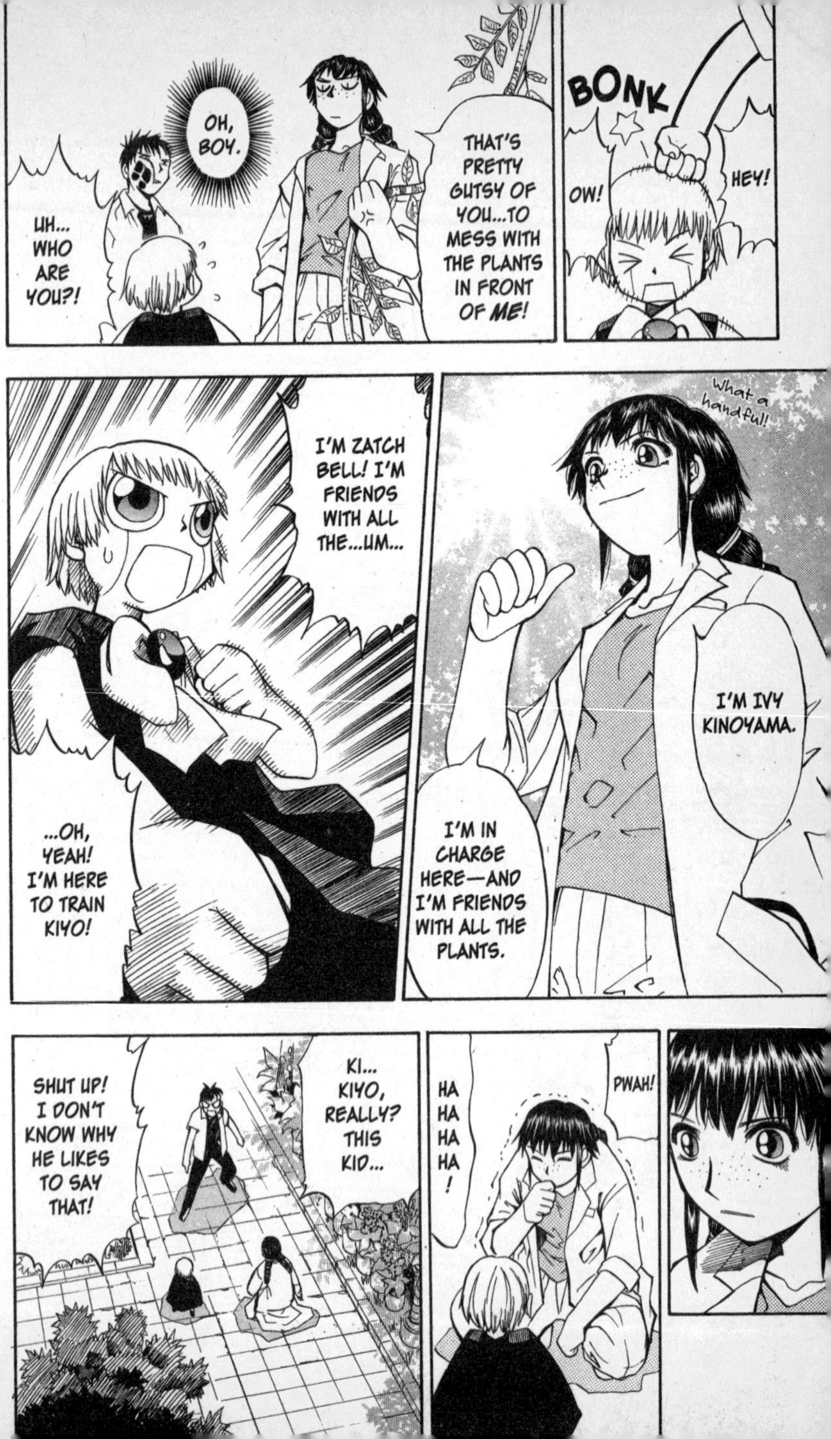
BONK
HEY!
OW!
THAT'S PRETTY GUTSY OF YOU...TO MESS WITH THE PLANTS IN FRONT OF ME!
OH, BOY.
UH... WHO ARE YOU?!
What a handful!
I'M IVY KINOYAMA.
I'M IN CHARGE HERE—AND I'M FRIENDS WITH ALL THE PLANTS.
I'M ZATCH BELL! I'M FRIENDS WITH ALL THE...UM...
...OH, YEAH! I'M HERE TO TRAIN KIYO!
PWAH!
HA HA HA HA!
KI... KIYO, REALLY? THIS KID...
SHUT UP! I DON'T KNOW WHY HE LIKES TO SAY THAT!

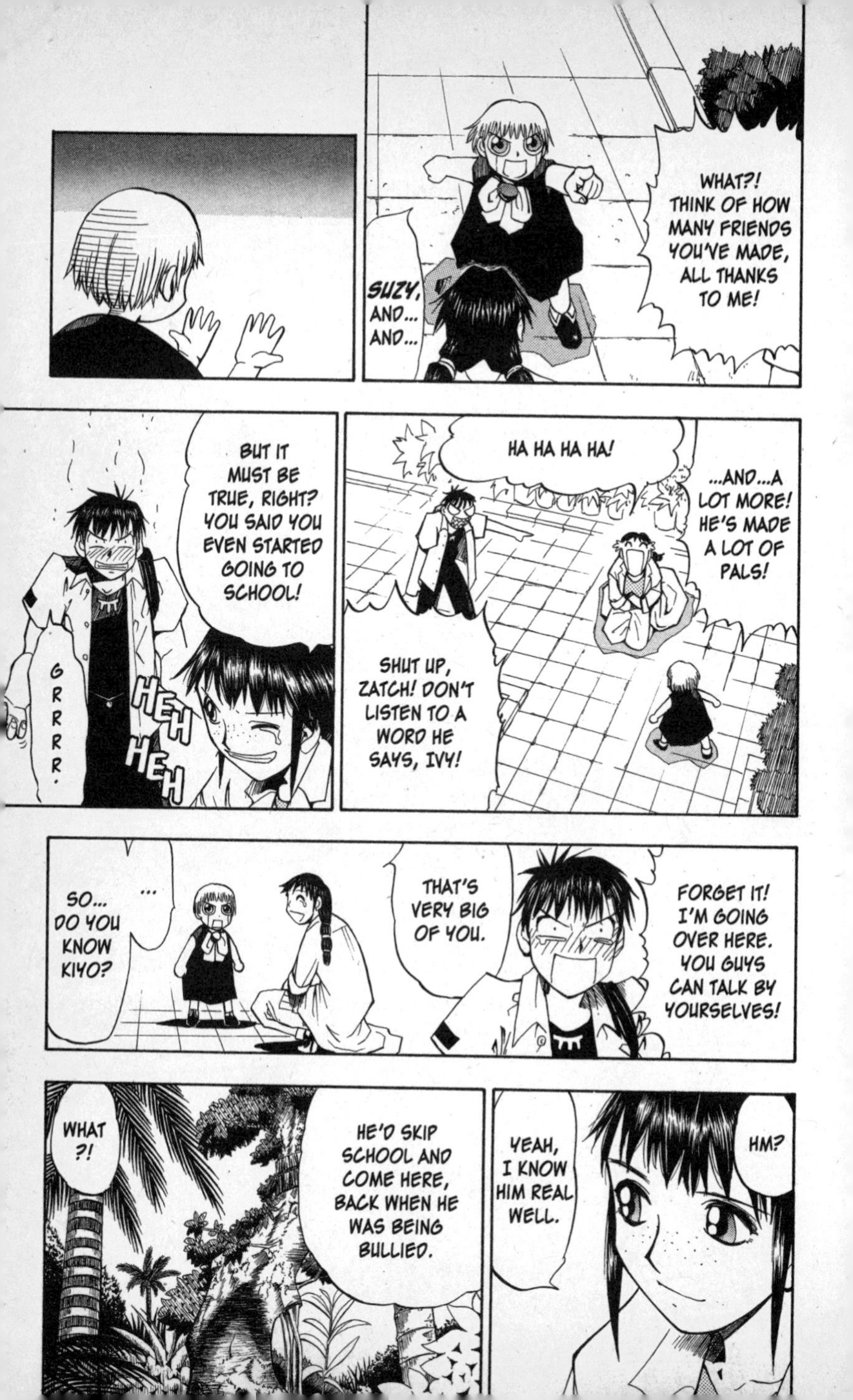
WHAT?! THINK OF HOW MANY FRIENDS YOU'VE MADE, ALL THANKS TO ME!
SUZY, AND... AND...
...AND...A LOT MORE! HE'S MADE A LOT OF PALS!
HA HA HA HA!
SHUT UP, ZATCH! DON'T LISTEN TO A WORD HE SAYS, IVY!
BUT IT MUST BE TRUE, RIGHT? YOU SAID YOU EVEN STARTED GOING TO SCHOOL!
HEH HEH
GRRRR.
FORGET IT! I'M GOING OVER HERE. YOU GUYS CAN TALK BY YOURSELVES!
THAT'S VERY BIG OF YOU.
...
SO... DO YOU KNOW KIYO?
HM?
YEAH, I KNOW HIM REAL WELL.
HE'D SKIP SCHOOL AND COME HERE, BACK WHEN HE WAS BEING BULLIED.
WHAT?!

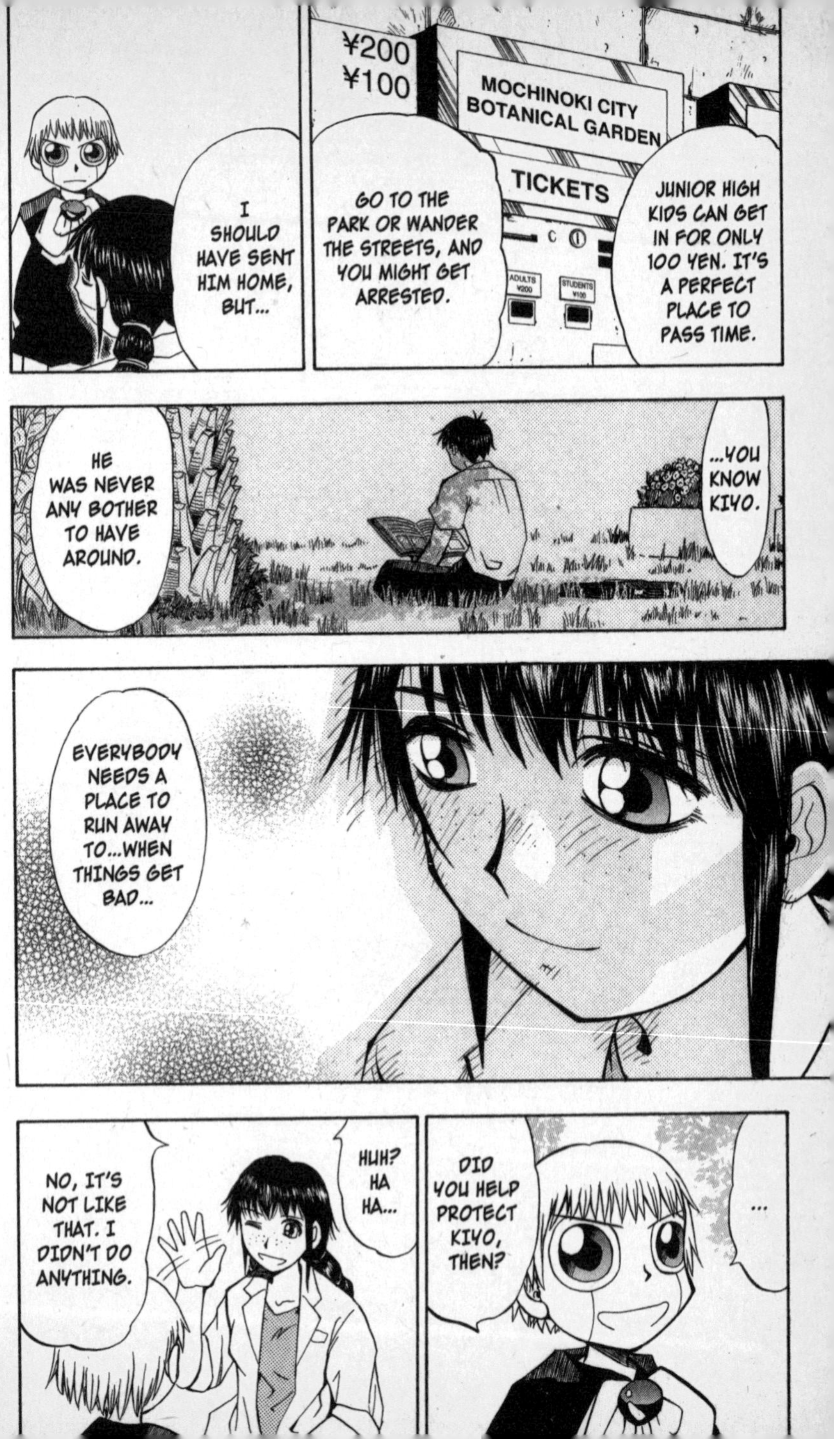
¥200
¥100
MOCHINOKI CITY BOTANICAL GARDEN
TICKETS
ADULTS ¥200
STUDENTS ¥100
JUNIOR HIGH KIDS CAN GET IN FOR ONLY 100 YEN. IT'S A PERFECT PLACE TO PASS TIME.
GO TO THE PARK OR WANDER THE STREETS, AND YOU MIGHT GET ARRESTED.
I SHOULD HAVE SENT HIM HOME, BUT...
...YOU KNOW KIYO.
HE WAS NEVER ANY BOTHER TO HAVE AROUND.
EVERYBODY NEEDS A PLACE TO RUN AWAY TO...WHEN THINGS GET BAD...
...
DID YOU HELP PROTECT KIYO, THEN?
HUH? HA HA...
NO, IT'S NOT LIKE THAT. I DIDN'T DO ANYTHING.

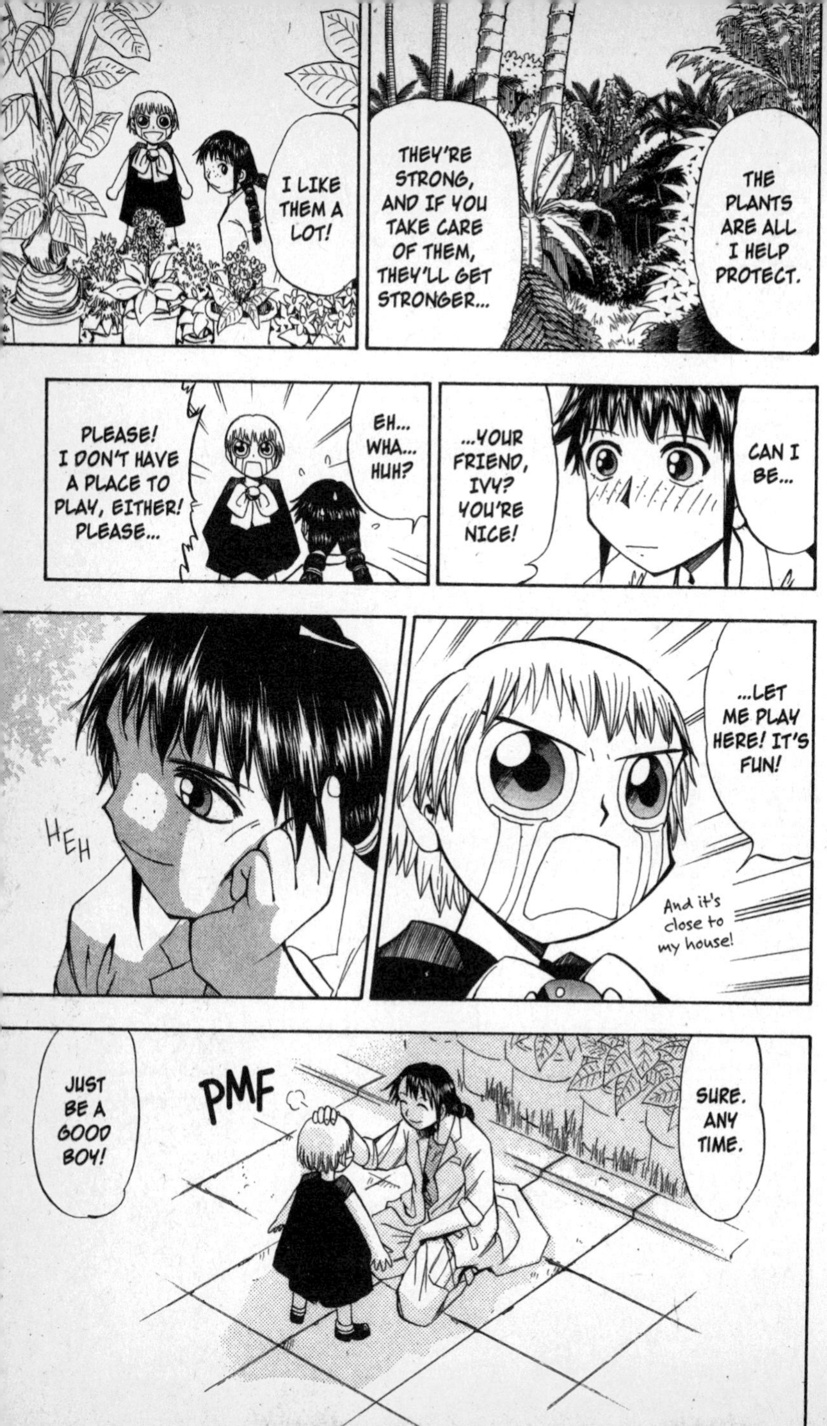
THE PLANTS ARE ALL I HELP PROTECT.
THEY'RE STRONG, AND IF YOU TAKE CARE OF THEM, THEY'LL GET STRONGER...
I LIKE THEM A LOT!
CAN I BE...
...YOUR FRIEND, IVY? YOU'RE NICE!
EH... WHA... HUH?
PLEASE! I DON'T HAVE A PLACE TO PLAY, EITHER! PLEASE...
...LET ME PLAY HERE! IT'S FUN!
And it's close to my house!
HEH
SURE. ANY TIME.
PMF
JUST BE A GOOD BOY!

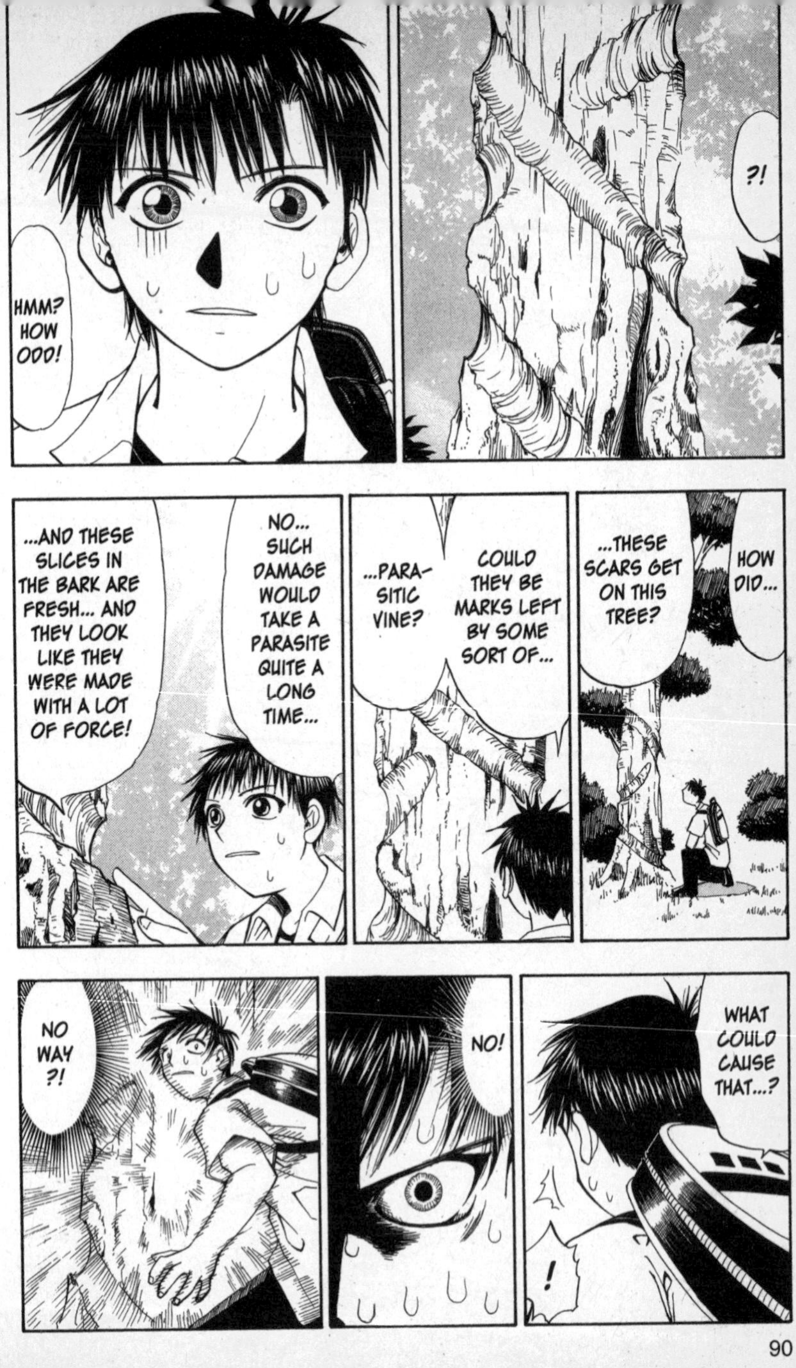
?!
HMM? HOW ODD!
HOW DID...
...THESE SCARS GET ON THIS TREE?
COULD THEY BE MARKS LEFT BY SOME SORT OF...
...PARA-SITIC VINE?
NO... SUCH DAMAGE WOULD TAKE A PARASITE QUITE A LONG TIME...
...AND THESE SLICES IN THE BARK ARE FRESH... AND THEY LOOK LIKE THEY WERE MADE WITH A LOT OF FORCE!
WHAT COULD CAUSE THAT...?
!
NO!
NO WAY ?!

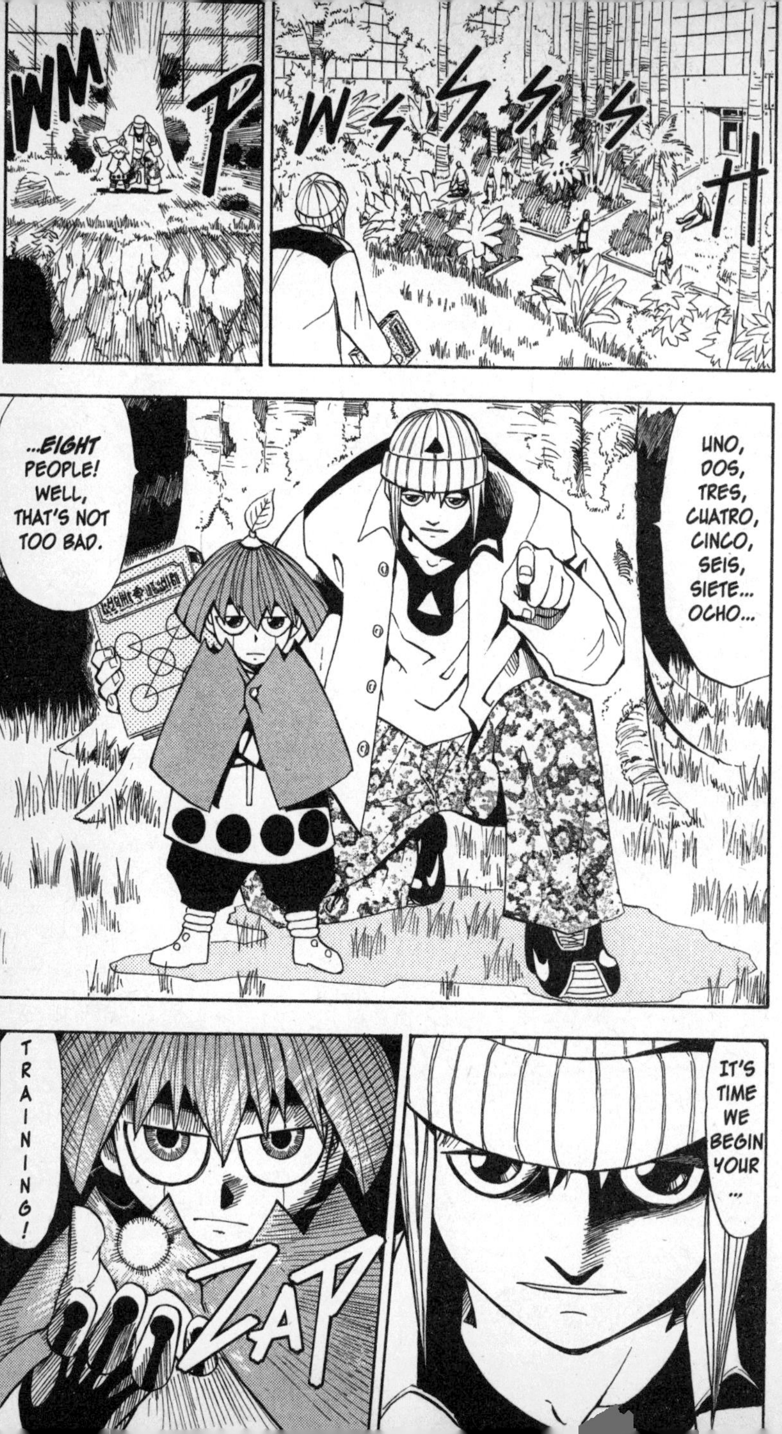
WM
PWSSSSH
UNO, DOS, TRES, CUATRO, CINCO, SEIS, SIETE... OCHO...
...EIGHT PEOPLE! WELL, THAT'S NOT TOO BAD.
IT'S TIME WE BEGIN YOUR ...
TRAINING!
ZAP

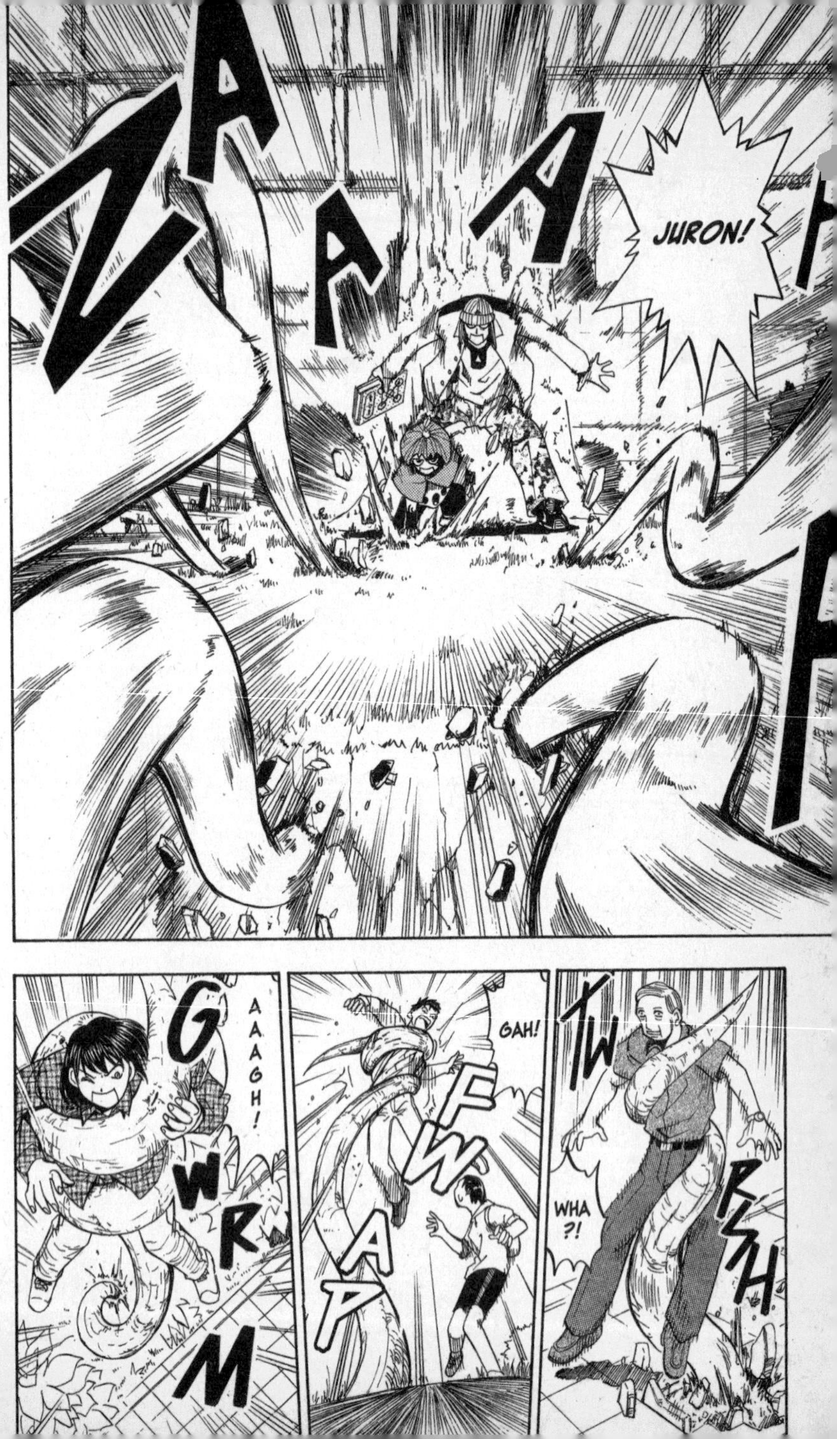
JURON!
ZAAAA
TW
WHA ?!
RSH.
GAH!
FWAAP
AAAGH!
GWRM

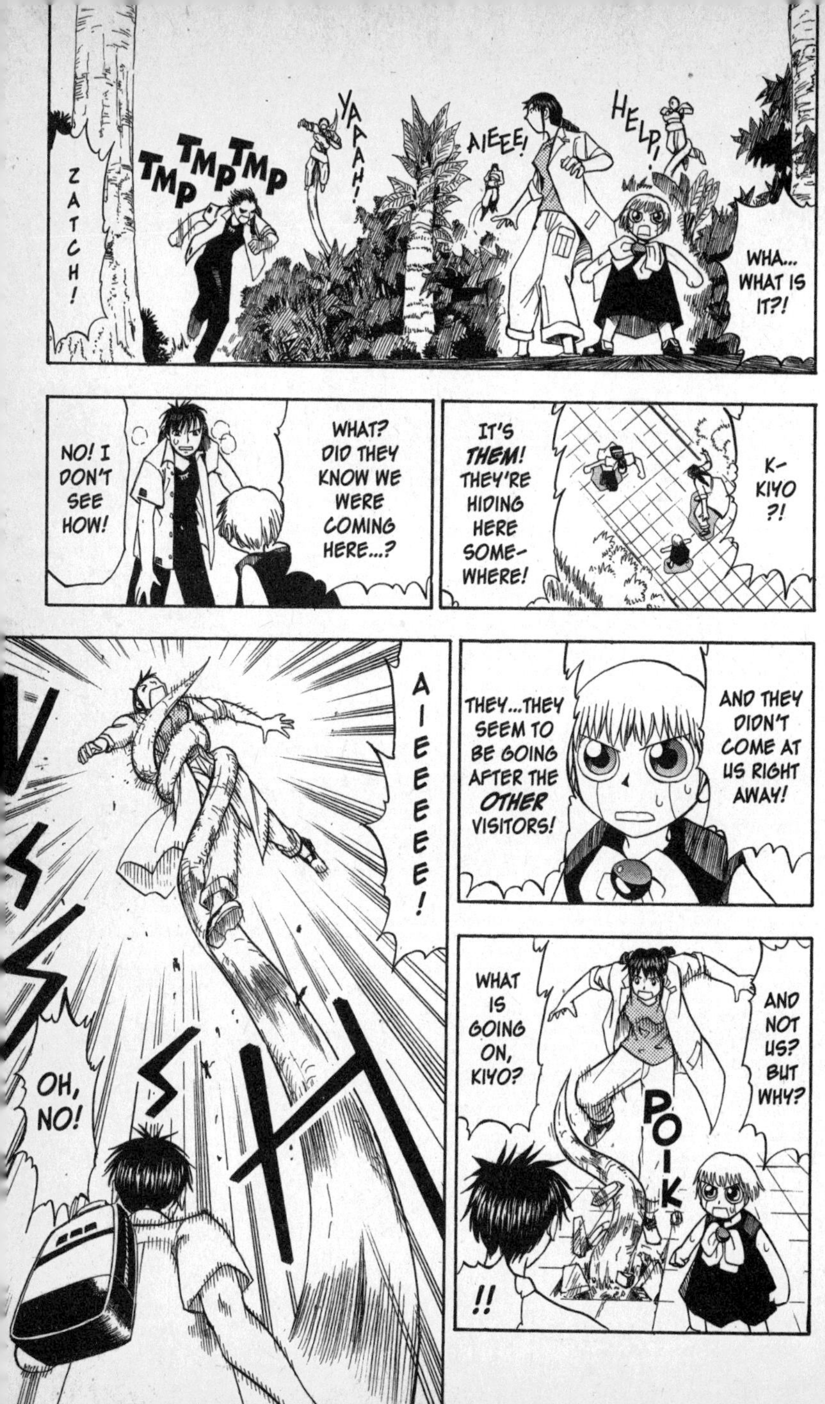
WHA... WHAT IS IT?!
HELP!
AIEEE!
YAAAH!
TMP TMP TMP TMP
ZATCH!
K-KIYO?!
IT'S THEM! THEY'RE HIDING HERE SOMEWHERE!
WHAT? DID THEY KNOW WE WERE COMING HERE...?
NO! I DON'T SEE HOW!
AND THEY DIDN'T COME AT US RIGHT AWAY!
THEY...THEY SEEM TO BE GOING AFTER THE OTHER VISITORS!
AND NOT US? BUT WHY?
WHAT IS GOING ON, KIYO?
POIK
!!
AIEEEEEE!
OH, NO!

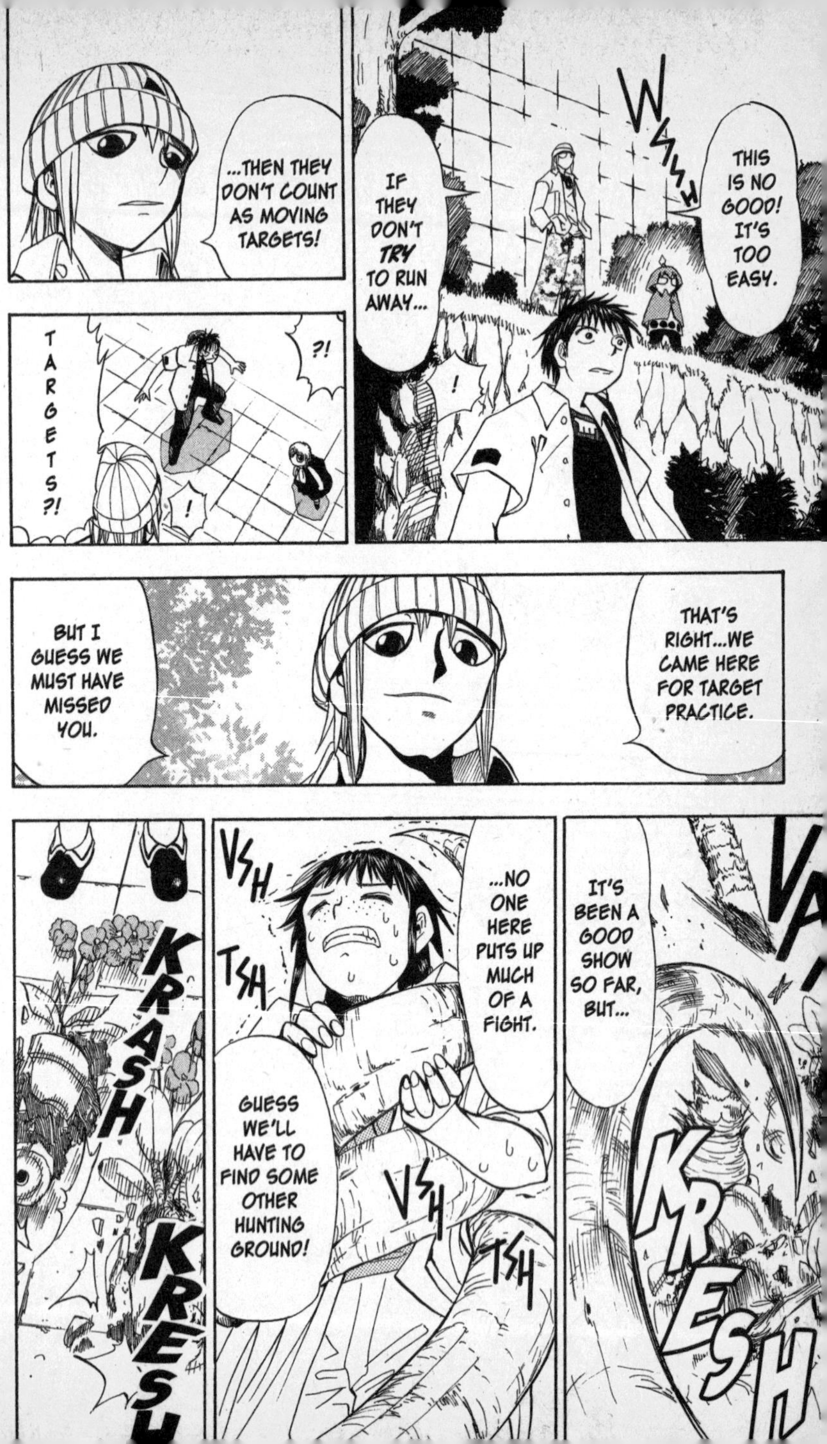

WSSSH
THIS IS NO GOOD! IT'S TOO EASY.
IF THEY DON'T TRY TO RUN AWAY...
!
...THEN THEY DON'T COUNT AS MOVING TARGETS!
?!
TARGETS?!
!
THAT'S RIGHT...WE CAME HERE FOR TARGET PRACTICE.
BUT I GUESS WE MUST HAVE MISSED YOU.
IT'S BEEN A GOOD SHOW SO FAR, BUT...
KRESH
VSH
TSH
...NO ONE HERE PUTS UP MUCH OF A FIGHT.
GUESS WE'LL HAVE TO FIND SOME OTHER HUNTING GROUND!
VSH
TSH
KRASH

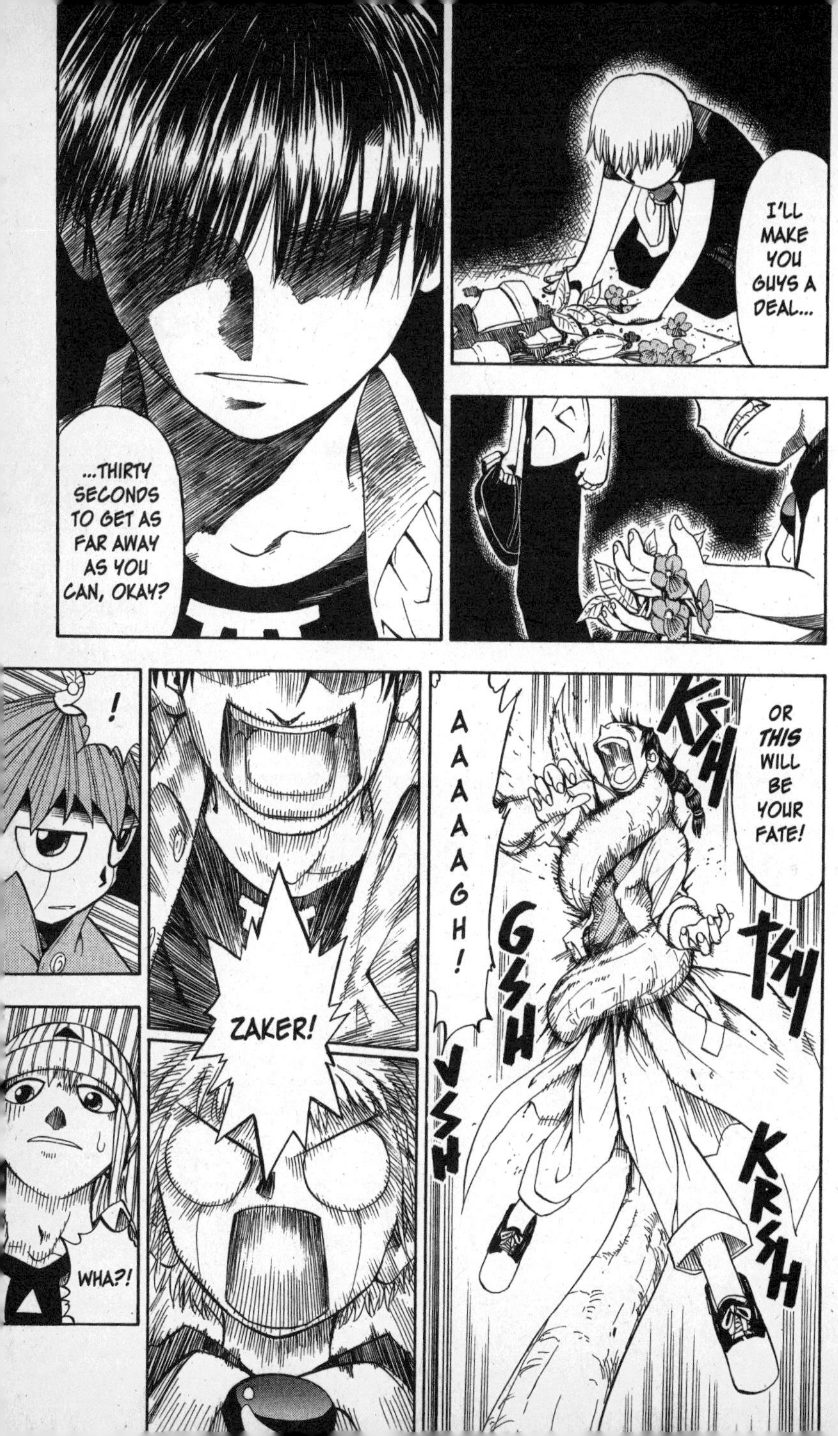
I'LL MAKE YOU GUYS A DEAL...
...THIRTY SECONDS TO GET AS FAR AWAY AS YOU CAN, OKAY?
OR THIS WILL BE YOUR FATE!
KSH
AAAAAAAGH!
GSH
TSH
VSH
KRSH
ZAKER!
!
WHA?!

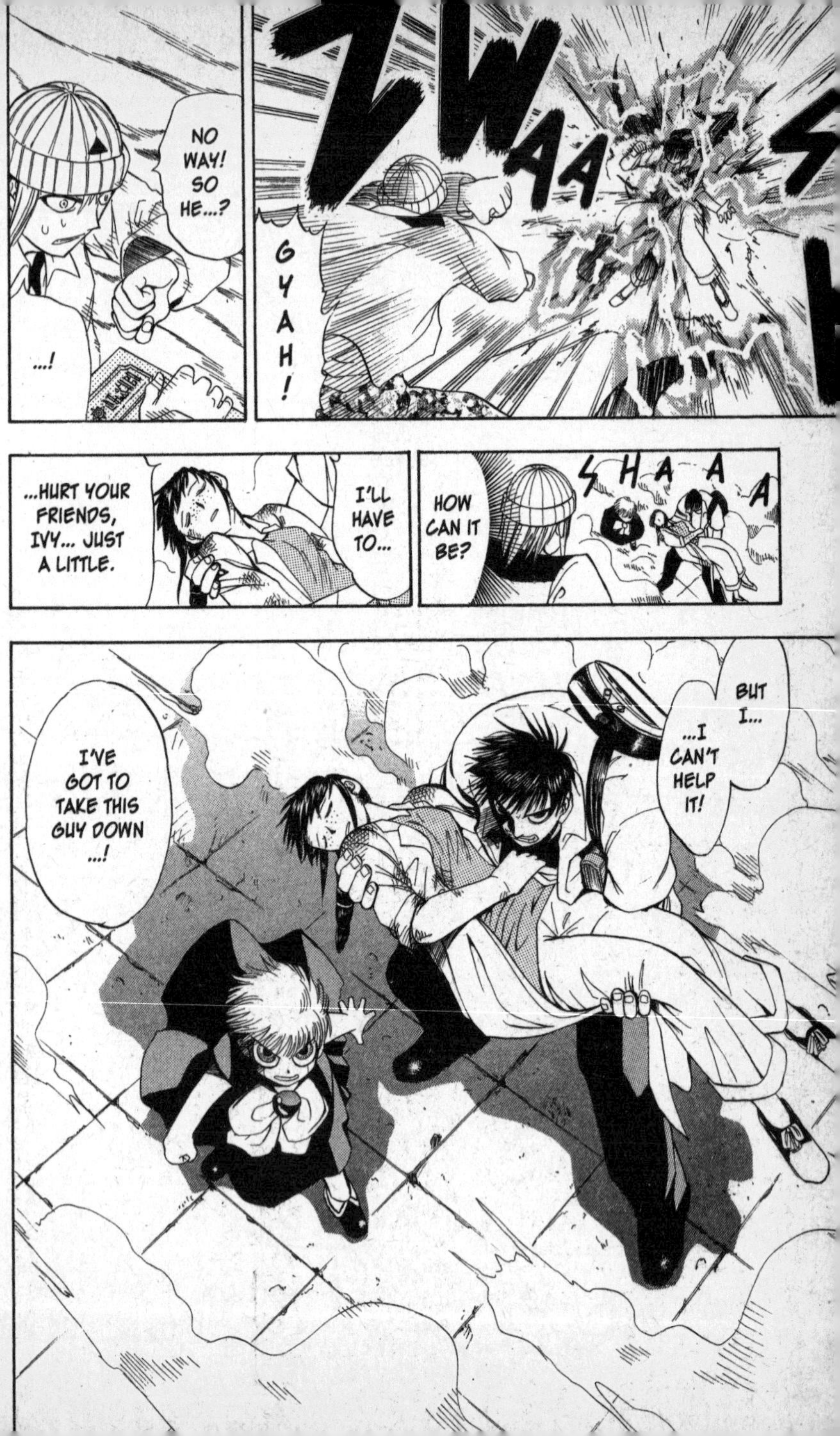
ZWAASH
GYAH!
NO WAY! SO HE...?
...!
SHAAAA
HOW CAN IT BE?
I'LL HAVE TO...
...HURT YOUR FRIENDS, IVY... JUST A LITTLE.
BUT I...
...I CAN'T HELP IT!
I'VE GOT TO TAKE THIS GUY DOWN ...!

LEVEL 14: A Heroic Heart

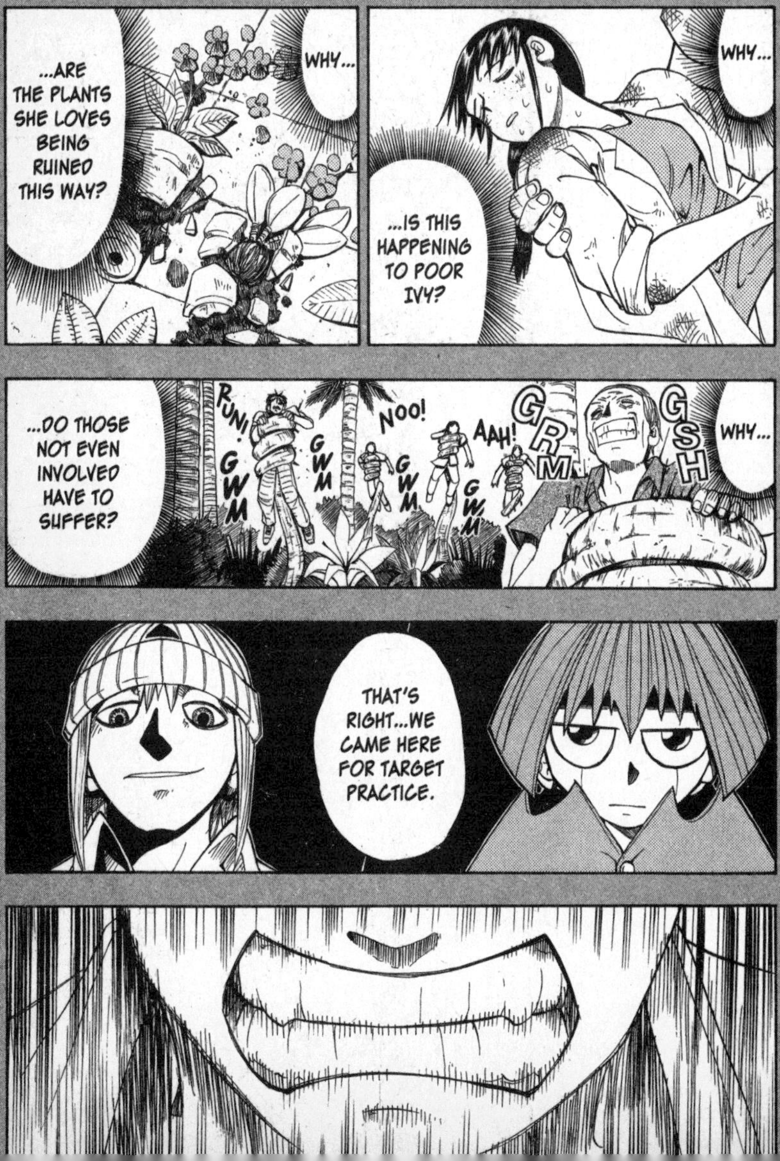
WHY...
...IS THIS HAPPENING TO POOR IVY?
WHY...
...ARE THE PLANTS SHE LOVES BEING RUINED THIS WAY?
WHY...
GSH
GRM
AAH!
GWM
NOO!
GWM
GWM
RUN!
GWM
...DO THOSE NOT EVEN INVOLVED HAVE TO SUFFER?
THAT'S RIGHT...WE CAME HERE FOR TARGET PRACTICE.

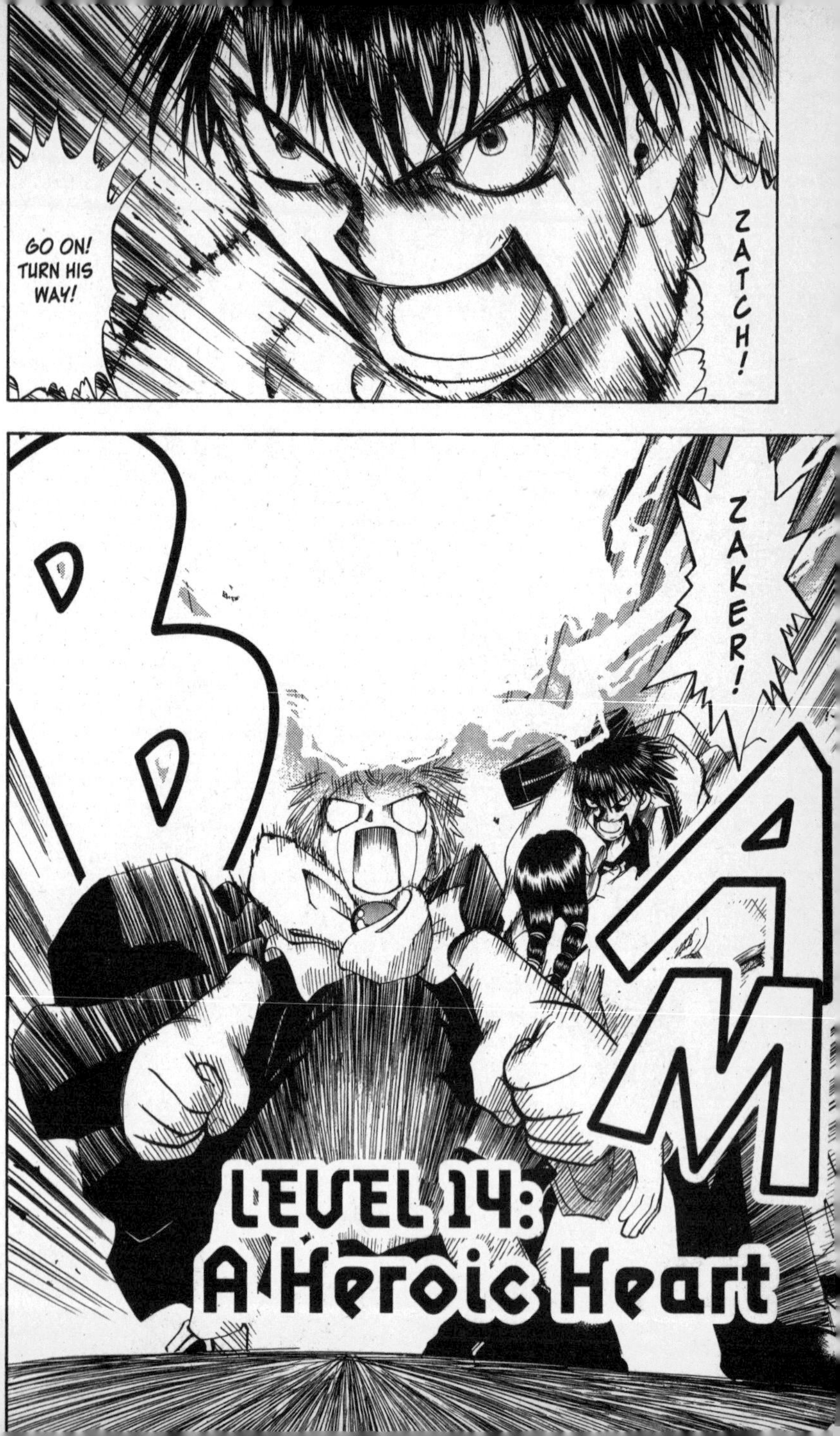
ZATCH!
GO ON! TURN HIS WAY!
ZAKER!
BAM
LEVEL 14: A Heroic Heart

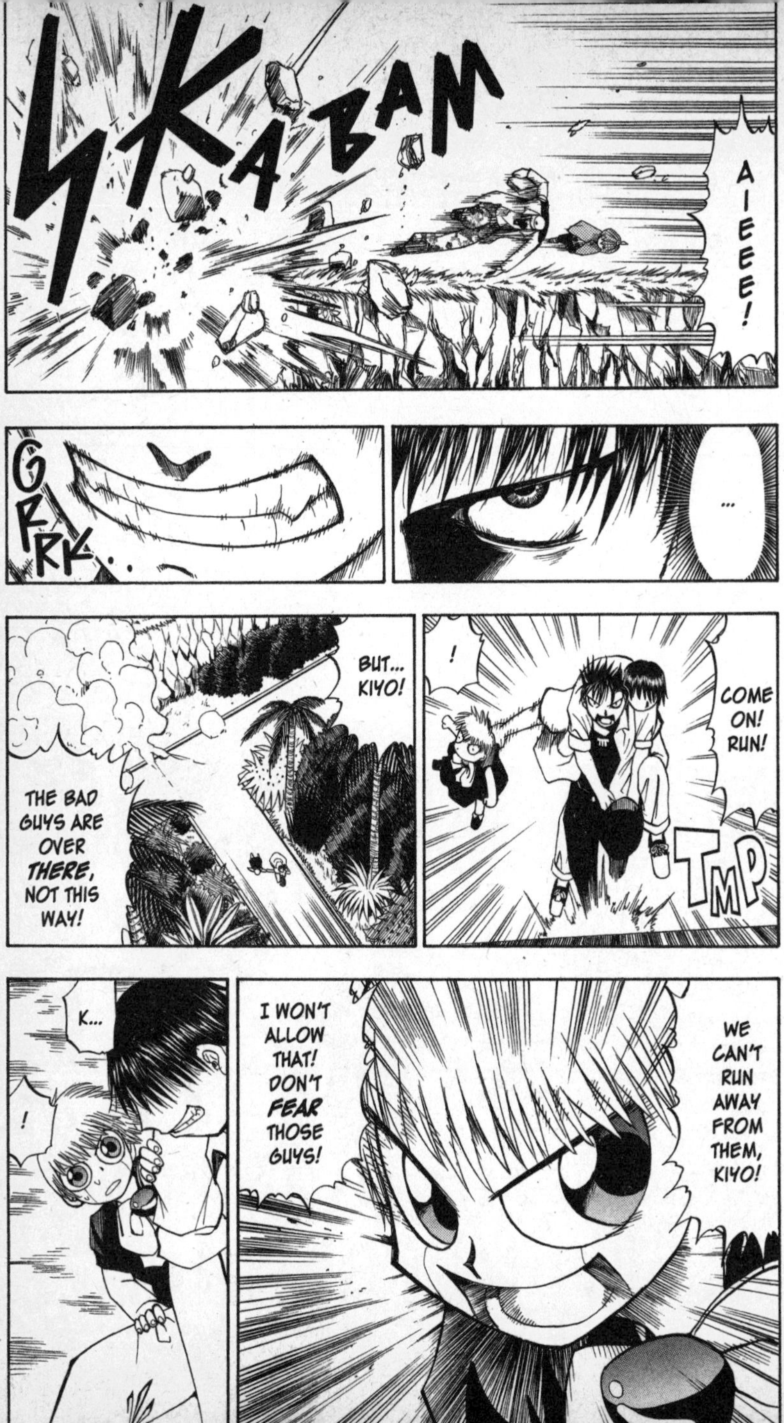
AIEEE!
SKABAM
...
GRRK
COME ON! RUN!
!
TMP
BUT... KIYO!
THE BAD GUYS ARE OVER **THERE**, NOT THIS WAY!
WE CAN'T RUN AWAY FROM THEM, KIYO!
I WON'T ALLOW THAT! DON'T **FEAR** THOSE GUYS!
K...
!

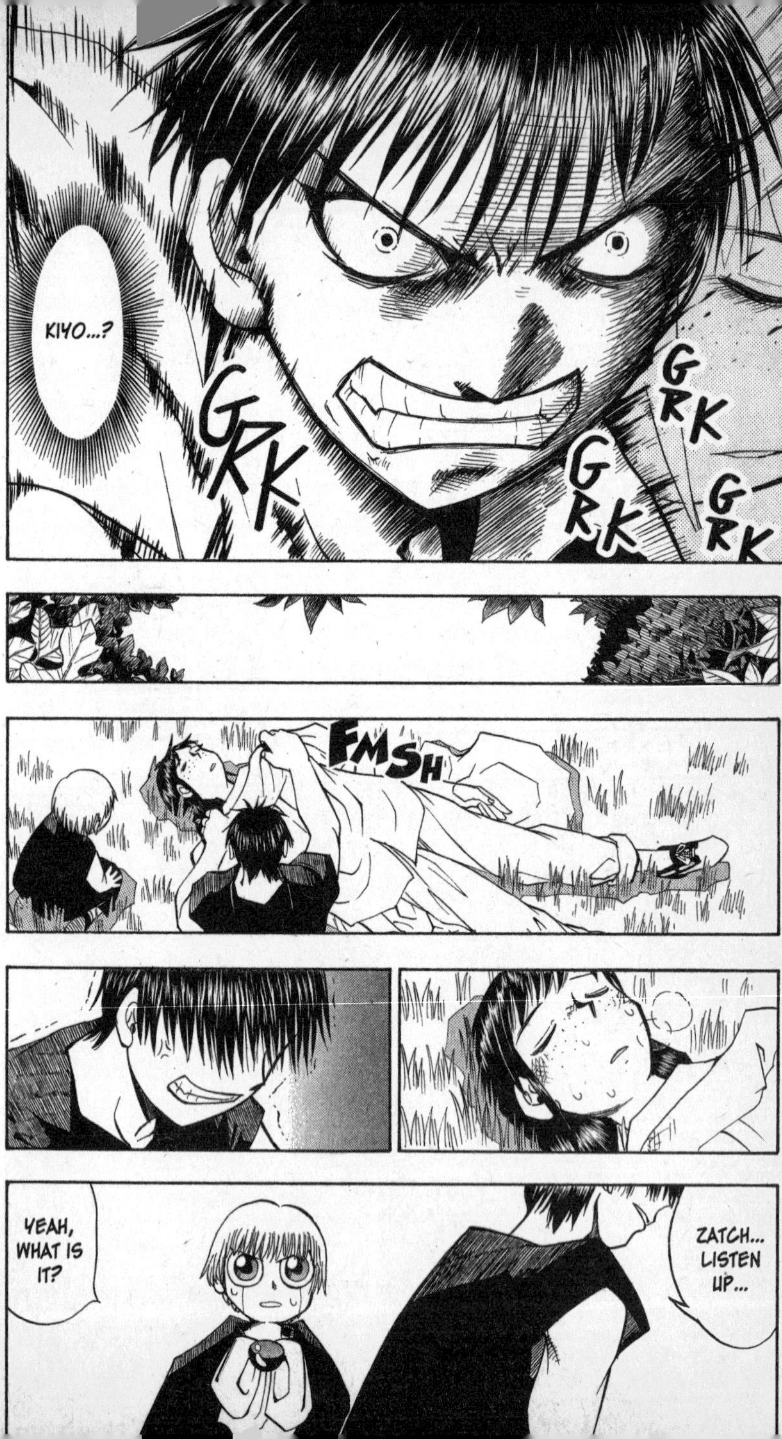
G RK
G RK
G RK
GRK
KIYO...?
FMSH
ZATCH... LISTEN UP...
YEAH, WHAT IS IT?

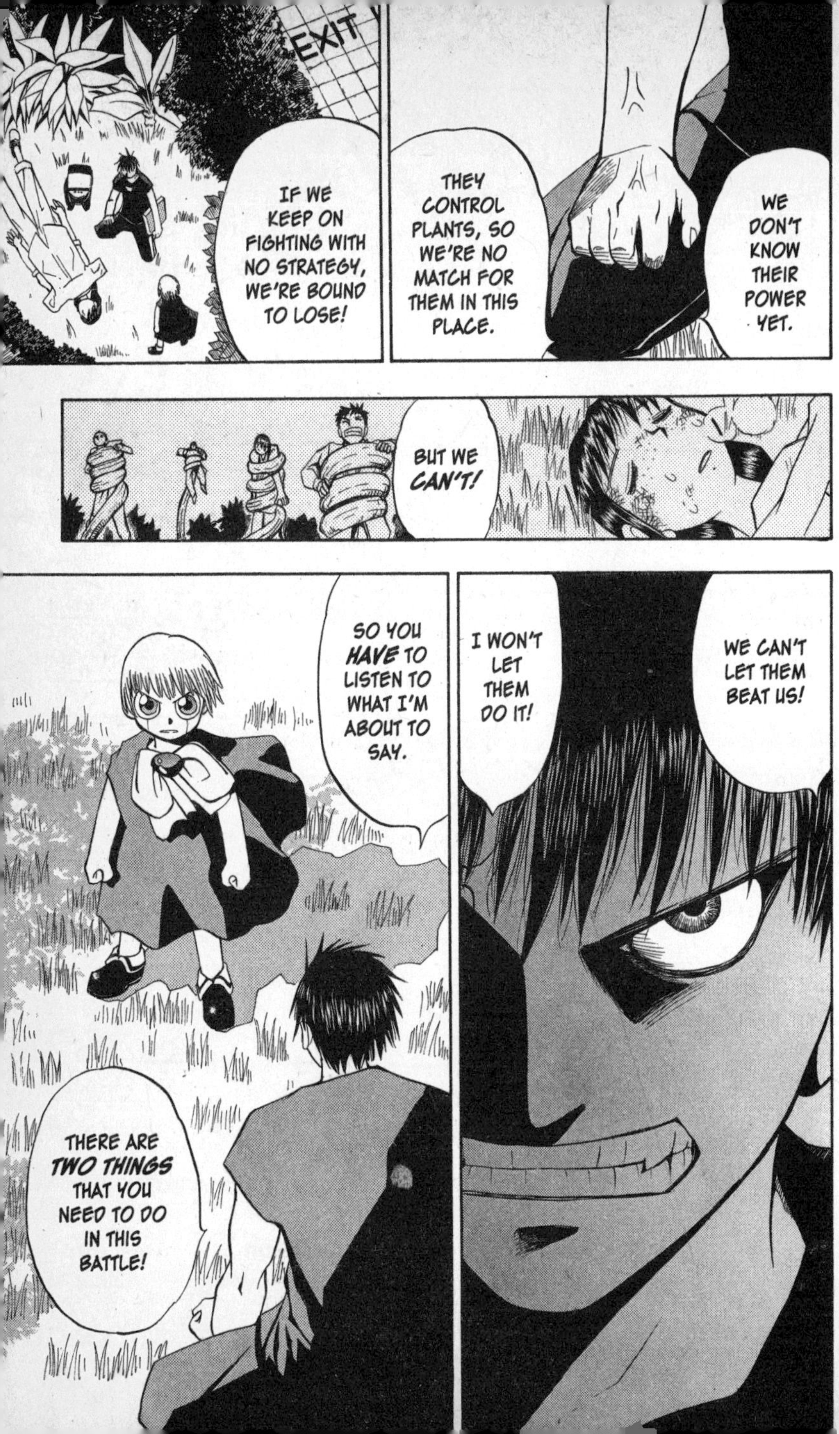
WE DON'T KNOW THEIR POWER YET.
THEY CONTROL PLANTS, SO WE'RE NO MATCH FOR THEM IN THIS PLACE.
IF WE KEEP ON FIGHTING WITH NO STRATEGY, WE'RE BOUND TO LOSE!
BUT WE CAN'T!
WE CAN'T LET THEM BEAT US!
I WON'T LET THEM DO IT!
SO YOU HAVE TO LISTEN TO WHAT I'M ABOUT TO SAY.
THERE ARE TWO THINGS THAT YOU NEED TO DO IN THIS BATTLE!

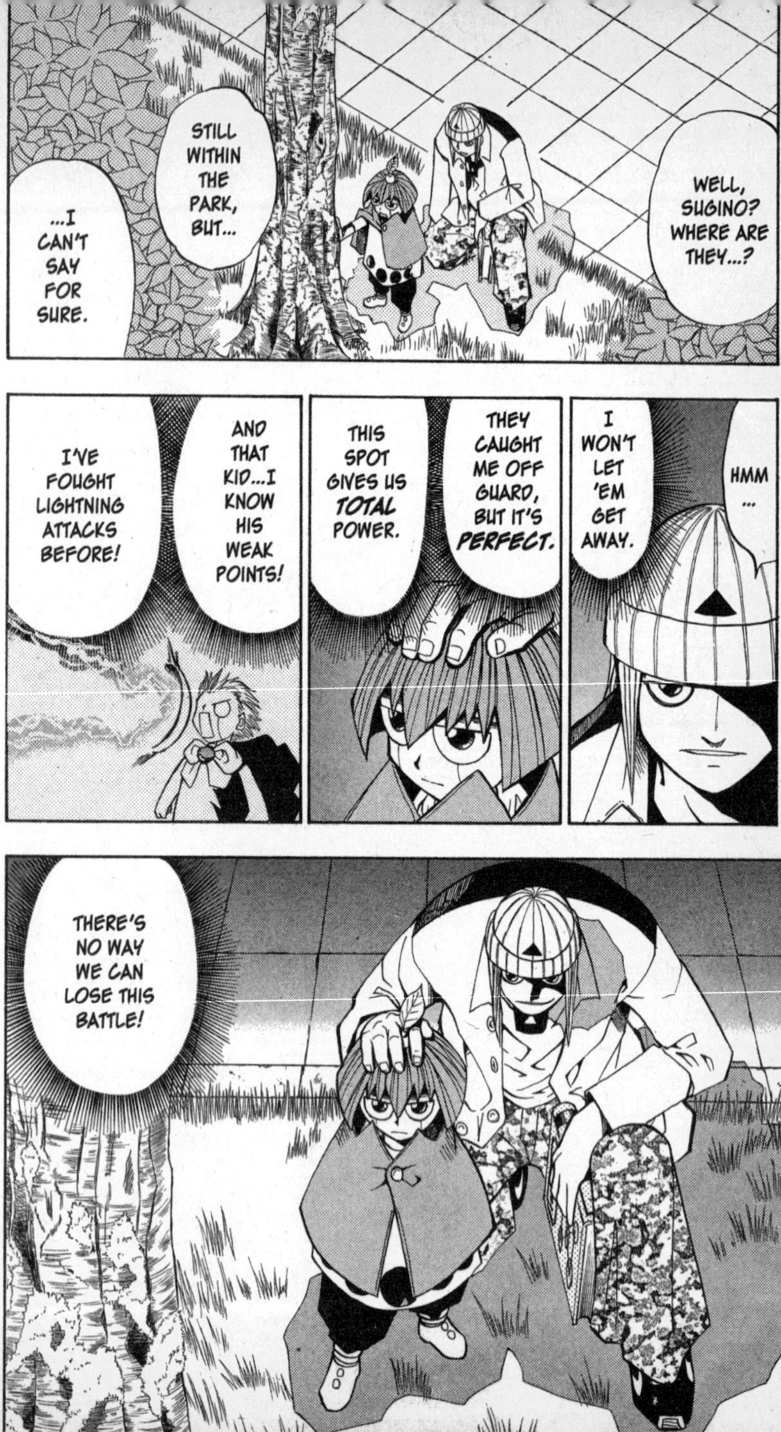
WELL, SUGINO? WHERE ARE THEY...?
STILL WITHIN THE PARK, BUT...
...I CAN'T SAY FOR SURE.
HMM ...
I WON'T LET 'EM GET AWAY.
THEY CAUGHT ME OFF GUARD, BUT IT'S PERFECT.
THIS SPOT GIVES US TOTAL POWER.
AND THAT KID...I KNOW HIS WEAK POINTS!
I'VE FOUGHT LIGHTNING ATTACKS BEFORE!
THERE'S NO WAY WE CAN LOSE THIS BATTLE!

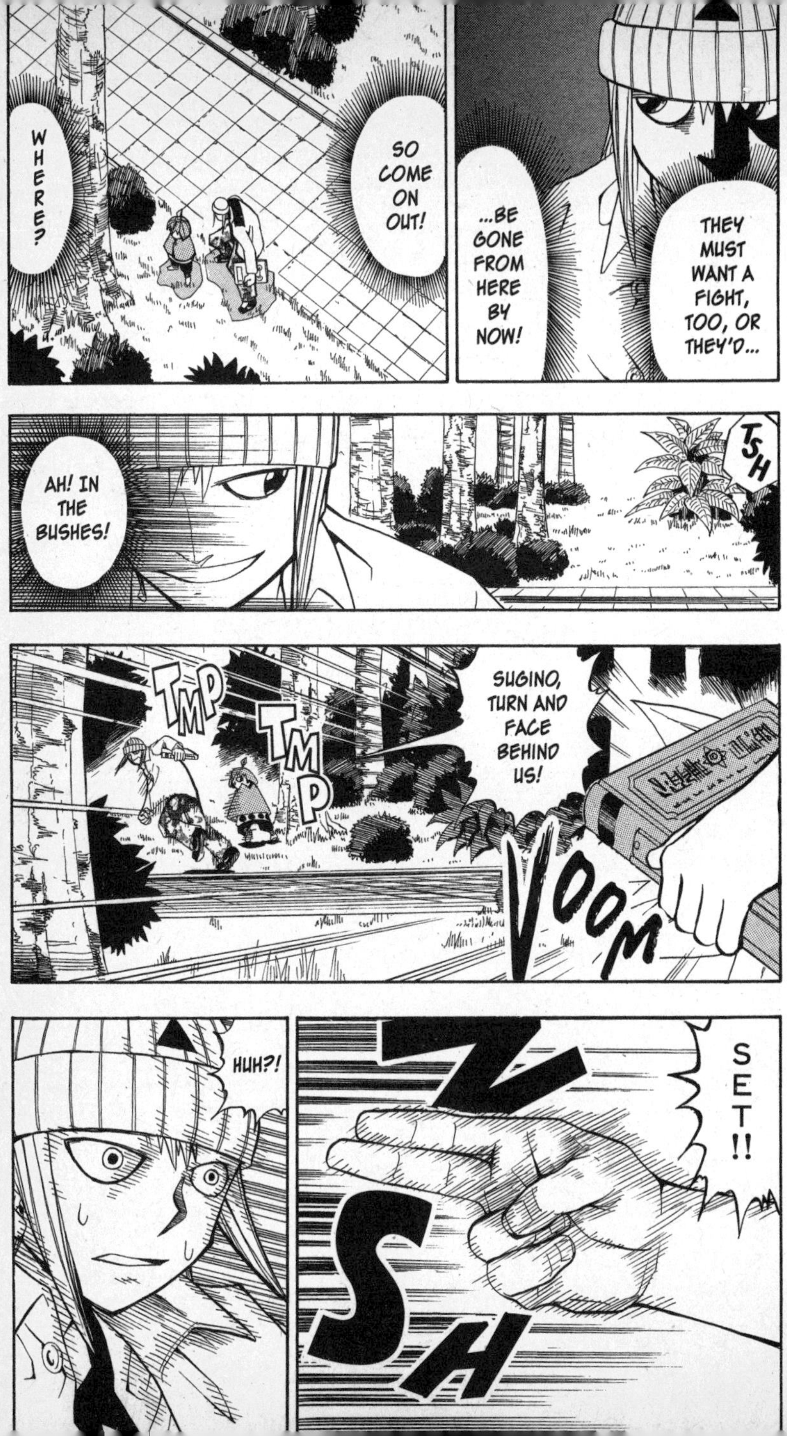
THEY MUST WANT A FIGHT, TOO, OR THEY'D...
...BE GONE FROM HERE BY NOW!
SO COME ON OUT!
WHERE?
TSH
AH! IN THE BUSHES!
SUGINO, TURN AND FACE BEHIND US!
TMP
TMP
VOOM
SET!!
ZSH
HUH?!

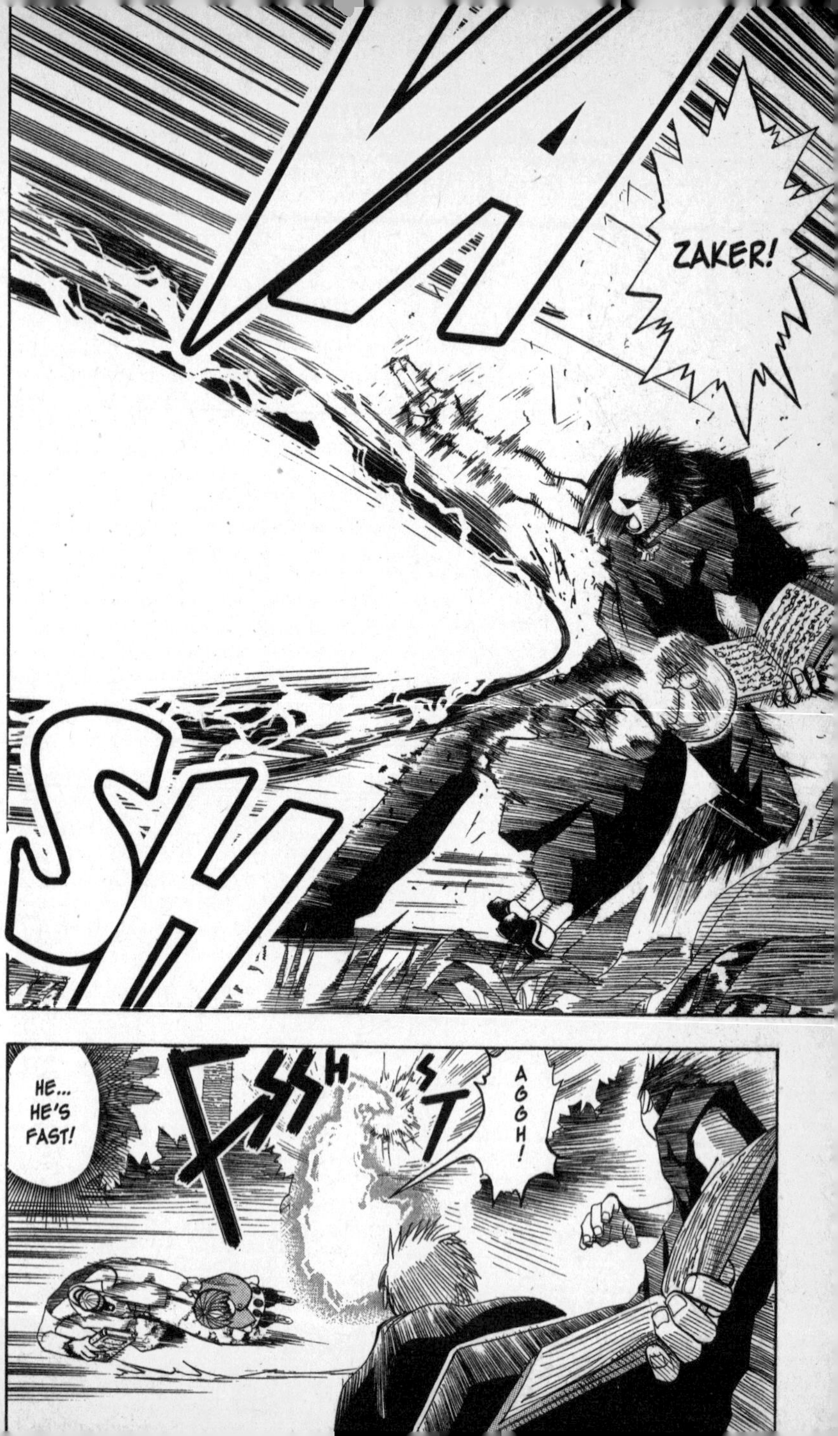
ZAKER!
AGGH!
HE... HE'S FAST!

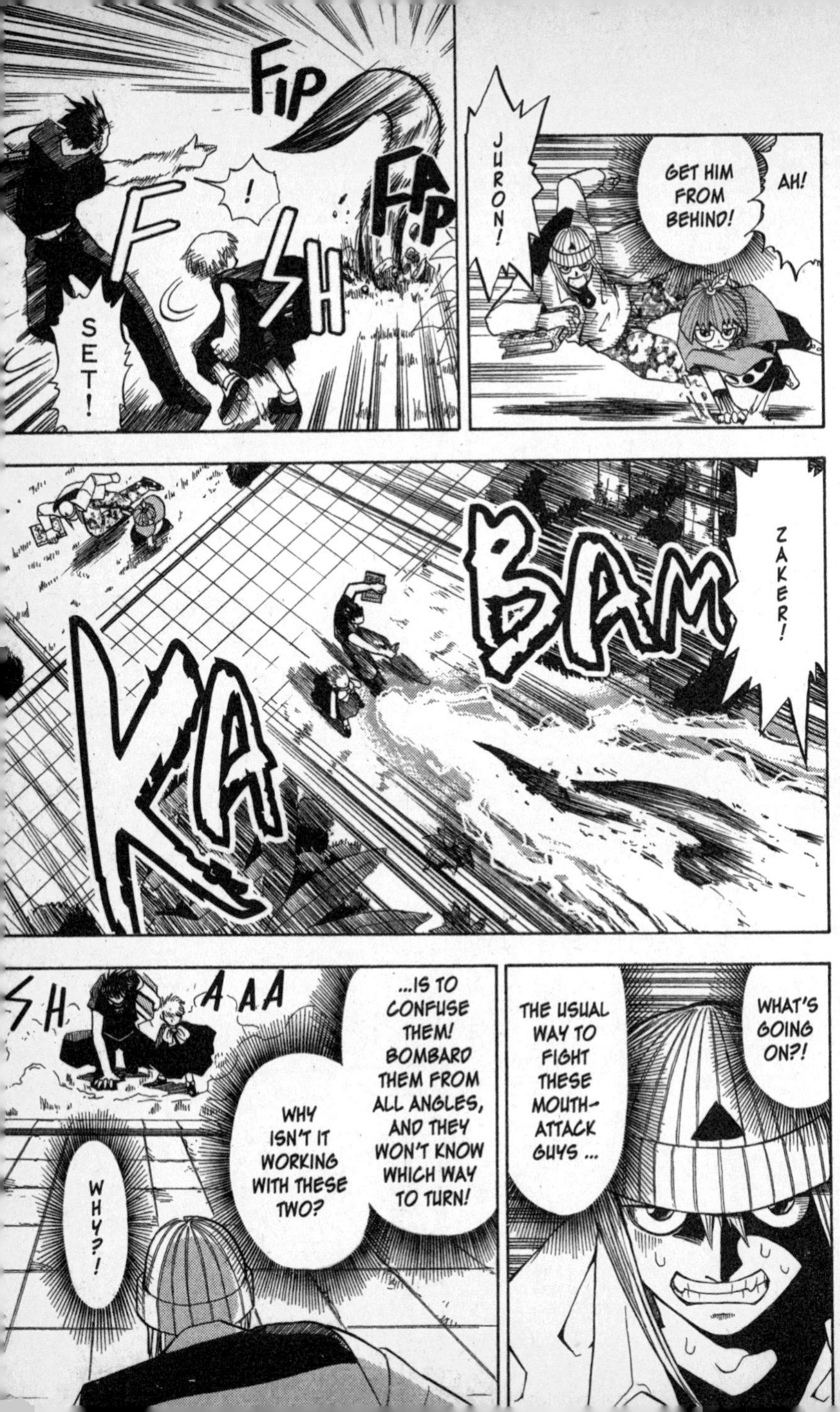
AH!
GET HIM FROM BEHIND!
JURON!
FIP
FAP
FIP
!
FSH
SET!
ZAKER!
BAM
KA
WHAT'S GOING ON?!
THE USUAL WAY TO FIGHT THESE MOUTH-ATTACK GUYS ...
...IS TO CONFUSE THEM! BOMBARD THEM FROM ALL ANGLES, AND THEY WON'T KNOW WHICH WAY TO TURN!
WHY ISN'T IT WORKING WITH THESE TWO?
AAA
SH
WHY?!

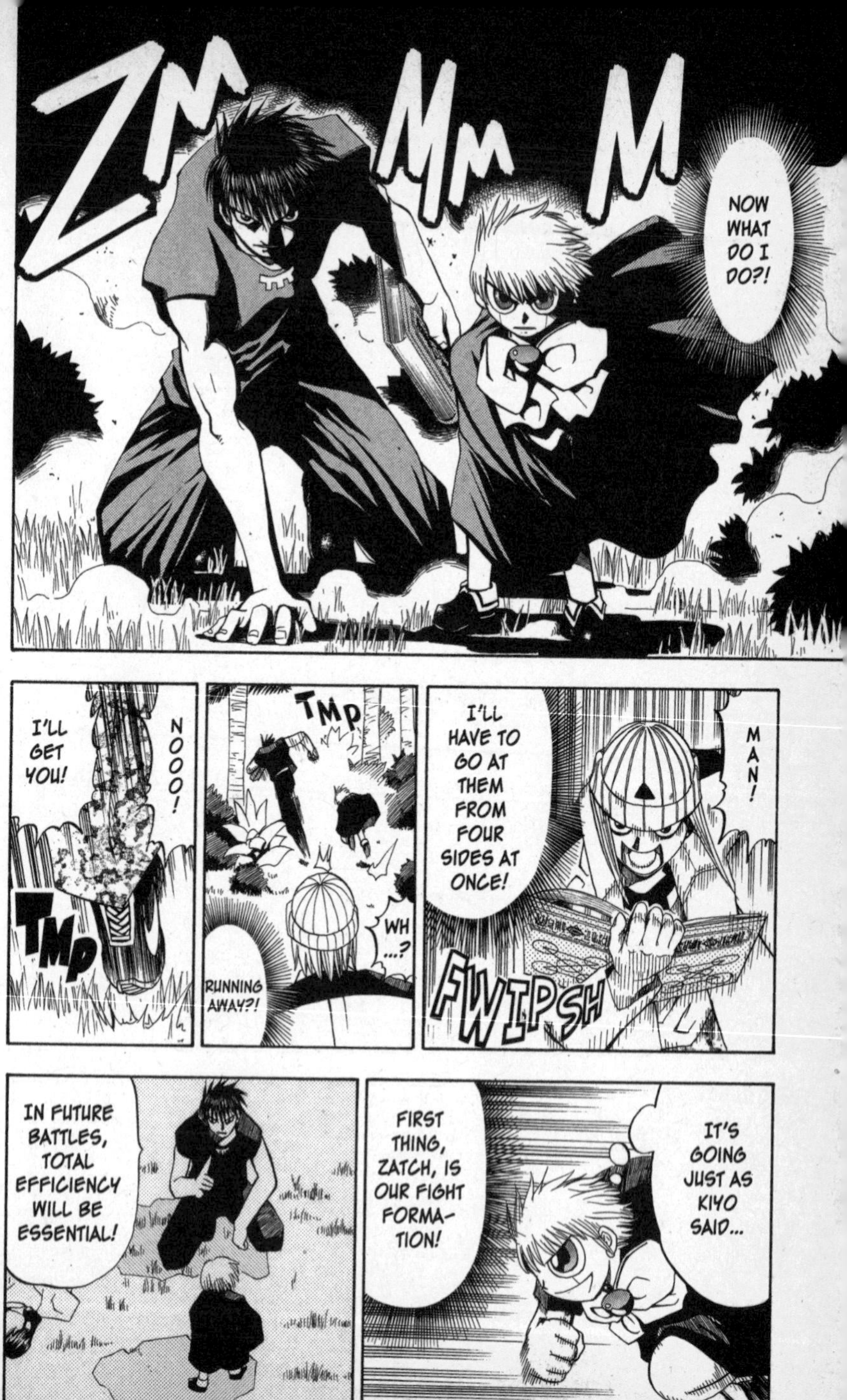
ZMMMMM
NOW WHAT DO I DO?!
MAN!
I'LL HAVE TO GO AT THEM FROM FOUR SIDES AT ONCE!
FWIPSH
TMP
WH ...?
RUNNING AWAY?!
NOOOO!
I'LL GET YOU!
TMP
IT'S GOING JUST AS KIYO SAID...
FIRST THING, ZATCH, IS OUR FIGHT FORMATION!
IN FUTURE BATTLES, TOTAL EFFICIENCY WILL BE ESSENTIAL!

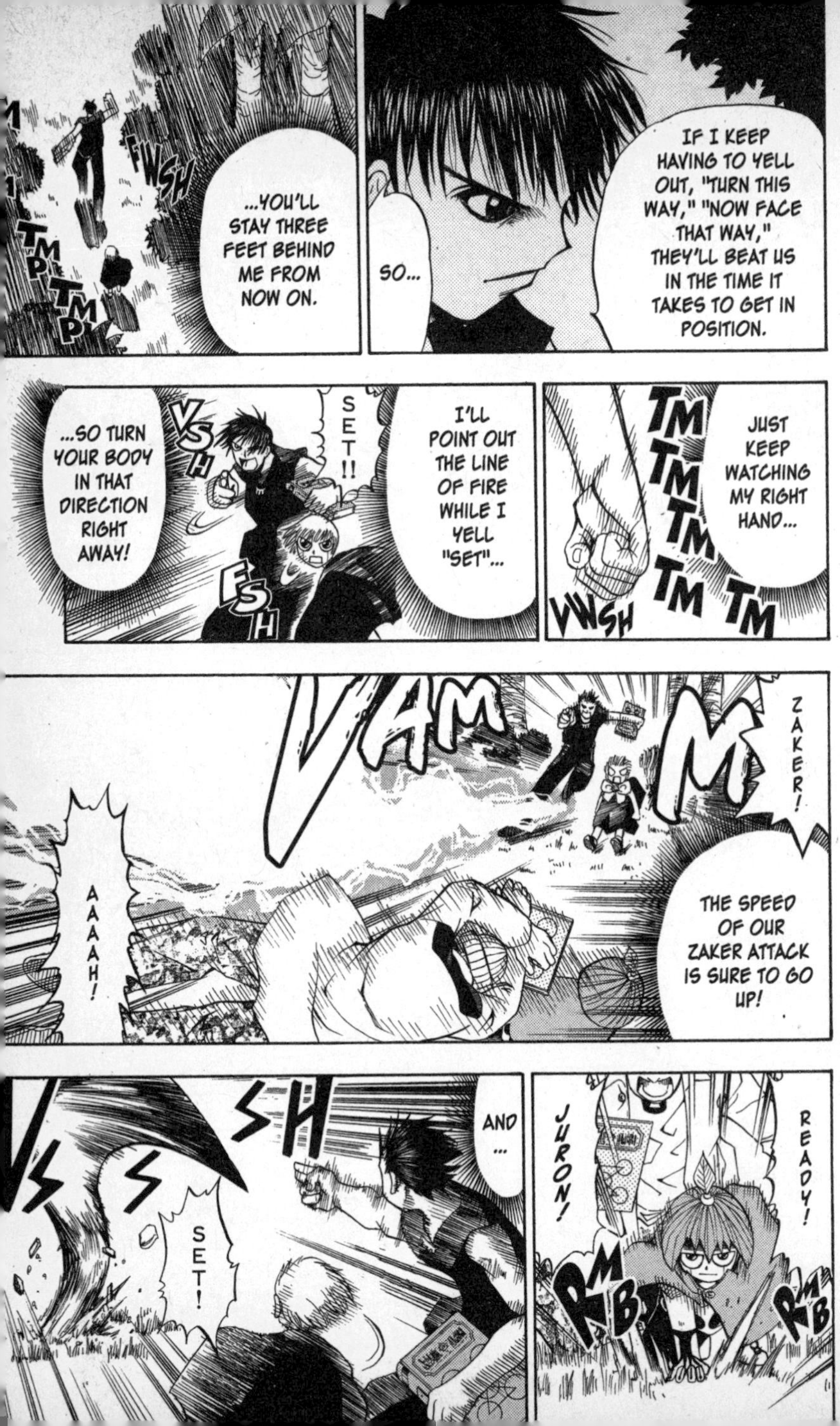
IF I KEEP HAVING TO YELL OUT, "TURN THIS WAY," "NOW FACE THAT WAY," THEY'LL BEAT US IN THE TIME IT TAKES TO GET IN POSITION.
SO...
...YOU'LL STAY THREE FEET BEHIND ME FROM NOW ON.
FWSH
TMP
TMP
TMP
JUST KEEP WATCHING MY RIGHT HAND...
TM TM TM TM TM TM
VWSH
I'LL POINT OUT THE LINE OF FIRE WHILE I YELL "SET"...
SET!!
VSH
...SO TURN YOUR BODY IN THAT DIRECTION RIGHT AWAY!
FSH
ZAKER!
VAMM
THE SPEED OF OUR ZAKER ATTACK IS SURE TO GO UP!
AAAAAH!
READY!
JURON!
RMB
RMB
AND...
SH
SET!
VS
S

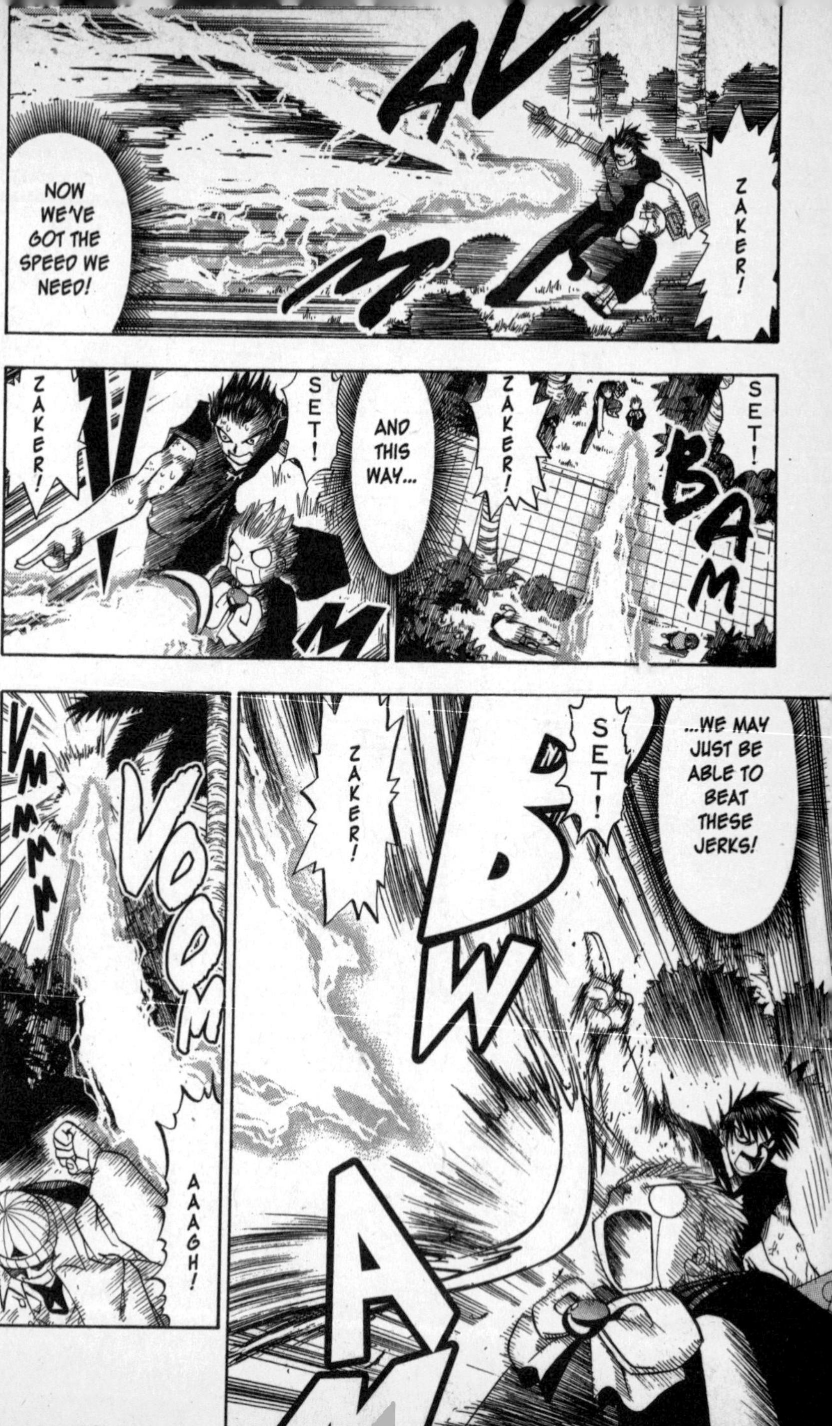
ZAKER!
NOW WE'VE GOT THE SPEED WE NEED!
AV
M
SET!
BAM
ZAKER!
AND THIS WAY...
SET!
ZAKER!
M
...WE MAY JUST BE ABLE TO BEAT THESE JERKS!
SET!
ZAKER!
BWAM
VOOM
VMMMM
AAAAGH!

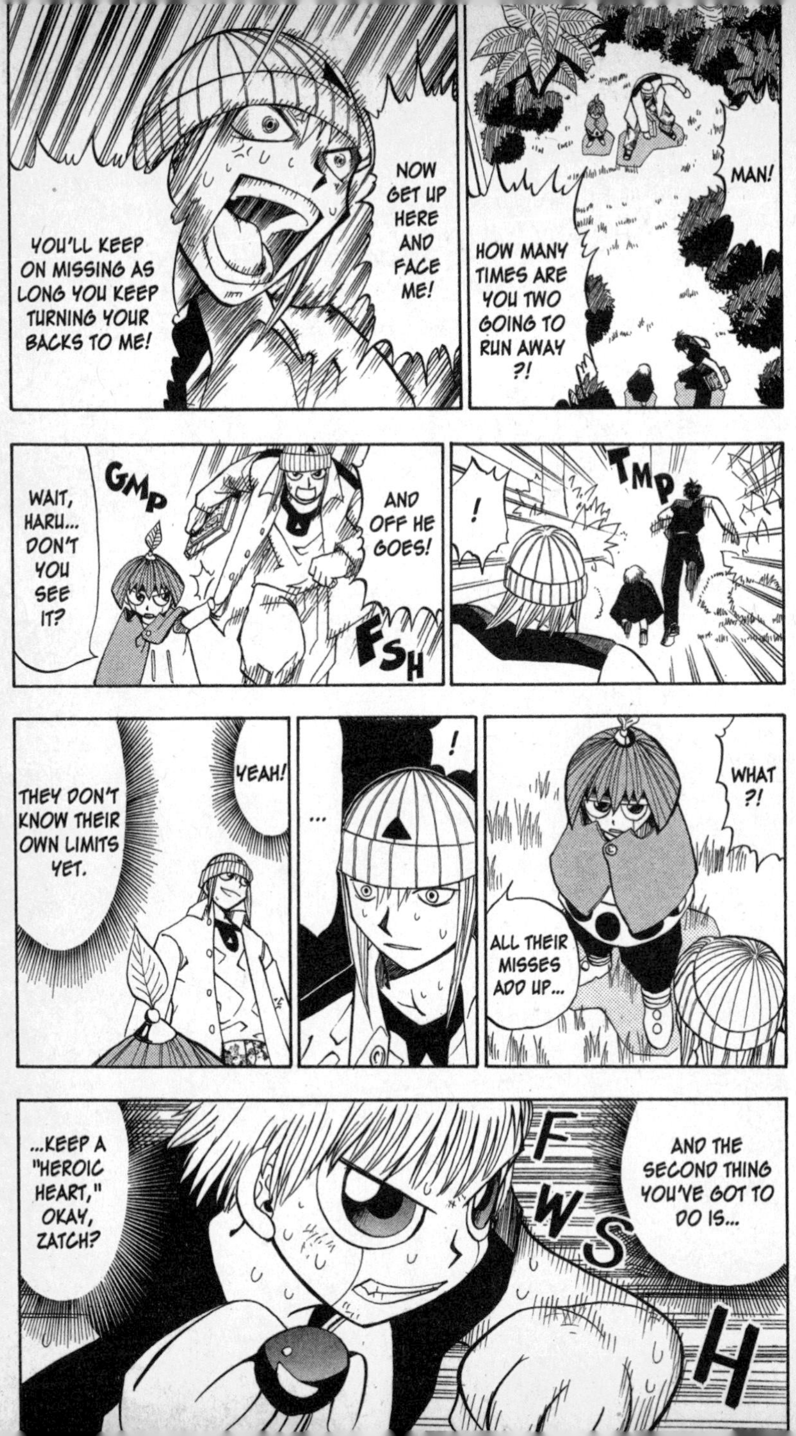
MAN!
HOW MANY TIMES ARE YOU TWO GOING TO RUN AWAY ?!
NOW GET UP HERE AND FACE ME!
YOU'LL KEEP ON MISSING AS LONG YOU KEEP TURNING YOUR BACKS TO ME!
TMP
!
AND OFF HE GOES!
FSH
GMP
WAIT, HARU... DON'T YOU SEE IT?
WHAT ?!
ALL THEIR MISSES ADD UP...
!
...
YEAH!
THEY DON'T KNOW THEIR OWN LIMITS YET.
AND THE SECOND THING YOU'VE GOT TO DO IS...
FWSH
...KEEP A "HEROIC HEART," OKAY, ZATCH?

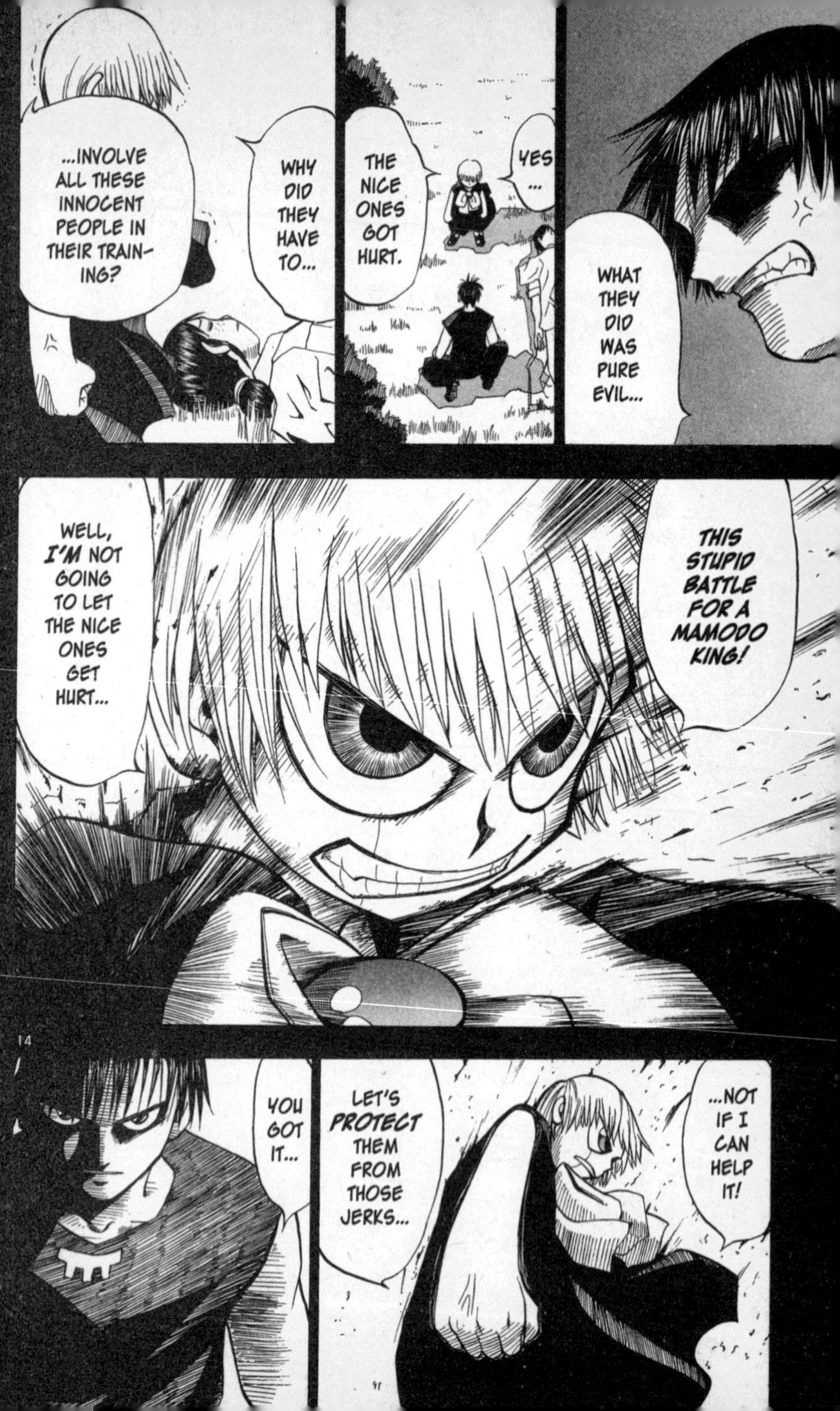
WHAT THEY DID WAS PURE EVIL...
YES...
THE NICE ONES GOT HURT.
WHY DID THEY HAVE TO...
...INVOLVE ALL THESE INNOCENT PEOPLE IN THEIR TRAINING?
THIS STUPID BATTLE FOR A MAMODO KING!
WELL, *I'M* NOT GOING TO LET THE NICE ONES GET HURT...
...NOT IF I CAN HELP IT!
LET'S *PROTECT* THEM FROM THOSE JERKS...
YOU GOT IT...

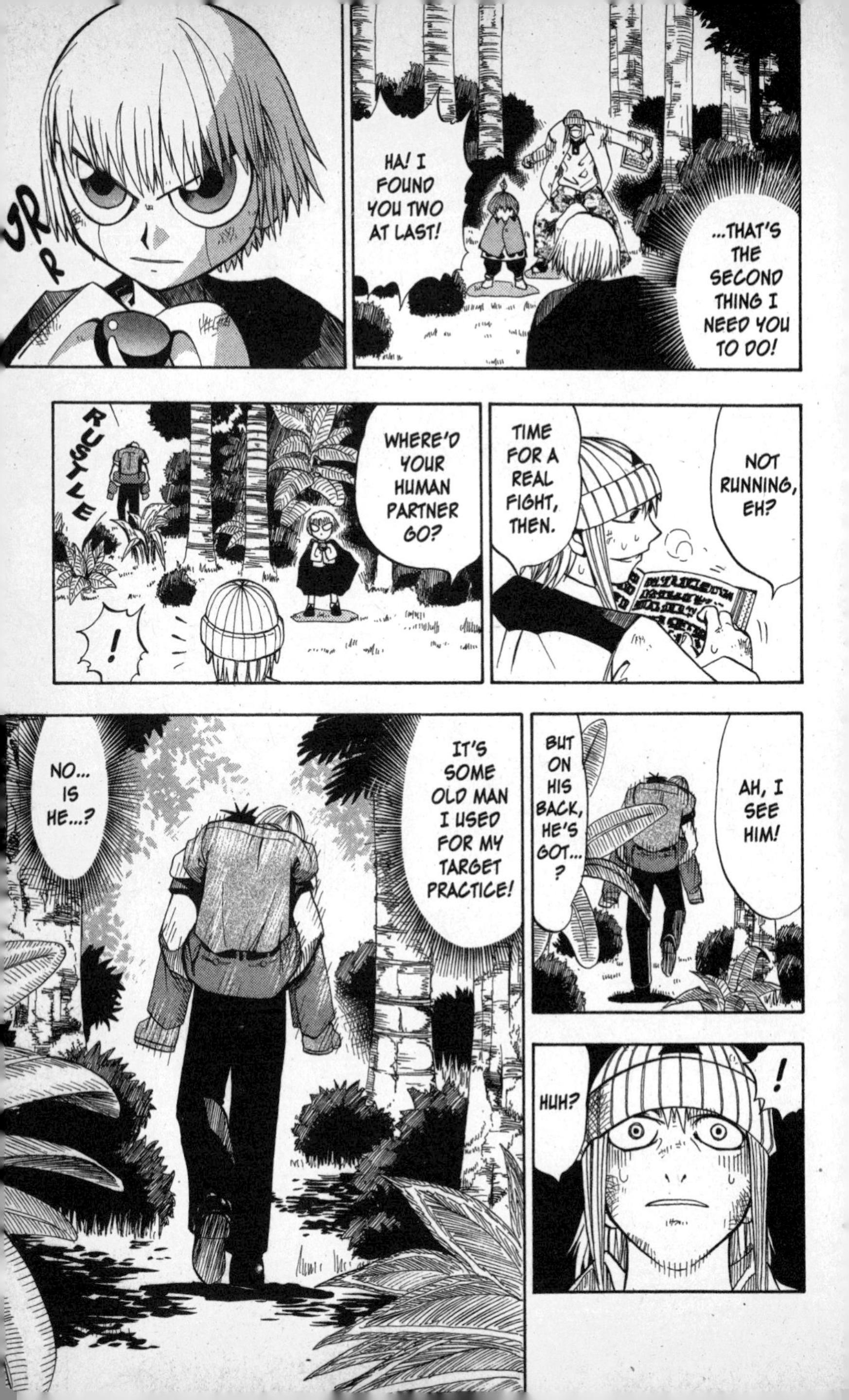
...THAT'S THE SECOND THING I NEED YOU TO DO!
HA! I FOUND YOU TWO AT LAST!
GRR
NOT RUNNING, EH?
TIME FOR A REAL FIGHT, THEN.
WHERE'D YOUR HUMAN PARTNER GO?
RUSTLE
!
AH, I SEE HIM!
BUT ON HIS BACK, HE'S GOT...?
!
HUH?
IT'S SOME OLD MAN I USED FOR MY TARGET PRACTICE!
NO... IS HE...?

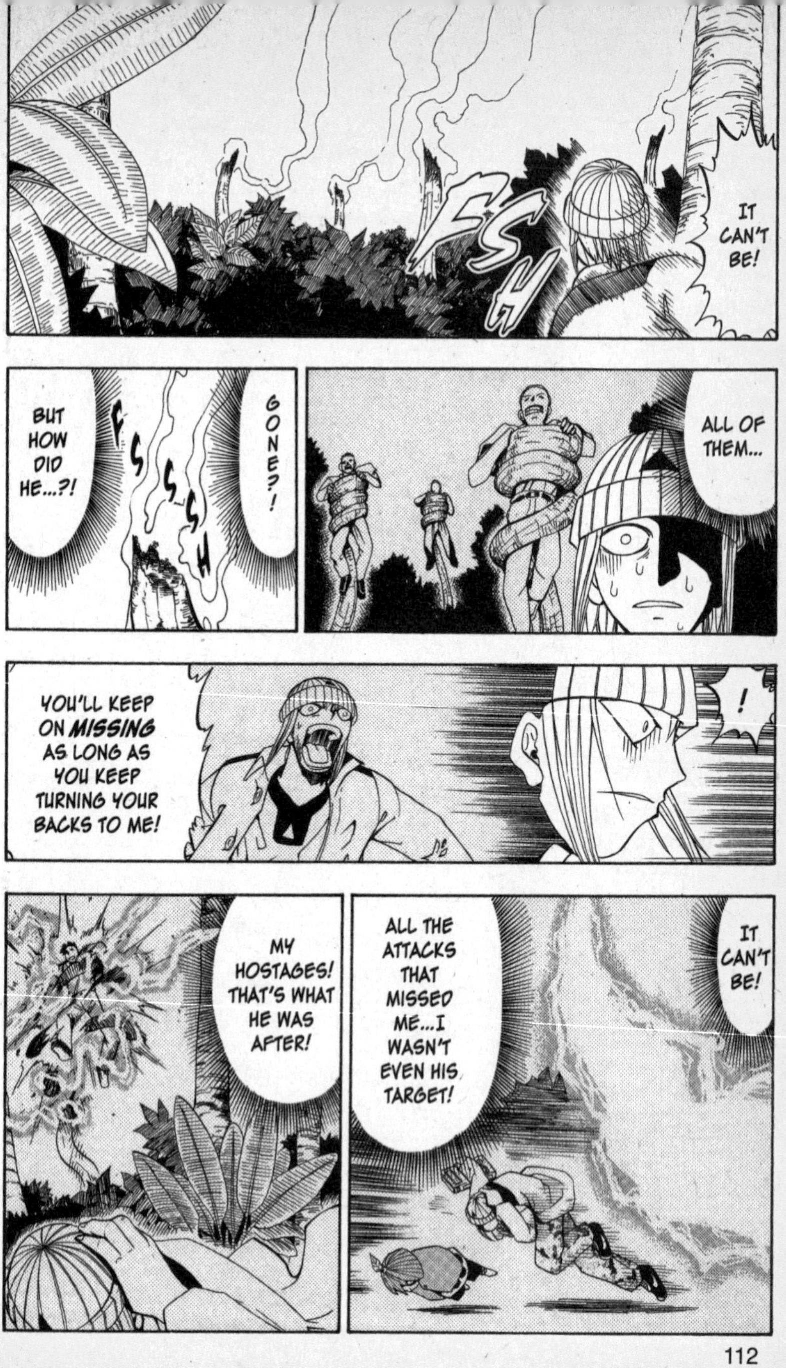
IT CAN'T BE!
FSH
ALL OF THEM...
GONE?!
FSSSH
BUT HOW DID HE...?!
!
YOU'LL KEEP ON *MISSING* AS LONG AS YOU KEEP TURNING YOUR BACKS TO ME!
IT CAN'T BE!
ALL THE ATTACKS THAT MISSED ME...I WASN'T EVEN HIS TARGET!
MY HOSTAGES! THAT'S WHAT HE WAS AFTER!

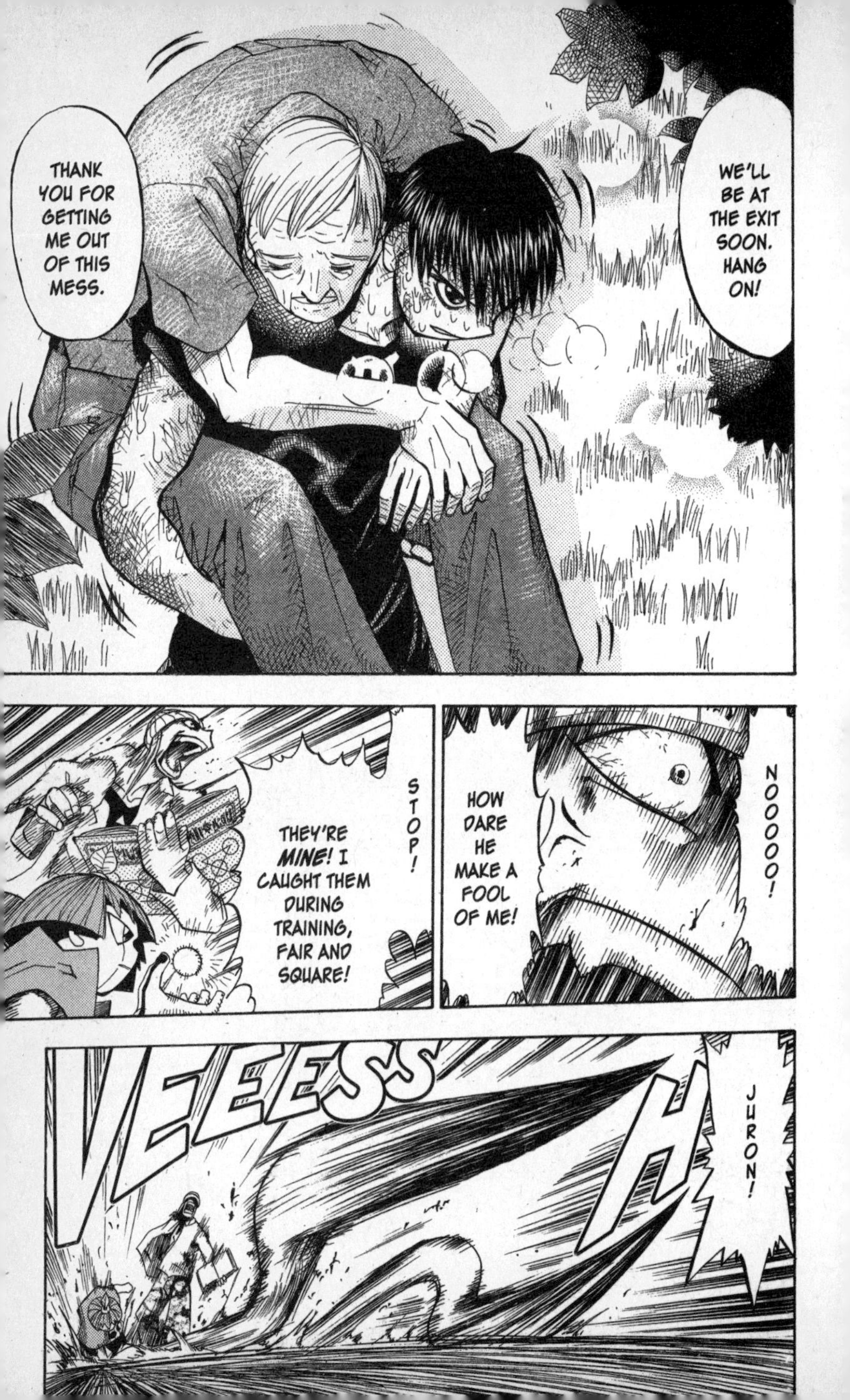
WE'LL BE AT THE EXIT SOON. HANG ON!
THANK YOU FOR GETTING ME OUT OF THIS MESS.
NOOOOOO!
HOW DARE HE MAKE A FOOL OF ME!
STOP!
THEY'RE *MINE*! I CAUGHT THEM DURING TRAINING, FAIR AND SQUARE!
JURON!
VEEESSH

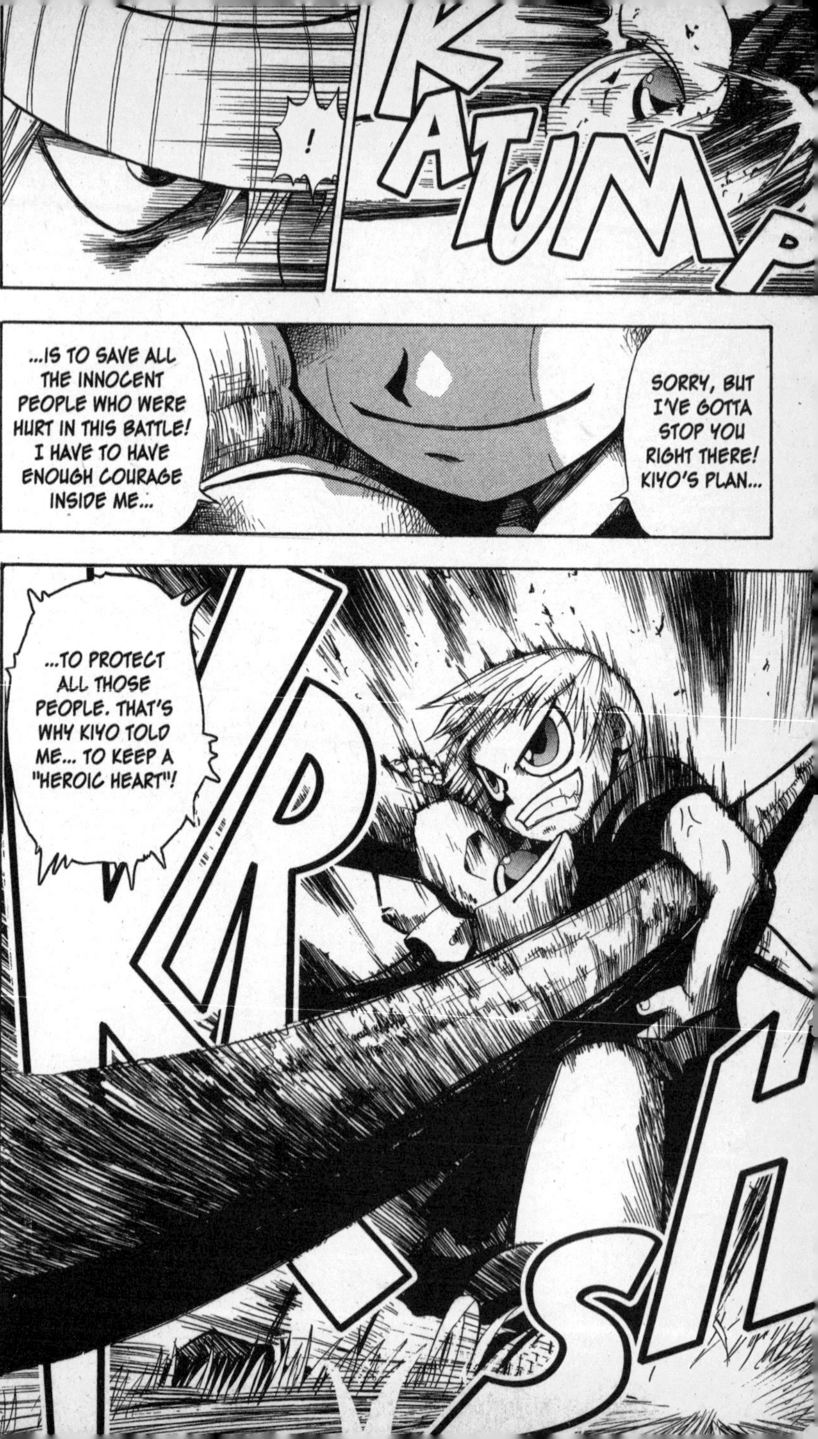
KATUMP
!
SORRY, BUT I'VE GOTTA STOP YOU RIGHT THERE! KIYO'S PLAN...
...IS TO SAVE ALL THE INNOCENT PEOPLE WHO WERE HURT IN THIS BATTLE! I HAVE TO HAVE ENOUGH COURAGE INSIDE ME...
...TO PROTECT ALL THOSE PEOPLE. THAT'S WHY KIYO TOLD ME... TO KEEP A "HEROIC HEART"!

LEVEL 15: The Limit of Strength

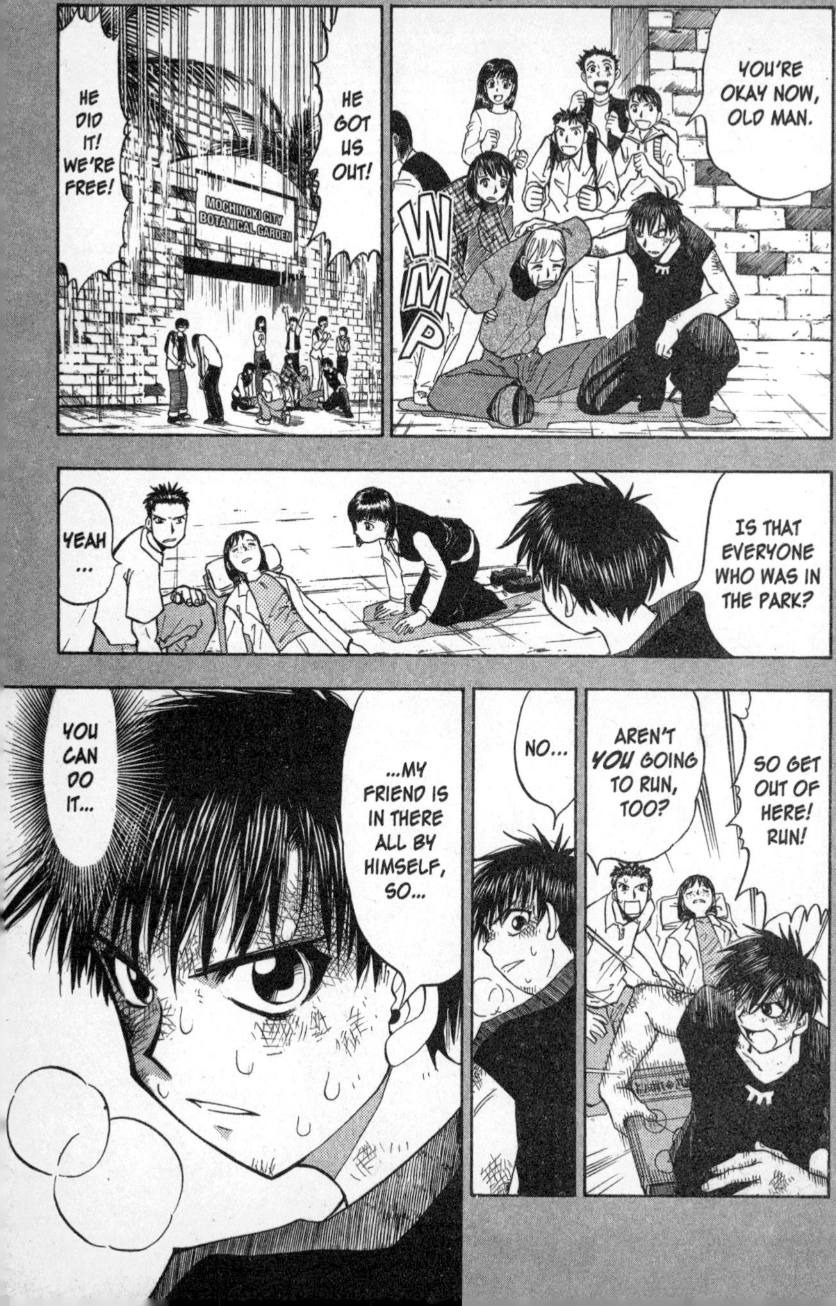

YOU'RE OKAY NOW, OLD MAN.
WMP
HE GOT US OUT!
HE DID IT! WE'RE FREE!
MOCHINOKI CITY BOTANICAL GARDEN
IS THAT EVERYONE WHO WAS IN THE PARK?
YEAH ...
SO GET OUT OF HERE! RUN!
AREN'T *YOU* GOING TO RUN, TOO?
NO...
...MY FRIEND IS IN THERE ALL BY HIMSELF, SO...
YOU CAN DO IT...

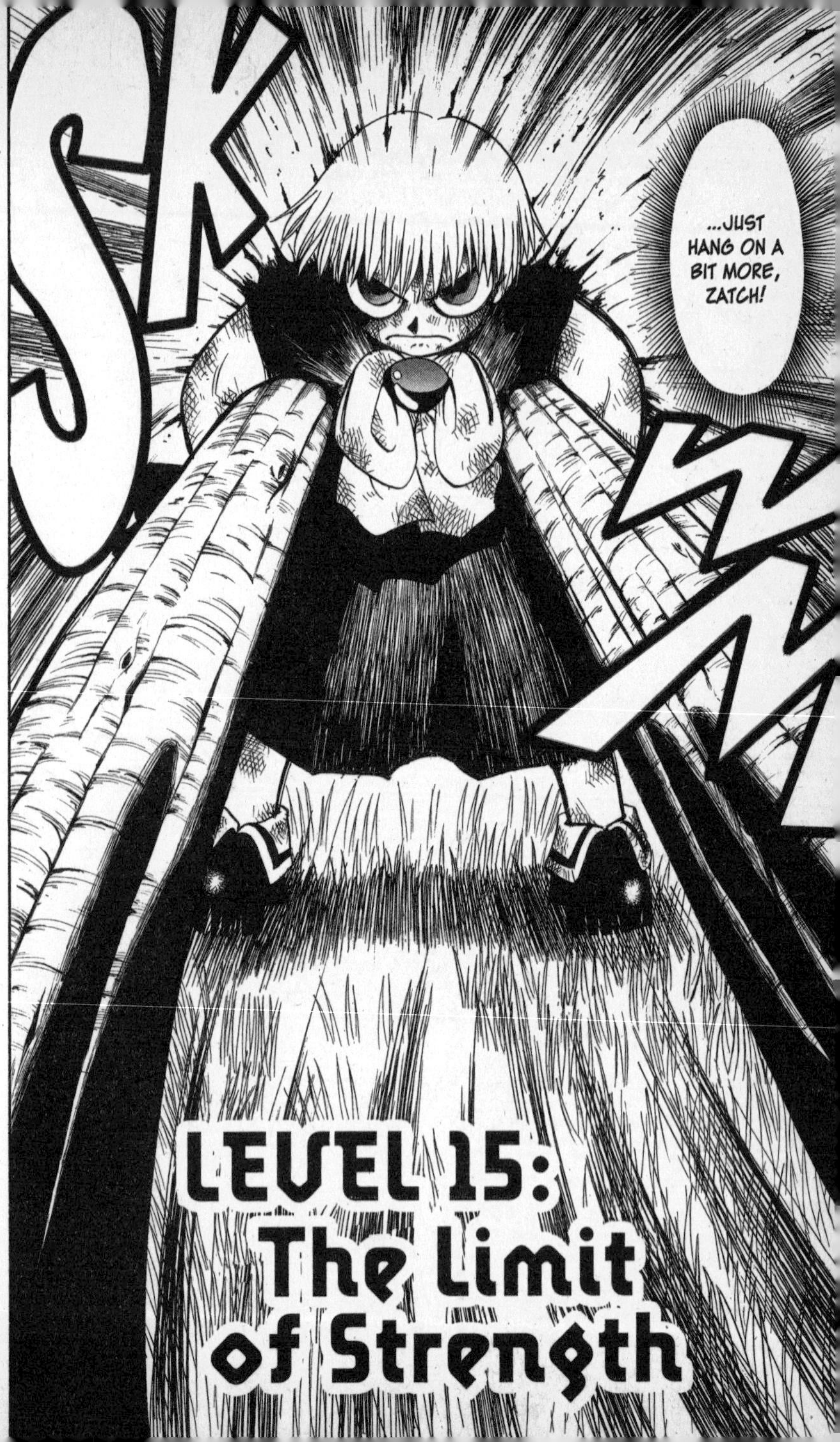
...JUST HANG ON A BIT MORE, ZATCH!

LEVEL 15: The Limit of Strength

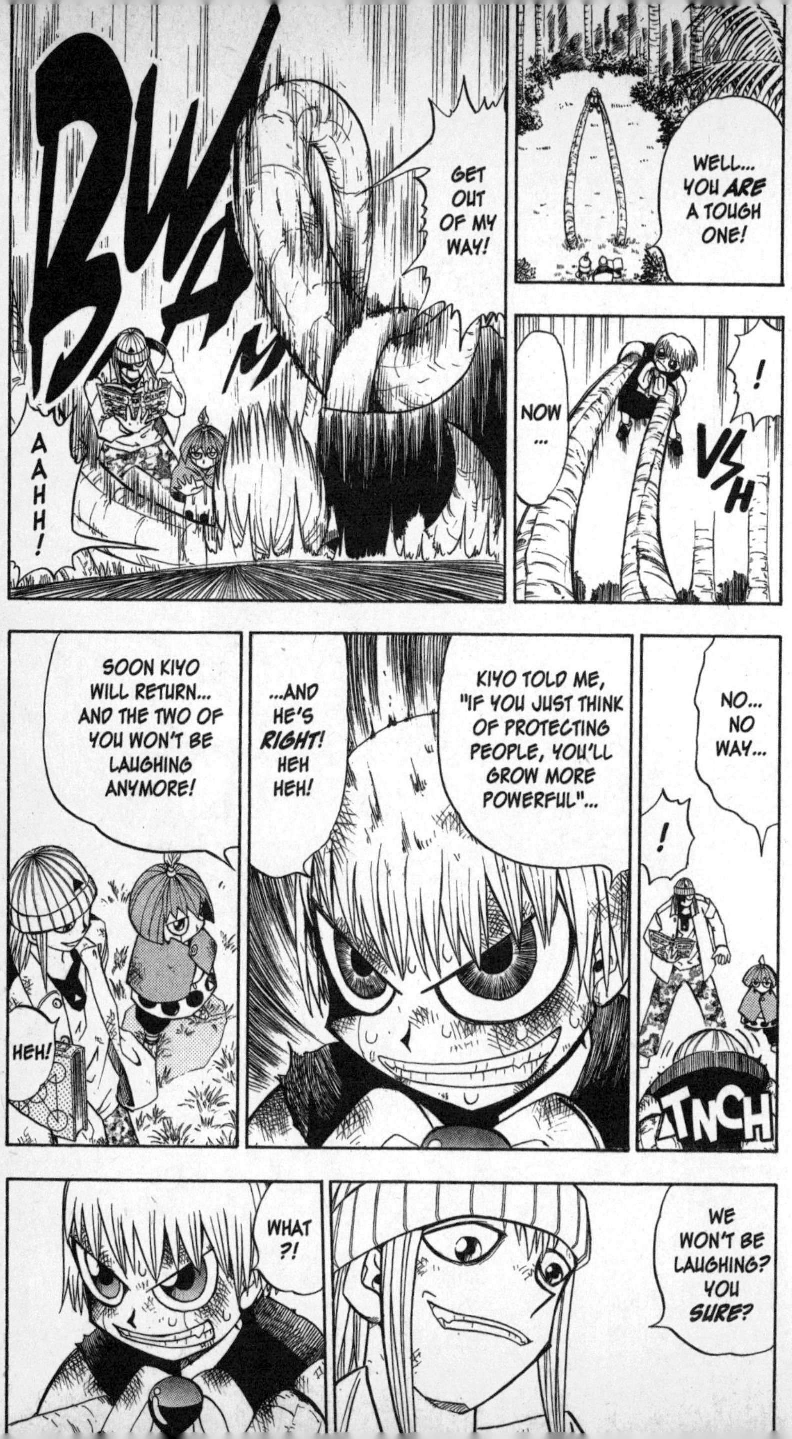
WELL... YOU ARE A TOUGH ONE!
!
NOW ...
VSH
GET OUT OF MY WAY!
BWAM
AAHH!
NO... NO WAY...
!
TNCH
KIYO TOLD ME, "IF YOU JUST THINK OF PROTECTING PEOPLE, YOU'LL GROW MORE POWERFUL"...
...AND HE'S RIGHT! HEH HEH!
SOON KIYO WILL RETURN... AND THE TWO OF YOU WON'T BE LAUGHING ANYMORE!
HEH!
WE WON'T BE LAUGHING? YOU SURE?
WHAT ?!

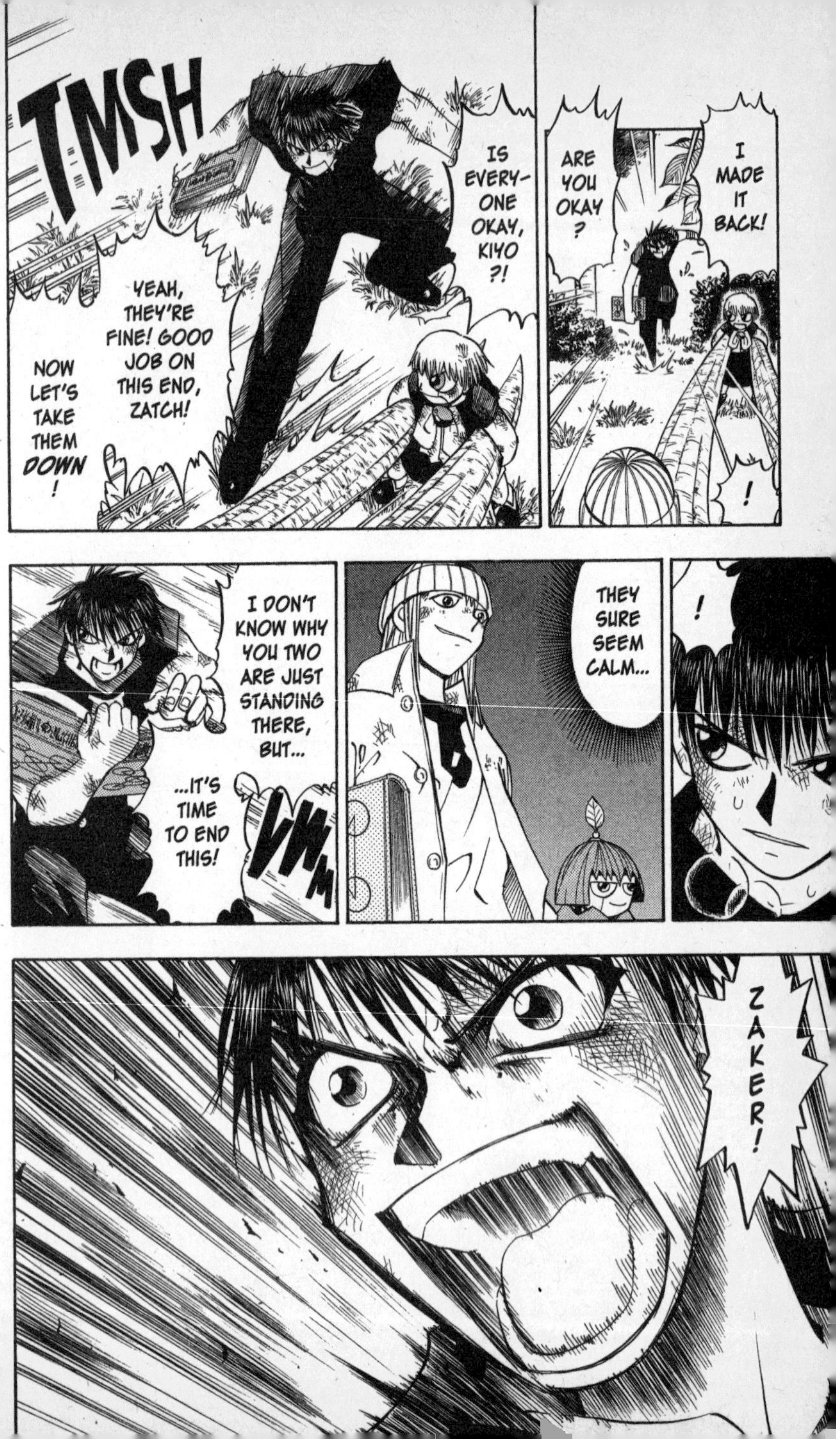
I MADE IT BACK!
ARE YOU OKAY?
!
IS EVERYONE OKAY, KIYO?!
TMSH
YEAH, THEY'RE FINE! GOOD JOB ON THIS END, ZATCH!
NOW LET'S TAKE THEM *DOWN*!
!
THEY SURE SEEM CALM...
I DON'T KNOW WHY YOU TWO ARE JUST STANDING THERE, BUT...
...IT'S TIME TO END THIS!
VWM
ZAKER!

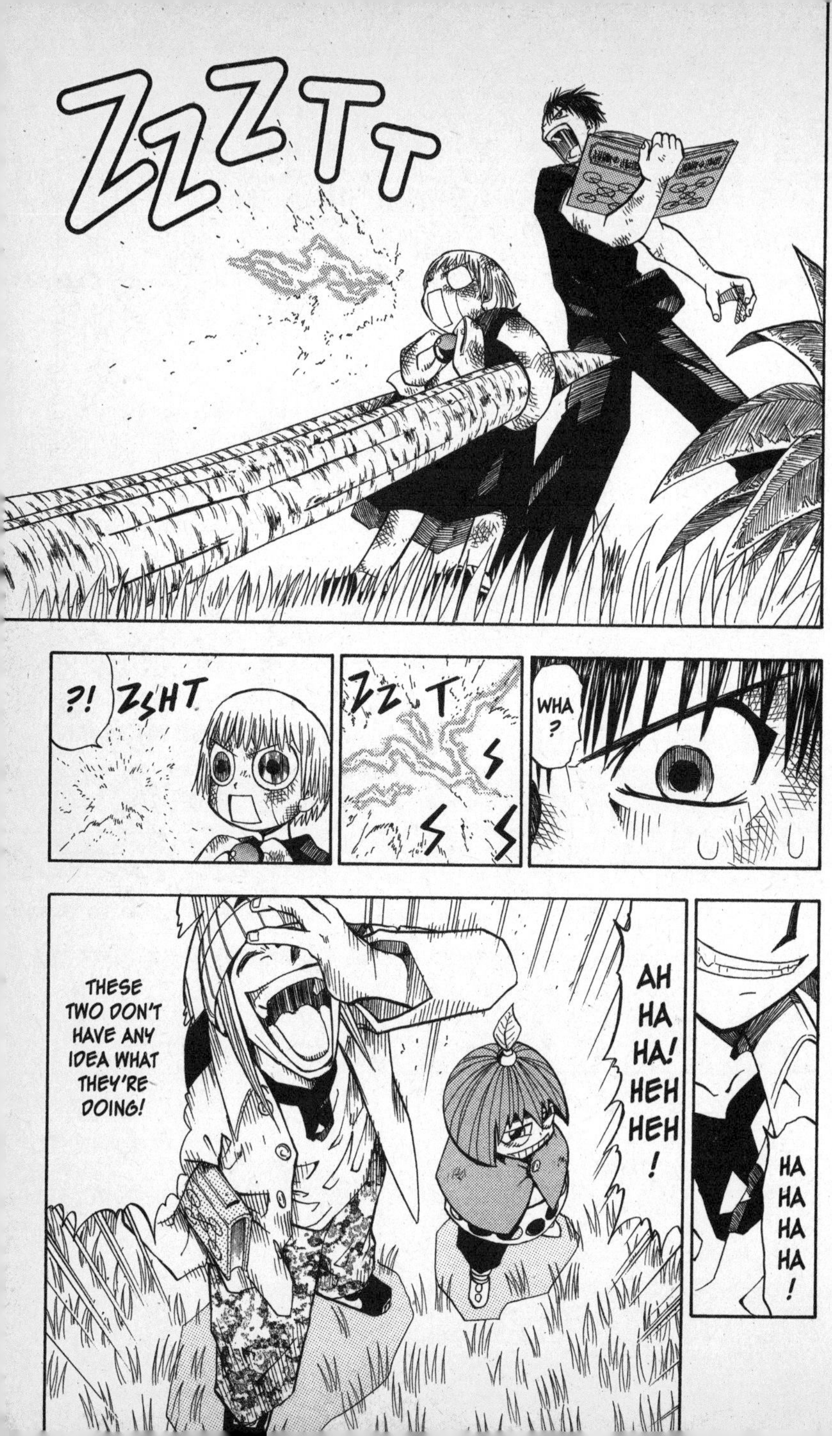
ZZZTT
WHA?
ZZ T
?!
ZSHT
HA HA HA HA!
AH HA HA! HEH HEH!
THESE TWO DON'T HAVE ANY IDEA WHAT THEY'RE DOING!

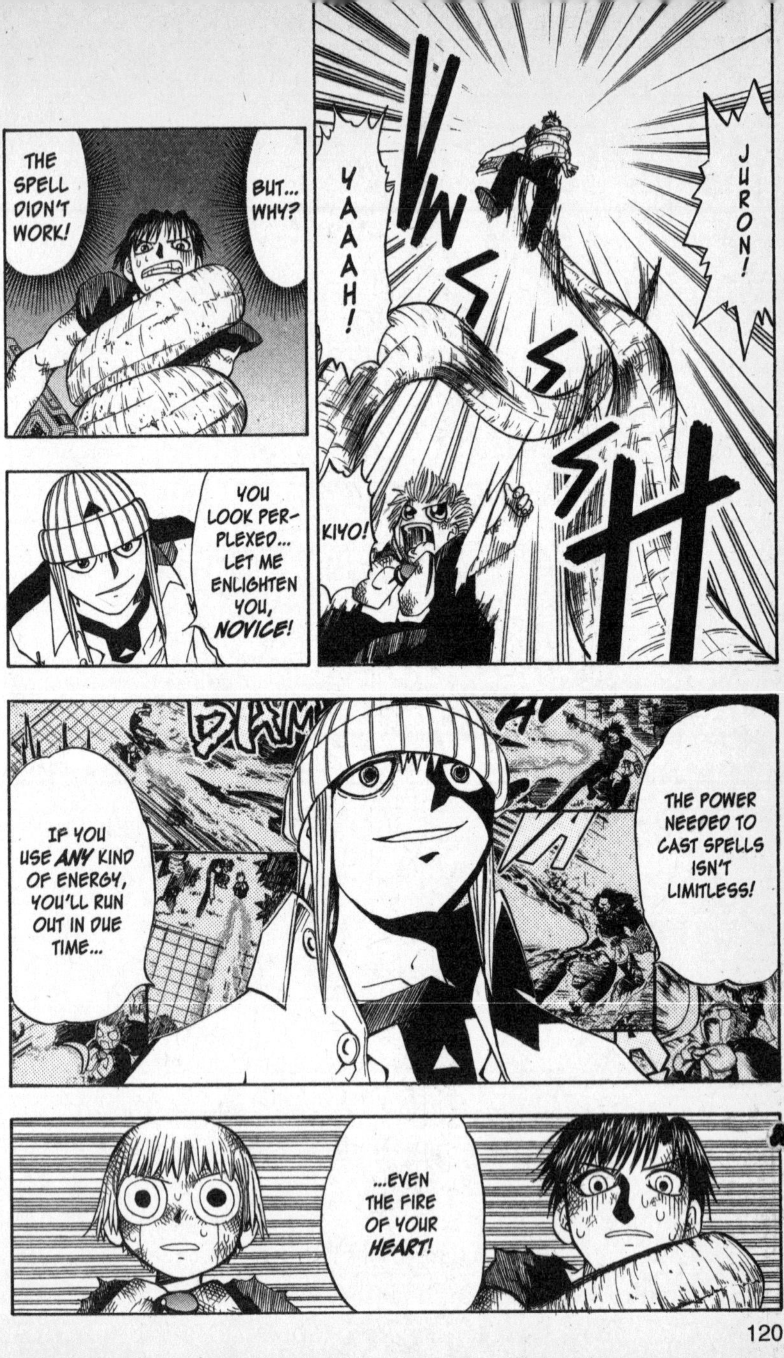
JURON!
YAAAAH!
VWSSSH
KIYO!
THE SPELL DIDN'T WORK!
BUT... WHY?
YOU LOOK PER-PLEXED... LET ME ENLIGHTEN YOU, NOVICE!
THE POWER NEEDED TO CAST SPELLS ISN'T LIMITLESS!
IF YOU USE ANY KIND OF ENERGY, YOU'LL RUN OUT IN DUE TIME...
...EVEN THE FIRE OF YOUR HEART!

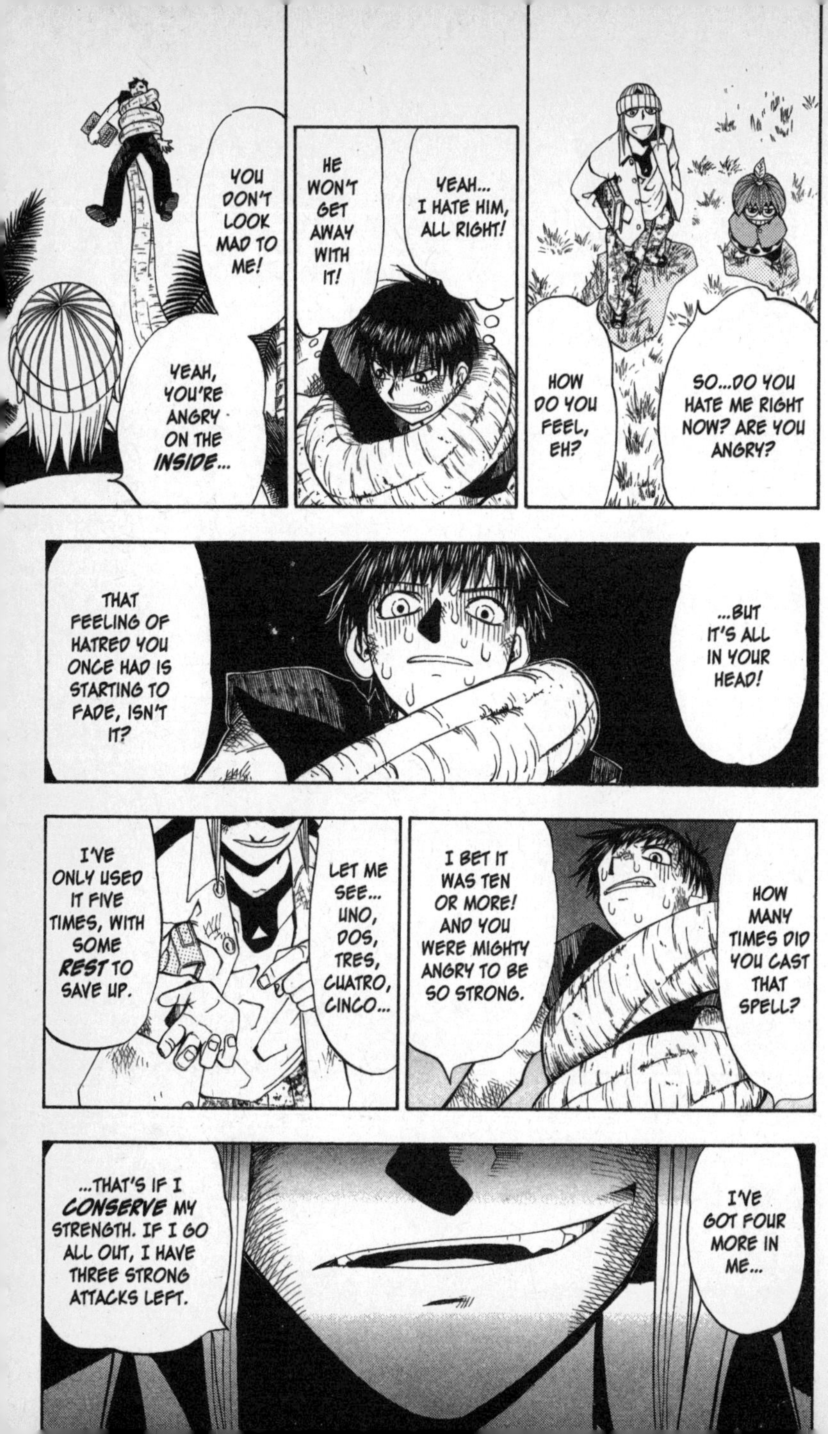
SO...DO YOU HATE ME RIGHT NOW? ARE YOU ANGRY?
HOW DO YOU FEEL, EH?
YEAH... I HATE HIM, ALL RIGHT!
HE WON'T GET AWAY WITH IT!
YOU DON'T LOOK MAD TO ME!
YEAH, YOU'RE ANGRY ON THE *INSIDE*...
...BUT IT'S ALL IN YOUR HEAD!
THAT FEELING OF HATRED YOU ONCE HAD IS STARTING TO FADE, ISN'T IT?
HOW MANY TIMES DID YOU CAST THAT SPELL?
I BET IT WAS TEN OR MORE! AND YOU WERE MIGHTY ANGRY TO BE SO STRONG.
LET ME SEE... UNO, DOS, TRES, CUATRO, CINCO...
I'VE ONLY USED IT FIVE TIMES, WITH SOME *REST* TO SAVE UP.
I'VE GOT FOUR MORE IN ME...
...THAT'S IF I *CONSERVE* MY STRENGTH. IF I GO ALL OUT, I HAVE THREE STRONG ATTACKS LEFT.

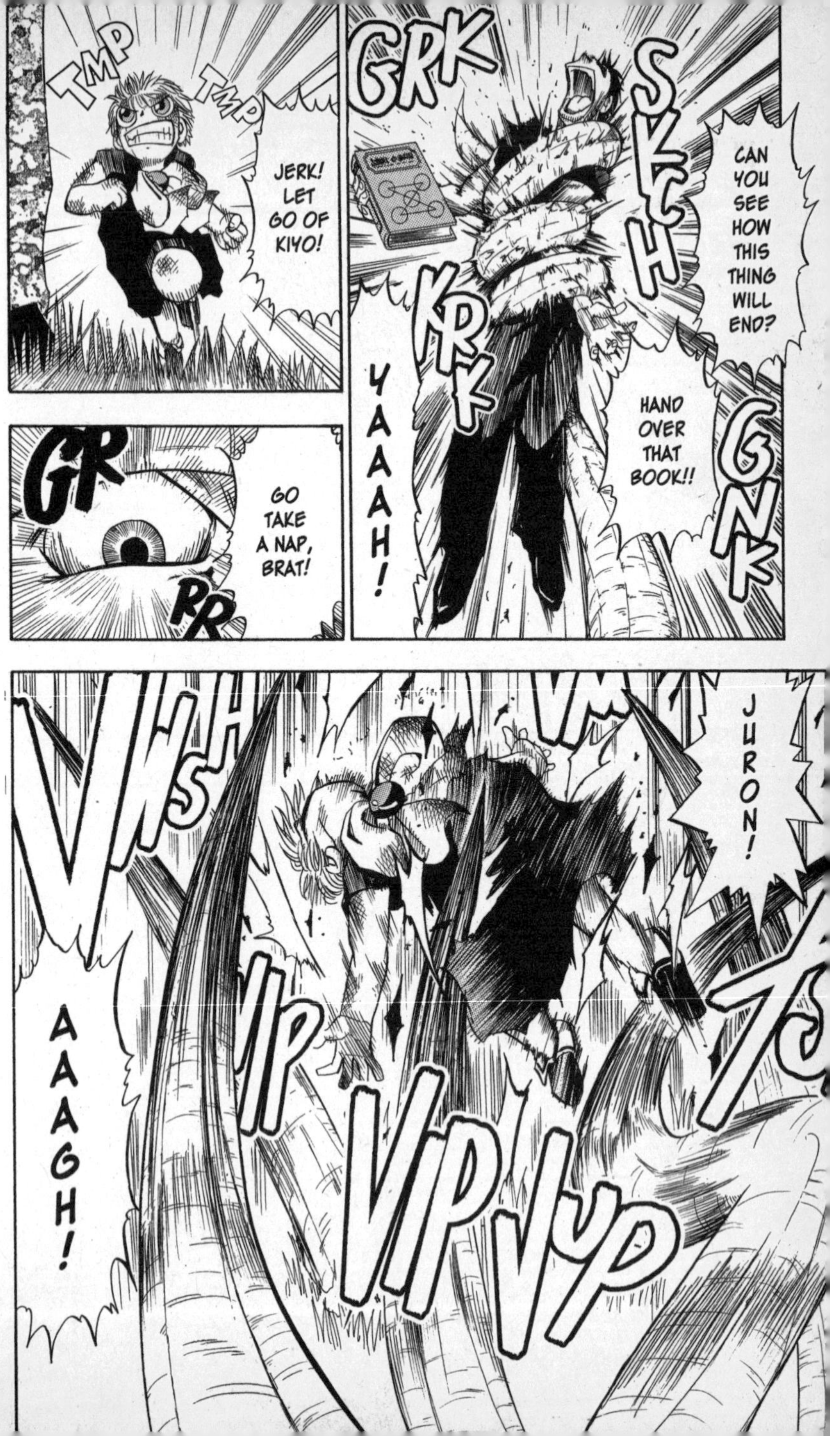
GRK
SKCH
CAN YOU SEE HOW THIS THING WILL END?
KRK
YAAAAH!
HAND OVER THAT BOOK!!
GNK
TMP
TMP
JERK! LET GO OF KIYO!
GR
GO TAKE A NAP, BRAT!
RR
JURON!
VIP
VIP
VYP
AAAGH!

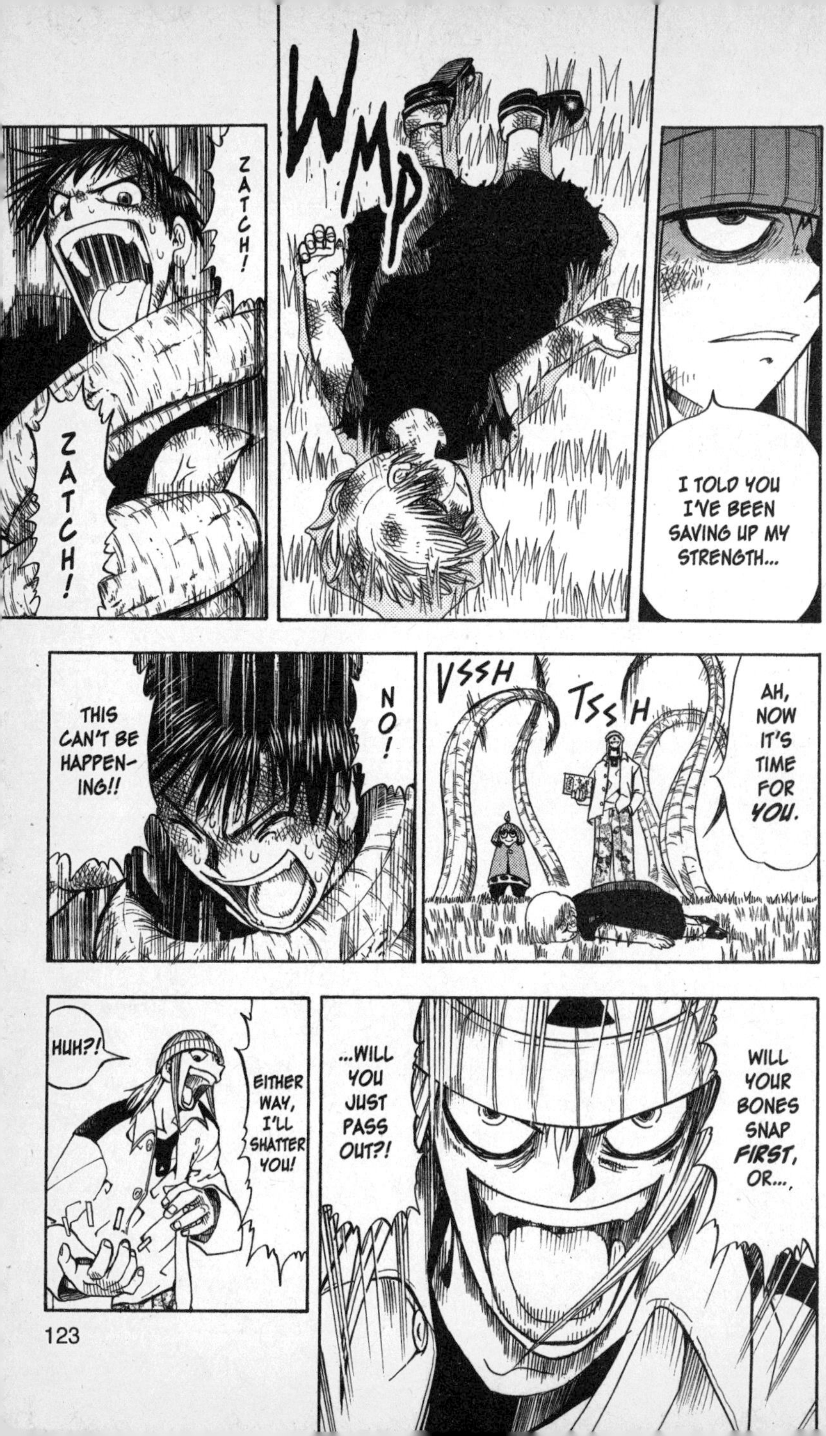
I TOLD YOU I'VE BEEN SAVING UP MY STRENGTH...
WMP
ZATCH!
ZATCH!
VSSH
TSSH
AH, NOW IT'S TIME FOR YOU.
NO!
THIS CAN'T BE HAPPENING!!
WILL YOUR BONES SNAP FIRST, OR...,
...WILL YOU JUST PASS OUT?!
EITHER WAY, I'LL SHATTER YOU!
HUH?!

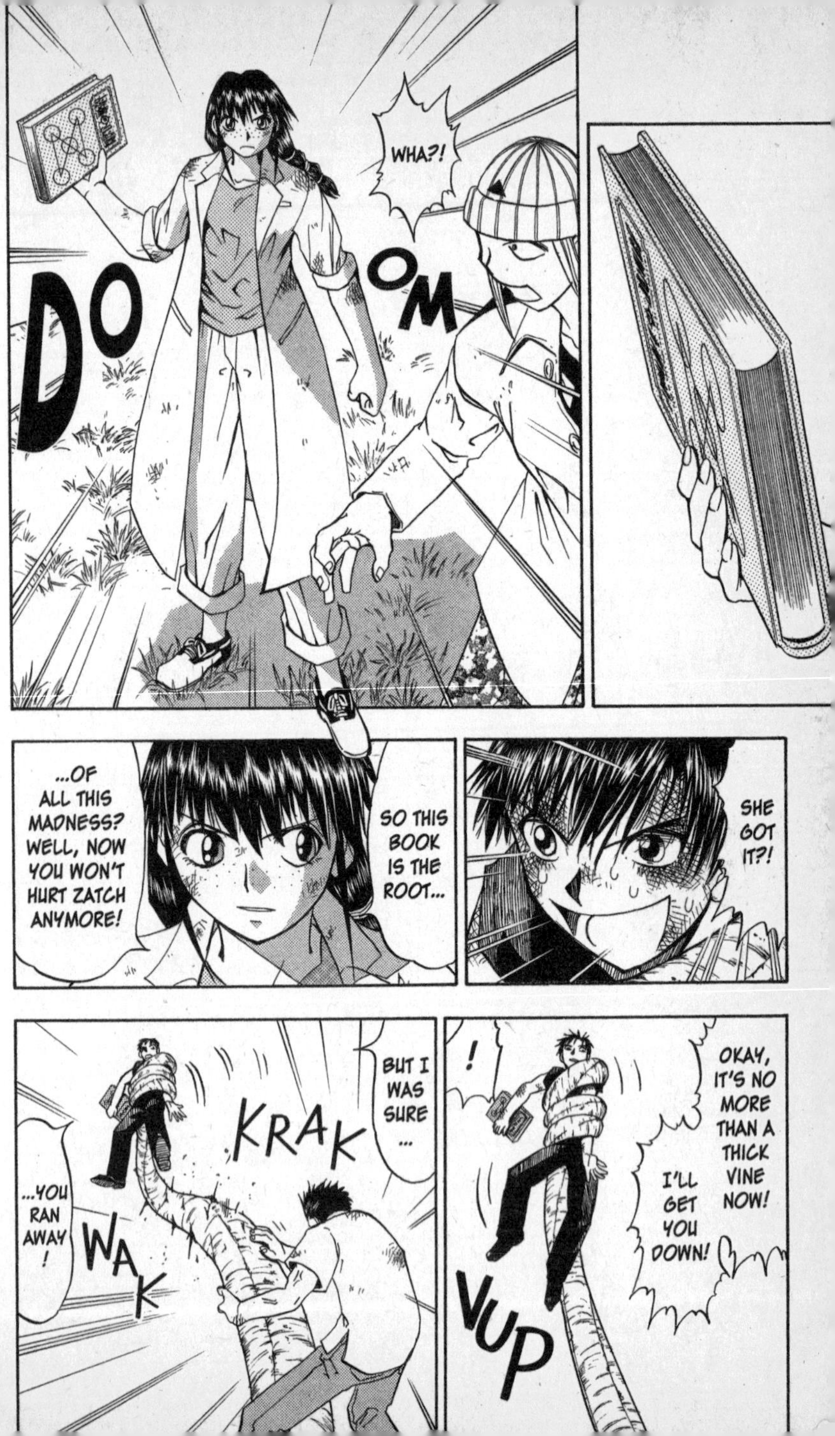
WHA?!
DOOM
SHE GOT IT?!
SO THIS BOOK IS THE ROOT...
...OF ALL THIS MADNESS? WELL, NOW YOU WON'T HURT ZATCH ANYMORE!
!
OKAY, IT'S NO MORE THAN A THICK VINE NOW!
I'LL GET YOU DOWN!
VUP
BUT I WAS SURE...
KRAK
...YOU RAN AWAY!
WAK

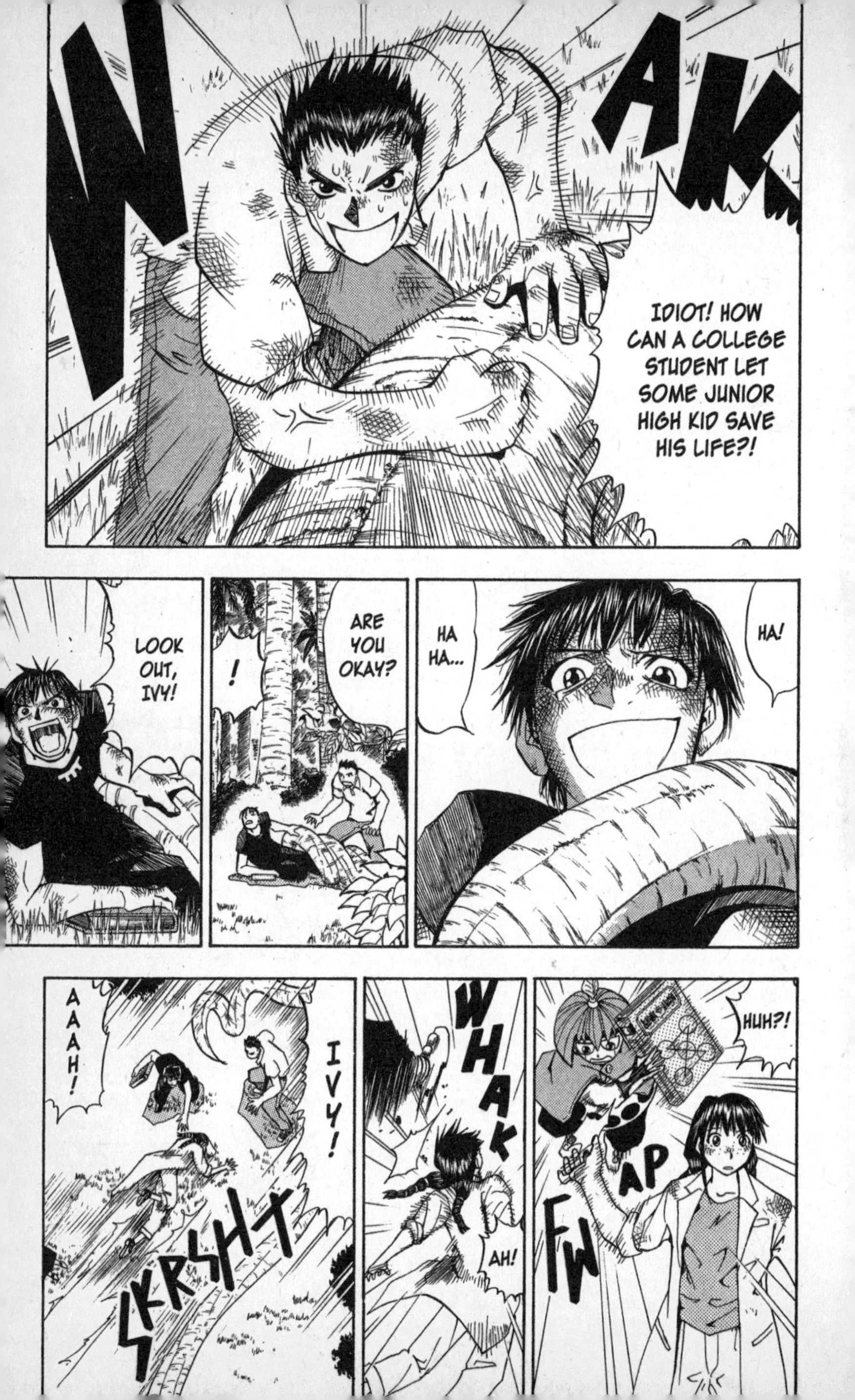
W
AK
IDIOT! HOW CAN A COLLEGE STUDENT LET SOME JUNIOR HIGH KID SAVE HIS LIFE?!
HA!
HA HA...
ARE YOU OKAY?
!
LOOK OUT, IVY!
HUH?!
FWAP
WHAK
AH!
IVY!
AAAAH!
SKRSHT

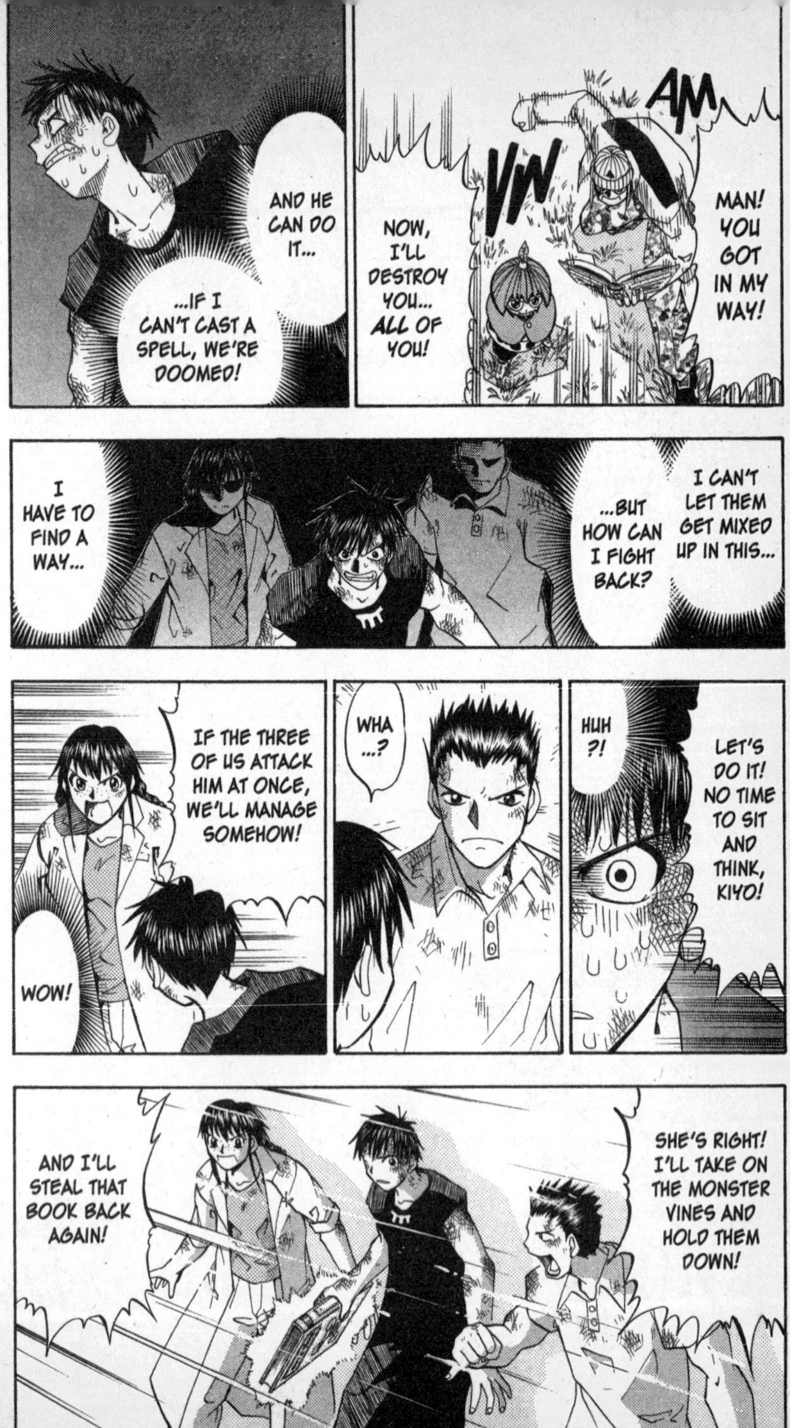
AM
VW
MAN! YOU GOT IN MY WAY!
NOW, I'LL DESTROY YOU... ALL OF YOU!
AND HE CAN DO IT...
...IF I CAN'T CAST A SPELL, WE'RE DOOMED!
I CAN'T LET THEM GET MIXED UP IN THIS...
...BUT HOW CAN I FIGHT BACK?
I HAVE TO FIND A WAY...
LET'S DO IT! NO TIME TO SIT AND THINK, KIYO!
HUH ?!
WHA ...?
IF THE THREE OF US ATTACK HIM AT ONCE, WE'LL MANAGE SOMEHOW!
WOW!
SHE'S RIGHT! I'LL TAKE ON THE MONSTER VINES AND HOLD THEM DOWN!
AND I'LL STEAL THAT BOOK BACK AGAIN!

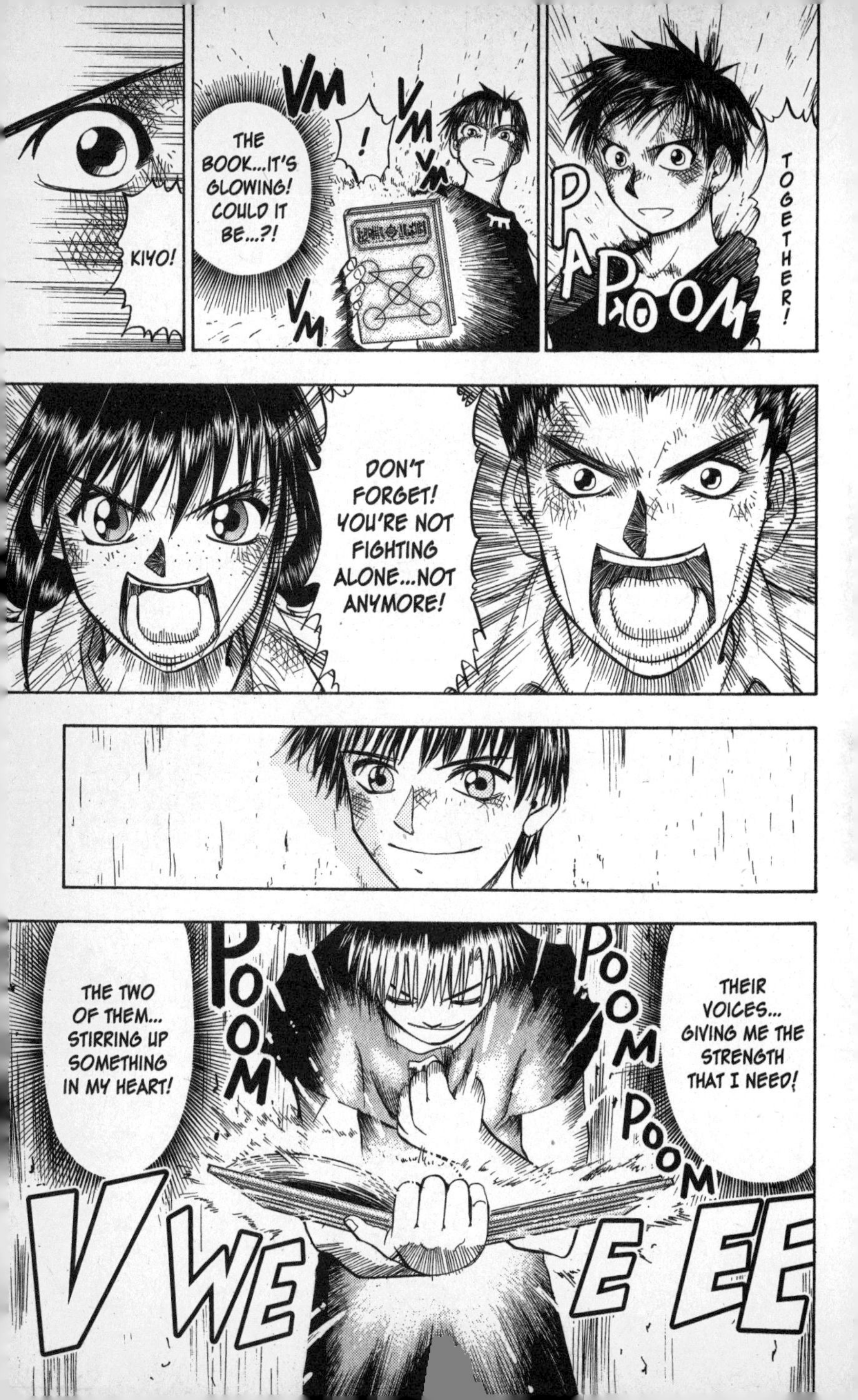
TOGETHER!
PAPOOM
VM
VM
VM
THE BOOK...IT'S GLOWING! COULD IT BE...?!
!
VM
KIYO!
DON'T FORGET! YOU'RE NOT FIGHTING ALONE...NOT ANYMORE!
THEIR VOICES... GIVING ME THE STRENGTH THAT I NEED!
POOM
POOM
THE TWO OF THEM... STIRRING UP SOMETHING IN MY HEART!
POOM
VWEEEE

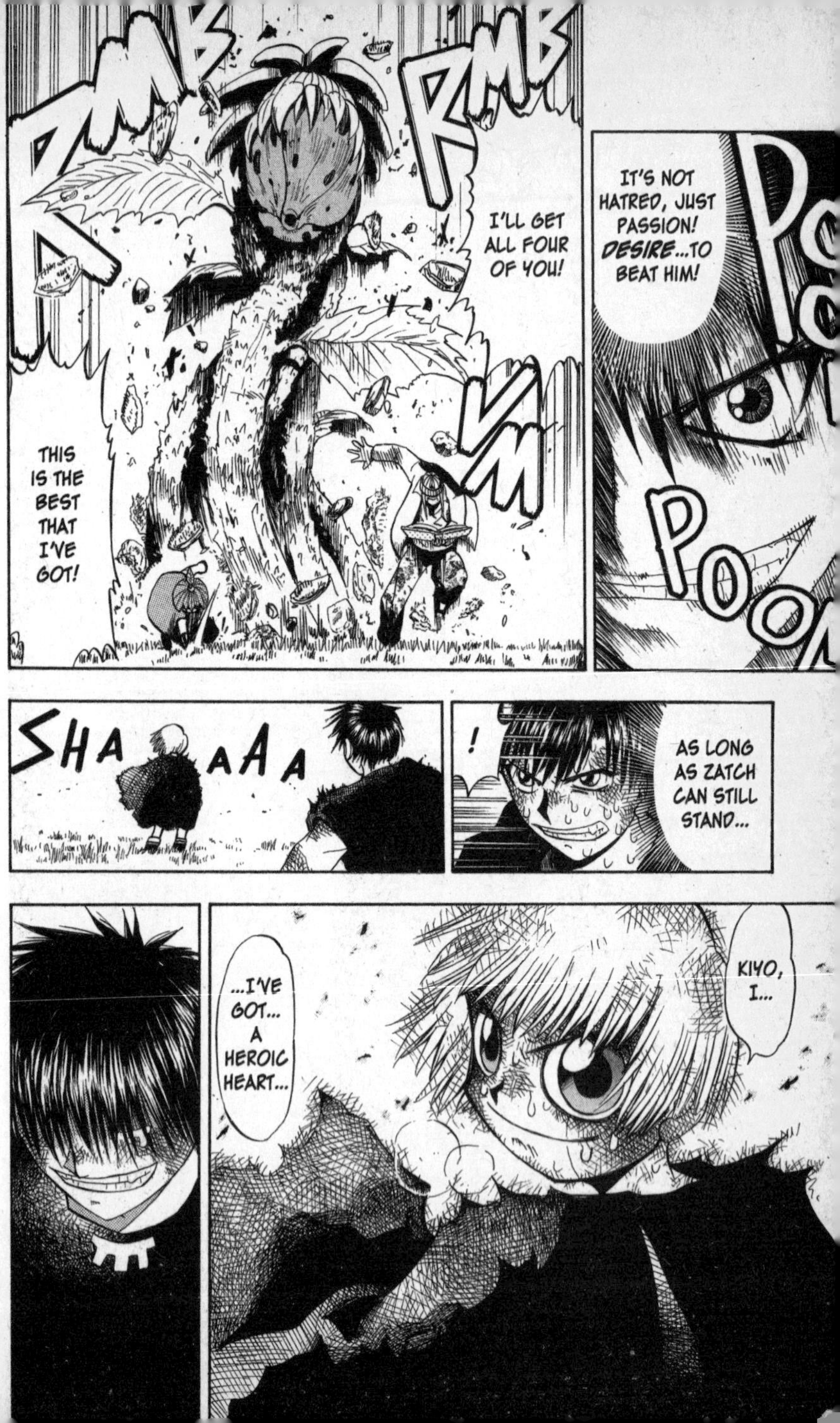
IT'S NOT HATRED, JUST PASSION! DESIRE...TO BEAT HIM!
POO
POOO
RMB
I'LL GET ALL FOUR OF YOU!
RMB
VM
THIS IS THE BEST THAT I'VE GOT!
!
AS LONG AS ZATCH CAN STILL STAND...
SHAAAAA
KIYO, I...
...I'VE GOT... A HEROIC HEART...

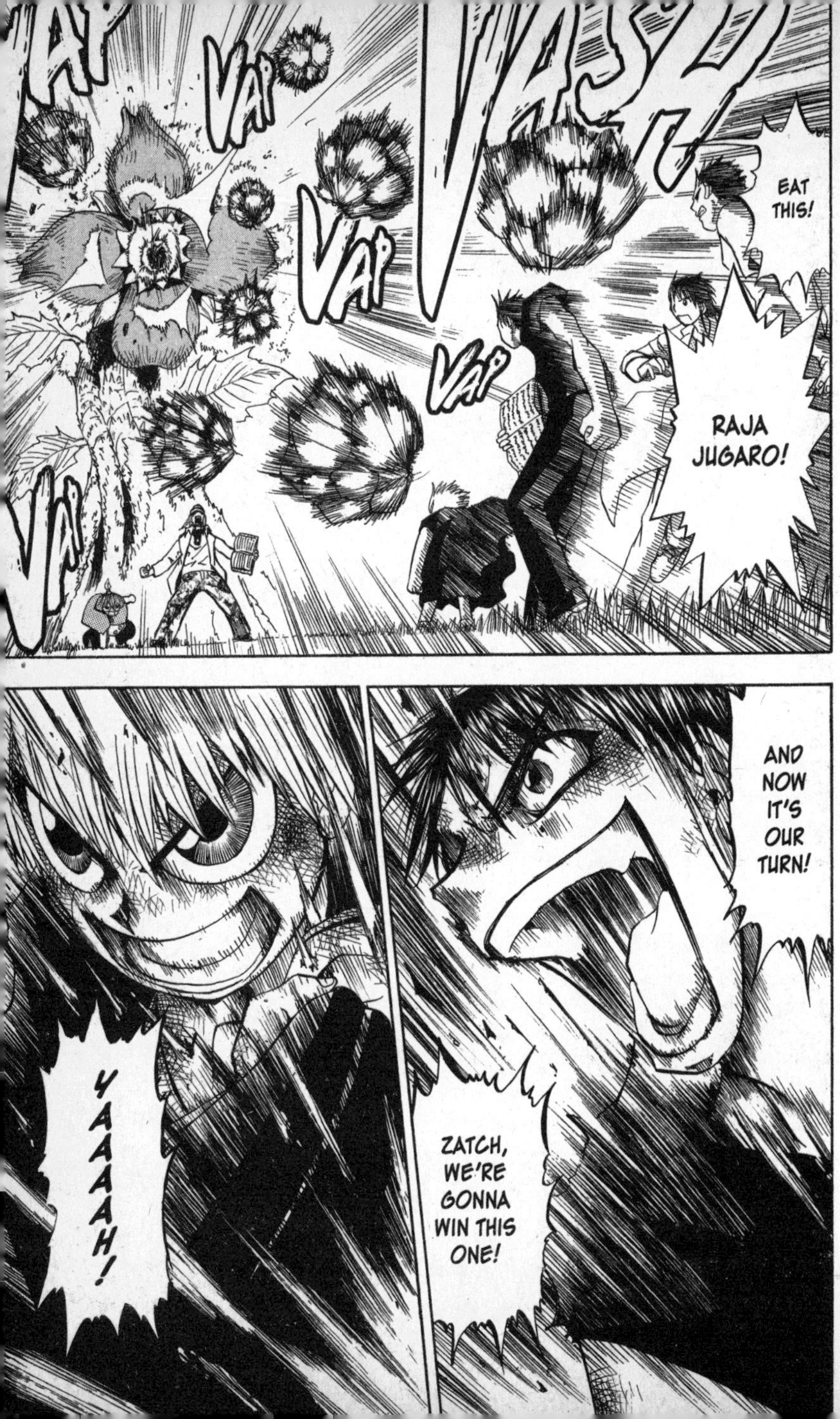
EAT THIS!
RAJA JUGARO!
VAP
VAP
VAP
VAP
VAP
AND NOW IT'S OUR TURN!
ZATCH, WE'RE GONNA WIN THIS ONE!
YAAAAAH!

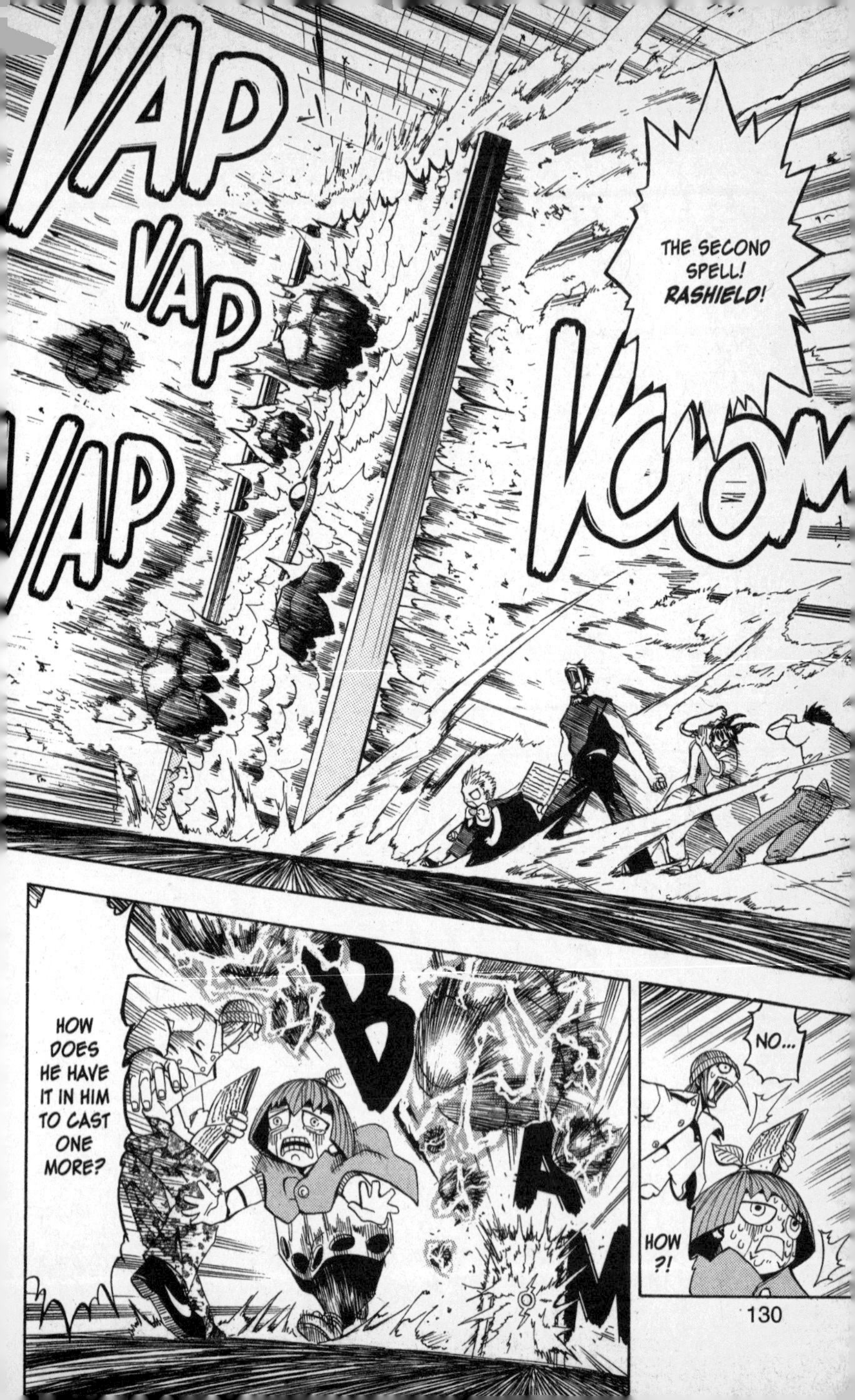
THE SECOND SPELL! RASHIELD!
VOOM
VAP
VAP
VAP
NO...
HOW ?!
BAM
HOW DOES HE HAVE IT IN HIM TO CAST ONE MORE?

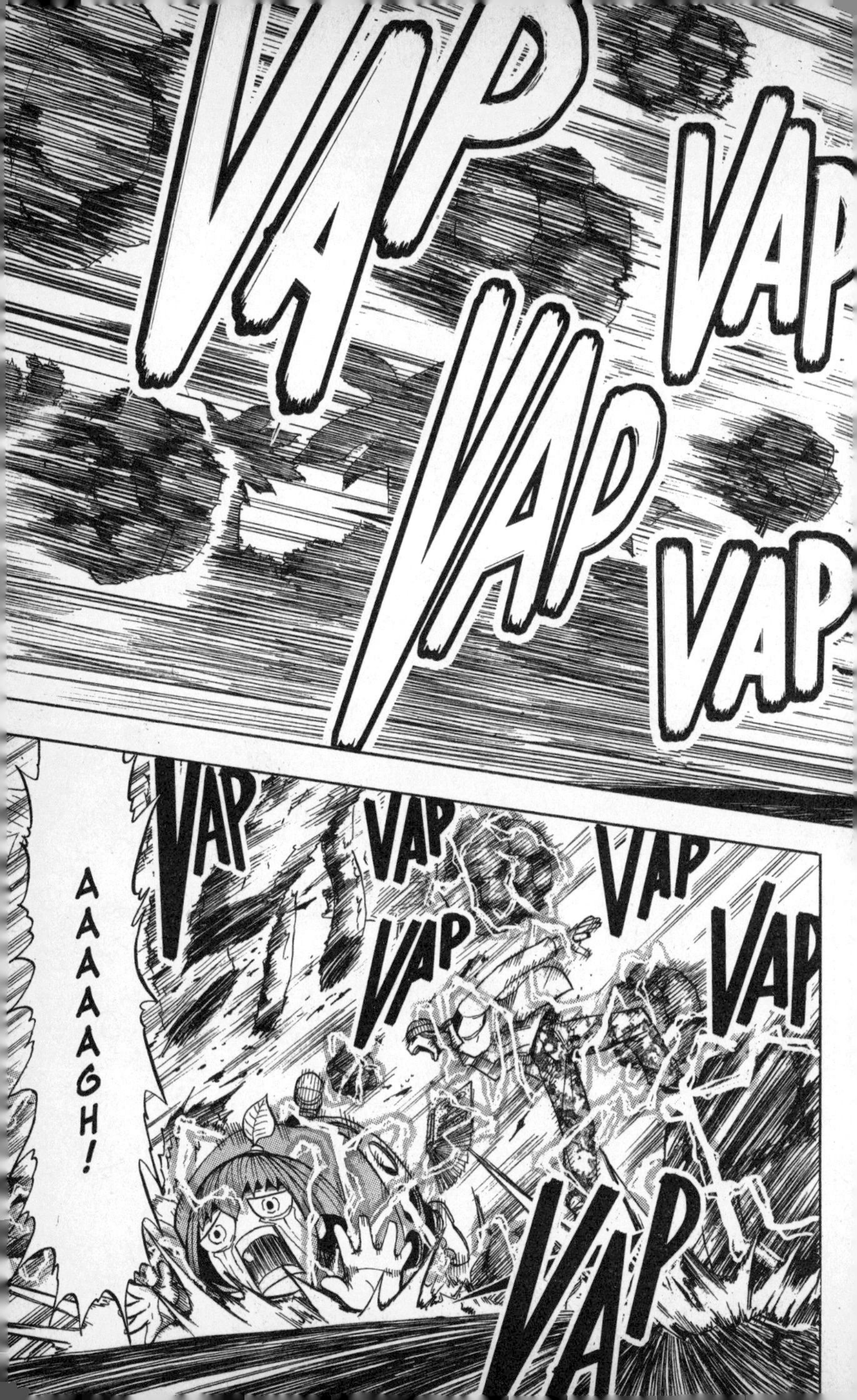
VAP
VAP
VAP
VAP
VAP
VAP
VAP
VAP
VAP
AAAAAGH!
VAP

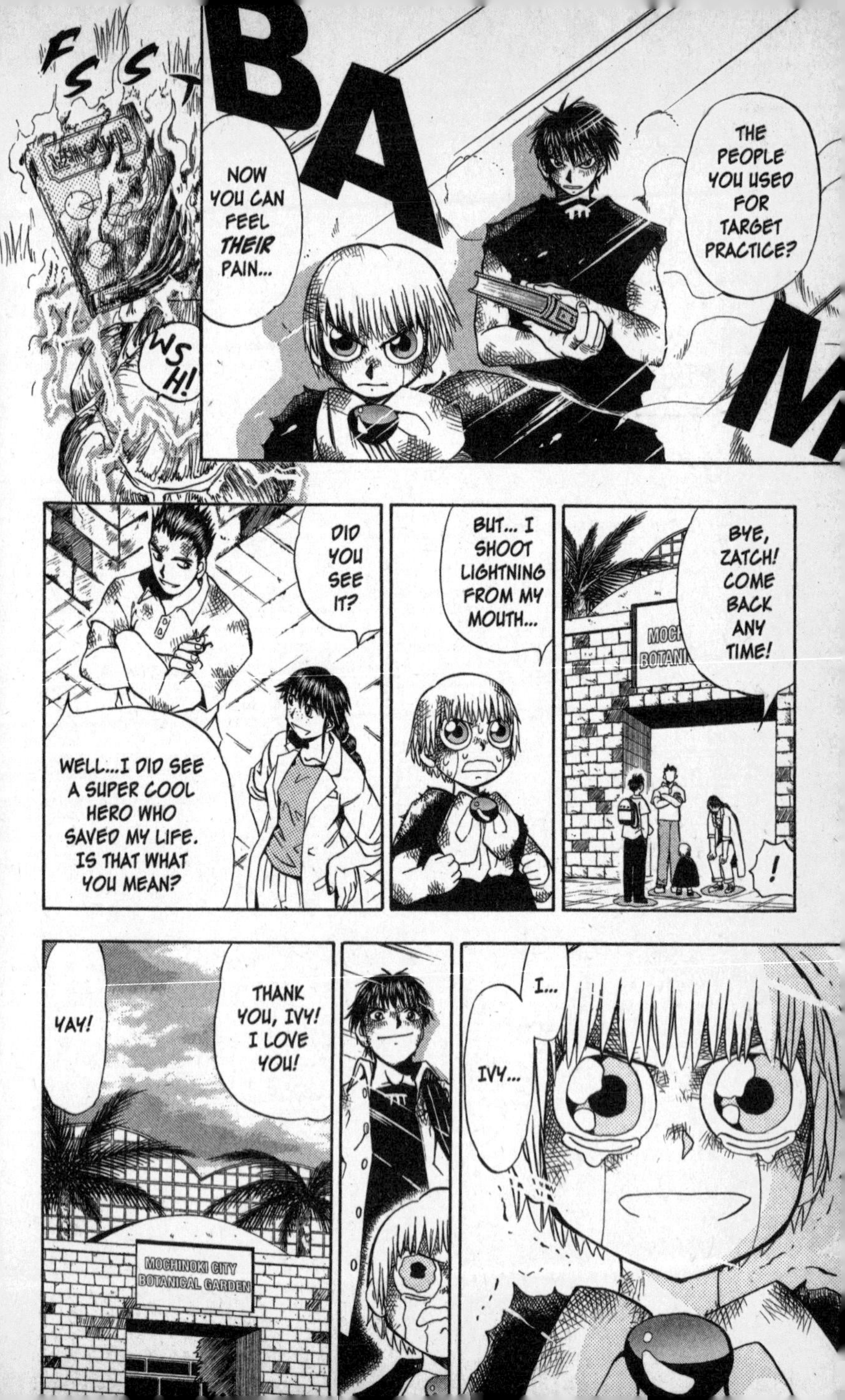

THE PEOPLE YOU USED FOR TARGET PRACTICE?
NOW YOU CAN FEEL *THEIR* PAIN...
BAM
FSST
WSH!
BYE, ZATCH! COME BACK ANY TIME!
!
BUT... I SHOOT LIGHTNING FROM MY MOUTH...
DID YOU SEE IT?
WELL...I DID SEE A SUPER COOL HERO WHO SAVED MY LIFE. IS THAT WHAT YOU MEAN?
I...
IVY...
THANK YOU, IVY! I LOVE YOU!
YAY!
MOCHINOKI CITY BOTANICAL GARDEN

LEVEL 16: A Real Family

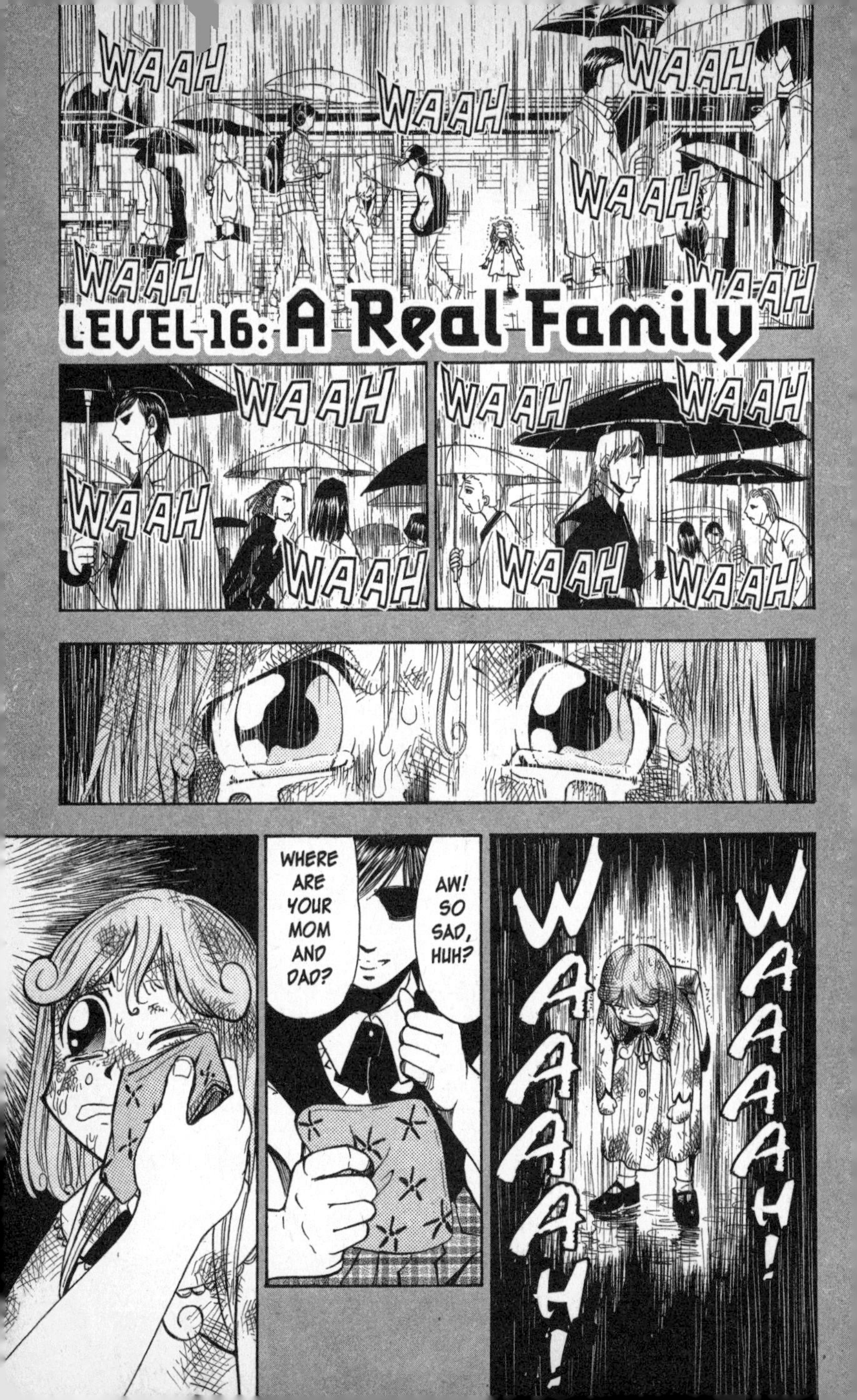
WAAH
WAAH
WAAH
WAAH
WAAH
WAAH
WAAH
WAAH
WAAH
WAAH
WAAH
WAAH
WAAH
WAAAAAH!
WAAAAAH!
AW! SO SAD, HUH?
WHERE ARE YOUR MOM AND DAD?

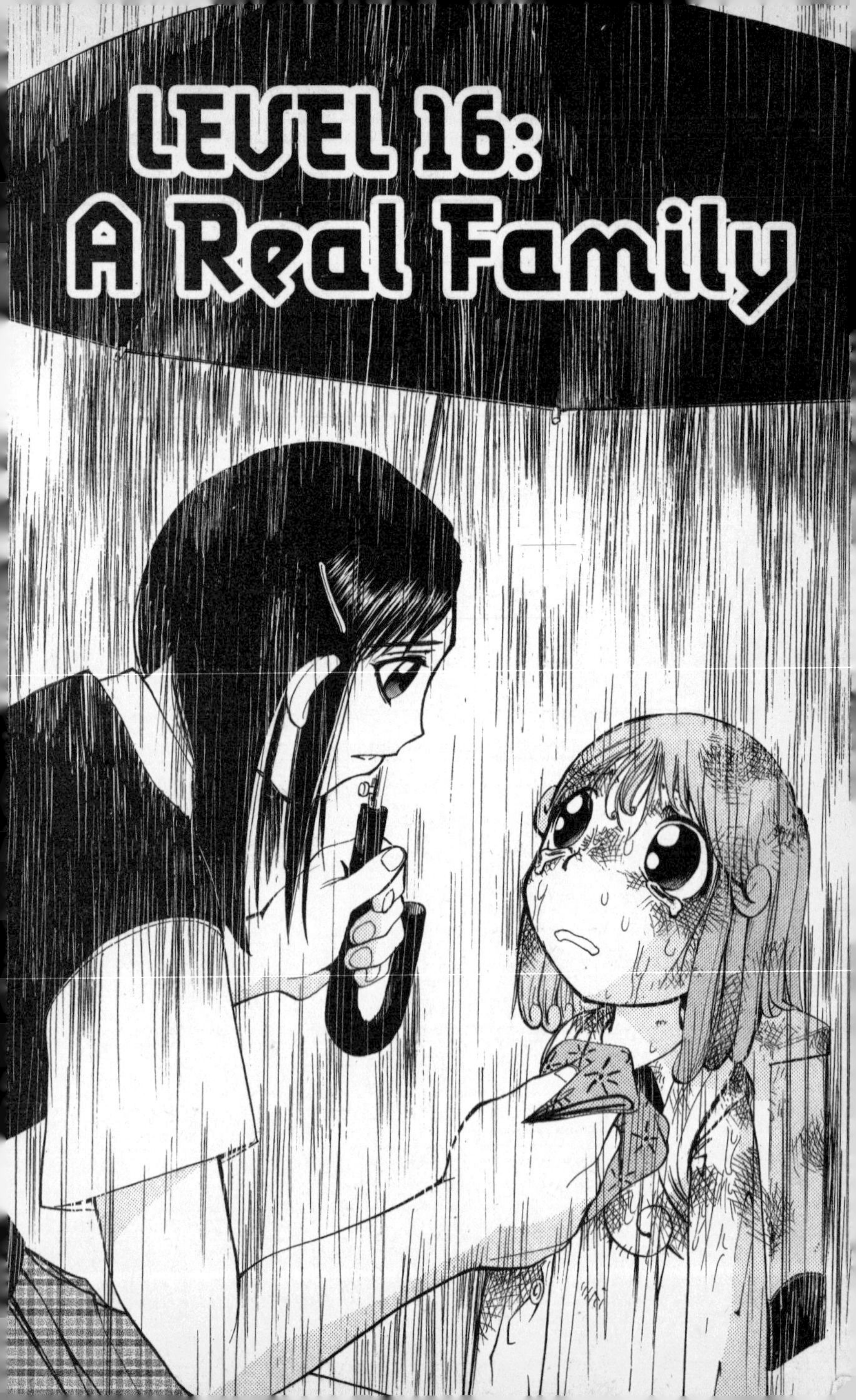
LEVEL 16:
A Real Family

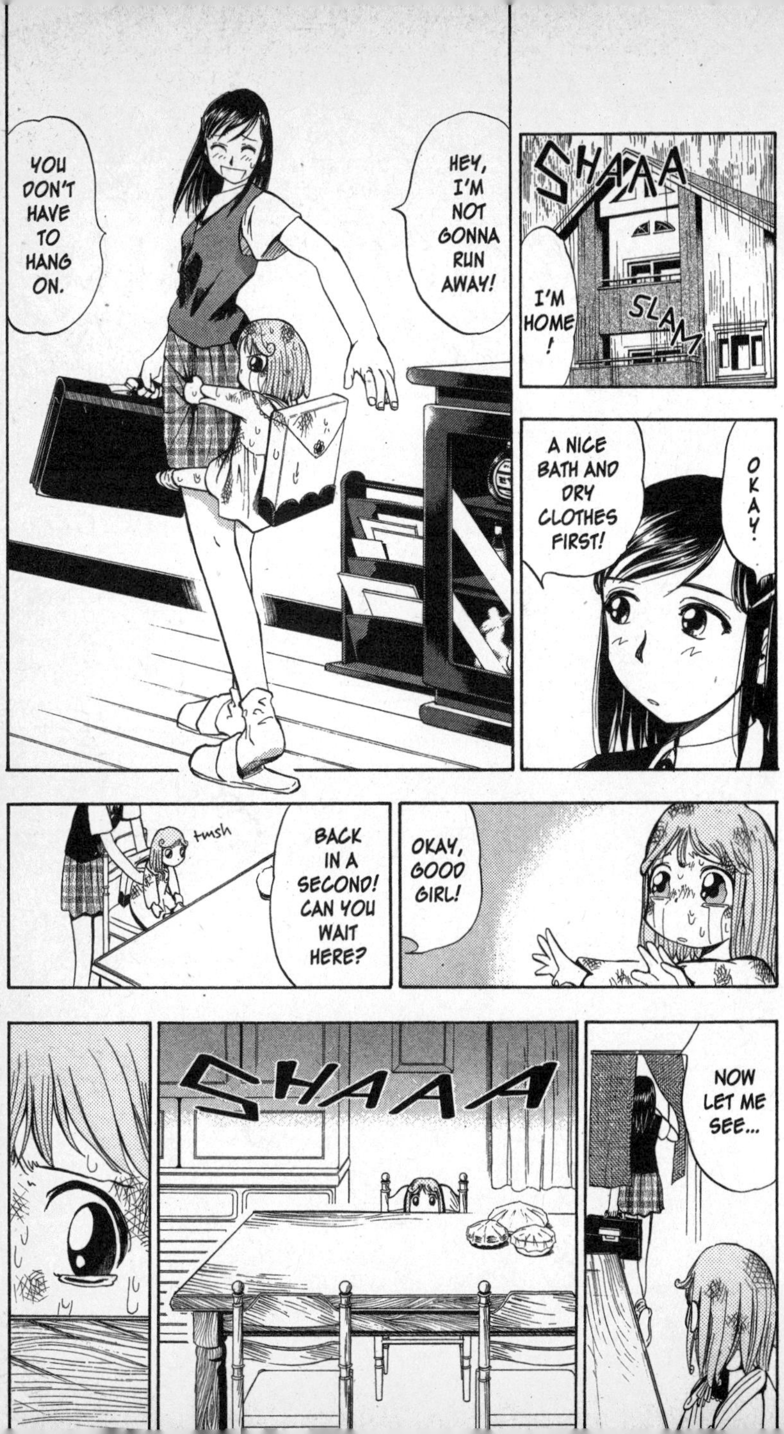
SHAAA
I'M HOME!
SLAM
OKAY.
A NICE BATH AND DRY CLOTHES FIRST!
HEY, I'M NOT GONNA RUN AWAY!
YOU DON'T HAVE TO HANG ON.
OKAY, GOOD GIRL!
BACK IN A SECOND! CAN YOU WAIT HERE?
tmsh
NOW LET ME SEE...
SHAAA

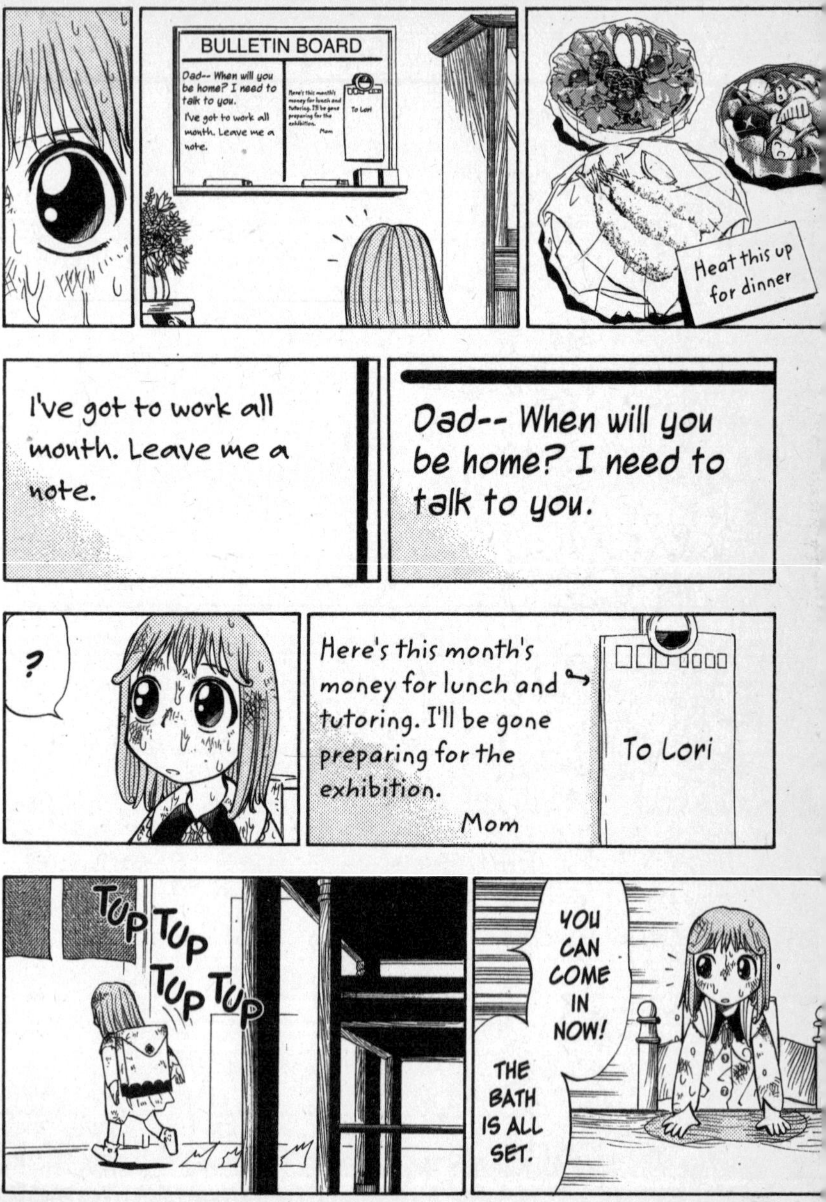
Heat this up for dinner
BULLETIN BOARD
Dad-- When will you be home? I need to talk to you.
I've got to work all month. Leave me a note.
To Lori
Dad-- When will you be home? I need to talk to you.
I've got to work all month. Leave me a note.
To Lori
Here's this month's money for lunch and tutoring. I'll be gone preparing for the exhibition.
Mom
?
YOU CAN COME IN NOW!
THE BATH IS ALL SET.
TUP TUP TUP TUP

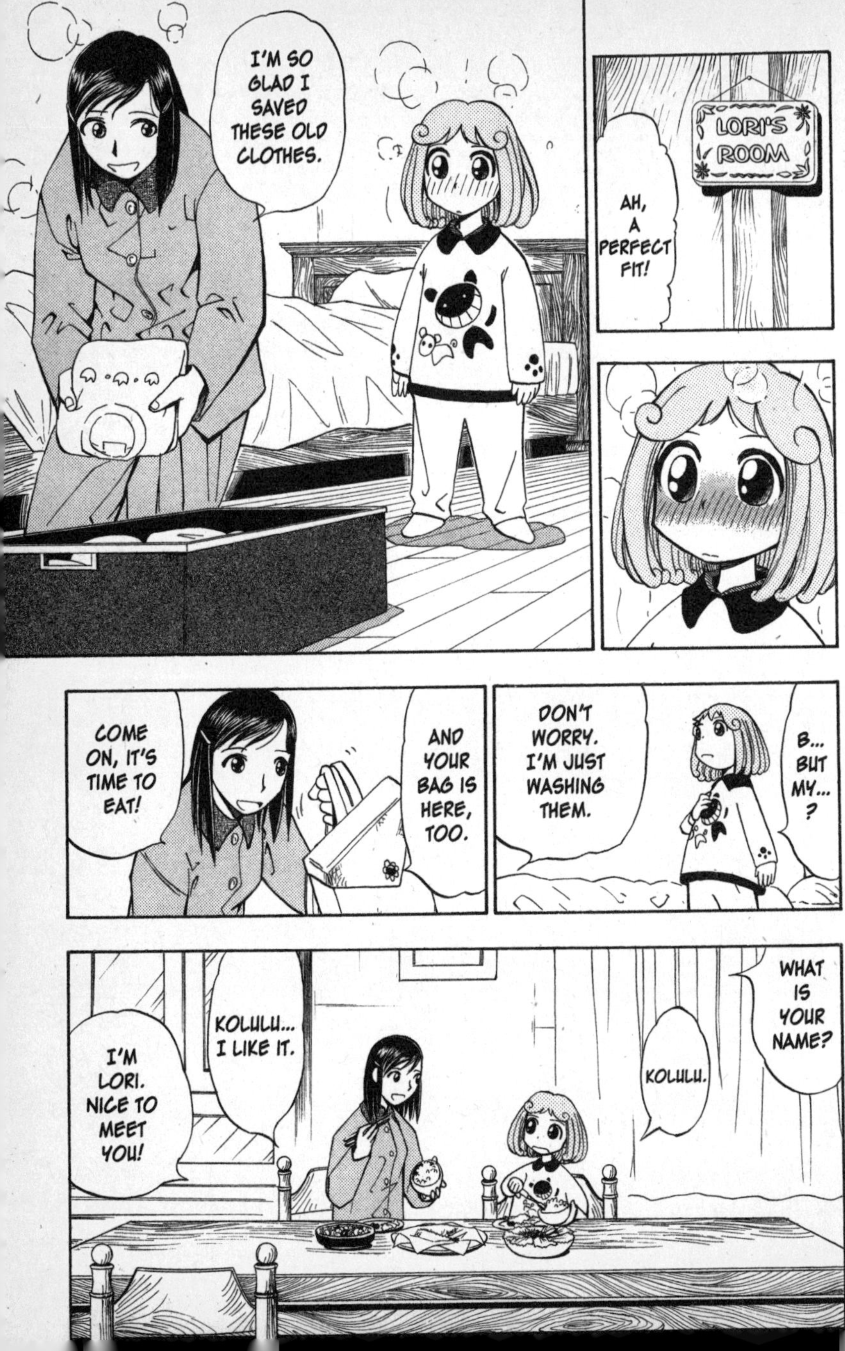
LORI'S ROOM
AH, A PERFECT FIT!
I'M SO GLAD I SAVED THESE OLD CLOTHES.
B... BUT MY...?
DON'T WORRY. I'M JUST WASHING THEM.
AND YOUR BAG IS HERE, TOO.
COME ON, IT'S TIME TO EAT!
WHAT IS YOUR NAME?
KOLULU.
KOLULU... I LIKE IT.
I'M LORI. NICE TO MEET YOU!

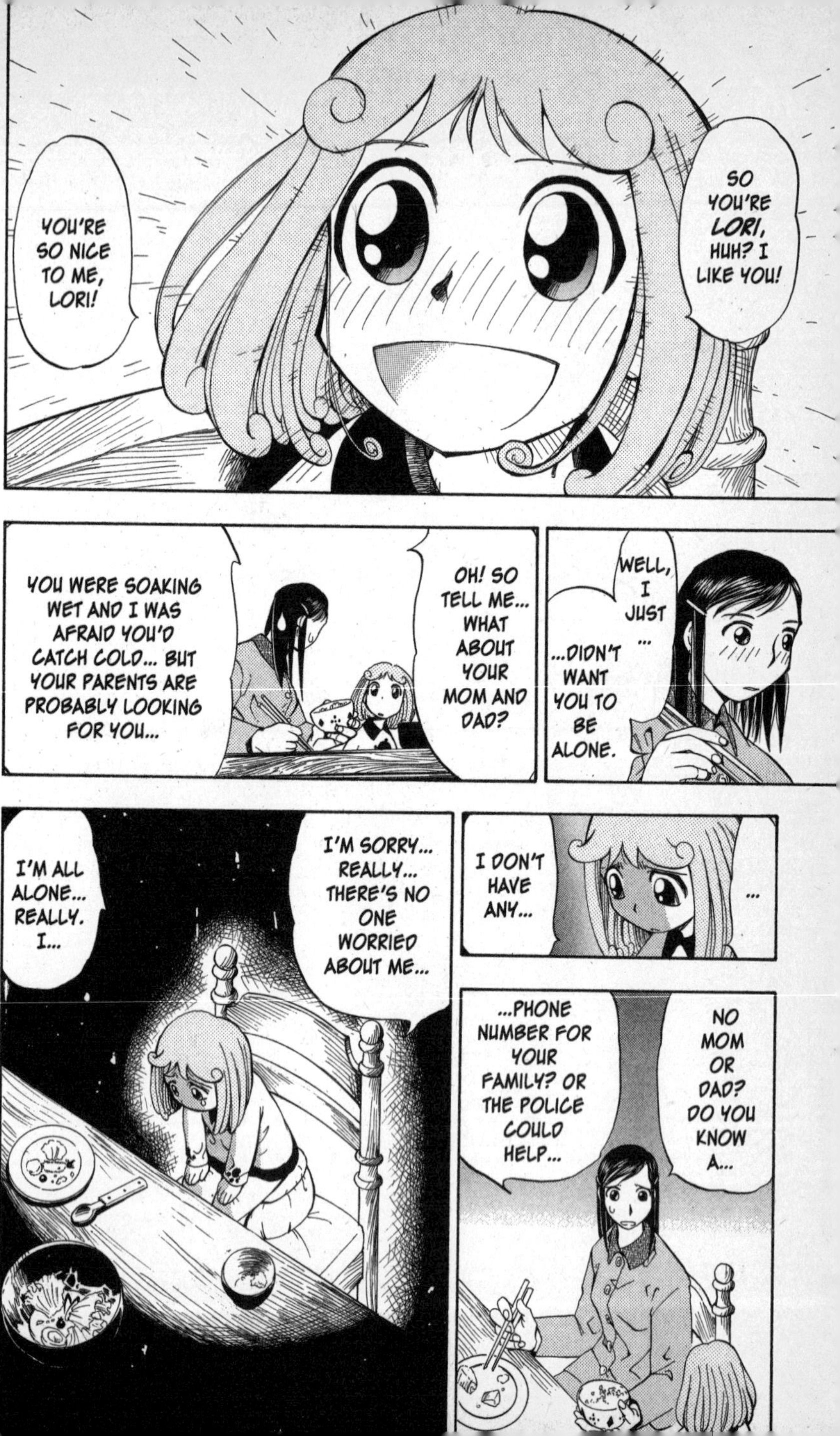
SO YOU'RE LORI, HUH? I LIKE YOU!
YOU'RE SO NICE TO ME, LORI!
WELL, I JUST ...
...DIDN'T WANT YOU TO BE ALONE.
OH! SO TELL ME... WHAT ABOUT YOUR MOM AND DAD?
YOU WERE SOAKING WET AND I WAS AFRAID YOU'D CATCH COLD... BUT YOUR PARENTS ARE PROBABLY LOOKING FOR YOU...
...
I DON'T HAVE ANY...
NO MOM OR DAD? DO YOU KNOW A...
...PHONE NUMBER FOR YOUR FAMILY? OR THE POLICE COULD HELP...
I'M SORRY... REALLY... THERE'S NO ONE WORRIED ABOUT ME...
I'M ALL ALONE... REALLY. I...

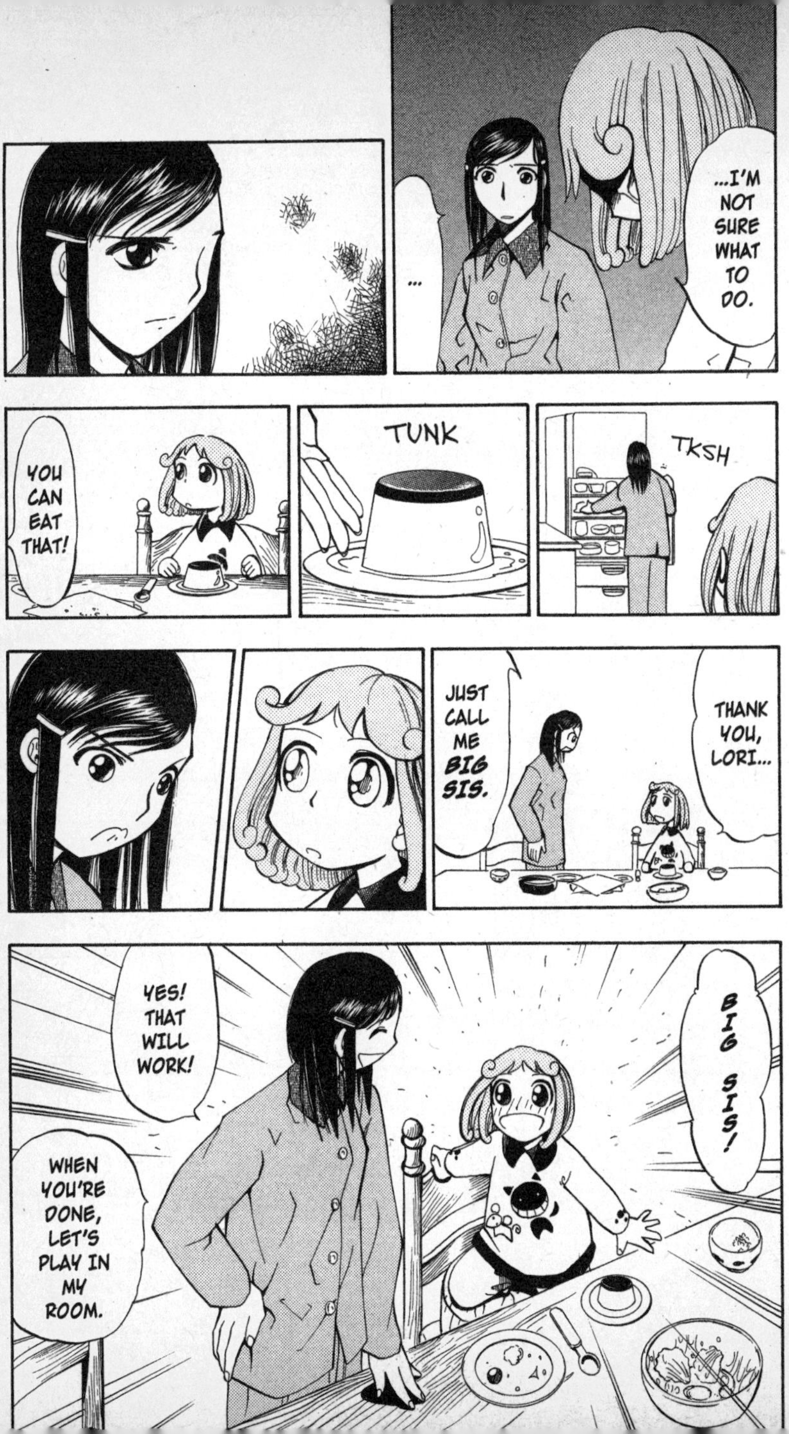
...I'M NOT SURE WHAT TO DO.
...
TKSH
TUNK
YOU CAN EAT THAT!
THANK YOU, LORI...
JUST CALL ME BIG SIS.
BIG SIS!
YES! THAT WILL WORK!
WHEN YOU'RE DONE, LET'S PLAY IN MY ROOM.

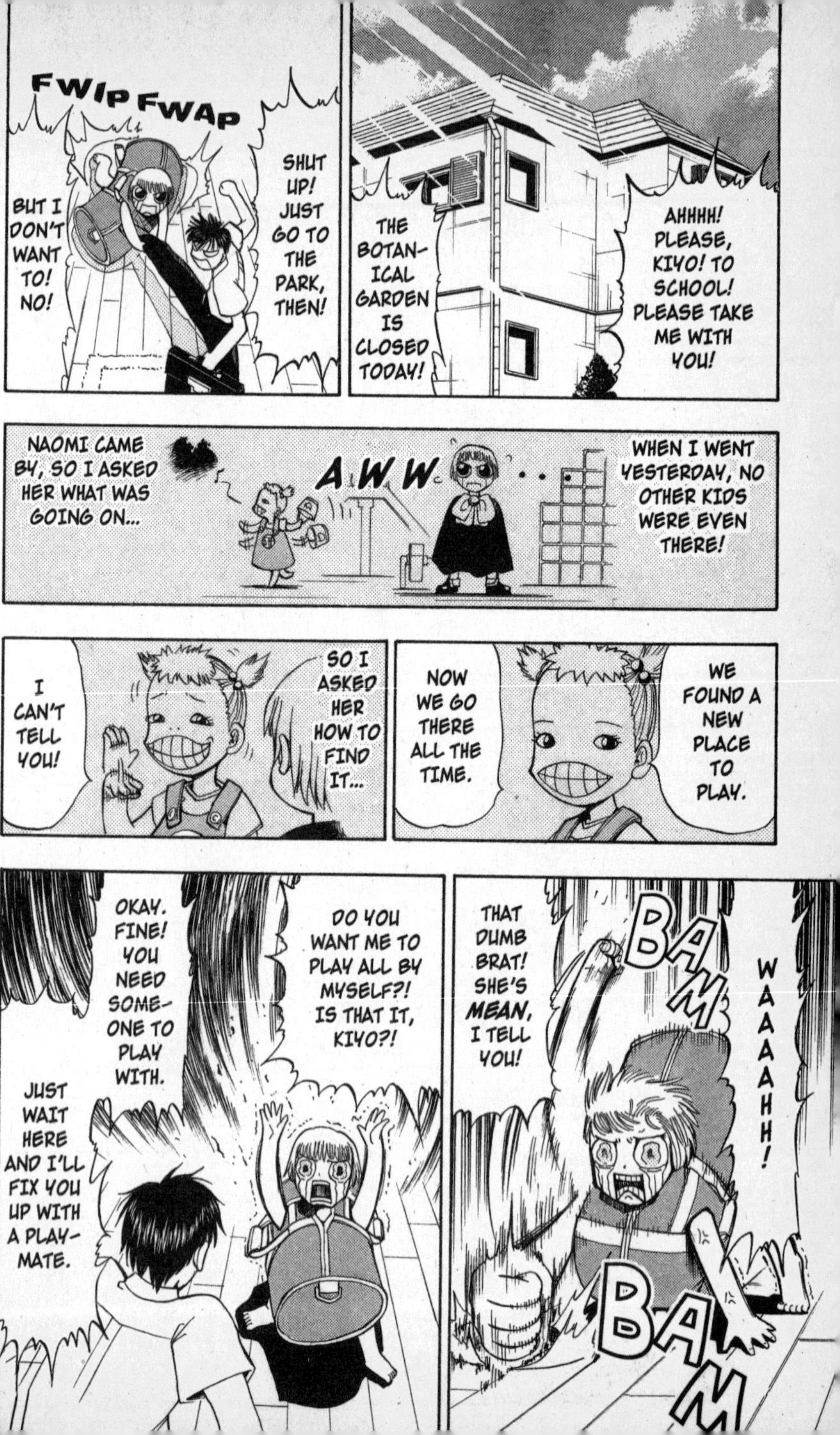
AHHHH! PLEASE, KIYO! TO SCHOOL! PLEASE TAKE ME WITH YOU!
THE BOTANICAL GARDEN IS CLOSED TODAY!
FWIP FWAP
SHUT UP! JUST GO TO THE PARK, THEN!
BUT I DON'T WANT TO! NO!
WHEN I WENT YESTERDAY, NO OTHER KIDS WERE EVEN THERE!
AWW
NAOMI CAME BY, SO I ASKED HER WHAT WAS GOING ON...
WE FOUND A NEW PLACE TO PLAY.
NOW WE GO THERE ALL THE TIME.
SO I ASKED HER HOW TO FIND IT...
I CAN'T TELL YOU!
WAAAAAHH!
BAM
THAT DUMB BRAT! SHE'S *MEAN*, I TELL YOU!
BAM
DO YOU WANT ME TO PLAY ALL BY MYSELF?! IS THAT IT, KIYO?!
OKAY. FINE! YOU NEED SOMEONE TO PLAY WITH.
JUST WAIT HERE AND I'LL FIX YOU UP WITH A PLAYMATE.

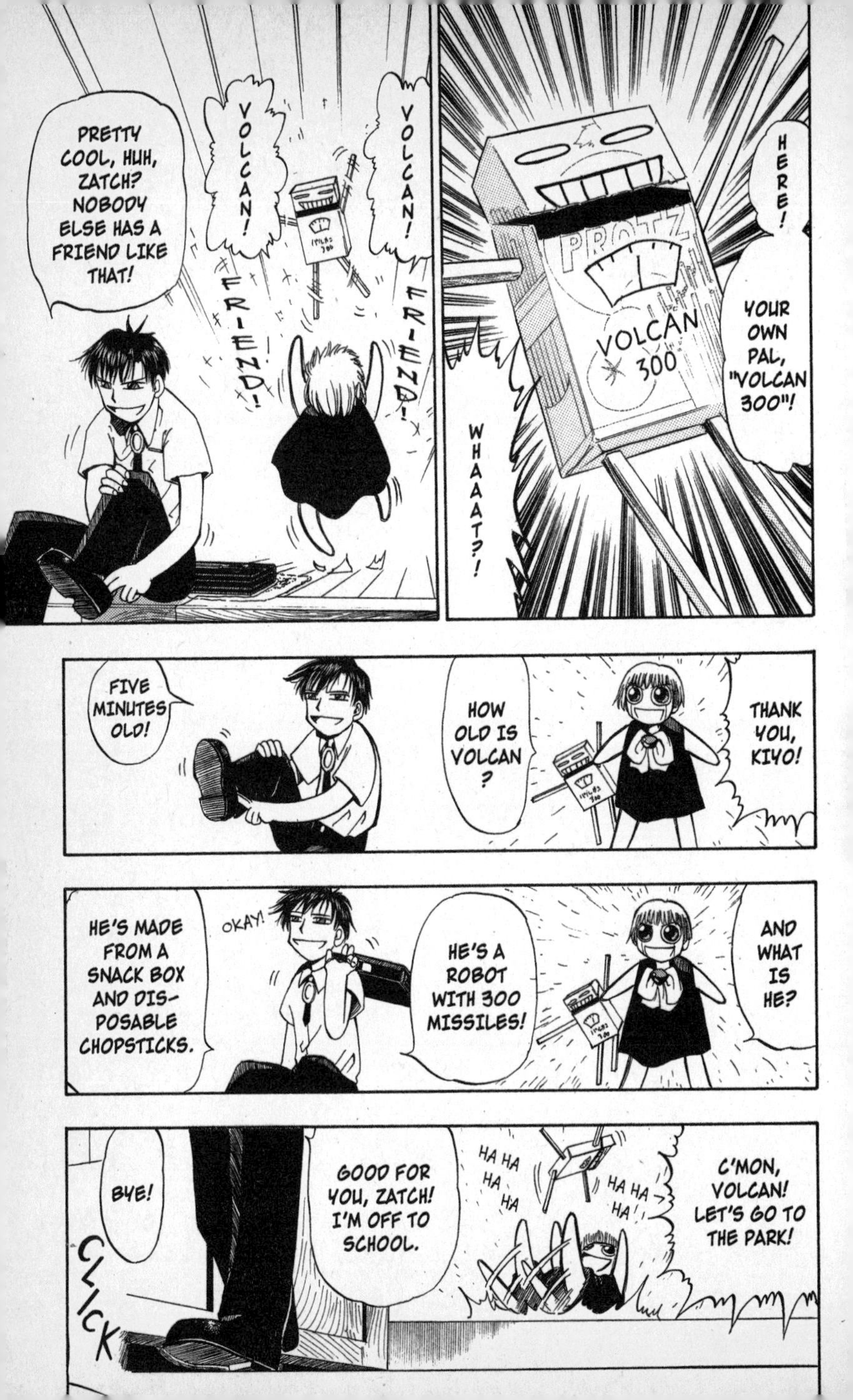
HERE!
YOUR OWN PAL, "VOLCAN 300"!
PROTZ
VOLCAN 300
WHAAAAT?!
VOLCAN!
VOLCAN!
FRIEND!
FRIEND!
PRETTY COOL, HUH, ZATCH? NOBODY ELSE HAS A FRIEND LIKE THAT!
THANK YOU, KIYO!
HOW OLD IS VOLCAN?
FIVE MINUTES OLD!
AND WHAT IS HE?
HE'S A ROBOT WITH 300 MISSILES!
OKAY!
HE'S MADE FROM A SNACK BOX AND DIS-POSABLE CHOPSTICKS.
C'MON, VOLCAN! LET'S GO TO THE PARK!
HA HA HA HA
HA HA HA HA
GOOD FOR YOU, ZATCH! I'M OFF TO SCHOOL.
BYE!
CLICK

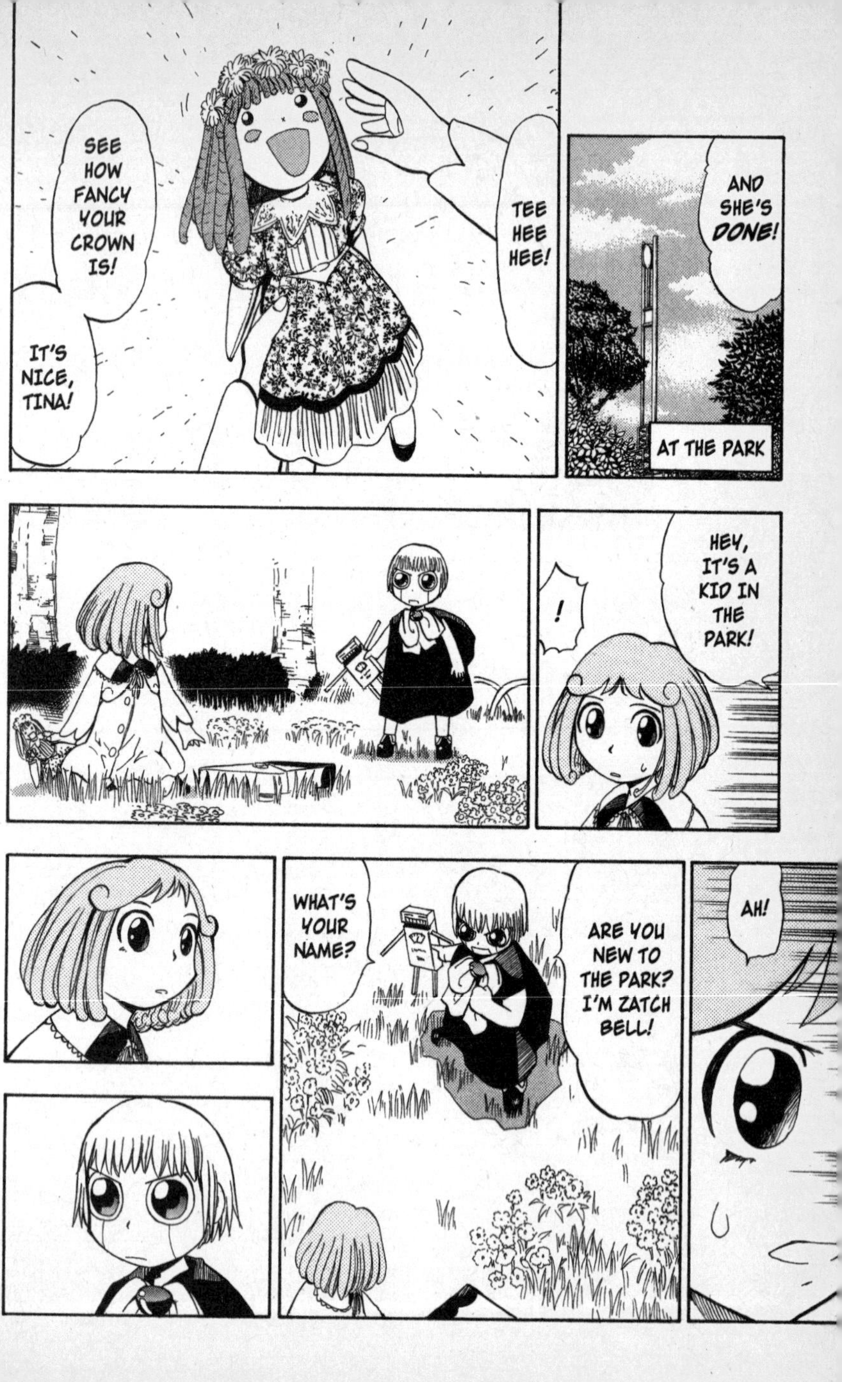
AT THE PARK
AND SHE'S *DONE!*
TEE HEE HEE!
SEE HOW FANCY YOUR CROWN IS!
IT'S NICE, TINA!
HEY, IT'S A KID IN THE PARK!
!
AH!
ARE YOU NEW TO THE PARK? I'M ZATCH BELL!
WHAT'S YOUR NAME?

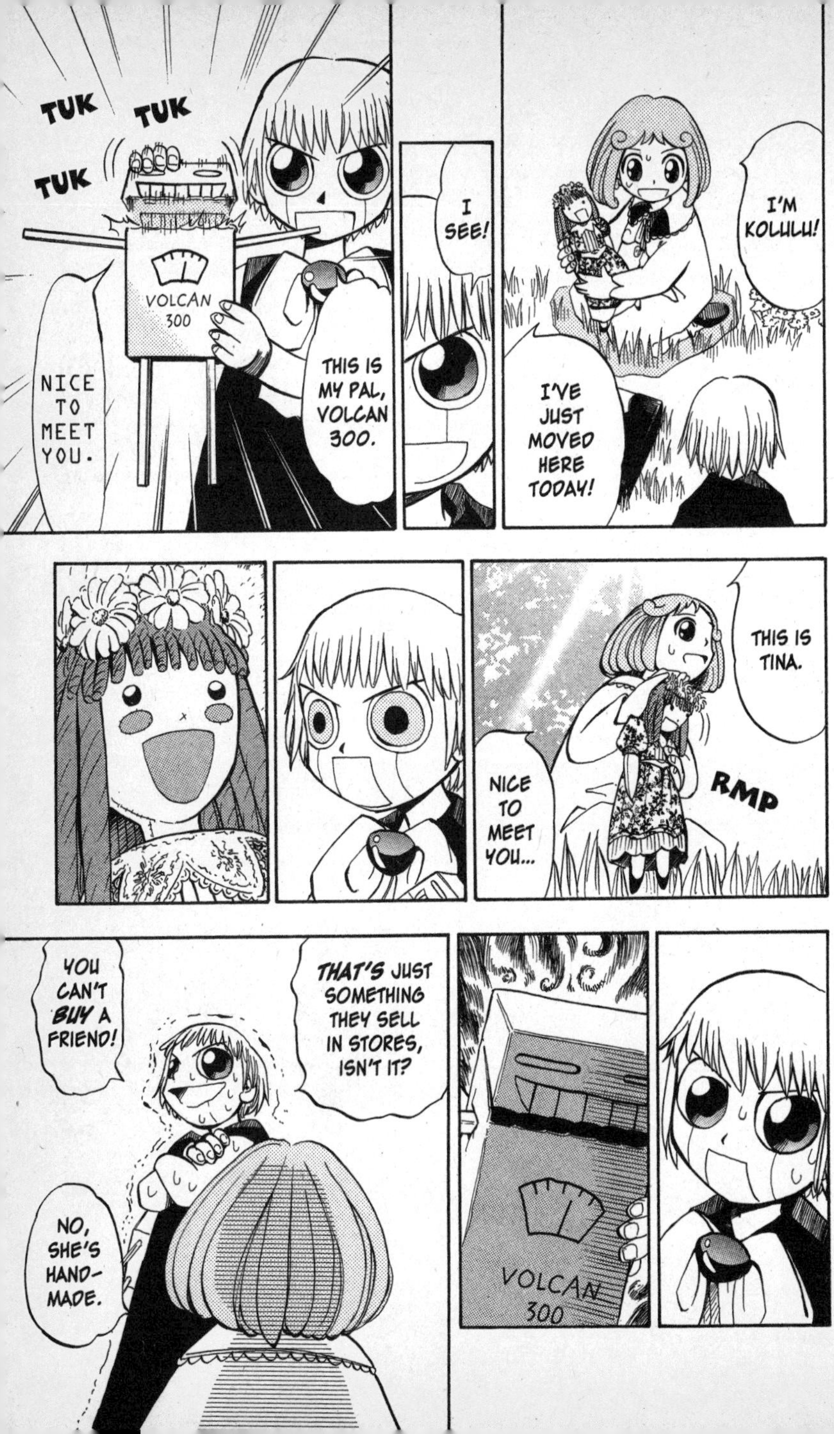
I'M KOLULU!
I'VE JUST MOVED HERE TODAY!
I SEE!
THIS IS MY PAL, VOLCAN 300.
TUK
TUK
TUK
VOLCAN 300
NICE TO MEET YOU.
THIS IS TINA.
RMP
NICE TO MEET YOU...
VOLCAN 300
THAT'S JUST SOMETHING THEY SELL IN STORES, ISN'T IT?
YOU CAN'T BUY A FRIEND!
NO, SHE'S HAND-MADE.

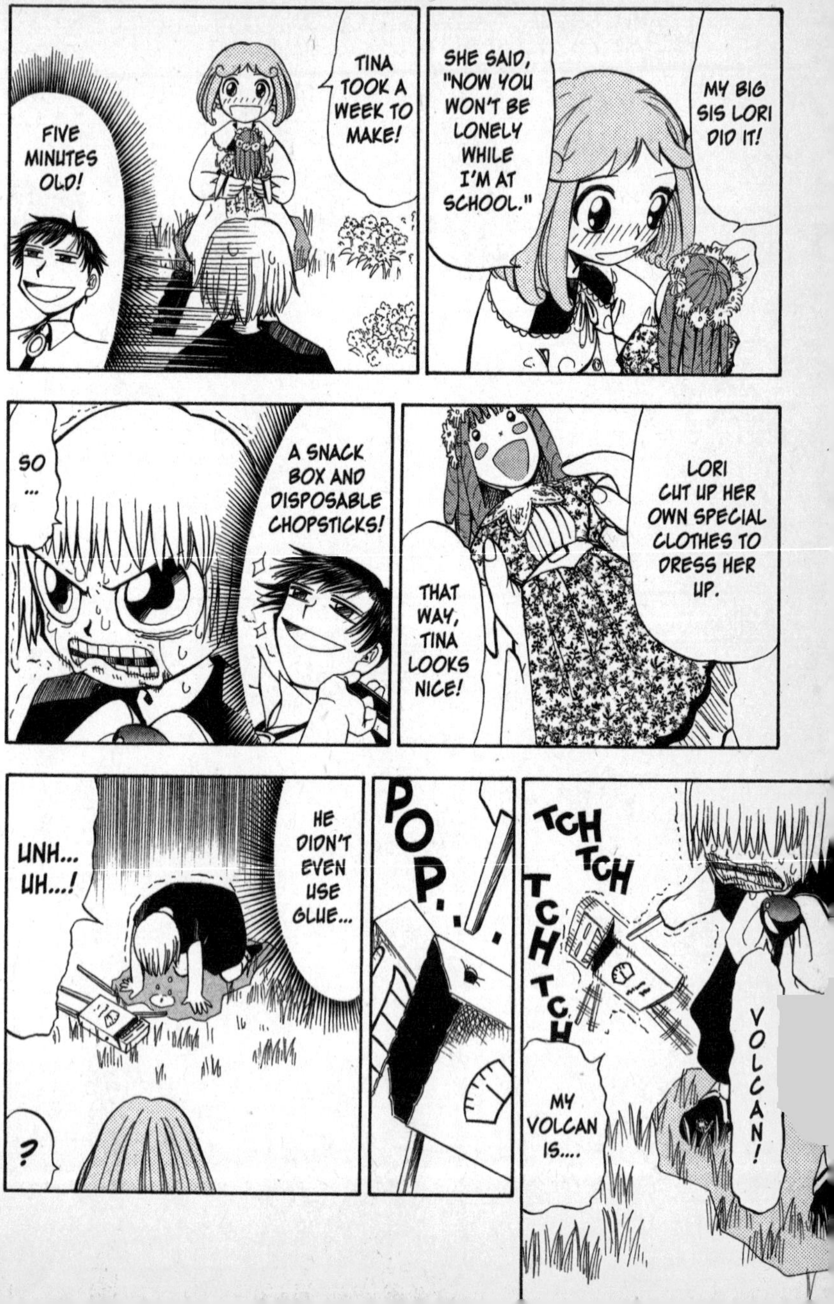
MY BIG SIS LORI DID IT!
SHE SAID, "NOW YOU WON'T BE LONELY WHILE I'M AT SCHOOL."
TINA TOOK A WEEK TO MAKE!
FIVE MINUTES OLD!
LORI CUT UP HER OWN SPECIAL CLOTHES TO DRESS HER UP.
THAT WAY, TINA LOOKS NICE!
A SNACK BOX AND DISPOSABLE CHOPSTICKS!
SO ...
TCH TCH TCH TCH TCH
VOLCAN!
MY VOLCAN IS....
POP...
HE DIDN'T EVEN USE GLUE...
UNH... UH...!
?

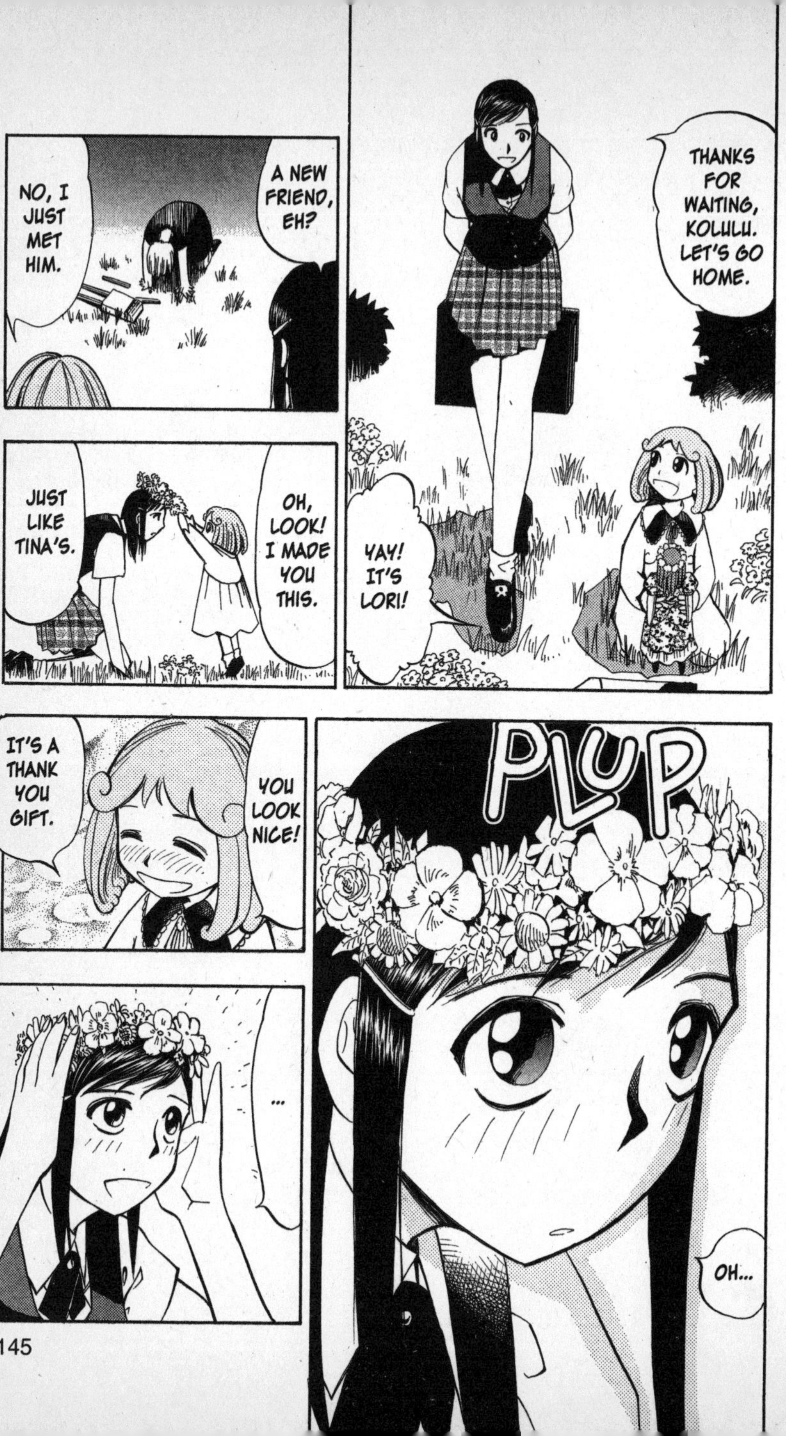
THANKS FOR WAITING, KOLULU. LET'S GO HOME.
YAY! IT'S LORI!
A NEW FRIEND, EH?
NO, I JUST MET HIM.
OH, LOOK! I MADE YOU THIS.
JUST LIKE TINA'S.
PLUP
OH...
YOU LOOK NICE!
IT'S A THANK YOU GIFT.
...

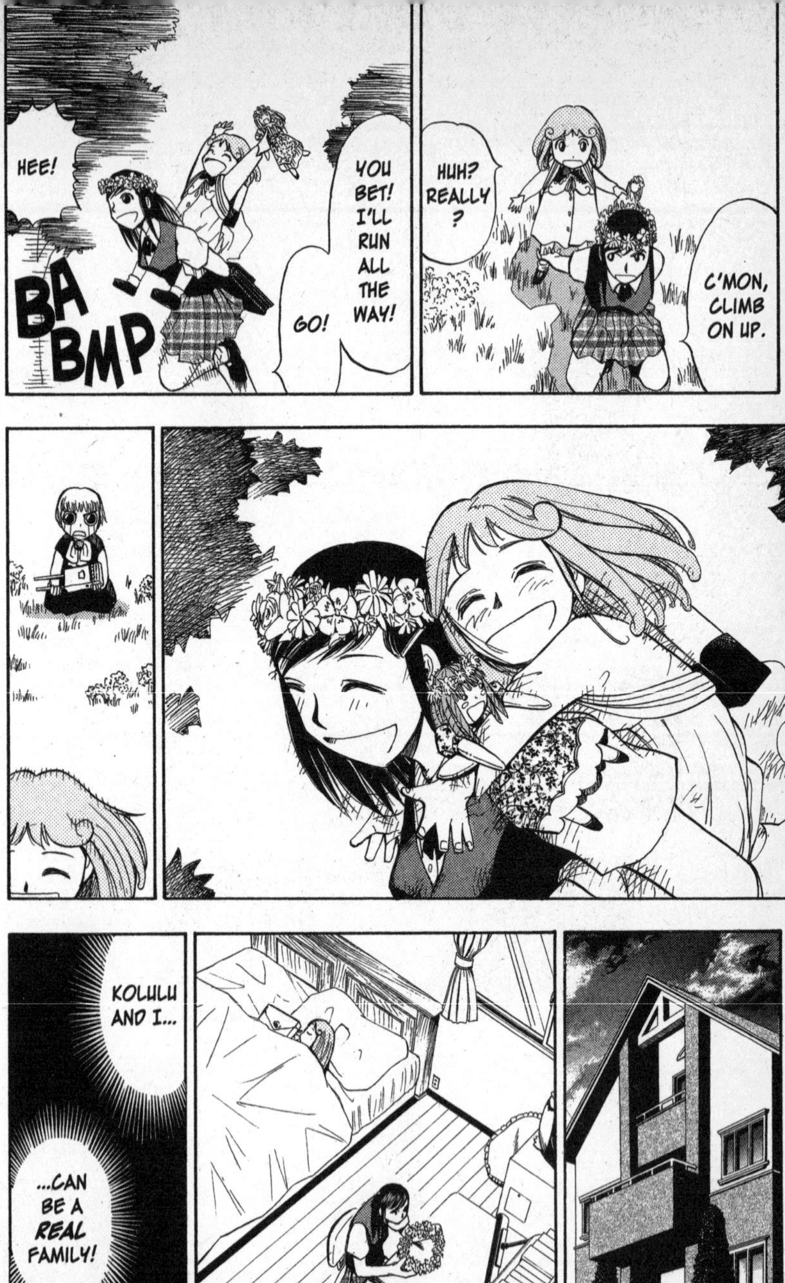
C'MON, CLIMB ON UP.
HUH? REALLY?
YOU BET! I'LL RUN ALL THE WAY!
GO!
HEE!
BA BMP
KOLULU AND I...
...CAN BE A REAL FAMILY!

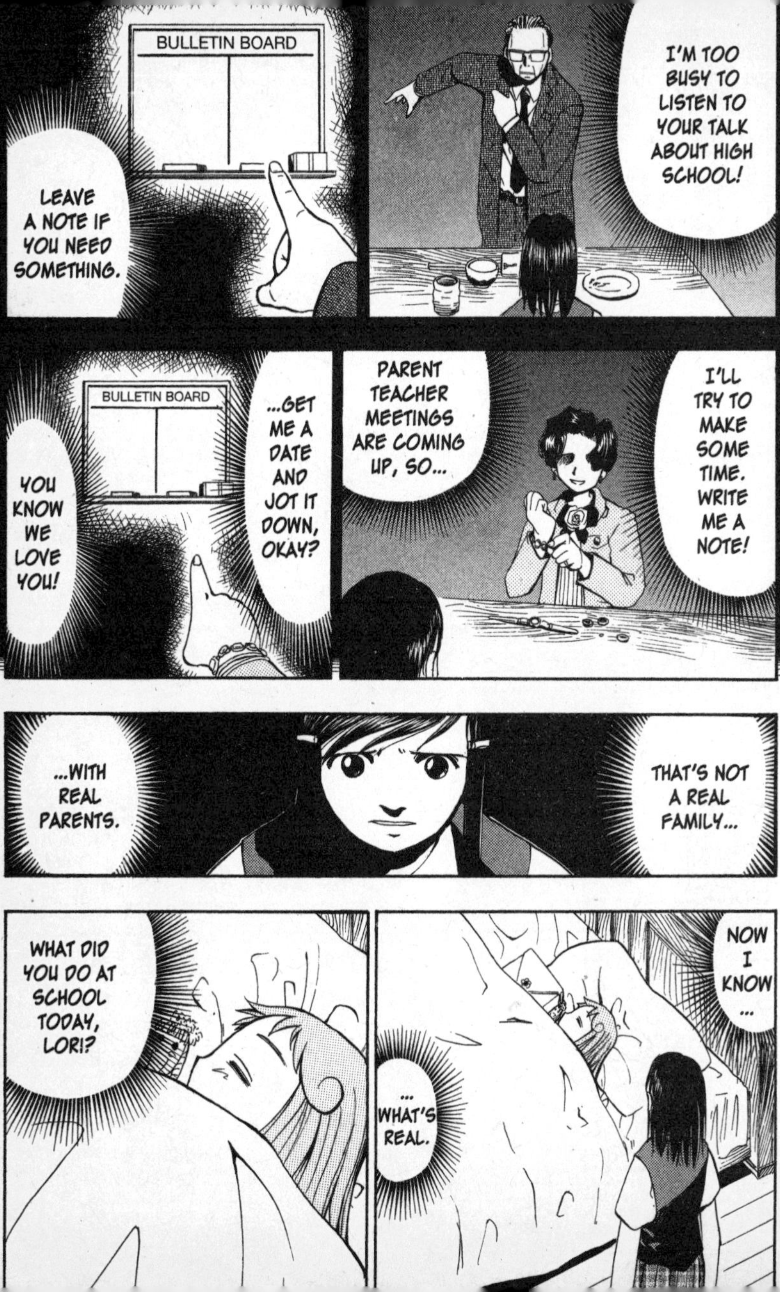
I'M TOO BUSY TO LISTEN TO YOUR TALK ABOUT HIGH SCHOOL!
BULLETIN BOARD
LEAVE A NOTE IF YOU NEED SOMETHING.
I'LL TRY TO MAKE SOME TIME. WRITE ME A NOTE!
PARENT TEACHER MEETINGS ARE COMING UP, SO...
...GET ME A DATE AND JOT IT DOWN, OKAY?
BULLETIN BOARD
YOU KNOW WE LOVE YOU!
THAT'S NOT A REAL FAMILY...
...WITH REAL PARENTS.
NOW I KNOW...
...WHAT'S REAL.
WHAT DID YOU DO AT SCHOOL TODAY, LORI?

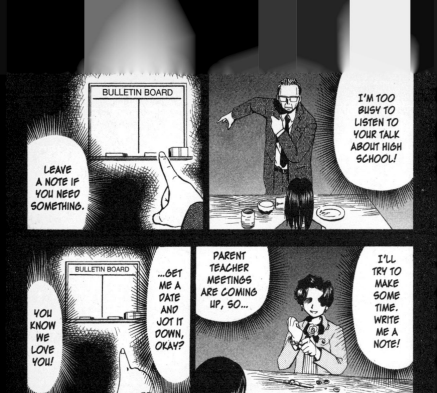

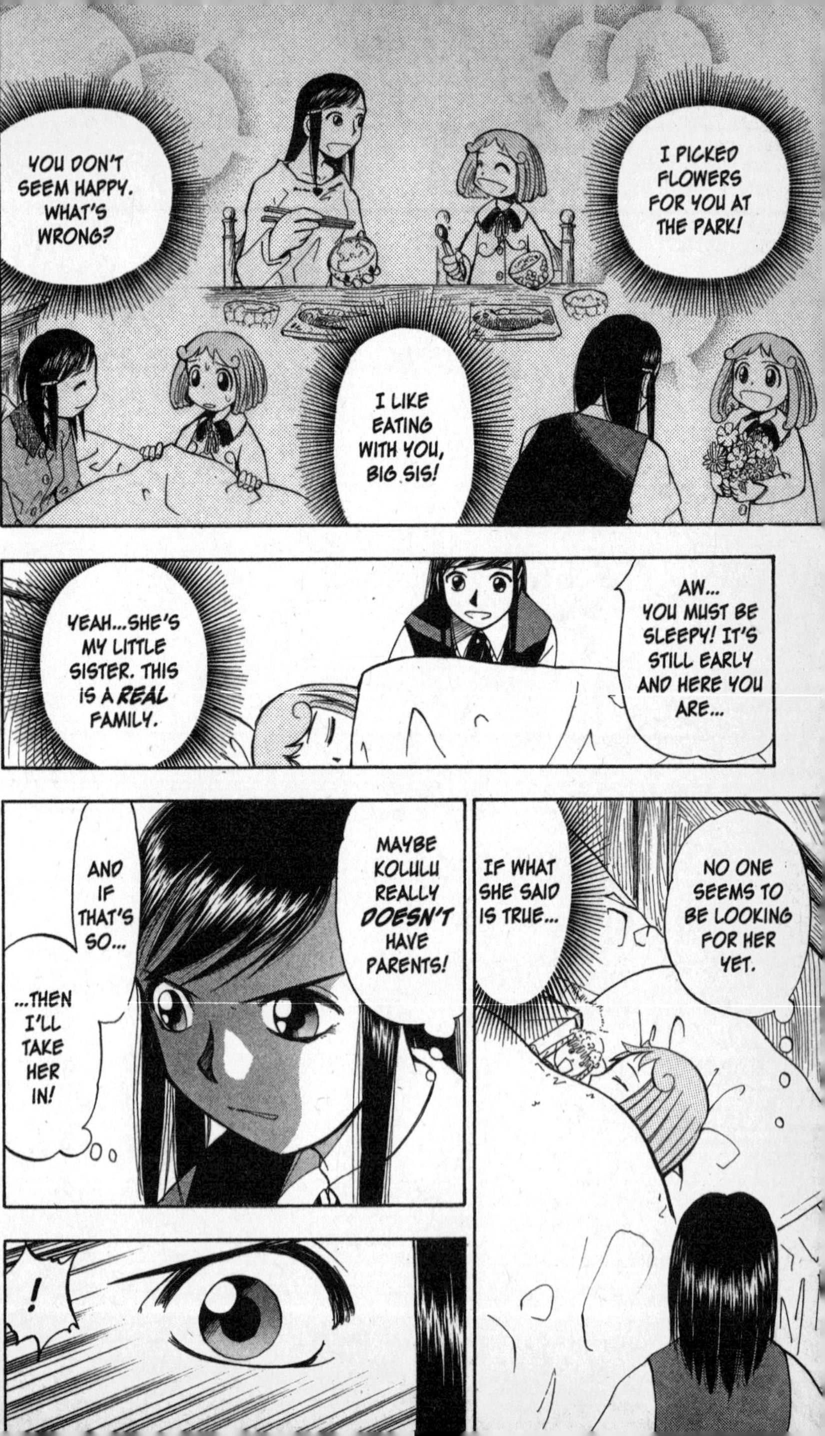
I PICKED FLOWERS FOR YOU AT THE PARK!
YOU DON'T SEEM HAPPY. WHAT'S WRONG?
I LIKE EATING WITH YOU, BIG SIS!
AW... YOU MUST BE SLEEPY! IT'S STILL EARLY AND HERE YOU ARE...
YEAH...SHE'S MY LITTLE SISTER. THIS IS A *REAL* FAMILY.
NO ONE SEEMS TO BE LOOKING FOR HER YET.
IF WHAT SHE SAID IS TRUE...
MAYBE KOLULU REALLY *DOESN'T* HAVE PARENTS!
AND IF THAT'S SO...
...THEN I'LL TAKE HER IN!
!

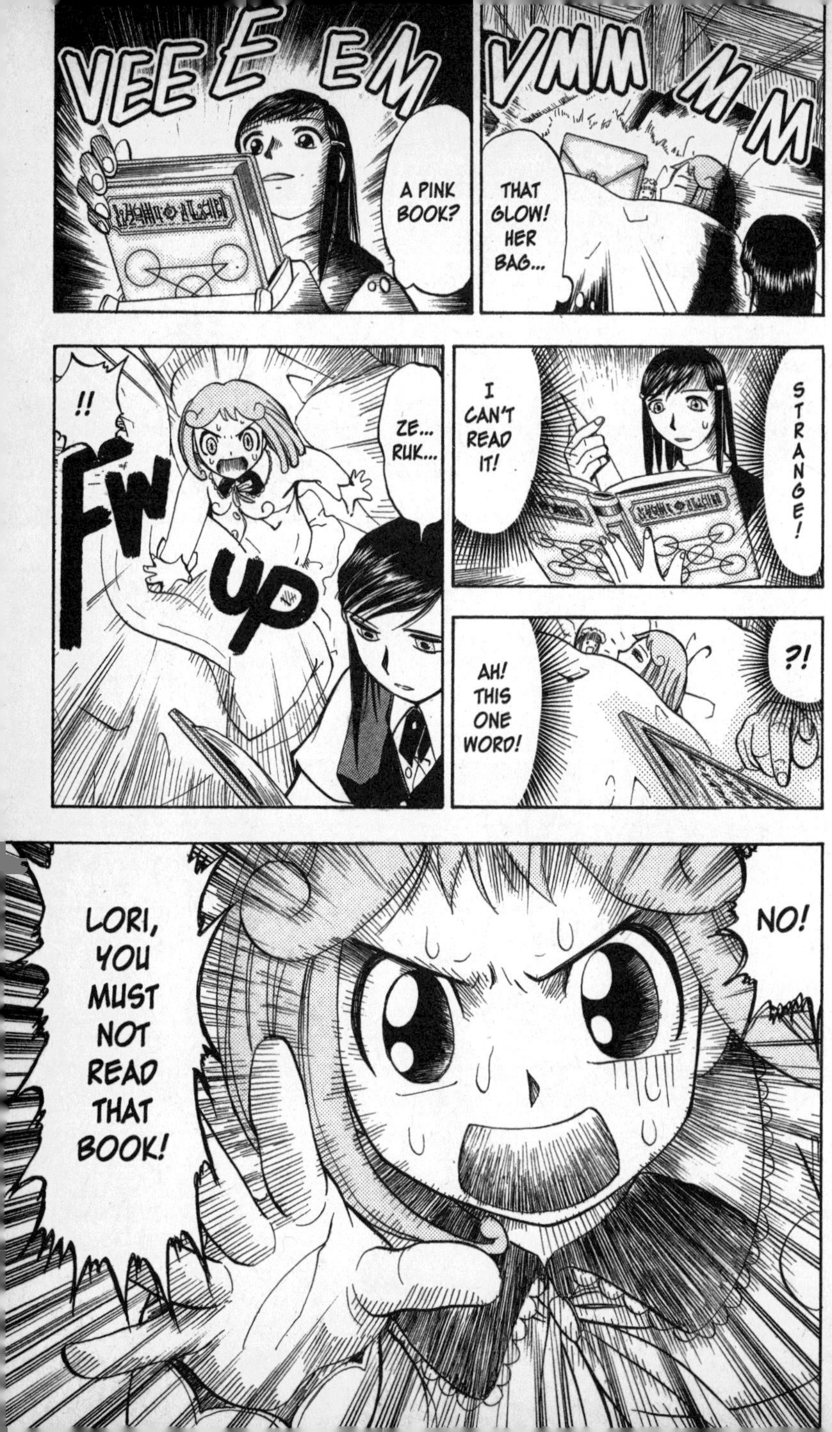
VEEE EM VMM MM M
THAT GLOW! HER BAG...
A PINK BOOK?
STRANGE!
I CAN'T READ IT!
?!
AH! THIS ONE WORD!
ZE... RUK...
!!
FWUP
NO!
LORI, YOU MUST NOT READ THAT BOOK!

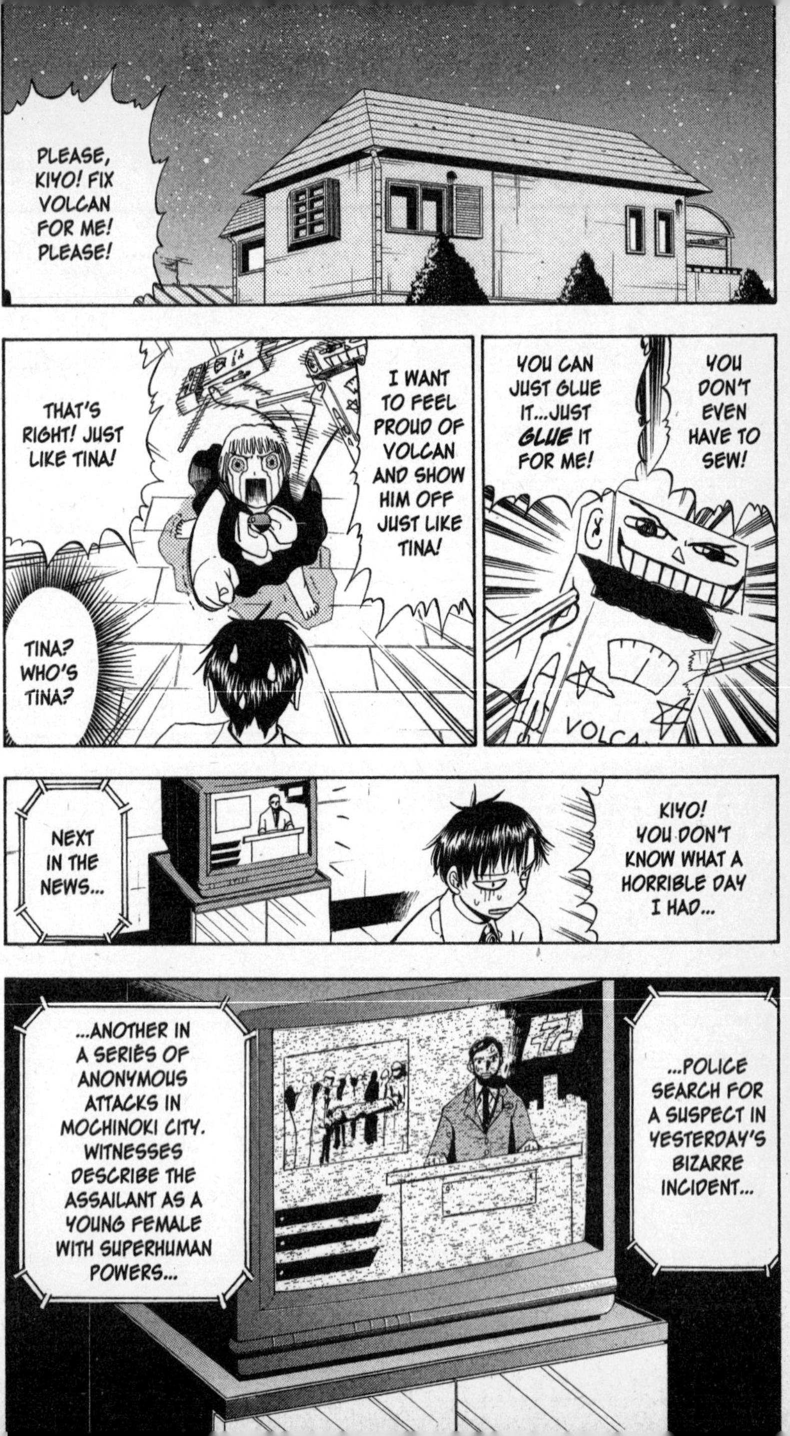
PLEASE, KIYO! FIX VOLCAN FOR ME! PLEASE!
YOU DON'T EVEN HAVE TO SEW!
YOU CAN JUST GLUE IT...JUST GLUE IT FOR ME!
VOLCAN
I WANT TO FEEL PROUD OF VOLCAN AND SHOW HIM OFF JUST LIKE TINA!
THAT'S RIGHT! JUST LIKE TINA!
TINA? WHO'S TINA?
KIYO! YOU DON'T KNOW WHAT A HORRIBLE DAY I HAD...
NEXT IN THE NEWS...
...POLICE SEARCH FOR A SUSPECT IN YESTERDAY'S BIZARRE INCIDENT...
...ANOTHER IN A SERIES OF ANONYMOUS ATTACKS IN MOCHINOKI CITY. WITNESSES DESCRIBE THE ASSAILANT AS A YOUNG FEMALE WITH SUPERHUMAN POWERS...

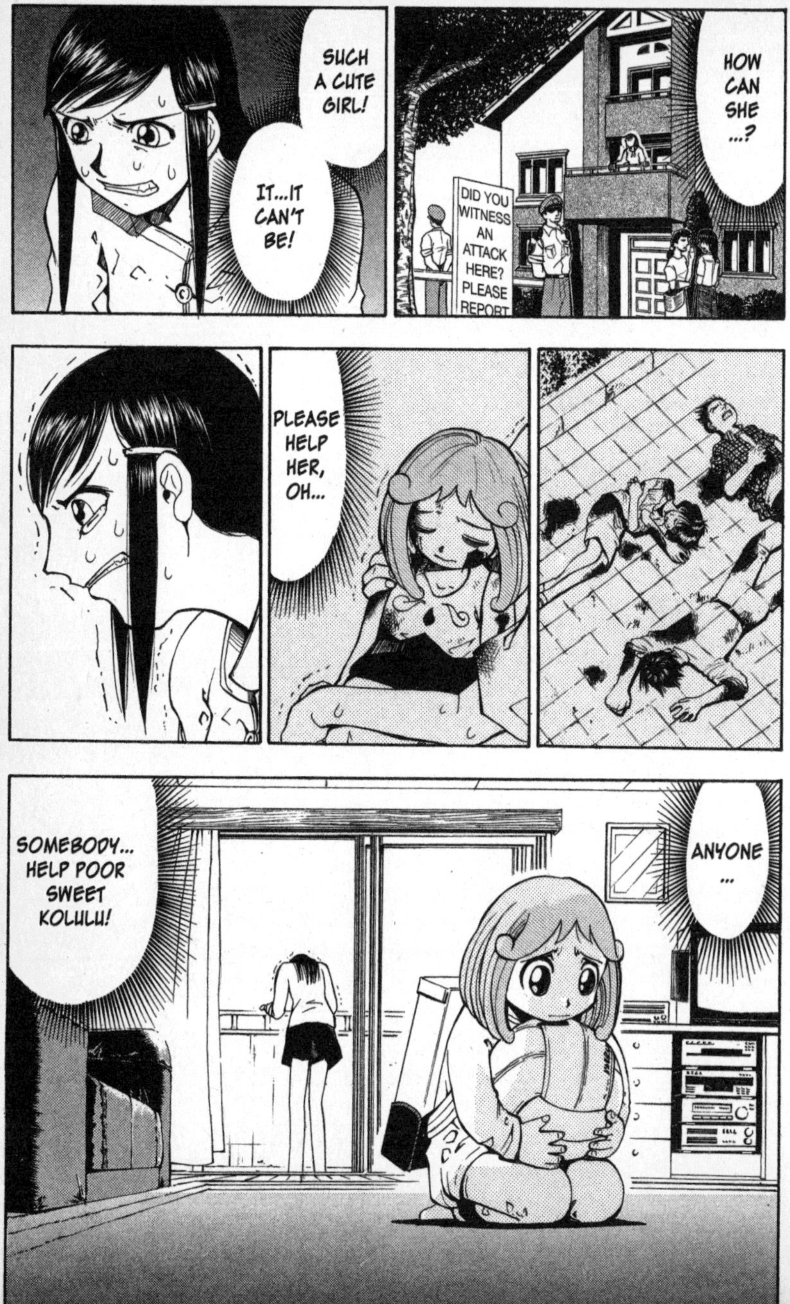
HOW CAN SHE ...?
DID YOU WITNESS AN ATTACK HERE? PLEASE REPORT
SUCH A CUTE GIRL!
IT...IT CAN'T BE!
PLEASE HELP HER, OH...
ANYONE ...
SOMEBODY... HELP POOR SWEET KOLULU!

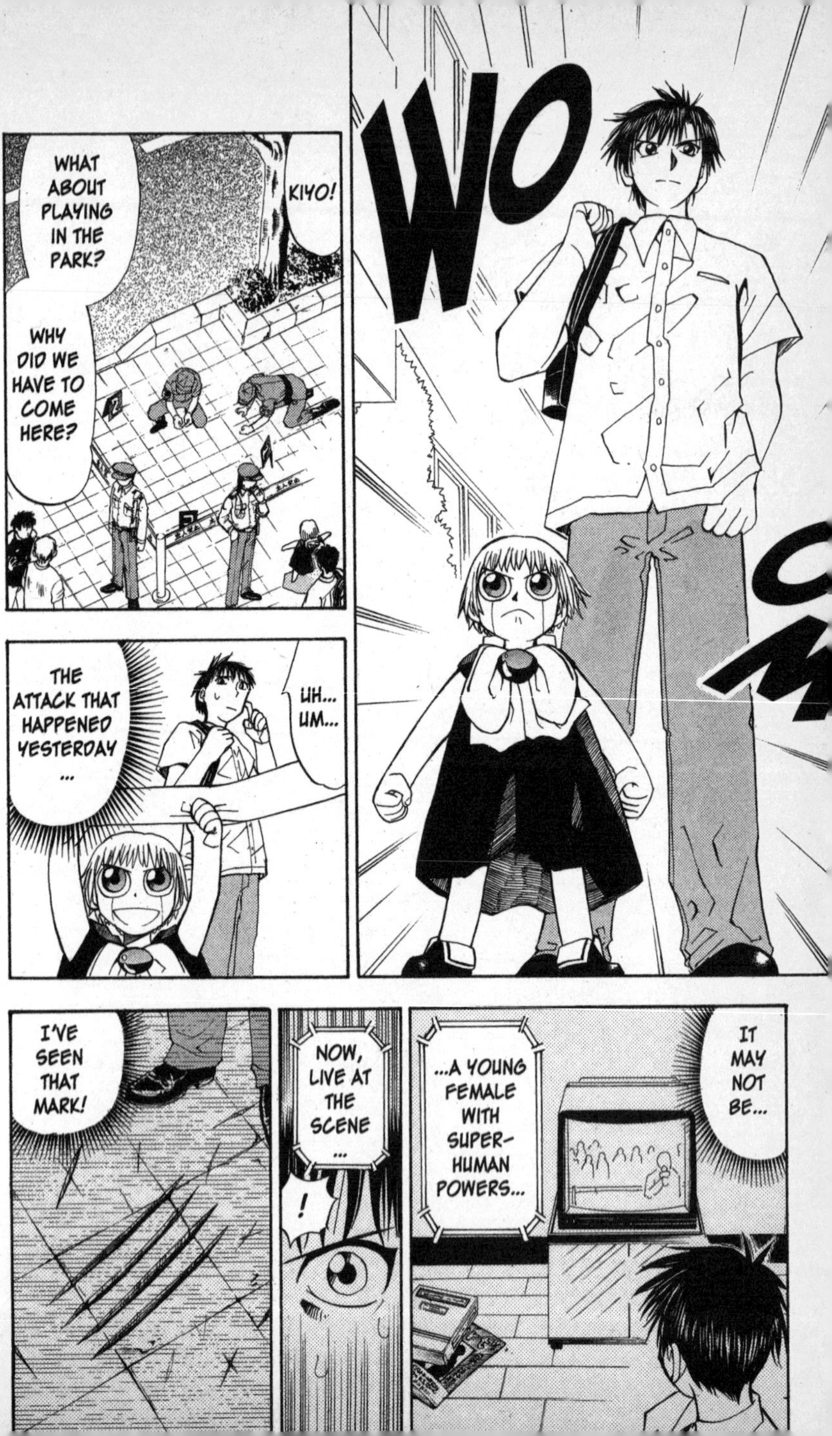
WO
KIYO!
WHAT ABOUT PLAYING IN THE PARK?
WHY DID WE HAVE TO COME HERE?
UH... UM...
THE ATTACK THAT HAPPENED YESTERDAY ...
IT MAY NOT BE...
...A YOUNG FEMALE WITH SUPER-HUMAN POWERS...
NOW, LIVE AT THE SCENE ...
!
I'VE SEEN THAT MARK!

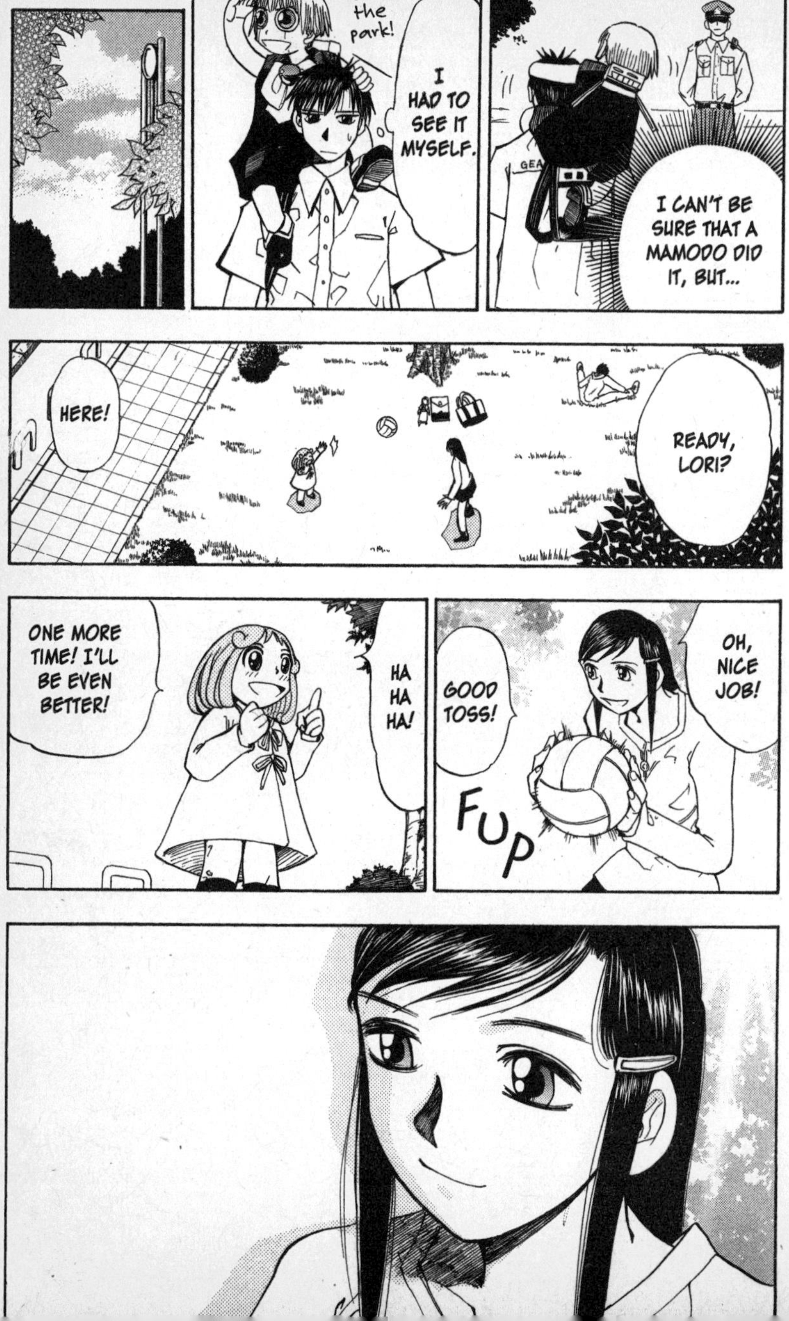
I CAN'T BE SURE THAT A MAMODO DID IT, BUT...
I HAD TO SEE IT MYSELF.
I can see the park!
READY, LORI?
HERE!
OH, NICE JOB!
GOOD TOSS!
FUP
HA HA HA!
ONE MORE TIME! I'LL BE EVEN BETTER!

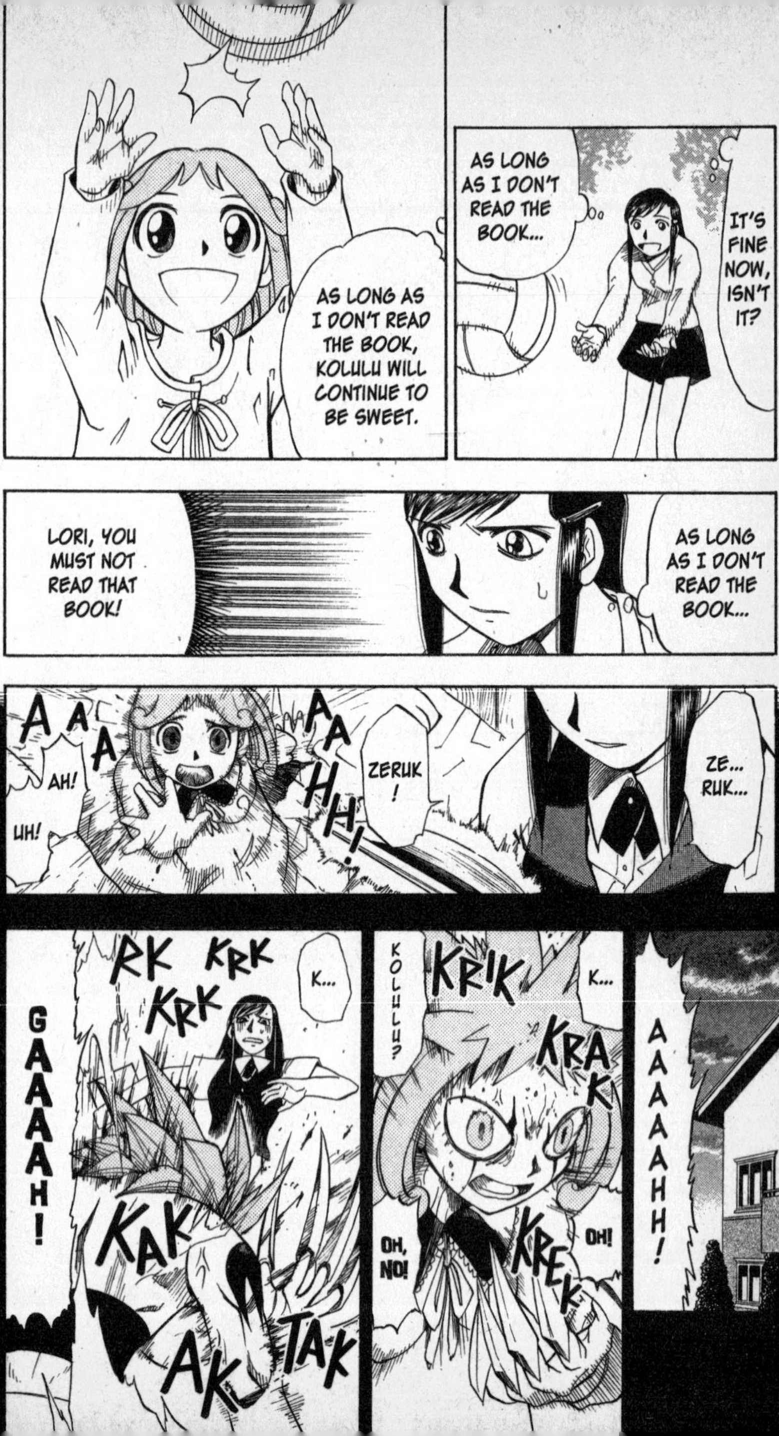
IT'S FINE NOW, ISN'T IT?
AS LONG AS I DON'T READ THE BOOK...
AS LONG AS I DON'T READ THE BOOK, KOLULU WILL CONTINUE TO BE SWEET.
AS LONG AS I DON'T READ THE BOOK...
LORI, YOU MUST NOT READ THAT BOOK!
ZE... RUK...
ZERUK!
AAHHH!
AAA
AH!
UH!
AAAAAAHH!
K...
KRIK
KOLULU?
KRAK
OH!
KREK
OH, NO!
K...
RK KRK
KRK
GAAAAAH!
KAK
TAK
AK

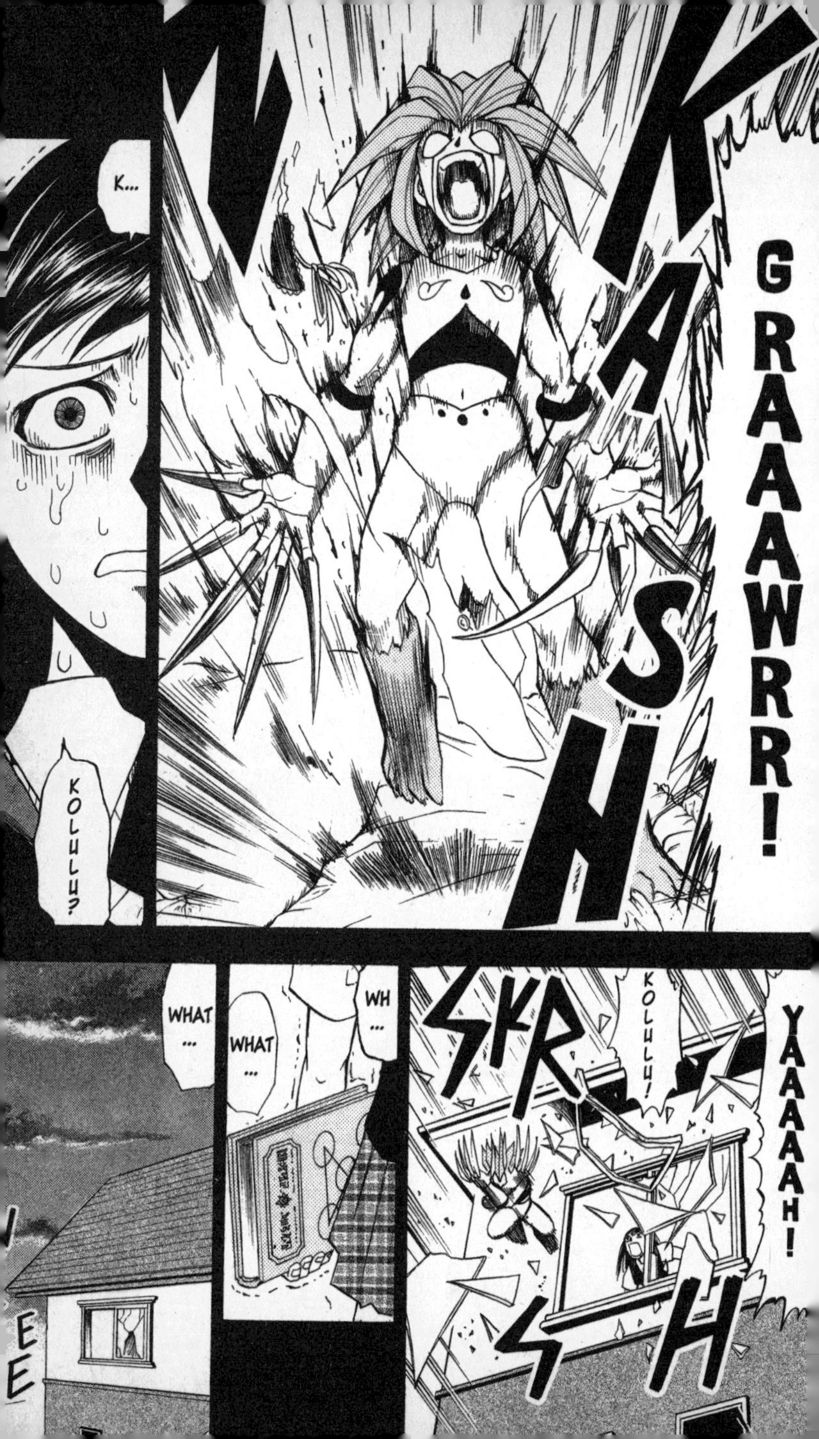
GRAAAWRRR!
K...
KOLULU?
YAAAAAH!
KOLULU!
SKR
SH
WH...
WHAT...
WHAT...

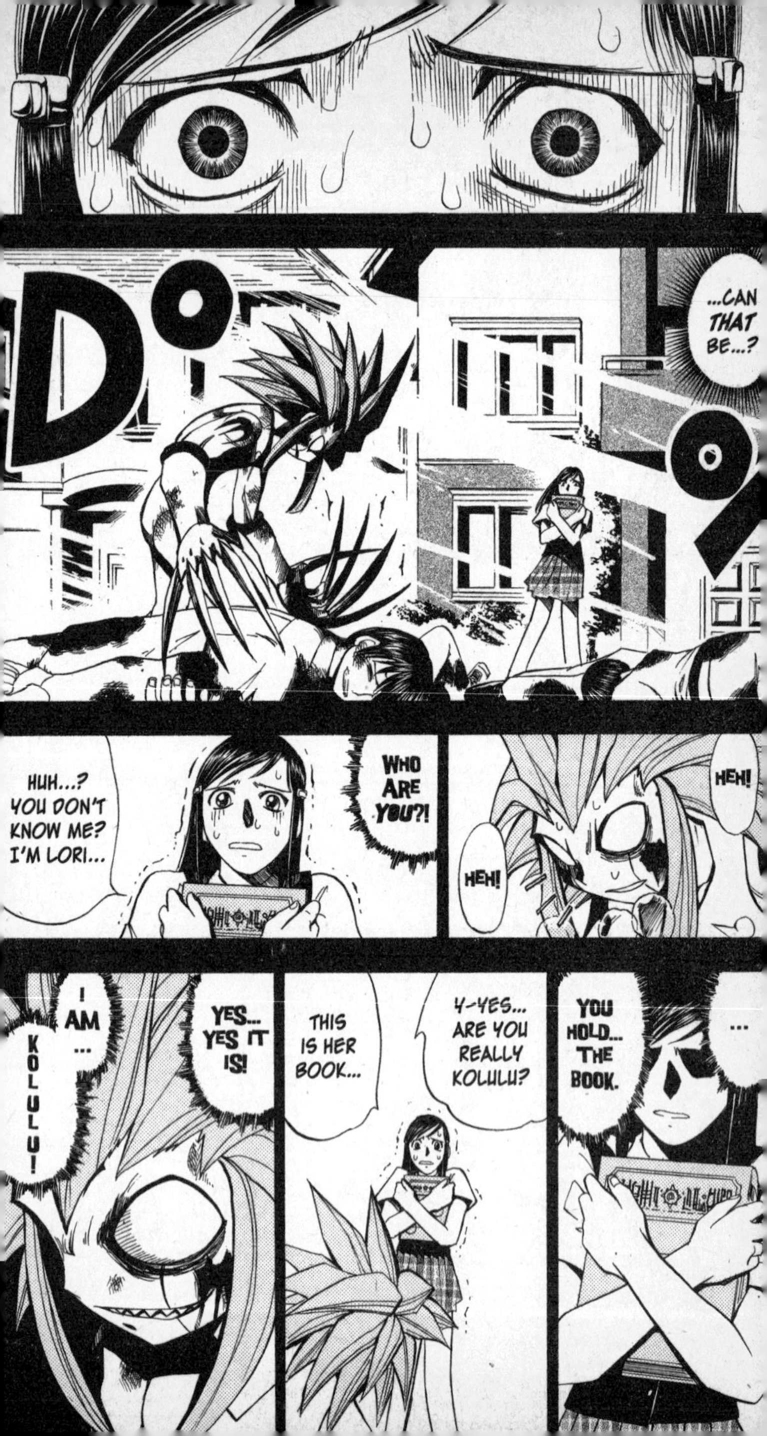
...CAN THAT BE...?
HEH!
HEH!
WHO ARE YOU?!
HUH...? YOU DON'T KNOW ME? I'M LORI...
...
YOU HOLD... THE BOOK.
Y-YES... ARE YOU REALLY KOLULU?
THIS IS HER BOOK...
YES... YES IT IS!
I AM ... KOLULU!

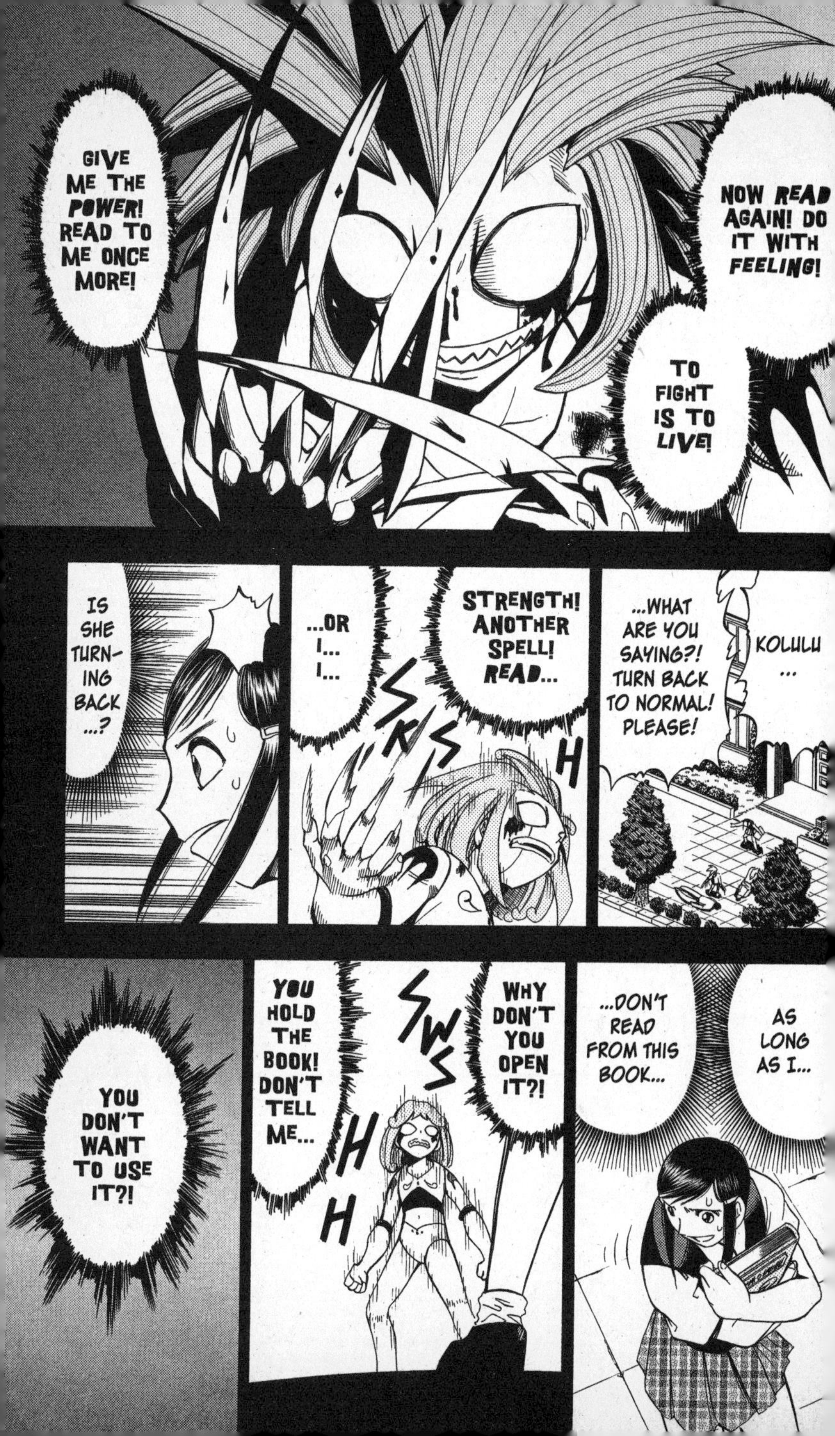
NOW READ AGAIN! DO IT WITH FEELING!
TO FIGHT IS TO LIVE!
GIVE ME THE POWER! READ TO ME ONCE MORE!
KOLULU ...
...WHAT ARE YOU SAYING?! TURN BACK TO NORMAL! PLEASE!
STRENGTH! ANOTHER SPELL! READ...
SKSH
...OR I... I...
IS SHE TURNING-ING BACK ...?
AS LONG AS I...
...DON'T READ FROM THIS BOOK...
WHY DON'T YOU OPEN IT?!
SWSH
HH
YOU HOLD THE BOOK! DON'T TELL ME...
YOU DON'T WANT TO USE IT?!

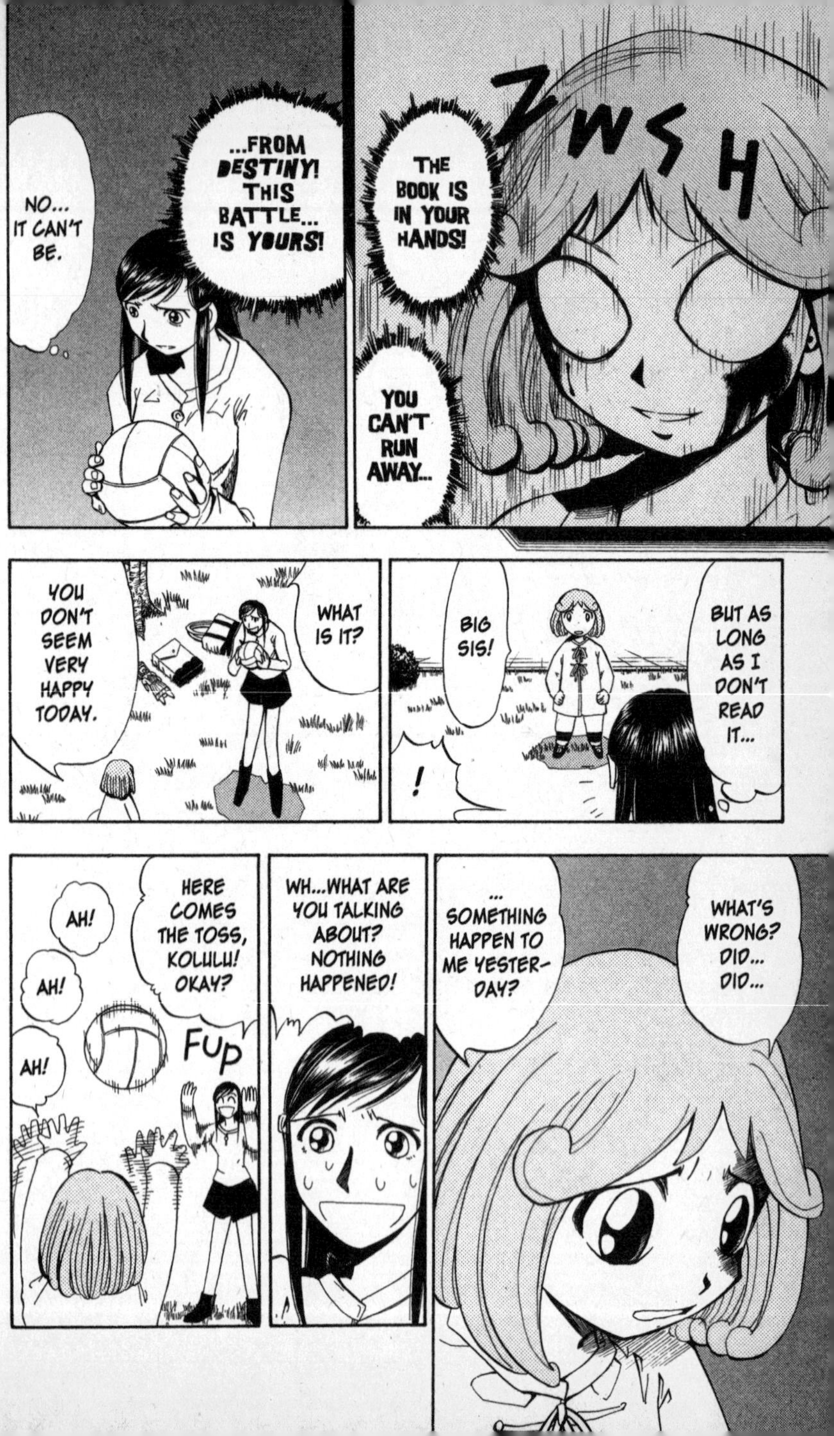
ZWSH
THE BOOK IS IN YOUR HANDS!
YOU CAN'T RUN AWAY...
...FROM DESTINY! THIS BATTLE... IS YOURS!
NO... IT CAN'T BE.
BUT AS LONG AS I DON'T READ IT...
BIG SIS!
!
WHAT IS IT?
YOU DON'T SEEM VERY HAPPY TODAY.
WHAT'S WRONG? DID... DID...
... SOMETHING HAPPEN TO ME YESTER-DAY?
WH...WHAT ARE YOU TALKING ABOUT? NOTHING HAPPENED!
HERE COMES THE TOSS, KOLULU! OKAY?
FUP
AH!
AH!
AH!

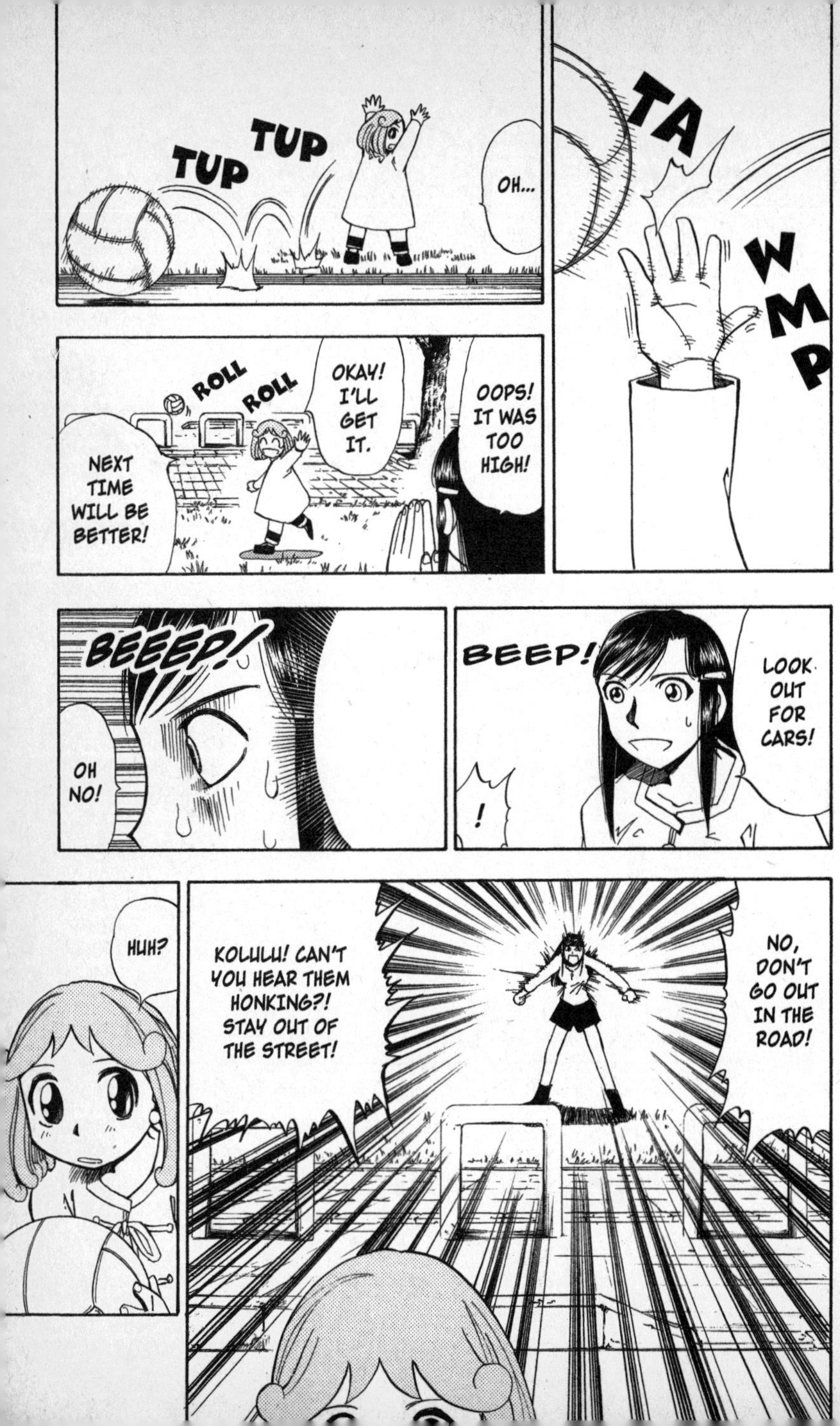
TA
WMP
OH...
TUP TUP
OOPS! IT WAS TOO HIGH!
OKAY! I'LL GET IT.
ROLL ROLL
NEXT TIME WILL BE BETTER!
LOOK OUT FOR CARS!
BEEP!
!
BEEEP!
OH NO!
NO, DON'T GO OUT IN THE ROAD!
KOLULU! CAN'T YOU HEAR THEM HONKING?! STAY OUT OF THE STREET!
HUH?

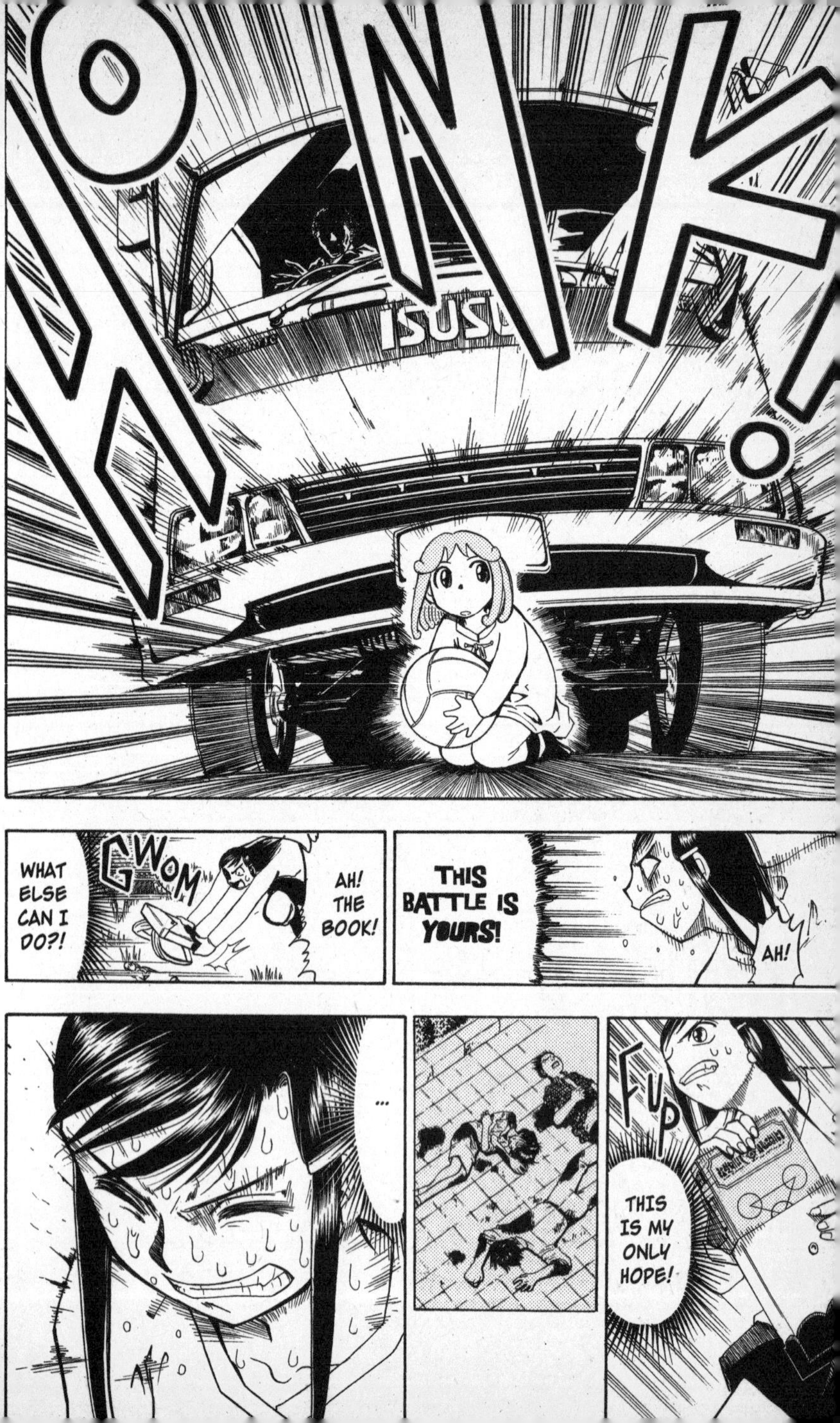
HONK!
ISUSU
THIS BATTLE IS YOURS!
AH!
AH! THE BOOK!
GWOM
WHAT ELSE CAN I DO?!
FUP
THIS IS MY ONLY HOPE!
...

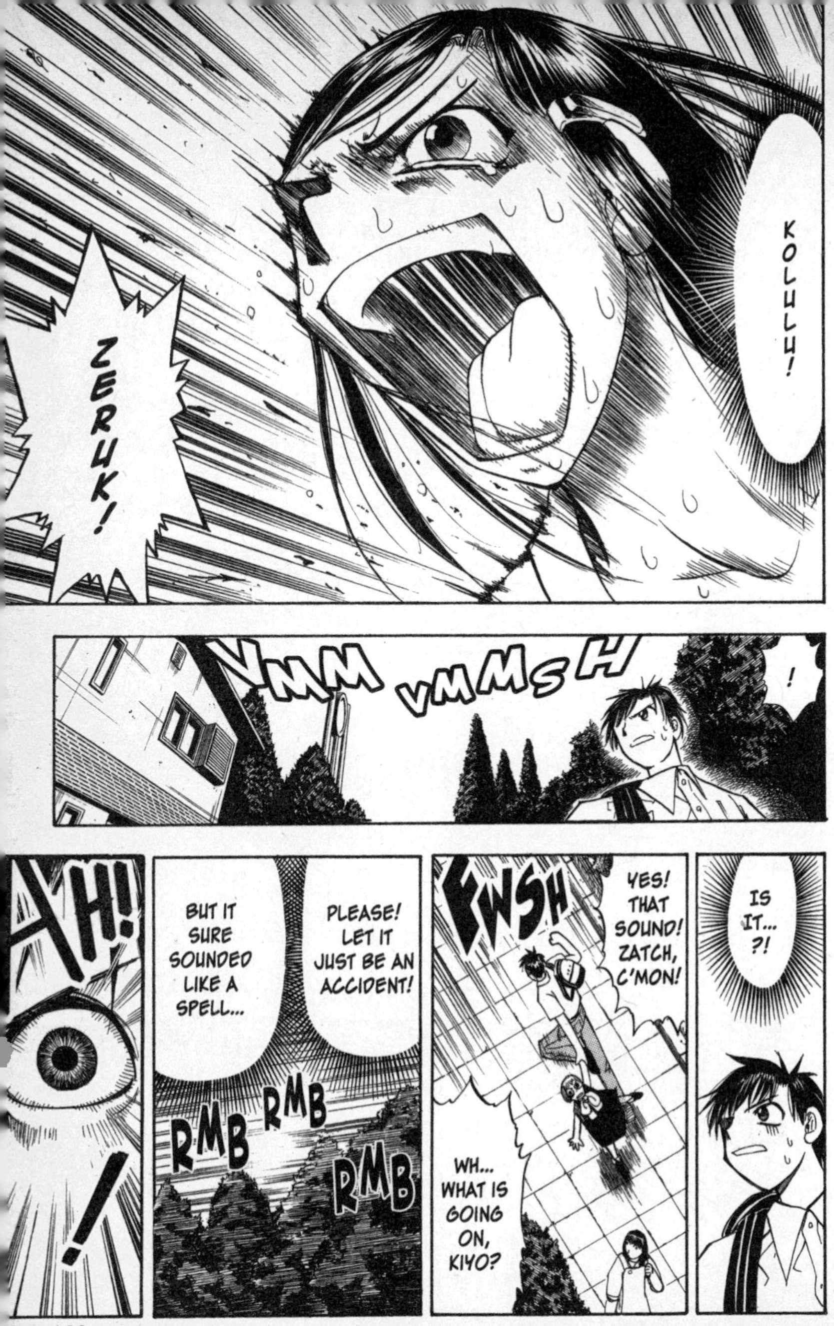
KOLULU!
ZERUK!
!
VMM VMMSH
IS IT...?!
YES! THAT SOUND! ZATCH, C'MON!
FWSH
WH... WHAT IS GOING ON, KIYO?
PLEASE! LET IT JUST BE AN ACCIDENT!
BUT IT SURE SOUNDED LIKE A SPELL...
RMB RMB RMB
AH!
!

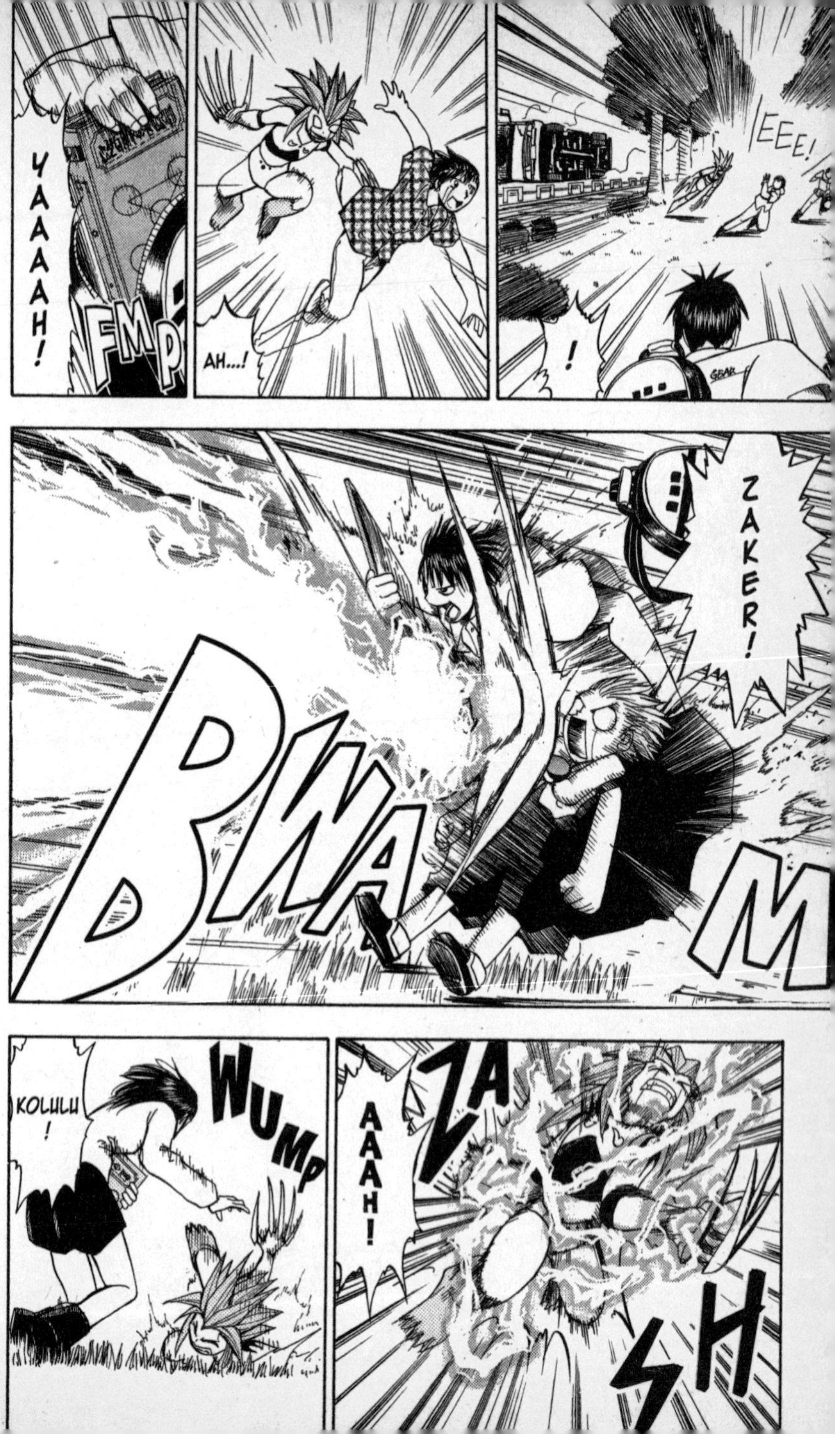
EEEE!
!
AH...!
YAAAAAH!
FMP
ZAKER!
BWAM
AAAAH!
ZA
SH
KOLULU!
WUMP

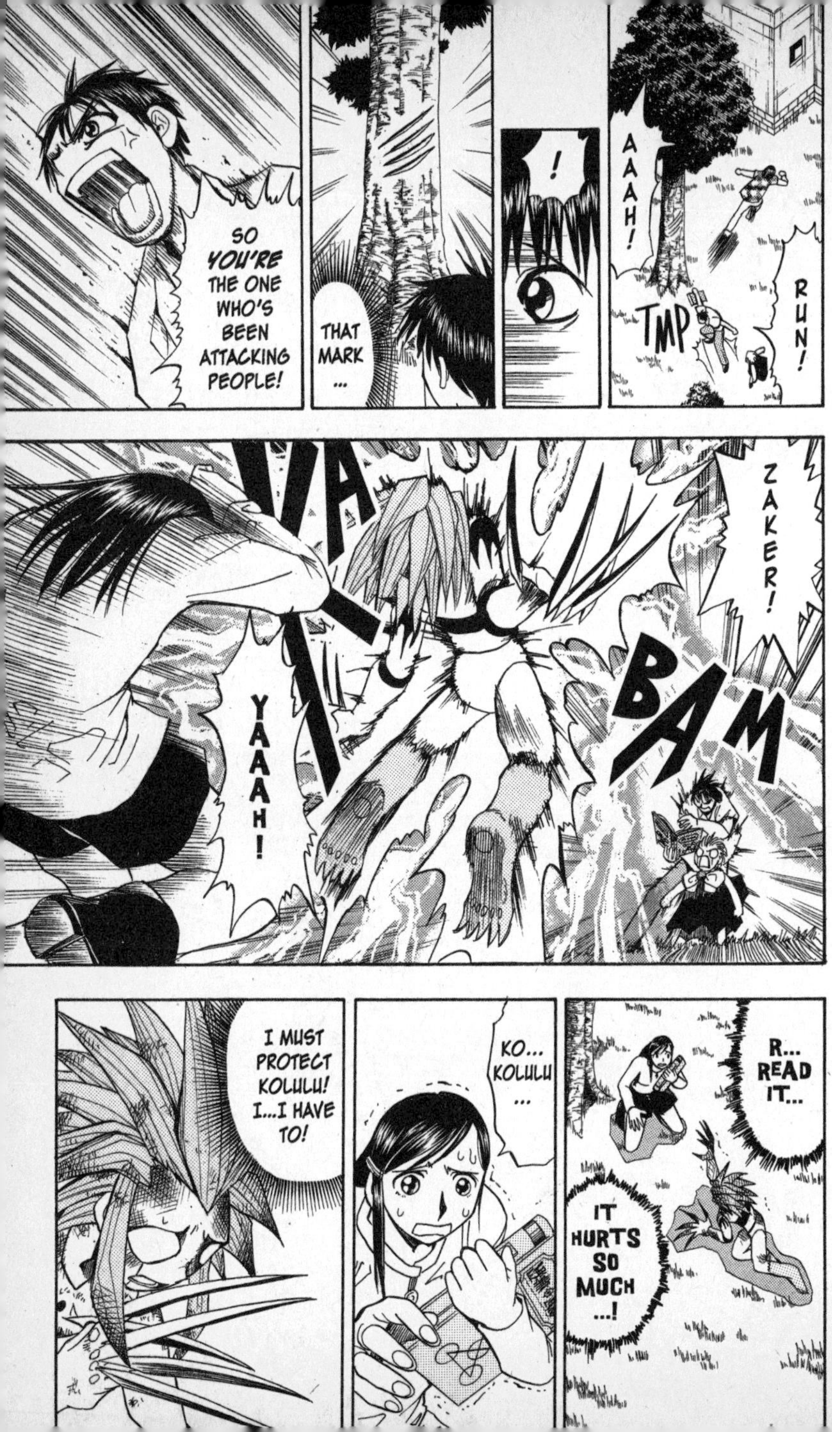
AAAAH!
RUN!
TMP
!
THAT MARK ...
SO YOU'RE THE ONE WHO'S BEEN ATTACKING PEOPLE!
ZAKER!
BAM
YA
YAAAAH!
R... READ IT...
IT HURTS SO MUCH ...!
KO... KOLULU ...
I MUST PROTECT KOLULU! I...I HAVE TO!

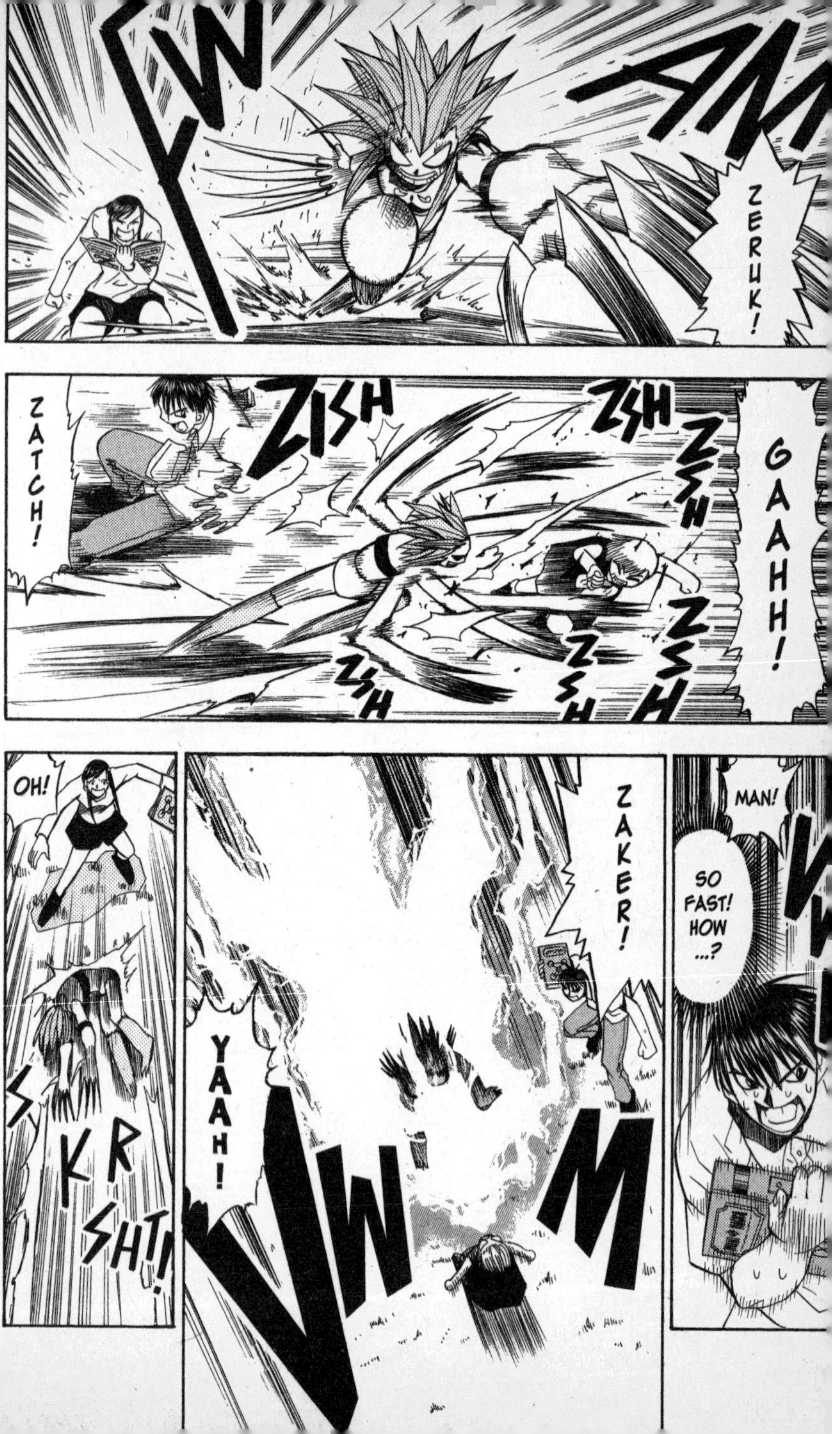
ZERUK!
GAAHH!
ZSH
ZSH
ZSH
ZSH
ZISH
ZATCH!
MAN!
SO FAST! HOW ...?
ZAKER!
YAAH!
OH!

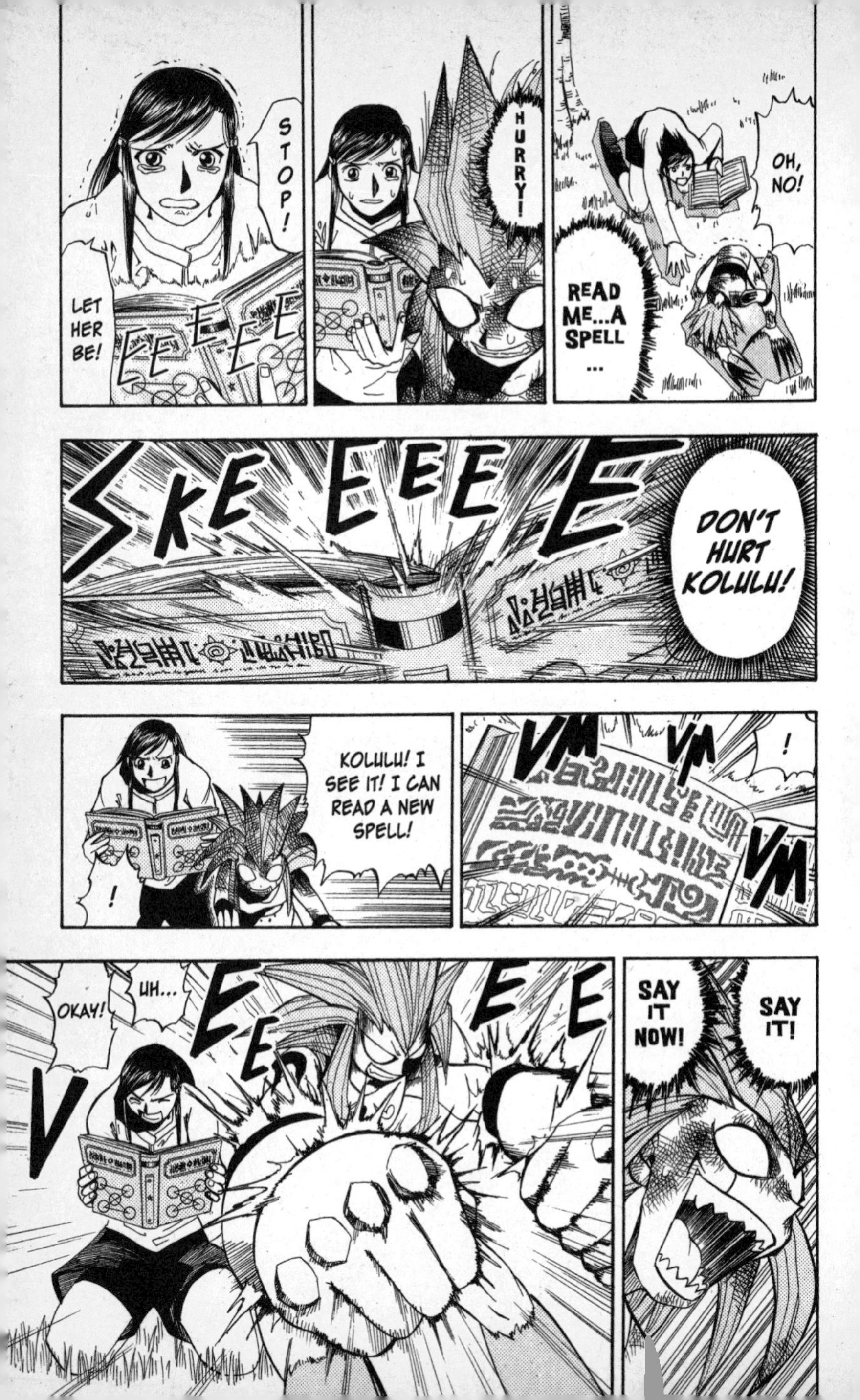
OH, NO!
READ ME...A SPELL ...
HURRY!
STOP!
LET HER BE!
EEEEE
SKEEEEE
DON'T HURT KOLULU!
!
VM VM VM
KOLULU! I SEE IT! I CAN READ A NEW SPELL!
!
SAY IT!
SAY IT NOW!
EEEE
UH...
OKAY!
V

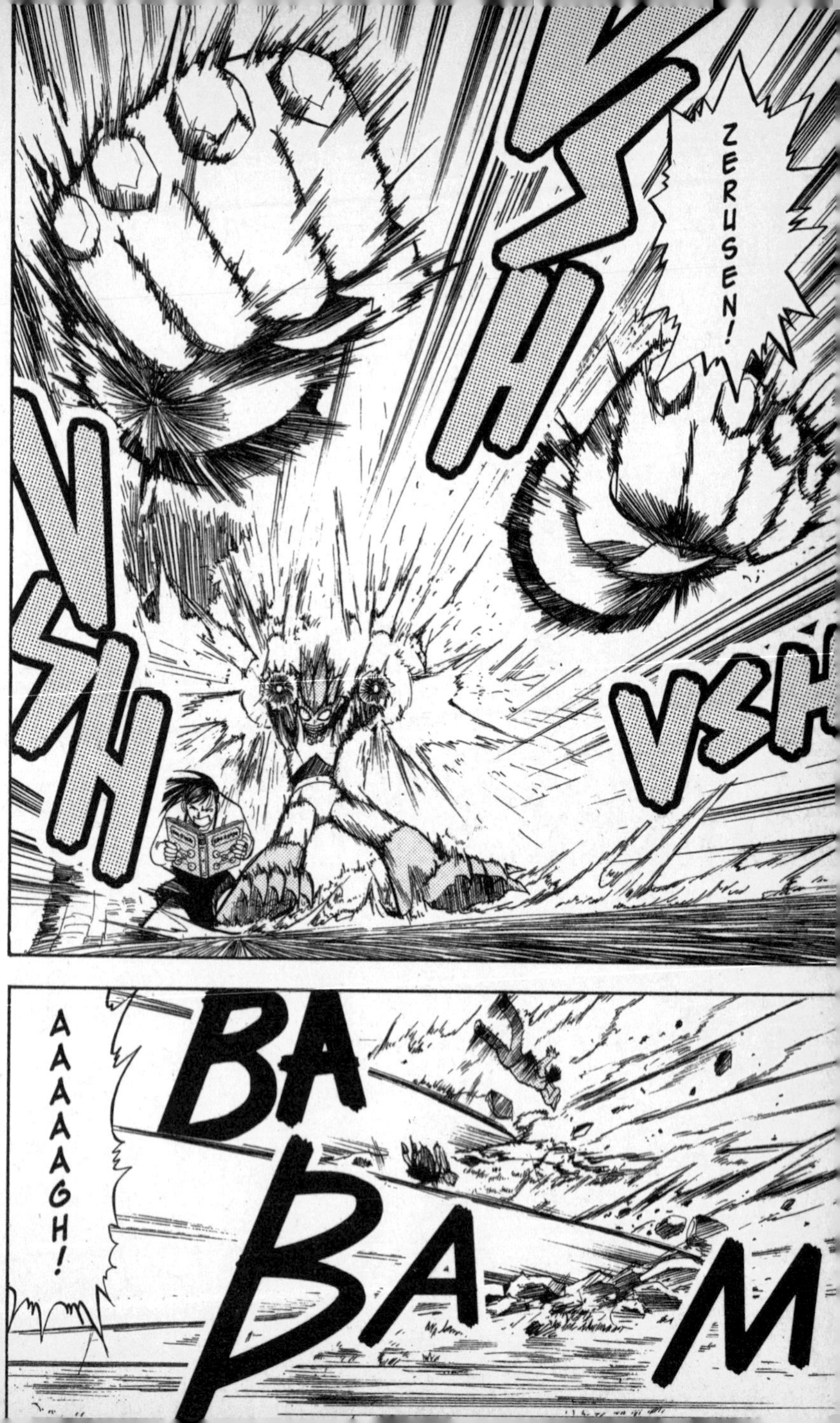
ZERUSEN!
VSH
VSH
VSH
BABAM
AAAAAAGH!

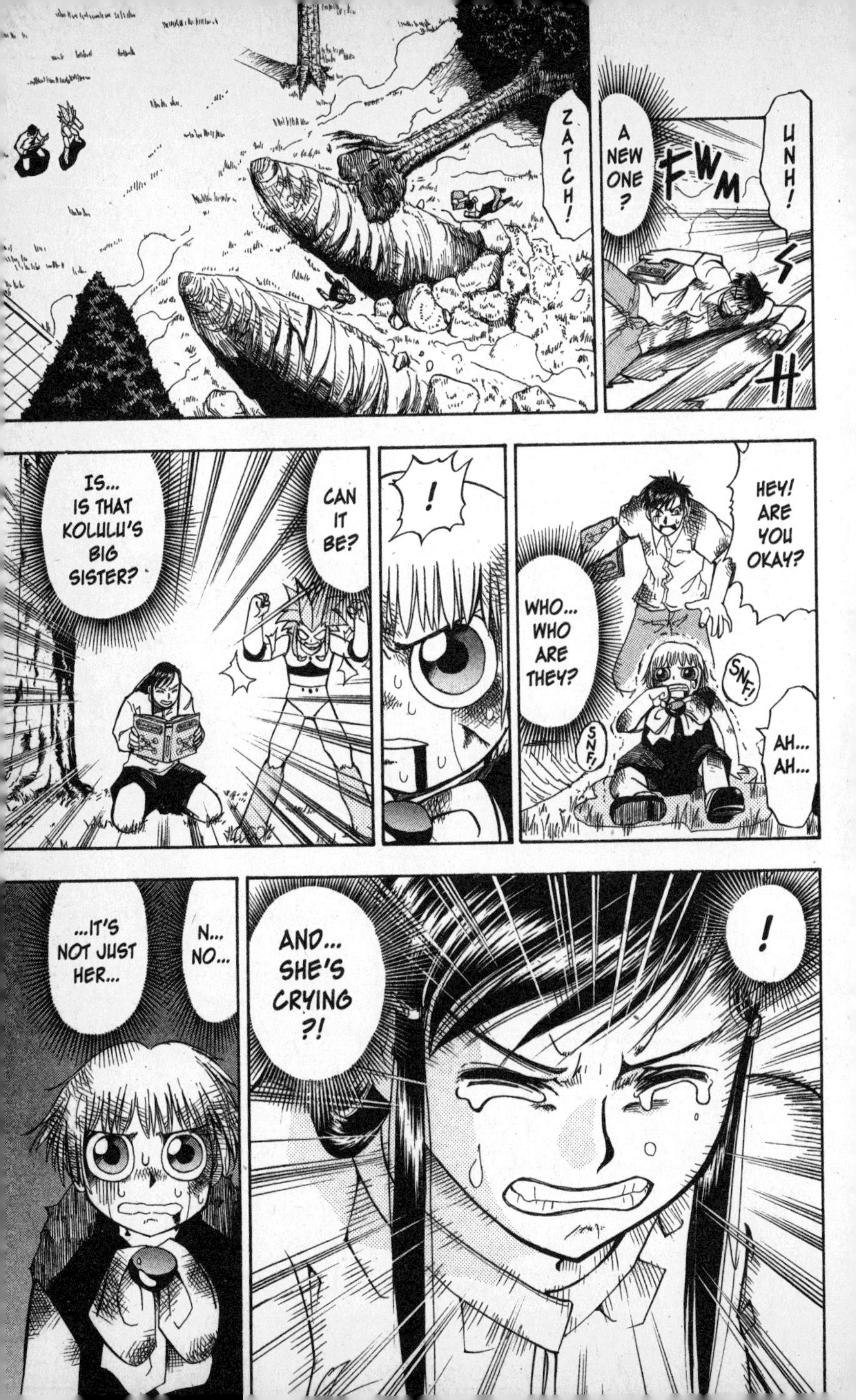
UNNH!
FWM
A NEW ONE?
ZATCH!
HEY! ARE YOU OKAY?
WHO... WHO ARE THEY?
SNF!
SNF!
AH... AH...
!
CAN IT BE?
IS... IS THAT KOLULU'S BIG SISTER?
!
AND... SHE'S CRYING?!
N... NO...
...IT'S NOT JUST HER...

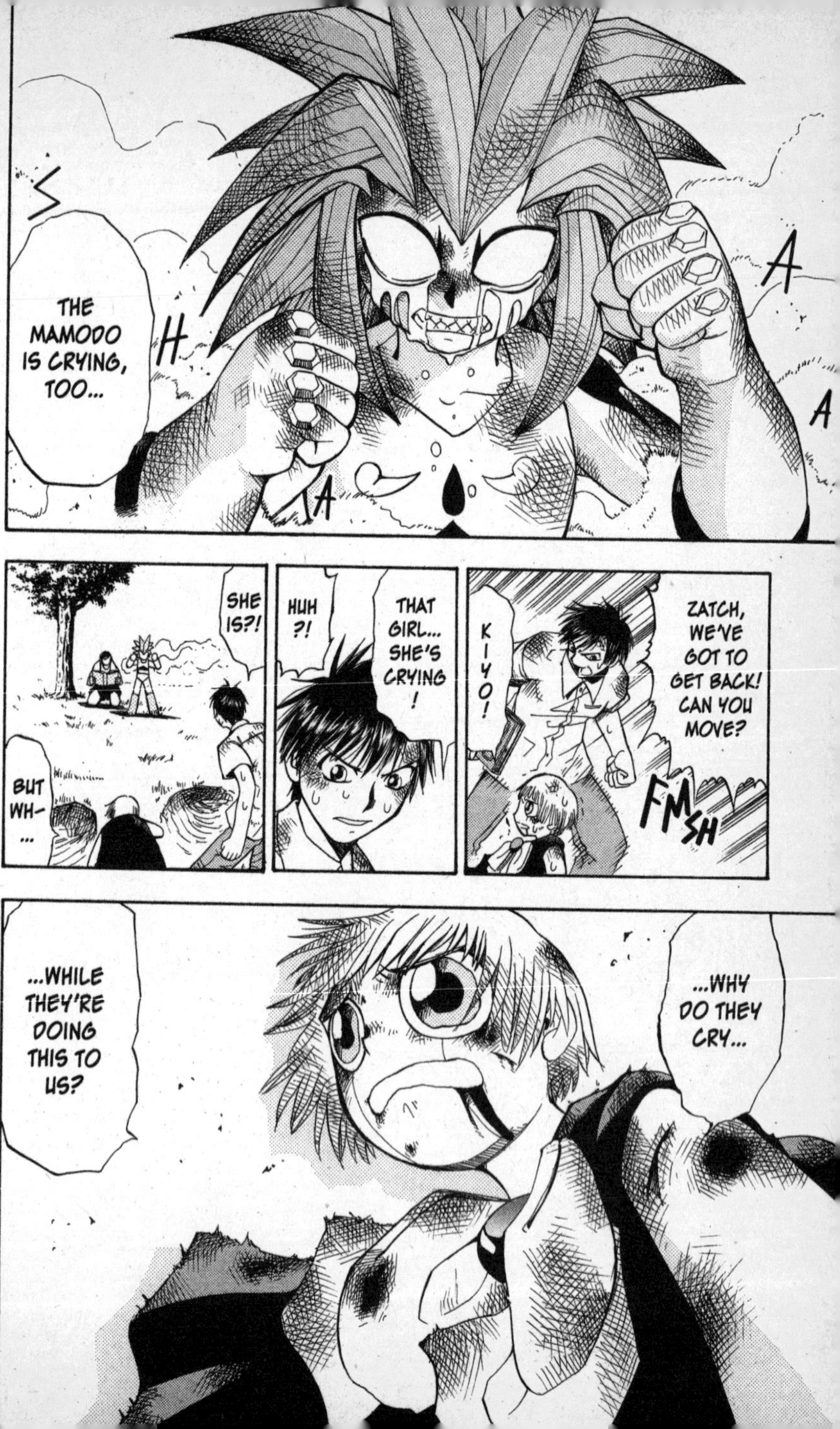
SHAAAA
THE MAMODO IS CRYING, TOO...
ZATCH, WE'VE GOT TO GET BACK! CAN YOU MOVE?
KIYO!
FMSH
THAT GIRL... SHE'S CRYING!
HUH?!
SHE IS?!
BUT WH-...
...WHY DO THEY CRY...
...WHILE THEY'RE DOING THIS TO US?

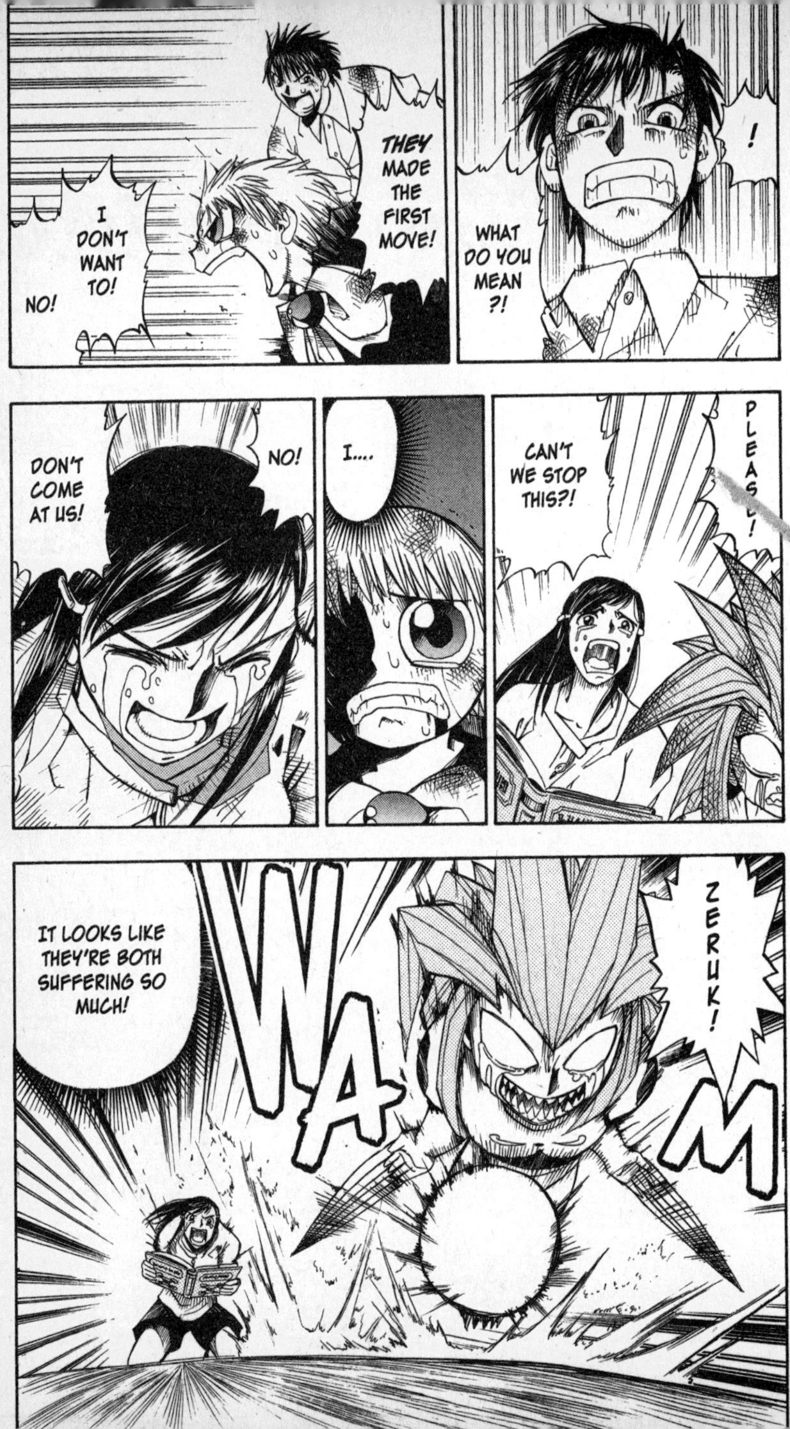
!
WHAT DO YOU MEAN ?!
THEY MADE THE FIRST MOVE!
I DON'T WANT TO!
NO!
PLEASE!
CAN'T WE STOP THIS?!
I....
NO!
DON'T COME AT US!
ZERUK!
WAM
IT LOOKS LIKE THEY'RE BOTH SUFFERING SO MUCH!

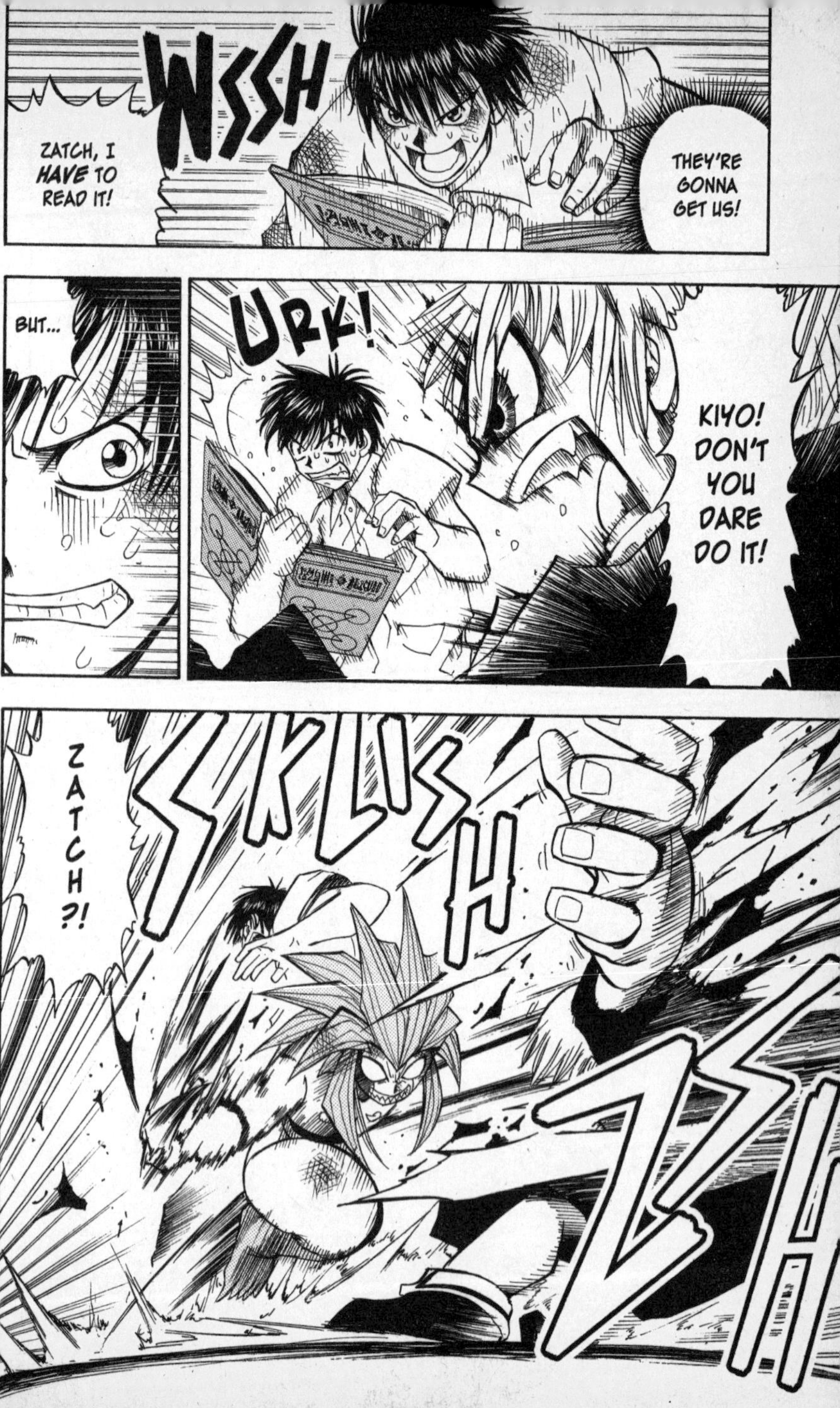
THEY'RE GONNA GET US!
WSSH
ZATCH, I HAVE TO READ IT!
KIYO! DON'T YOU DARE DO IT!
URK!
BUT...
SKLISH
ZATCH?!

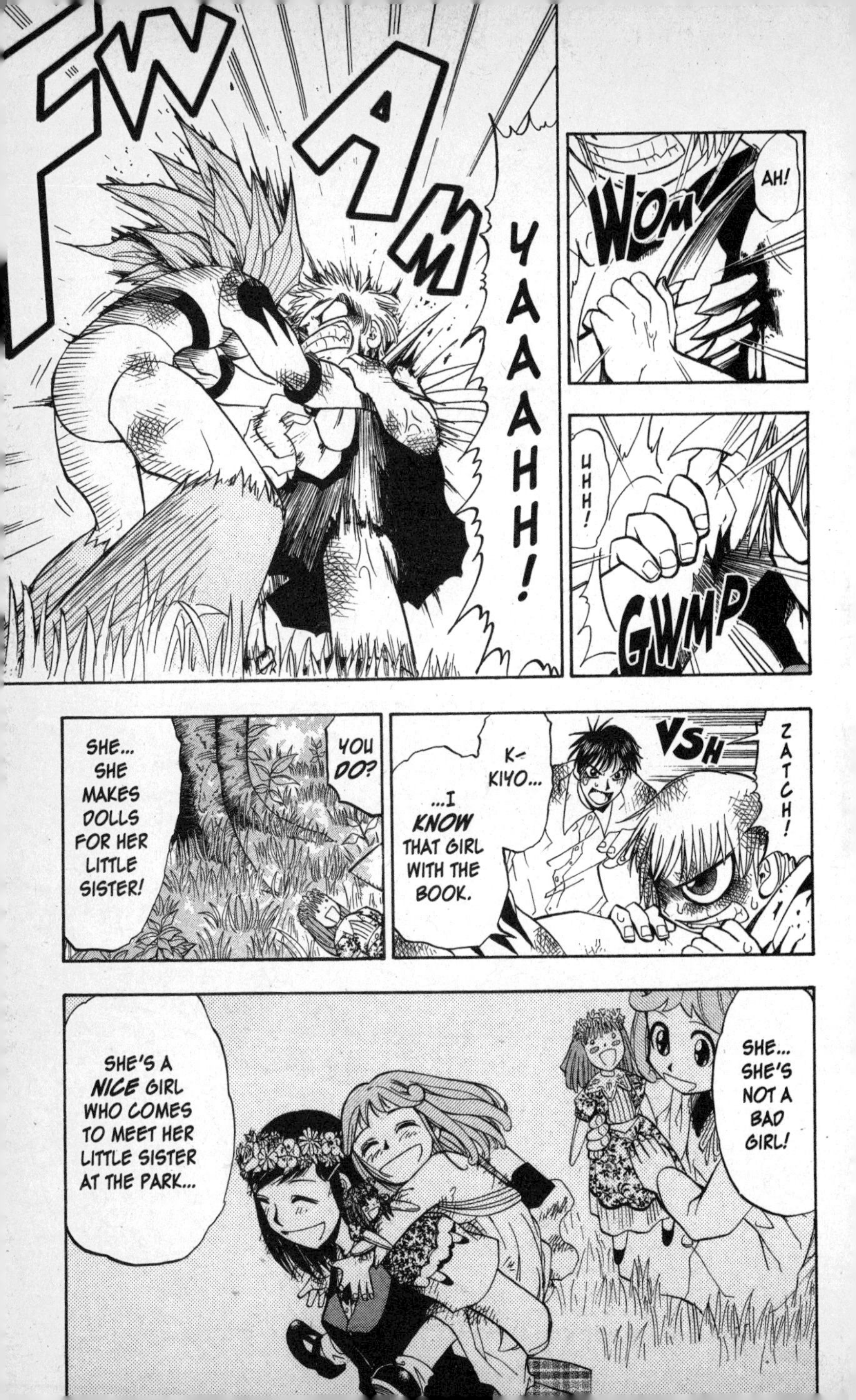
AH!
WOM
UHH!
GWMP
FWAM
YAAAAHH!
ZATCH!
VSH
K-KIYO...
...I KNOW THAT GIRL WITH THE BOOK.
YOU DO?
SHE... SHE MAKES DOLLS FOR HER LITTLE SISTER!
SHE... SHE'S NOT A BAD GIRL!
SHE'S A NICE GIRL WHO COMES TO MEET HER LITTLE SISTER AT THE PARK...

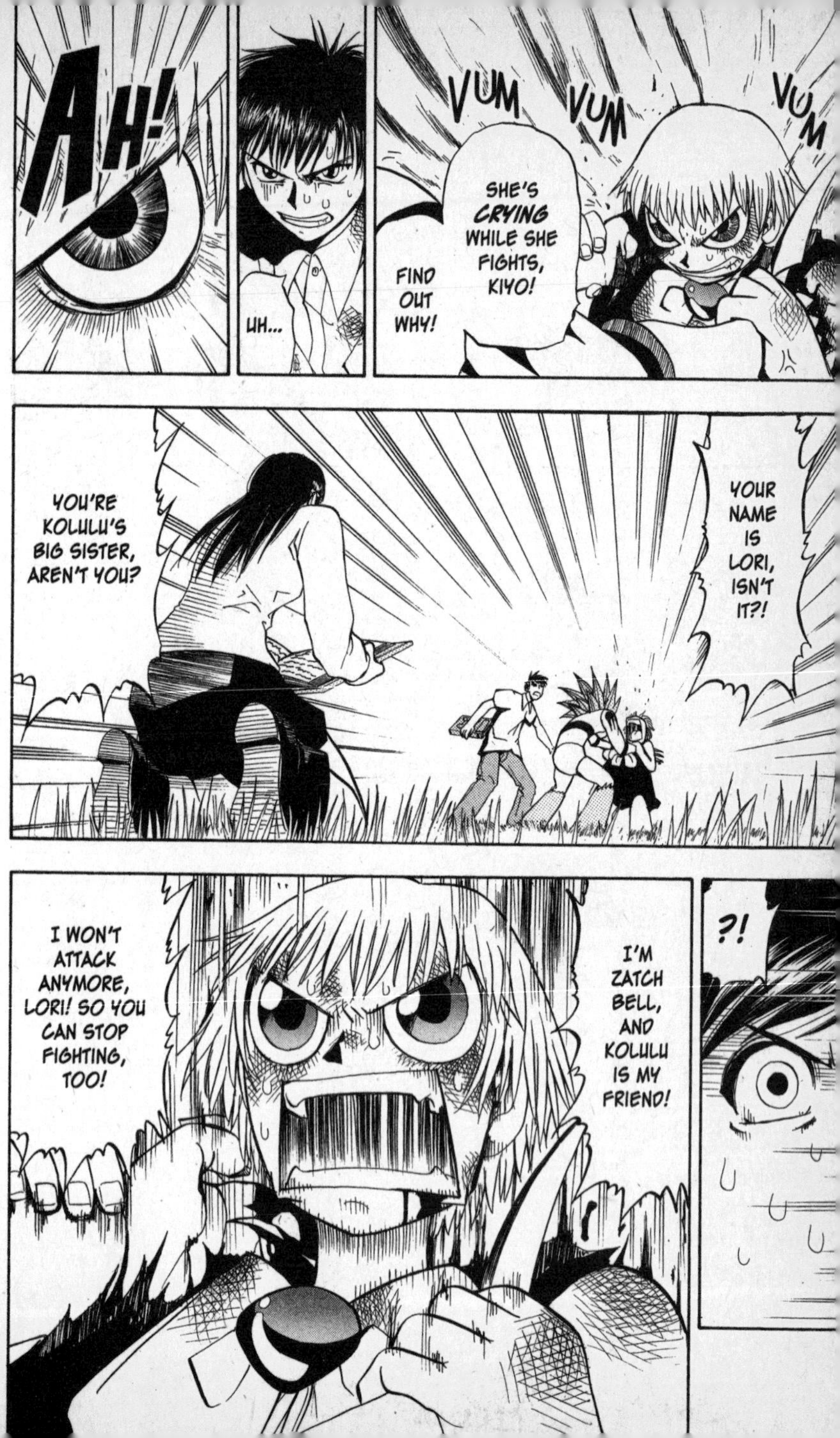
VUM
VUM
VUM
SHE'S CRYING WHILE SHE FIGHTS, KIYO!
FIND OUT WHY!
UH...
AH!
YOUR NAME IS LORI, ISN'T IT?!
YOU'RE KOLULU'S BIG SISTER, AREN'T YOU?
?!
I'M ZATCH BELL, AND KOLULU IS MY FRIEND!
I WON'T ATTACK ANYMORE, LORI! SO YOU CAN STOP FIGHTING, TOO!

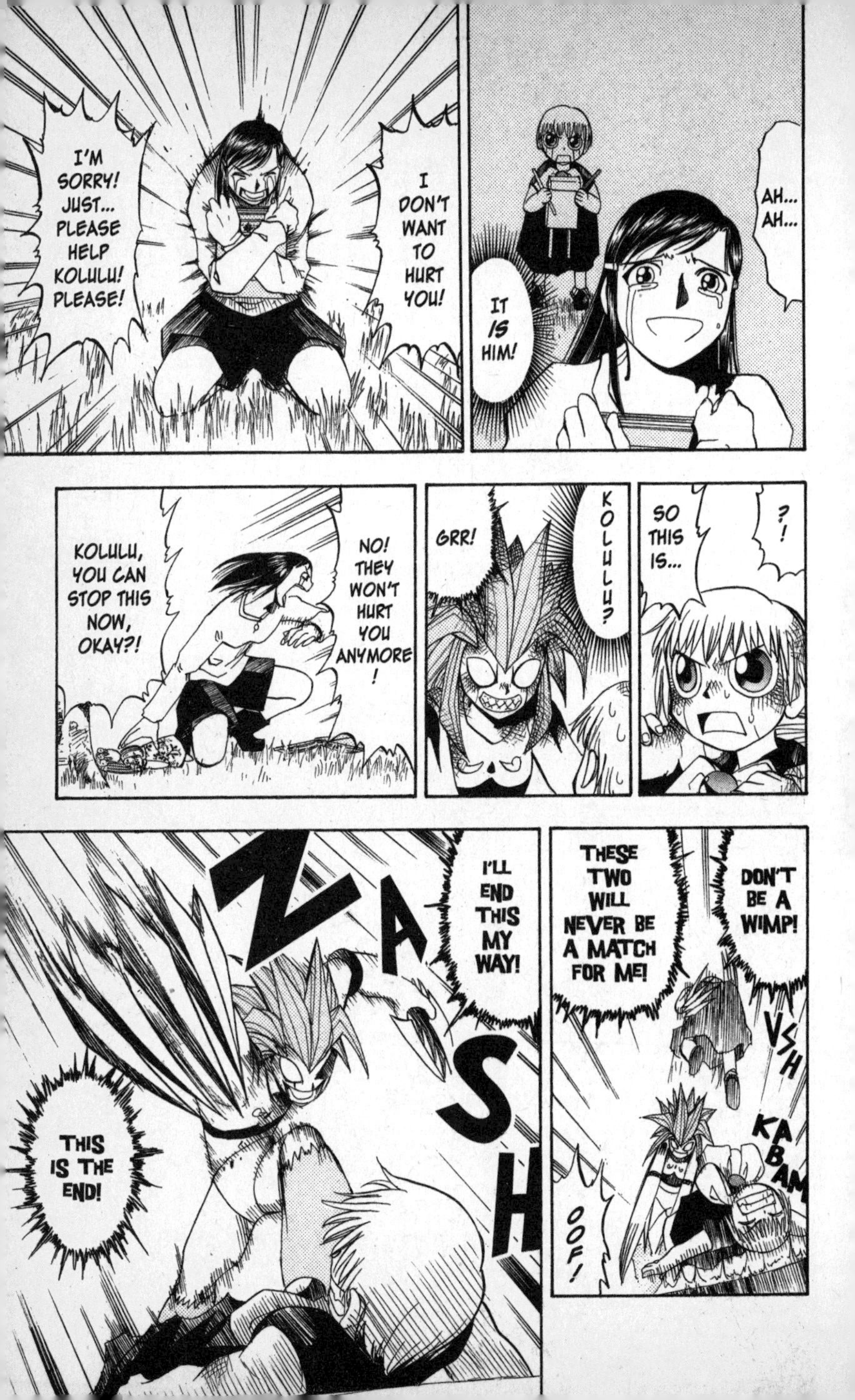
AH... AH...
IT IS HIM!
I DON'T WANT TO HURT YOU!
I'M SORRY! JUST... PLEASE HELP KOLULU! PLEASE!
?!
SO THIS IS...
KOLULU?
GRR!
NO! THEY WON'T HURT YOU ANYMORE!
KOLULU, YOU CAN STOP THIS NOW, OKAY?!
DON'T BE A WIMP!
THESE TWO WILL NEVER BE A MATCH FOR ME!
VSH
KABAM
OOF!
I'LL END THIS MY WAY!
ZASH
THIS IS THE END!

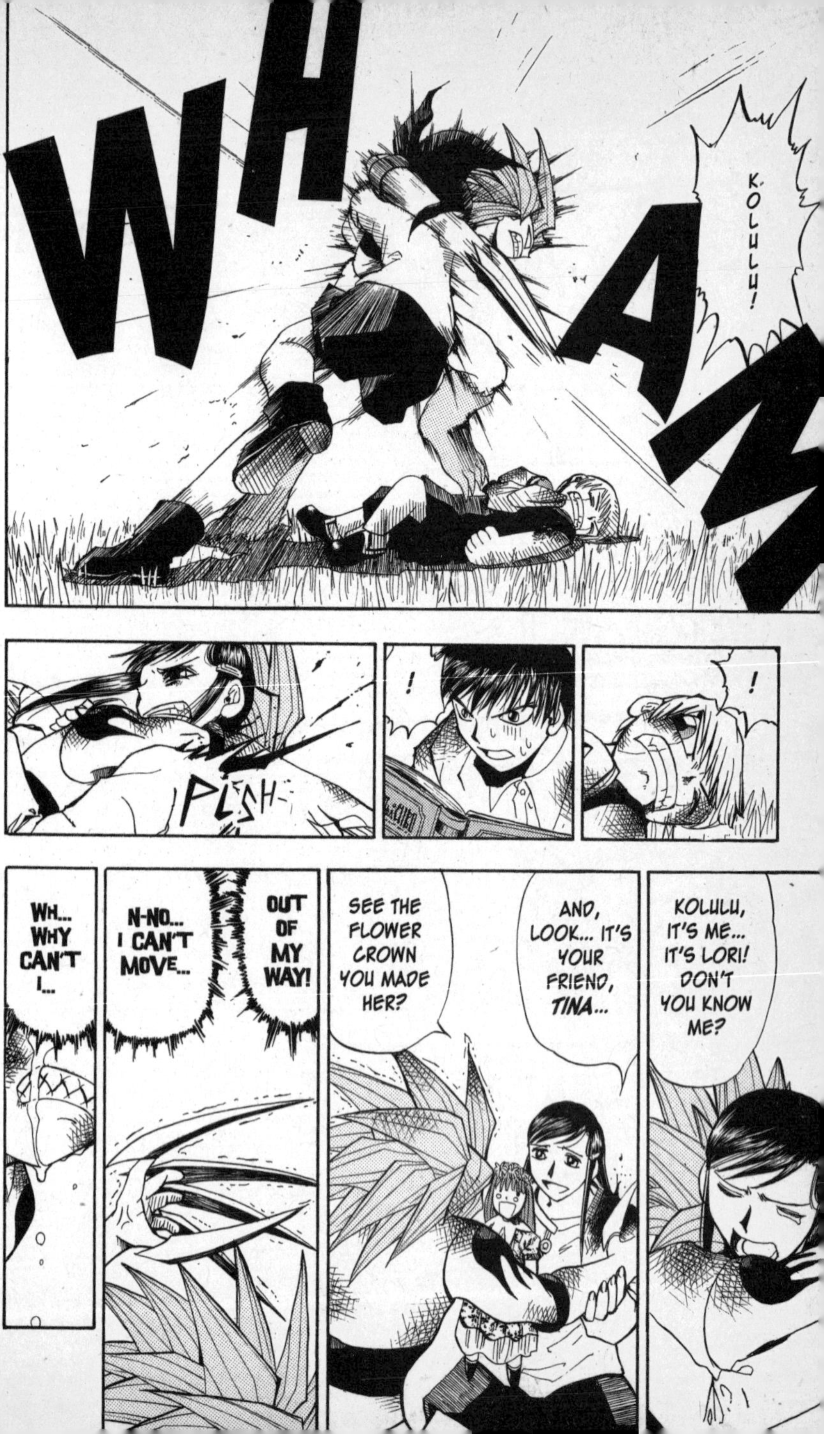
KOLULU!
WHAM
!
!
PLSH
KOLULU, IT'S ME... IT'S LORI! DON'T YOU KNOW ME?
AND, LOOK... IT'S YOUR FRIEND, TINA...
SEE THE FLOWER CROWN YOU MADE HER?
OUT OF MY WAY!
N-NO... I CAN'T MOVE...
WH... WHY CAN'T I...

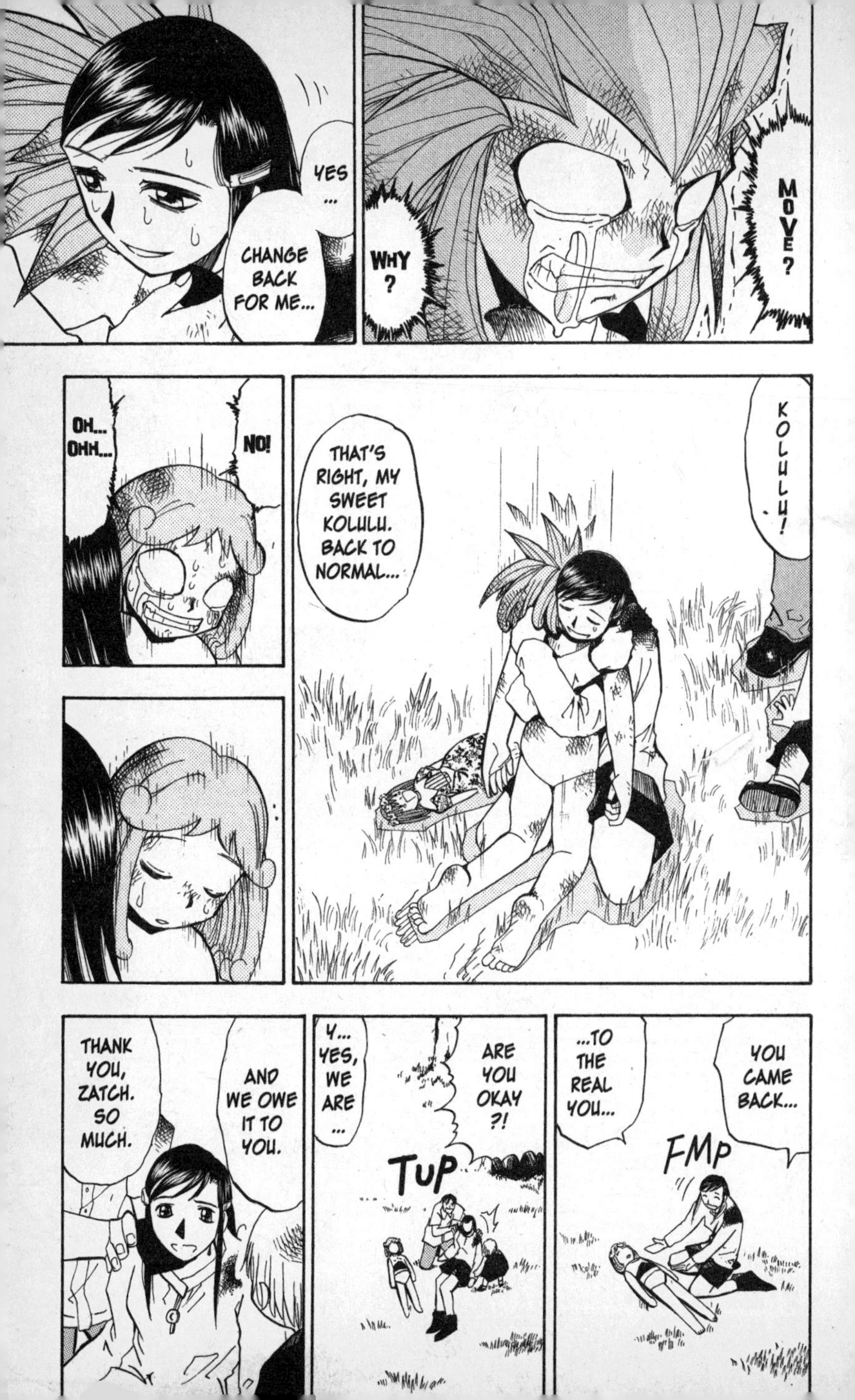
MOVE?
WHY?
YES...
CHANGE BACK FOR ME...
KOLULU!
THAT'S RIGHT, MY SWEET KOLULU. BACK TO NORMAL...
NO!
OH... OHH...
YOU CAME BACK...
...TO THE REAL YOU...
FMP
ARE YOU OKAY?!
Y... YES, WE ARE...
TUP
AND WE OWE IT TO YOU.
THANK YOU, ZATCH. SO MUCH.

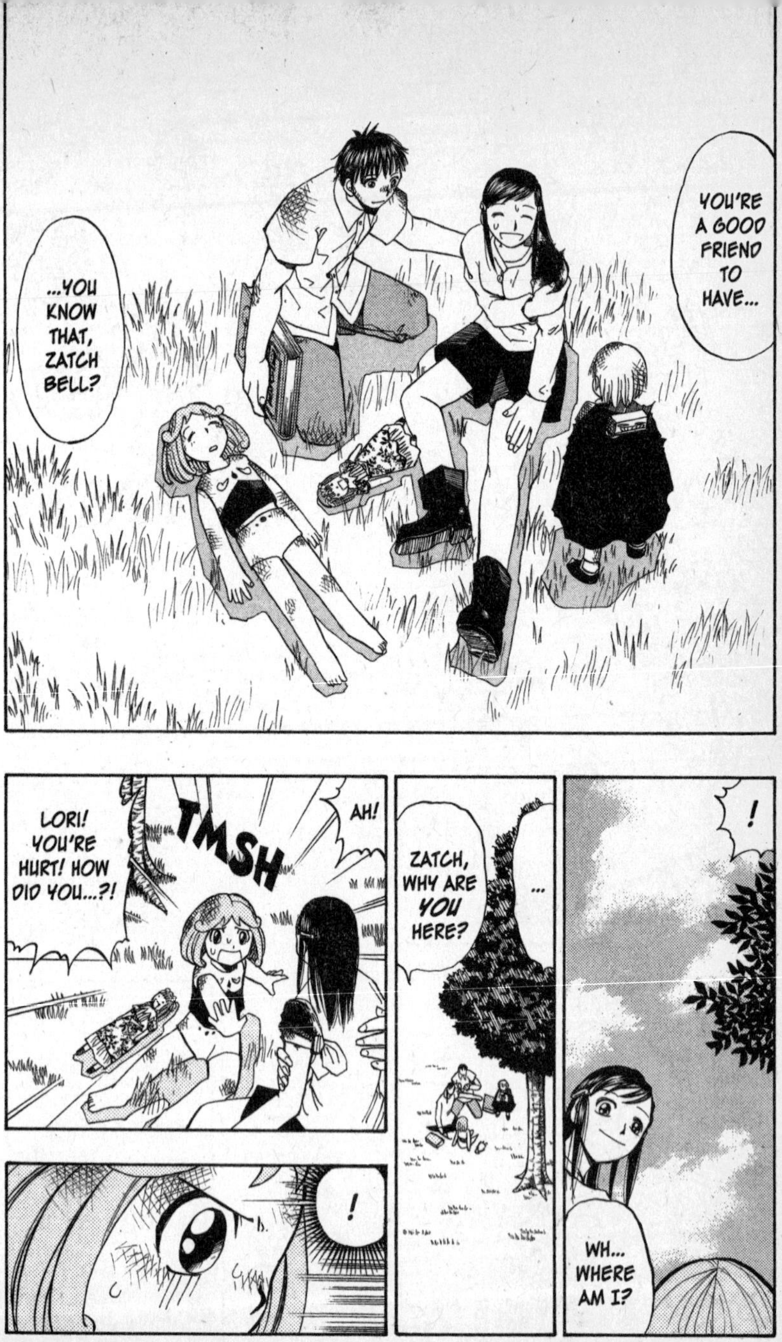
YOU'RE A GOOD FRIEND TO HAVE...
...YOU KNOW THAT, ZATCH BELL?
!
WH... WHERE AM I?
...
ZATCH, WHY ARE YOU HERE?
AH!
TMSH
LORI! YOU'RE HURT! HOW DID YOU...?!
!

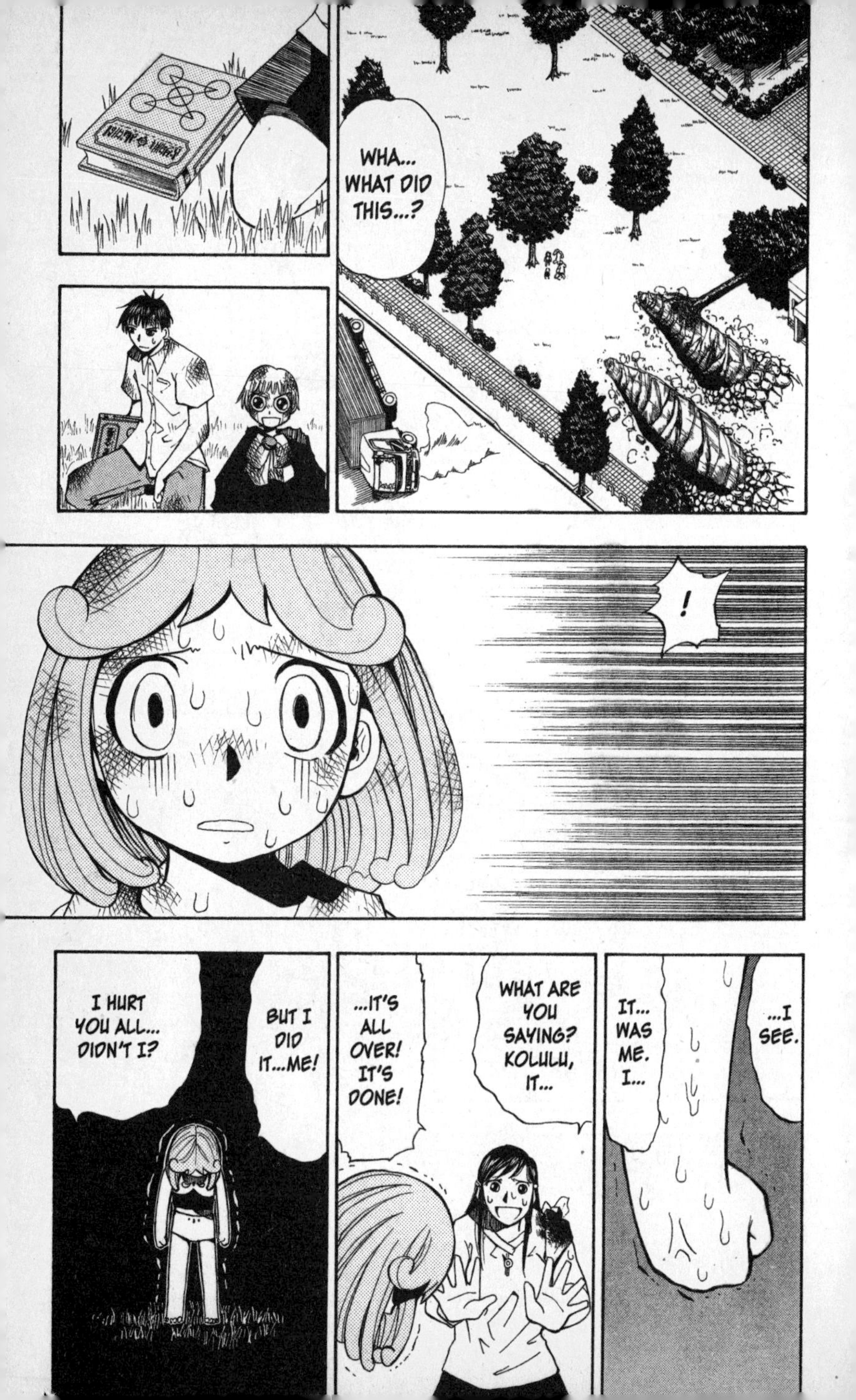
WHA... WHAT DID THIS...?
!
...I SEE.
IT... WAS ME. I...
WHAT ARE YOU SAYING? KOLULU, IT...
...IT'S ALL OVER! IT'S DONE!
BUT I DID IT...ME!
I HURT YOU ALL... DIDN'T I?

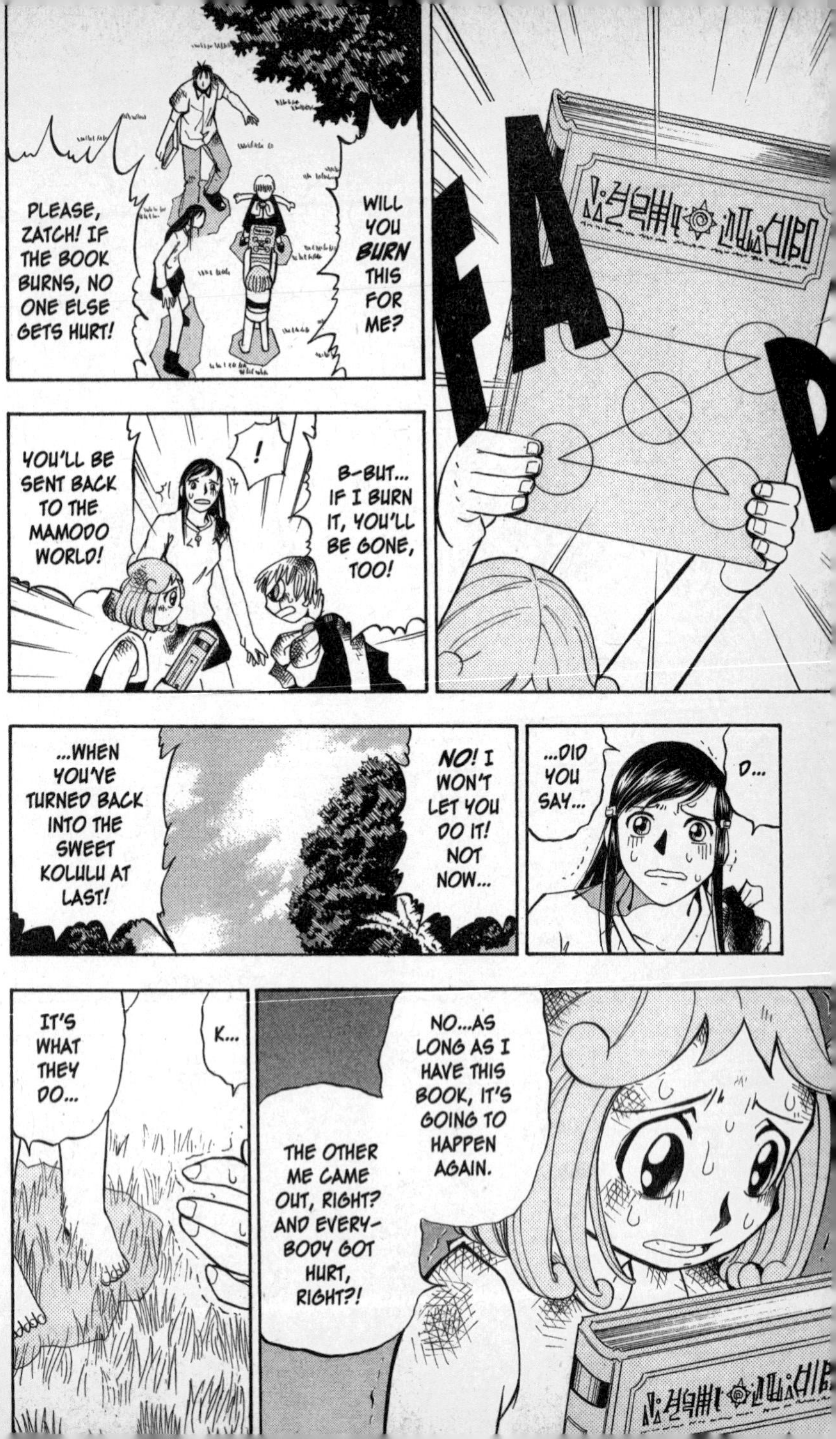
FA
WILL YOU BURN THIS FOR ME?
PLEASE, ZATCH! IF THE BOOK BURNS, NO ONE ELSE GETS HURT!
!
B-BUT... IF I BURN IT, YOU'LL BE GONE, TOO!
YOU'LL BE SENT BACK TO THE MAMODO WORLD!
D...
...DID YOU SAY...
NO! I WON'T LET YOU DO IT! NOT NOW...
...WHEN YOU'VE TURNED BACK INTO THE SWEET KOLULU AT LAST!
NO...AS LONG AS I HAVE THIS BOOK, IT'S GOING TO HAPPEN AGAIN.
THE OTHER ME CAME OUT, RIGHT? AND EVERY-BODY GOT HURT, RIGHT?!
K...
IT'S WHAT THEY DO...

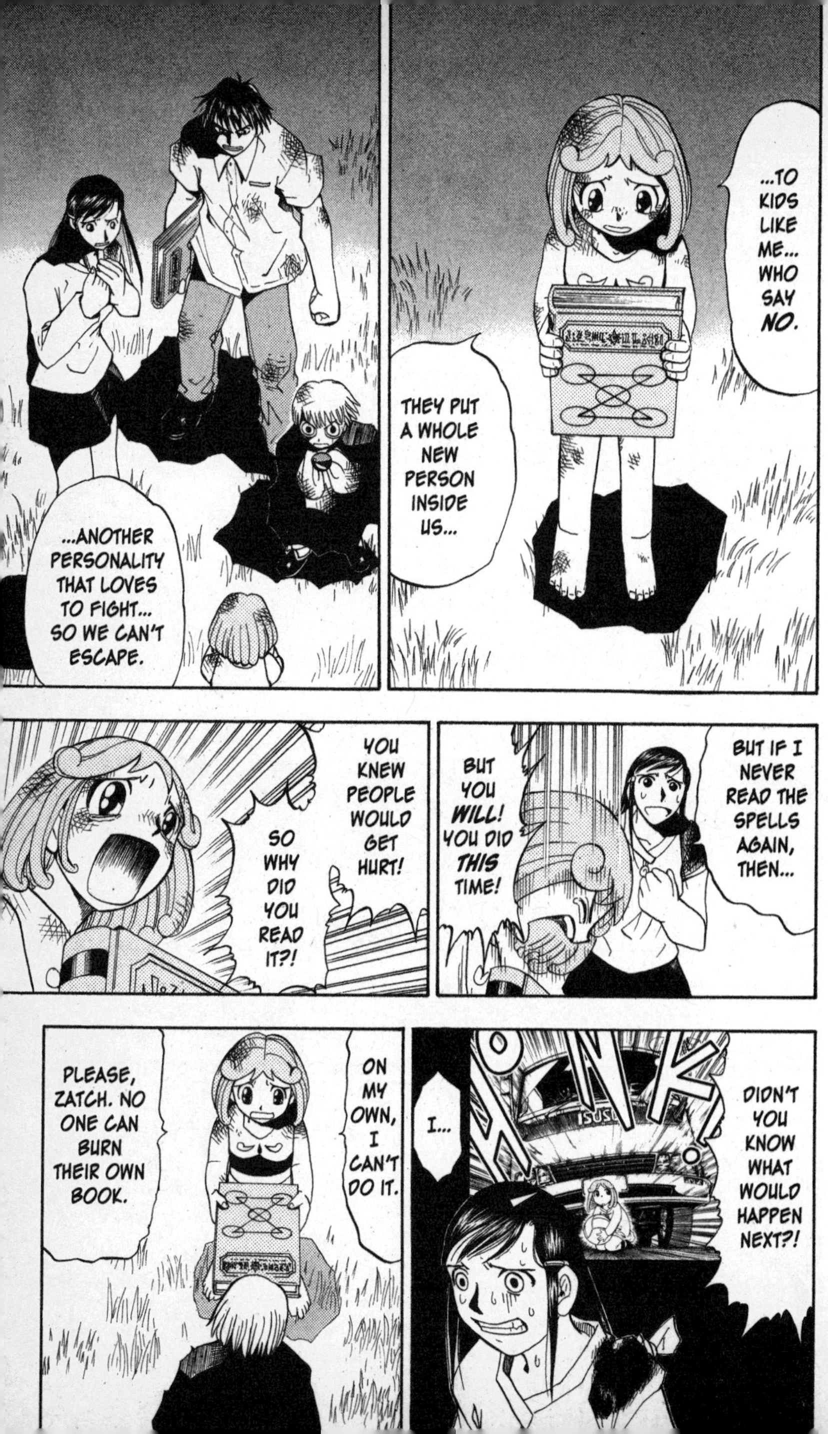
...TO KIDS LIKE ME... WHO SAY *NO*.
THEY PUT A WHOLE NEW PERSON INSIDE US...
...ANOTHER PERSONALITY THAT LOVES TO FIGHT... SO WE CAN'T ESCAPE.
BUT IF I NEVER READ THE SPELLS AGAIN, THEN...
BUT YOU *WILL*! YOU DID *THIS* TIME!
YOU KNEW PEOPLE WOULD GET HURT!
SO WHY DID YOU READ IT?!
DIDN'T YOU KNOW WHAT WOULD HAPPEN NEXT?!
I...
ON MY OWN, I CAN'T DO IT.
PLEASE, ZATCH. NO ONE CAN BURN THEIR OWN BOOK.

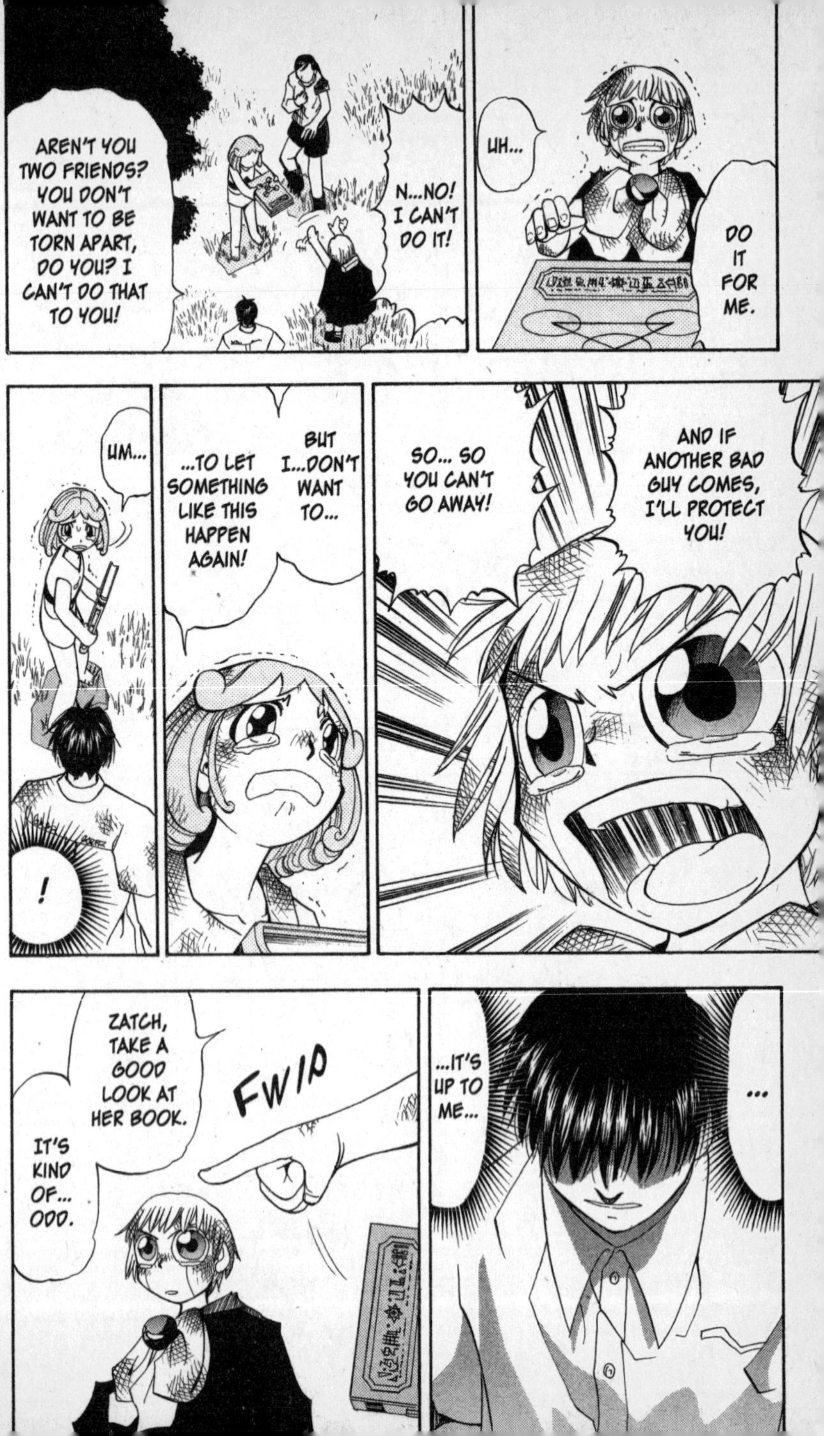
DO IT FOR ME.
UH...
N...NO! I CAN'T DO IT!
AREN'T YOU TWO FRIENDS? YOU DON'T WANT TO BE TORN APART, DO YOU? I CAN'T DO THAT TO YOU!
AND IF ANOTHER BAD GUY COMES, I'LL PROTECT YOU!
SO... SO YOU CAN'T GO AWAY!
BUT I...DON'T WANT TO...
...TO LET SOMETHING LIKE THIS HAPPEN AGAIN!
UM...
!
...
...IT'S UP TO ME...
ZATCH, TAKE A GOOD LOOK AT HER BOOK.
FWIP
IT'S KIND OF... ODD.

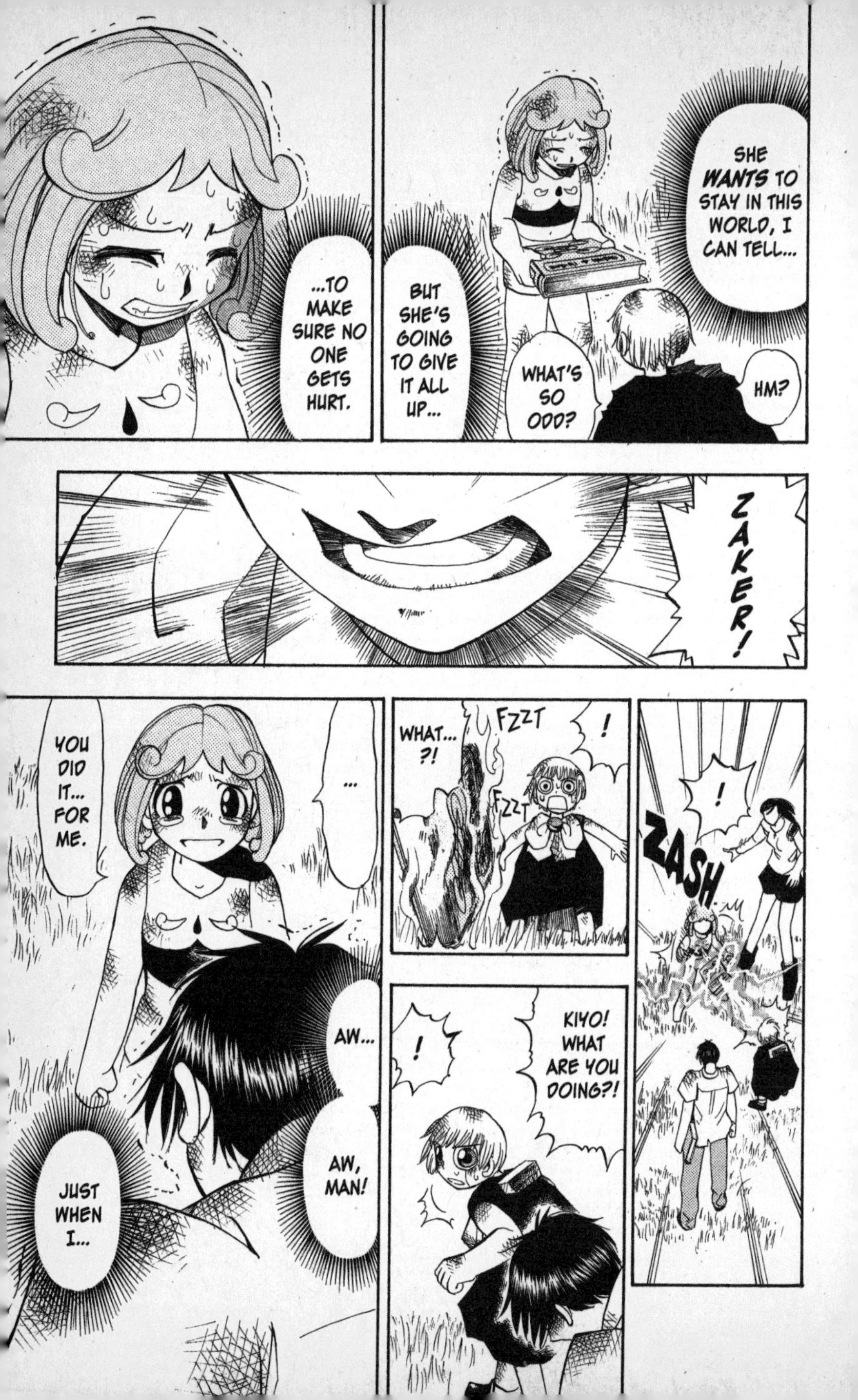
SHE WANTS TO STAY IN THIS WORLD, I CAN TELL...
HM?
WHAT'S SO ODD?
BUT SHE'S GOING TO GIVE IT ALL UP...
...TO MAKE SURE NO ONE GETS HURT.
ZAKER!
!
ZASH
!
FZZT
WHAT... ?!
FZZT
KIYO! WHAT ARE YOU DOING?!
!
...
YOU DID IT... FOR ME.
AW...
AW, MAN!
JUST WHEN I...

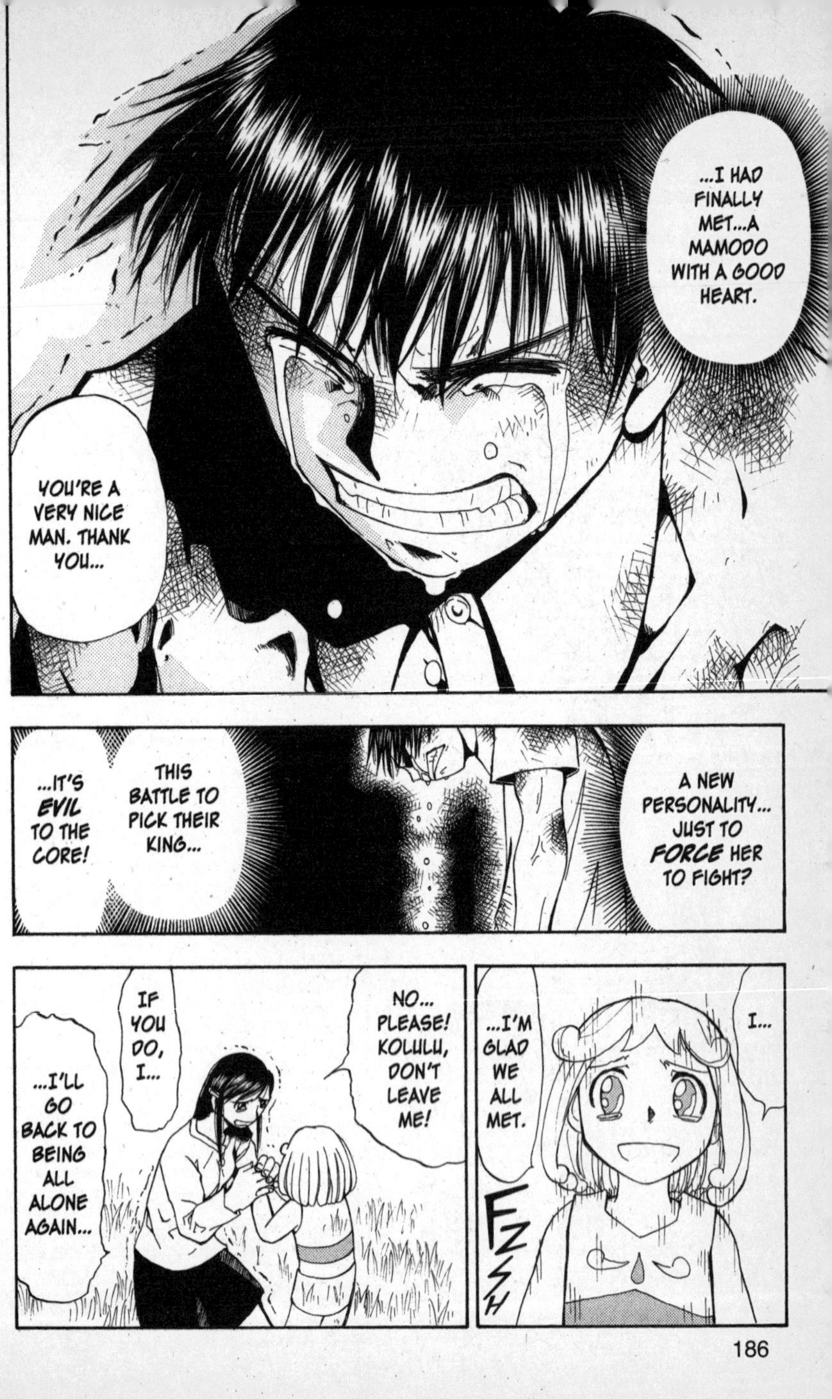
...I HAD FINALLY MET...A MAMODO WITH A GOOD HEART.
YOU'RE A VERY NICE MAN. THANK YOU...
A NEW PERSONALITY... JUST TO *FORCE* HER TO FIGHT?
THIS BATTLE TO PICK THEIR KING...
...IT'S *EVIL* TO THE CORE!
I...
...I'M GLAD WE ALL MET.
FZSSH
NO... PLEASE! KOLULU, DON'T LEAVE ME!
IF YOU DO, I...
...I'LL GO BACK TO BEING ALL ALONE AGAIN...

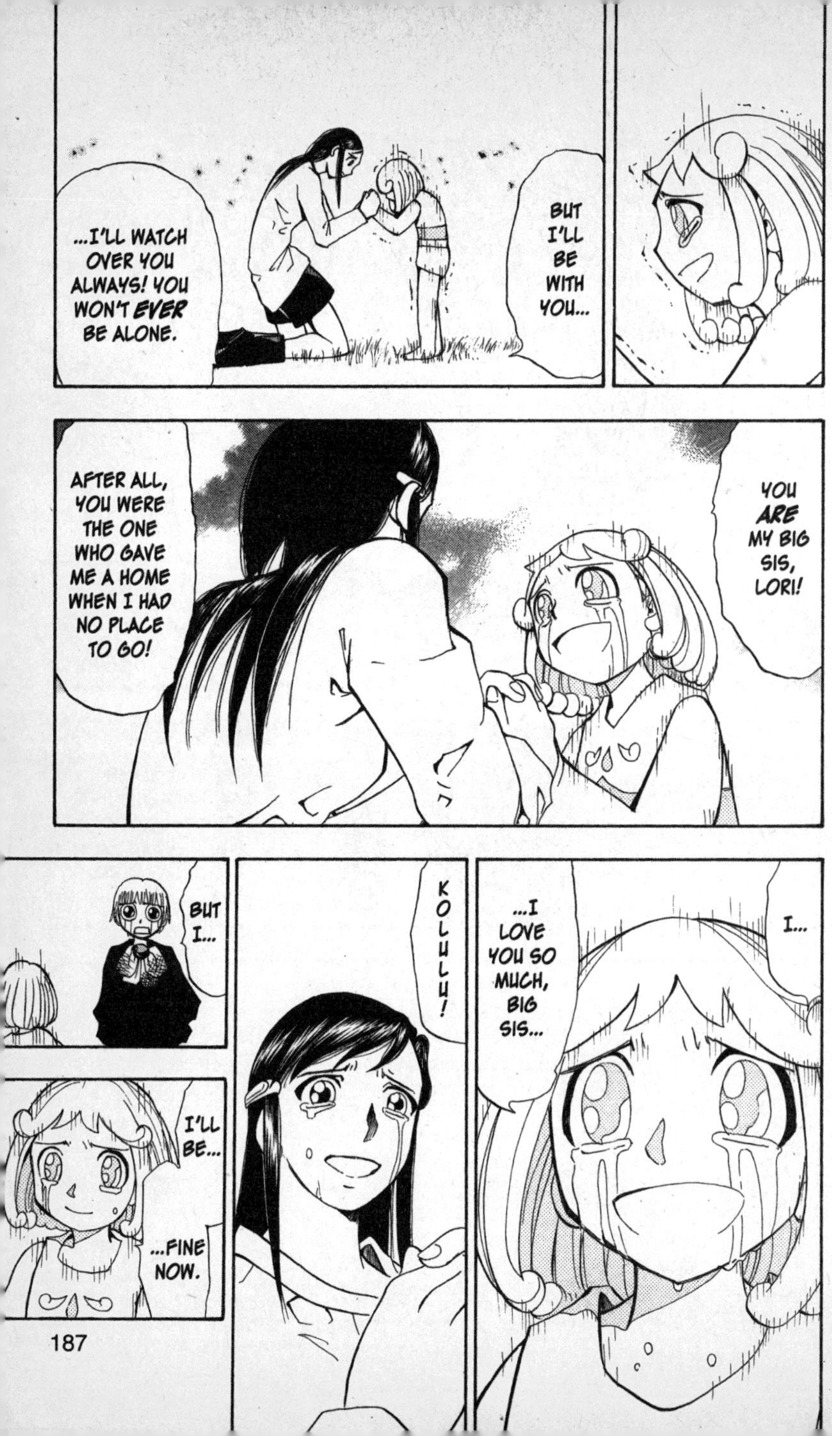
BUT I'LL BE WITH YOU...
...I'LL WATCH OVER YOU ALWAYS! YOU WON'T *EVER* BE ALONE.
YOU *ARE* MY BIG SIS, LORI!
AFTER ALL, YOU WERE THE ONE WHO GAVE ME A HOME WHEN I HAD NO PLACE TO GO!
I...
...I LOVE YOU SO MUCH, BIG SIS...
KOLULU!
BUT I...
I'LL BE...
...FINE NOW.

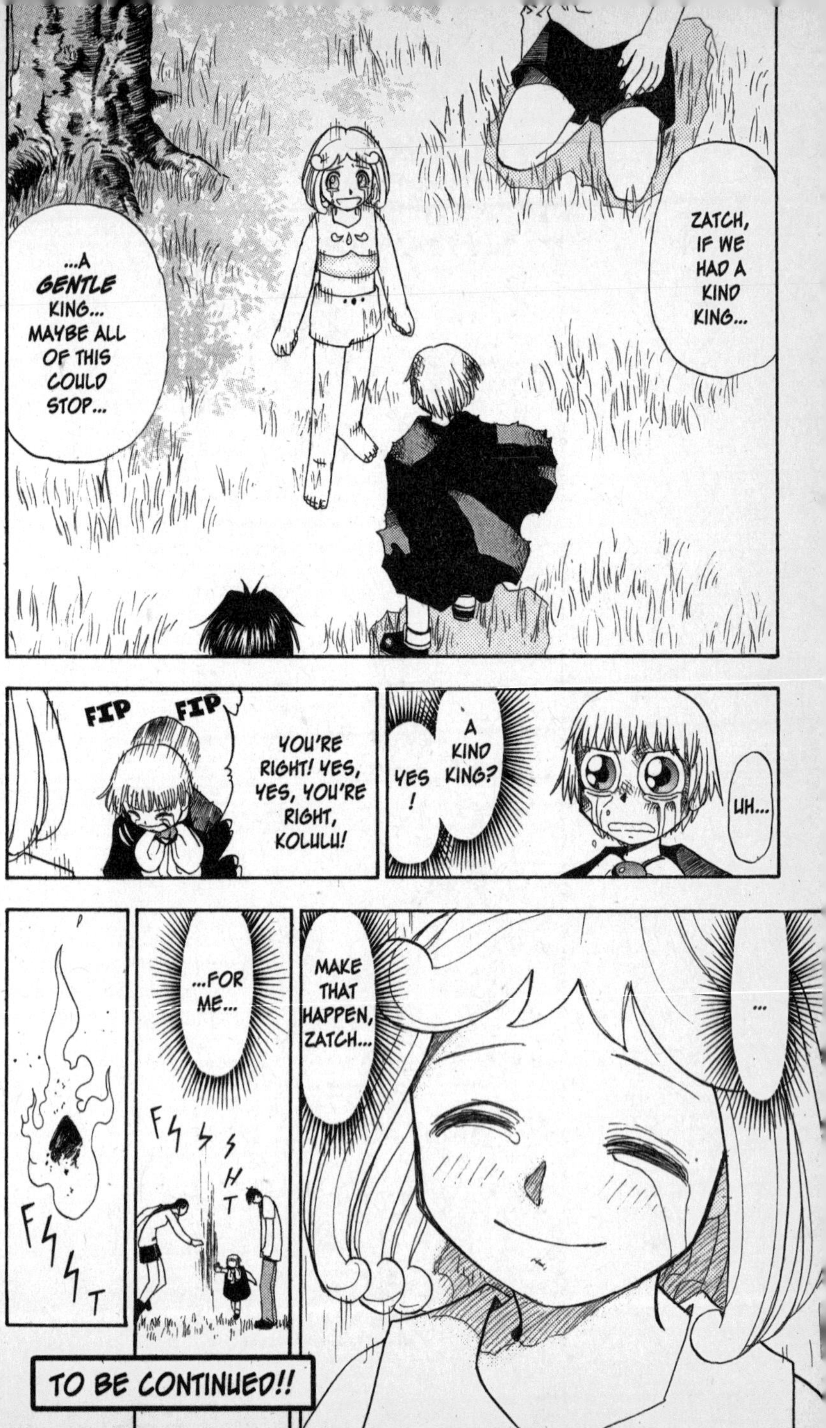
ZATCH, IF WE HAD A KIND KING...
...A GENTLE KING... MAYBE ALL OF THIS COULD STOP...
UH...
A KIND KING?
YES!
FIP FIP
YOU'RE RIGHT! YES, YES, YOU'RE RIGHT, KOLULU!
...
MAKE THAT HAPPEN, ZATCH...
...FOR ME...
FSSHT
FSST
TO BE CONTINUED!!

ZATCH & SUZY

BY MAKOTO RAIKU

...NOT A MELON OR TANGERINE IN SIGHT.

SO...

A BARE TREE IS ALL.

PAPAYA?

BUT... BUT...

YOU SEE... IT'S A BOTANICAL GARDEN...

だんだんとマンガ家らしく…

MAKOTO RAIKU

Yep, I look the part of a real manga artist…

Zatch loves yellowtail. Not tuna—yellowtail.
He even had a yellowtail slung over his shoulder
the day he met Kiyo. He especially likes fatty
winter yellowtail…

ZATCH BELL!

Video Game
Coming Fall 2005!

www.Zatch-Bell.com
www.BandaiGames.com

PlayStation.2
NINTENDO GAMECUBE.
GAME BOY ADVANCE

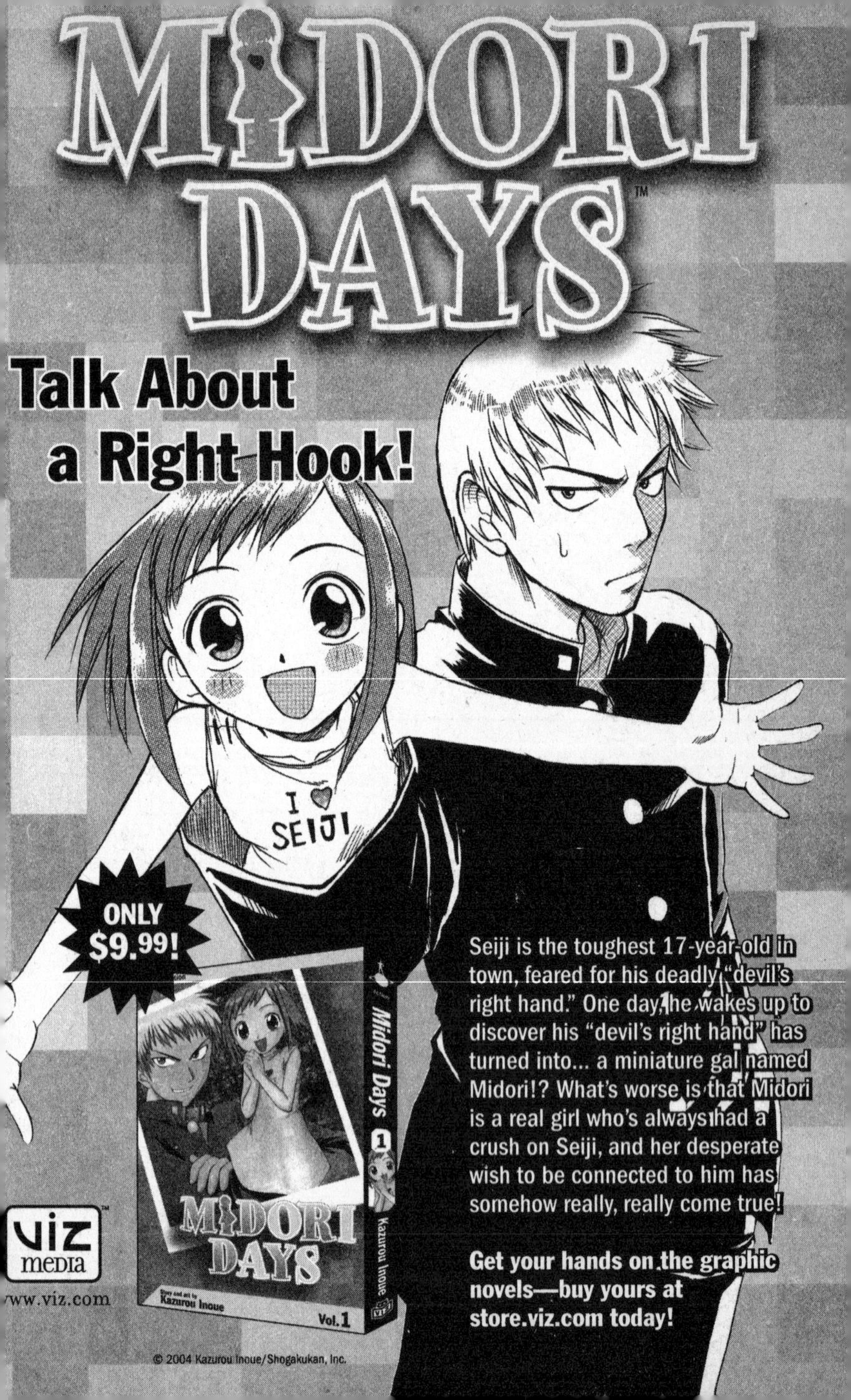
MIDORI DAYS™
Talk About a Right Hook!
I ♥ SEIJI
ONLY $9.99!
Midori Days 1
Kazurou Inoue
MIDORI DAYS
Story and art by Kazurou Inoue
Vol. 1
VIZ MEDIA™
www.viz.com
Seiji is the toughest 17-year-old in town, feared for his deadly "devil's right hand." One day, he wakes up to discover his "devil's right hand" has turned into... a miniature gal named Midori!? What's worse is that Midori is a real girl who's always had a crush on Seiji, and her desperate wish to be connected to him has somehow really, really come true!
Get your hands on the graphic novels—buy yours at store.viz.com today!
© 2004 Kazurou Inoue/Shogakukan, Inc.

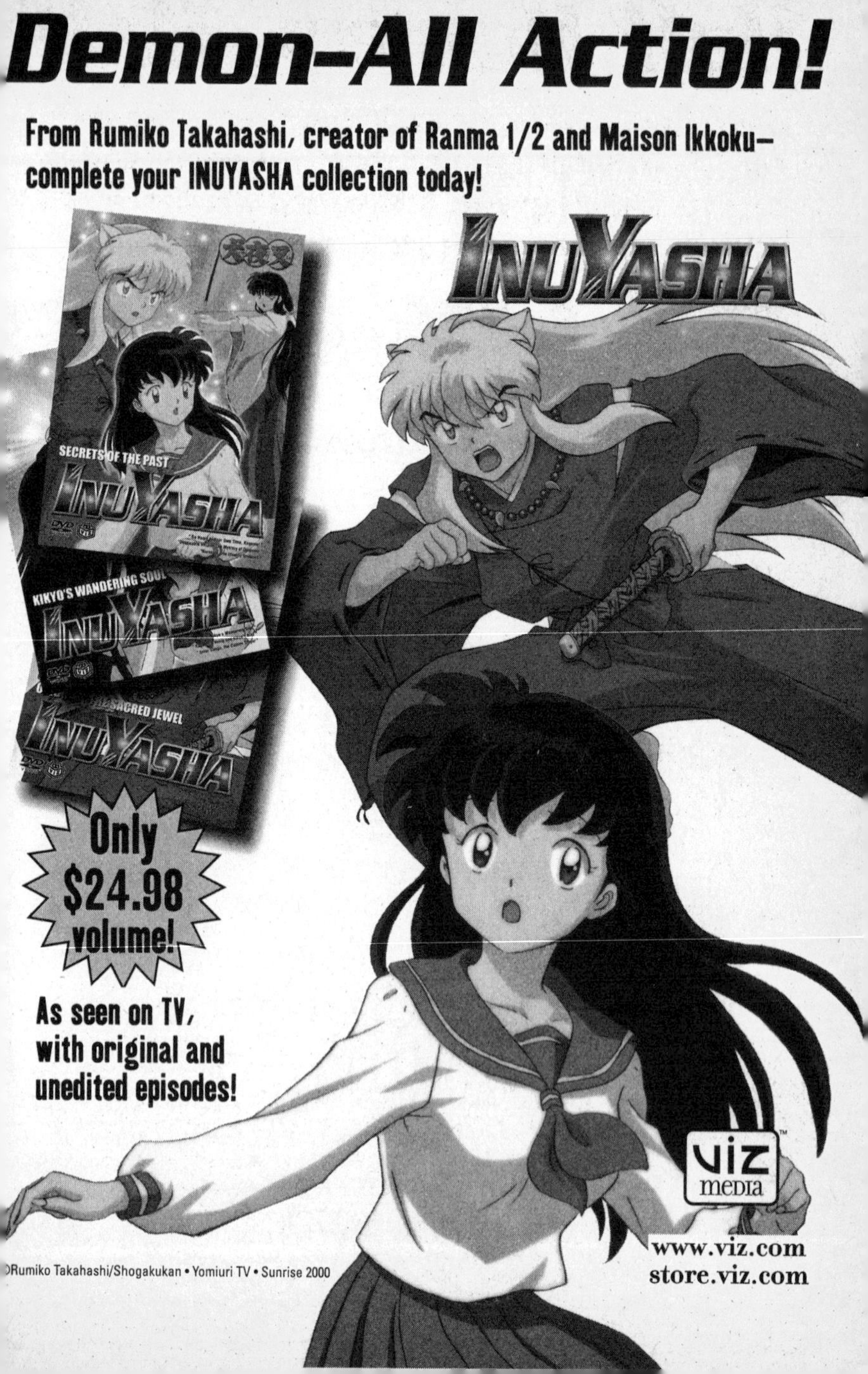

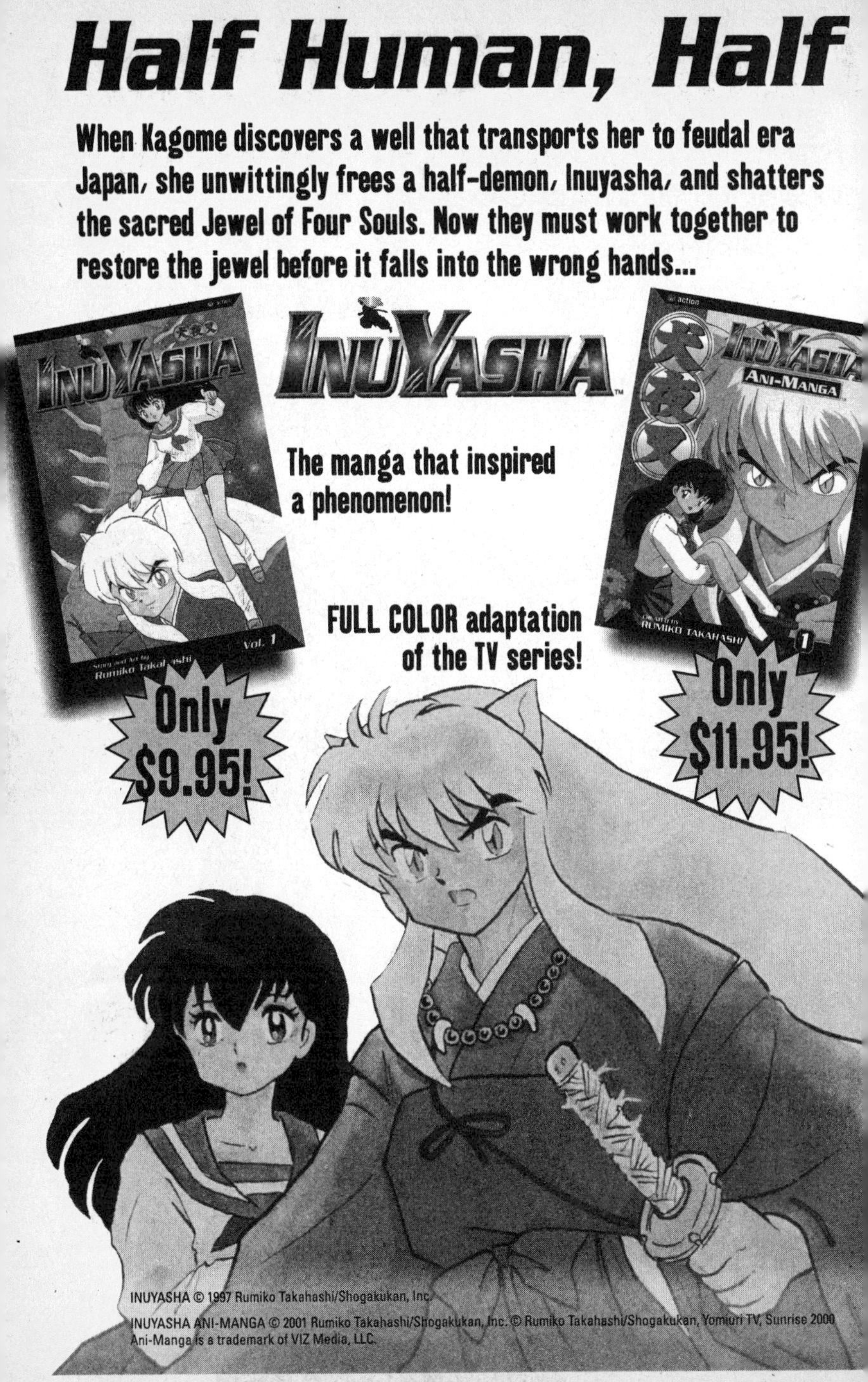
Half Human, Half
When Kagome discovers a well that transports her to feudal era Japan, she unwittingly frees a half-demon, Inuyasha, and shatters the sacred Jewel of Four Souls. Now they must work together to restore the jewel before it falls into the wrong hands...
INUYASHA
The manga that inspired a phenomenon!
Only $9.95!
FULL COLOR adaptation of the TV series!
INUYASHA ANI-MANGA
RUMIKO TAKAHASHI
Only $11.95!
INUYASHA © 1997 Rumiko Takahashi/Shogakukan, Inc.
INUYASHA ANI-MANGA © 2001 Rumiko Takahashi/Shogakukan, Inc. © Rumiko Takahashi/Shogakukan, Yomiuri TV, Sunrise 2000
Ani-Manga is a trademark of VIZ Media, LLC.

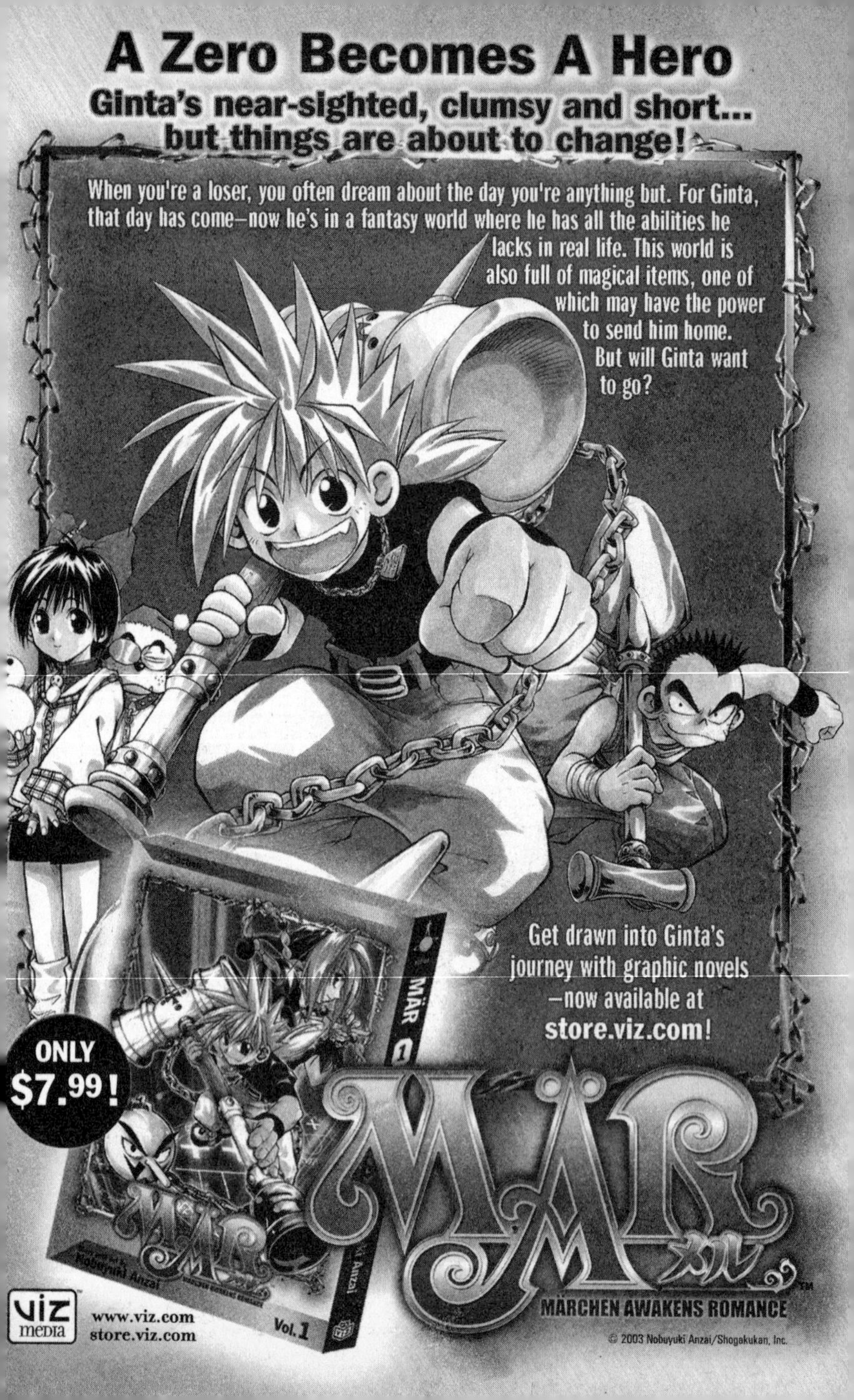
A Zero Becomes A Hero
Ginta's near-sighted, clumsy and short... but things are about to change!
When you're a loser, you often dream about the day you're anything but. For Ginta, that day has come—now he's in a fantasy world where he has all the abilities he lacks in real life. This world is also full of magical items, one of which may have the power to send him home. But will Ginta want to go?
Get drawn into Ginta's journey with graphic novels —now available at store.viz.com!
ONLY $7.99!
MÄR
Nobuyuki Anzai
Vol. 1
MÄR
MÄRCHEN AWAKENS ROMANCE
viz media
www.viz.com
store.viz.com
© 2003 Nobuyuki Anzai/Shogakukan, Inc.

STUDENTS BY DAY, DEMON-FIGHTERS BY NIGHT!

KEKKAISHI
【けっかいし】

Teenagers Yoshimori and Tokine are "kekkaishi"—demon-fighters that battle bad beings side-by-side almost every night. They also quarrel with each other, but their biggest fight is the one between their families. Can Yoshimori and Tokine fight together long enough to end their families' ancient rivalry and save the world?

Join this modern-day Romeo and Juliet adventure—graphic novels now available at *store.viz.com*!

ONLY $9.99!

Story and Art by
YELLOW TANABE

© 2004 Yellow Tanabe/Shogakukan, Inc.

VIZ MEDIA

www.viz.com
store.viz.com

LOVE MANGA? LET US KNOW!

☐ Please do NOT send me information about VIZ Media products, news and events, special offers, or other information.

☐ Please do NOT send me information from VIZ Media's trusted business partners.

Name: _____

Address: _____

City: _____ **State:** _____ **Zip:** _____

E-mail: _____

☐ Male ☐ Female **Date of Birth** (mm/dd/yyyy): ___/___/___ (Under 13? Parental consent required)

What race/ethnicity do you consider yourself? (check all that apply)

☐ White/Caucasian ☐ Black/African American ☐ Hispanic/Latino

☐ Asian/Pacific Islander ☐ Native American/Alaskan Native ☐ Other: _____

What VIZ title(s) did you purchase? (indicate title(s) purchased) _____

_____

What other VIZ titles do you own? _____

_____

Reason for purchase: (check all that apply)

☐ Special offer ☐ Favorite title / author / artist / genre

☐ Gift ☐ Recommendation ☐ Collection

☐ Read excerpt in VIZ manga sampler ☐ Other _____

Where did you make your purchase? (please check one)

☐ Comic store ☐ Bookstore ☐ Grocery Store

☐ Convention ☐ Newsstand ☐ Video Game Store

☐ Online (site:_____) ☐ Other _____

How many manga titles have you purchased in the last year? How many were VIZ titles?

STAFFORDSHIRE LIBRARY AND INFORMATION SERVICES
Please return or renew by the last date shown

		BURTON LIBRARY, HIGH STREET
		BURTON ON TRENT. TEL: 239556
JUL 08		CHILDREN'S LIBRARY
18. SEP 08	2 8 NOV 2014	
28. APR 09		
13. MAY 09		
17. 07. 09		
11. AUG 11		
09 DEC 09		

If not required by other readers, this item may may be renewed
in person, by post or telephone, online or by email.
To renew, either the book or ticket are required

24 HOUR RENEWAL LINE 0845 33 00 740

media   Poughkeepsie, NY 12601